Fertility, Wealth, and Politics in Three Southwest German Villages 1650–1900

STUDIES IN CENTRAL EUROPEAN HISTORIES

GENERAL EDITORS

Thomas A. Brady Jr.
University of California, Berkeley

Roger Chickering
Georgetown University

BOARD OF EDITORS

Jan de Vries
University of California, Berkeley

Susan Karant-Nunn
Portland State University

H. C. Erik Midelfort
University of Virginia

David Sabean
University of California, Los Angeles

Charles Ingrao
Purdue University

Jonathan Sperber
University of Missouri

Atina Grossmann
Columbia University

Peter Hayes
Northwestern University

PUBLISHED

Communal Reformation
Peter Blickle

*Protestant Politics: Jacob Sturm (1489–1553)
and the German Reformation*
Thomas A. Brady Jr.

*Military System and Social Life in Old Regime
Prussia, 1713–1807*
Otto Büsch

*Karl Lamprecht:
A German Academic Life (1856–1915)*
Roger Chickering

*Conflicting Visions of Reform: German Lay
Propaganda Pamphlets, 1519–1530*
Miriam Usher Chrisman

*Migration and Urbanization
in the Ruhr Valley, 1821–1914*
James H. Jackson Jr.

*Revolution from the Right:
Politics, Class, and the
Rise of Nazism in Saxony,
1919–1933*
Benjamin Lapp

German Encounters with Modernity
Catherine Roper

*Charity and Economy in the Orphanages of
Early Modern Augsburg*
Thomas Max Safley

*German Villages in Crisis: Rural Life in
Hesse Kassel and the Thirty Years' War
1580–1720*
John Theibault

*Communities and Conflict in
Early Modern Colmar: 1575–1730*
Peter G. Wallace

Fertility, Wealth, and Politics in Three Southwest German Villages 1650–1900

Ernest Benz

Humanities Press, Inc.
A subsidiary of Brill Academic Publishers
Boston

Humanities Press, Inc.
A subsidiary of Brill Academic Publishers
112 Water Street, Suite 400, Boston, MA 02109
Toll free 877-999-7575

©1999 by Humanities Press, Inc.

Library of Congress Cataloging-in-Publication Data

Benz, Ernest, 1954–
    Fertility, wealth, and politics in three Southwest German villages, 1650–1900 / Ernest Benz.
    p. cm. — (Studies in Central European histories)
    Includes bibliographical references and index.
    ISBN 0-391-04093-6 (cloth)
    1. Family size—Germany—Kappel-Grafenhausen—History.
    2. Fertility, Human—Germany—Kappel-Grafenhausen—History.
    3. Family size—Germany—Rust—History. 4. Fertility, Human—
Germany—Rust—History. I. Title. II. Series.
HQ762.G2K372   1999
304.6'34'09434—dc21   99-22627
                                              CIP

All rights reserved. No part of this publication may be reproduced or transmitted, in any form or by any means, without written permission from the publisher.

Printed in the United States of America

Contents

List of Tables	ix
List of Figures	xi
List of Maps	xiii
Acknowledgments	xv
Abbreviations	xvii
1. A Starting Point	1
2. Land and People	12
War and Peace	12
Emigration	18
The Logic of Population Pressure	20
3. Agriculture and Industry	27
Farming and Labour	27
The Artisanate	34
Outsiders	38
Commerce	39
Professions	40
Local Positions	41
Industry	42
4. Heirs and Heiresses	52
Malthus and Oedipus	52
Inheritance	54
Can The Oedipal Model Be Saved?	63
5. Malthusians and Neomalthusians	69
Illegitimacy	69
The Sartoris	73
Age at First Marriage	80

6. Natural Fertility and Family Limitation	87
The Classical Theory of Family Limitation	87
Estimating the Percentage Limiting	95
The Course of Marital Fertility in Grafenhausen, Kappel, and Rust	97
7. Proprietors and Notables	110
Fertility Control for Farming and Labour	111
Family Limitation among Artisans	115
Other Occupations	118
Notables	121
8. Fragmentation and Accumulation	131
The Refined Morcellement Hypothesis	131
The Land Market	136
The Lifetime Career of Landholding	140
Grafenhausen and Kappel Compared	143
9. Rich and Poor	152
Grafenhausen	152
Kappel	158
Rust	163
The Refined Morcellement Hypothesis Evaluated	169
10. Subjects and Citizens	175
The Ruster Rebellion	178
The Reichenweier Tithe	180
The Restless Minds of Grafenhausen	182
The Revolution of 1848	186
11. Anticlericals and Ultramontanes	199
Models of Secularization	199
Church and State	202
The Jewish Community in Rust	206
Old Catholicism in Kappel	207
Federal Elections 1868–1912	214
12. Localities and Parties	230
Notable Politics 1871–1901	231

The Fertility of Electors	244
Party Politics 1905–1920	247
Did Politics Matter?	251
13. Innovation and Diffusion	261
Bibliography	270
Index	284

List of Tables

2.3	Distribution of children's ages at death in documented marriages, by date of parents' wedding	17
3.1	Distribution of occupations in Grafenhausen, Kappel, and Rust combined	28
4.2	Average change in the Land tax assessment of a married man, At the wedding of a child, At the wedding of a son, At the wedding of a daughter, At the wedding of a youngest son, and At the death of a wife, in late nineteenth-century Kappel and Rust	59
5.2	Distributions of occupations of Lovers of unwed mothers, Fathers of unwed mothers, and Future husbands of unwed mothers, compared to the Overall occupational distribution	71
6.1	Average interval, in years, Between wedding and first legitimate birth, Between all confinements but the last two, and Between the second-last and last confinements in documented completed families, by date of wedding	93
6.2	Simplified checklist of measures of fertility and their interpretation	97
6.3	Average age of wife at last birth and Final birth interval, both in years, together with the Number of legitimate children in documented completed families in Grafenhausen, by date of wedding	98
6.4	Average age of wife at last birth and Final birth interval, both in years, together with the Number of legitimate children in documented completed families in Kappel, by date of wedding	99
6.6	Average age of wife at last birth and Final birth interval, both in years, together with the Number of legitimate children in documented completed families in Rust, by date of wedding	101
7.2	Average age of wife at last birth and Final birth interval, both in years, together with the Number of legitimate children in documented completed families engaged in Farming and Labour, by date of wedding	112
7.6	Average age of wife at last birth and Final birth interval, both in years, together with the Number of legitimate children in documented completed families in artisanal occupational categories, by date of wedding	117
7.8	Mortality and fertility in documented marriages formed 1875–1899 and engaged in Industry, Labour, or neither	120

LIST OF TABLES

8.1	Distributions of Holders of mortgages and Mortgages held in Rust in 1827, by the character, location, and occupation of the mortgagee	139
9.1	Comparison, for rich and poor couples, of Average age of wife at last birth and Final birth interval, both in years, together with the Number of legitimate children in mature documented completed families in Grafenhausen, by marriage cohort and age of bride	153
9.2	Comparison, across economic categories, of Average age of wife at last birth and Final birth interval, both in years, together with the Number of legitimate children in mature documented completed families in Grafenhausen, by year of source and age of bride	155
9.5	Comparison, for rich and poor couples, of Average age of wife at last birth and Final birth interval, both in years, together with the Number of legitimate children in mature documented completed families in Kappel, by date of wedding and age of bride	159
9.9	Comparison, for rich and poor couples, of Average age of wife at last birth and Final birth interval, both in years, together with the Number of legitimate children in mature documented completed families in Rust, by date of wedding and age of bride	166
10.1	Fertility of documented marriages of Voters in the 11 March 1824 municipal election in Grafenhausen, by political faction	185
10.2	Fertility of documented marriages of All husbands and Notable husbands Signing 2 March 1848 petition in Kappel	188
10.3	Fertility of documented marriages of Radical and Moderate electors in Ettenheim and Kenzingen ridings from 1846 to 1850	192
10.4	Distributions of occupations of Radical and Moderate electors in Ettenheim and Kenzingen ridings from 1846 to 1850	193
11.1	Outcome of the 1903 German federal election and the 1905 Baden provincial election in selected polls in Ettenheim-Emmendingen-Lahr riding	200
11.2	Fertility of documented marriages of Voters in the 4 September 1865 district election in Grafenhausen, by political faction	205
11.3	Distributions of husbands' occupations in Kappel, by religion 1875-1890	209
11.4	Fertility of documented marriages of Old Catholics and Roman Catholics in Kappel, by wife's date of birth	212
12.1	Fertility of documented marriages of Voters in provincial elections of 1889 and 1893 in Grafenhausen, by voting record	240
12.2	Distributions of occupations of National Liberal and Centre electors in Ettenheim-Kenzingen riding from 1871 to 1901	245
12.3	Fertility of documented marriages of Electors in Ettenheim-Kenzingen riding from 1871 to 1901, by party and religion	246

List of Figures

2.1	The populations of Grafenhausen, Kappel, and Rust 1593–1969	13
4.1	Case histories of three inheritances in Rust in the 1760s	56
4.3	Average holdings of married couples as a fraction of the village average, by the age of the husband	60
5.1	Percentage of births out of wedlock in Grafenhausen, Kappel, and Rust combined, by decade of birth from 1650–9 to 1910–9	70
5.3	The Sartori family tree	73
5.4	Average age of wife at first marriage in documented marriages in Grafenhausen, Kappel, and Rust, by date of wedding	81
6.5	The shape of family limitation in Grafenhausen and in Kappel	100
6.7	The shape of family limitation overall and in Rust	102
7.1	Average age of wife at second-last confinement in documented completed families in Farming and Labour categories, by date of wedding	112
7.3	The shape of family limitation in the Farming and Labour categories	113
7.4	Average age at first marriage of husbands and wives in documented marriages in Farming and Labour categories, by date of wedding	114
7.5	Average age of wife at second-last confinement in documented completed families in artisanal occupational categories, by date of wedding	116
7.7	The shape of family limitation in combined Affluent and Substantial categories and in the Craft category	118
7.9	Average age of wife at second-last confinement in documented completed families, by status and by date of wedding	124
7.10	The shape of family limitation by status	125
7.11	m index of family limitation in documented marriages beginning 1875–1899 according to occupation and status, and by OSB	126
9.3	Average age of wife at second-last confinement for rich and poor couples in mature documented completed families in Grafenhausen, by date of wedding	156
9.4	The shape of family limitation among rich and poor in Grafenhausen	157
9.6	Average age of wife at second-last confinement for rich and poor couples in mature documented completed families in Kappel, by date of wedding	160
9.7	The shape of family limitation among rich and poor in Kappel	162

9.8	Average age of wife at second-last confinement for rich and poor couples in mature documented completed families in Rust, by date of wedding	165
9.10	The shape of family limitation among rich and poor in Rust	168
11.5	Difference between Centre and National Liberal vote as a percentage of the number of eligible voters in Grafenhausen, Kappel, and Rust, in federal elections from 1868 to 1912	219
12.4	Difference between Centre and National Liberal vote as a percentage of the number of eligible voters in Grafenhausen, Kappel, and Rust in provincial elections from 1889 to 1913	250

List of Maps

1.1	The Rhine Plain	5
2.2	Grafenhausen, Kappel, and Rust	15
3.2	Ettenheim County	32

Acknowledgments

As one who preens himself on self-sufficiency, I find the list of acknowledgements embarrassingly long. None the less, each of the following individuals helped in one or more ways with substantive or technical work. I extend thanks to them and to all those whose names I never learned or did not retain.

(1) Albert Kobele, without whom there would have been no OSBs to study, for his introductions, advice, and hospitality

(2) John Knodel, for sharing the results of his research over the years, including drafts of *Demographic Behavior in the Past*

(3) custodians and workers in archives, for patience, access, and advice

    (a) in the villages themselves: mayors Raimund Halter (Kappel-Grafenhausen), Erich Spoth (Rust), Günter Gorecky (Rust), and Herbert Blattmann (Münchweier); municipal clerks Albert Uhl (Grafenhausen), Michael Gula (Grafenhausen), Stefan Schludecker (Rust), Hartwig Busshardt (Herbolzheim), Rupert Weber (Ringsheim); priests Wolfgang Jörger (Grafenhausen), Werner Pohl (Grafenhausen), Karl Schillinger (Kappel), Anton Uhrenbacher (Rust), Konrad Czech (Rust), Antonius Schmidt (Rust), and their households; Ottmar Mutz (Grafenhausen), Cornelia Fischer (Grafenhausen), Eleonore Dietz (Kappel-Grafenhausen), Edmund Edelmann (Kappel), Franz Klauser (Kappel), Tobias Korta (Kappel), Alfred Baumann (Rust), Martin Spoth (Rust), Leopold Greber (Ettenheim), Bernhard Uttenweiler (Ettenheim), Friedrich Hinn (Herbolzheim), Walter Geppert (Herbolzheim), Edgar Hellwig (Herbolzheim);

    (b) at the Generallandesarchiv in Karlsruhe: Reinhold Rupp, Christiana Scheuble, Heinz Leonhardt, Hiltburg Köckert, Rainer Trunk, Martina Heine, Paul Neumaier, Hans Müller;

    (c) at the Staatsarchiv in Freiburg: Anneliese Müller, Erdmuthe Krieg, Jochen Rees, Paul Waldherr, Uwe Fahrer, Manfred Herb;

    (d) at the archive of the archdiocese in Freiburg: Ulrike Dehn, Franz Hundsnurscher, Monika Ritter;

(4) at the University of Toronto: Margarita Orszag, most prominently for administering the financial side of the computer work; Pat Pearson, Don McNaughton, and Gaetan Godin, who worked for Ned Shorter as research assistants on projects that eventually flowed into my thesis; Roni Moravan, for untangling at least as many problems as University of Toronto Computing Services created; and Bert Hall, for discussing the technology, or lack thereof, involved in various activities in the early modern period.

For part of the period during which my research was carried out, I received

Ontario Graduate Scholarships and Social Sciences and Humanities Research Council of Canada Doctoral Fellowships.

(5) The book draws extensively on my Ph.D. thesis, defended in December 1987 at the University of Toronto. The defence committee included Ned Shorter, John Knodel, Julian Dent, David Levine, Thomas McIntire, and Jim Retallack. I have benefitted then and since from conversations with each of them.

(6) For *Studies in Cental European Histories*, Tom Brady and an anonymous reviewer watched over the manuscript in different but timely ways. The staff at Humanities Press and Brill Academic Publishers have done their part unobtrusively. Bill George oversaw the conversion of numerous charts into their current eminently readable form.

To the living and the dead, to the named and the unnamed, I express my gratitude once again.

Abbreviations

ADBR	Archives départementales du Bas-Rhin Strasbourg
BvB A	Böcklin family archive (currently in Staatsarchiv Freiburg)
Gem A Grafenhausen	Grafenhausen section of Kappel-Grafenhausen municipal archive
Gem A Kappel	Kappel section of Kappel-Grafenhausen municipal archive
Gem A Rust	Rust municipal archive
GLA	Generallandesarchiv Karlsruhe
Ord A	Archiepiscopal Ordinariatsarchiv Freiburg
OSB *Grafenhausen*	Albert Köbele, *Ortssippenbuch Grafenhausen*, third edition (Grafenhausen, 1971)
OSB *Kappel*	Albert Köbele, *Dorfsippenbuch Kappel am Rhein*, second edition (Grafenhausen, 1969)
OSB *Rust*	Albert Köbele, *Ortssippenbuch Rust* (Grafenhausen, 1969) References to OSB family histories are given by the numeral assigned to that entry by the OSB compiler. References to page numbers, on the other hand, are preceded by "page".
Pf A Grafenhausen	Grafenhausen parish archive
Pf A Kappel	Kappel parish archive
Pf A Rust	Rust parish archive
St A	Staatsarchiv Freiburg

1

A Starting Point

That fertility is a domain in its own right is both a presupposition and an implication of this book. The presupposition, that fertility is a topic worthy of study, is less debated. Whether the implication of such study should be to emphasize the independence of fertility is more controversial. Yet one upshot of this intensive investigation of three centuries of births in southwest German villages is enhanced appreciation of the autonomy of fertility. Family limitation was a starting point in history, less a response than an initiative.

Both chronologically and geographically, the onset of fertility transition in these villages fell between the exceptional efforts of eighteenth-century France[1] and the halving of birth rates in the rest of Europe in the generations around 1900. Considerably earlier than most Europeans, then, many of these peasants began to practise family limitation. Rather than allow physiology to set the end of childbearing, individuals chose the time themselves. By halting reproduction, they produced a new population. In re-fashioning themselves, they fashioned the future. From that perspective, the specialized history of fertility sheds light on the history of humanity as a whole. To that extent the presupposition is borne out.

The implication is more sweeping, in that it challenges the idea that family limitation was a simple outgrowth of broader trends, a significant effect of a still more significant cause. This book takes great care in investigating how decisions regarding fertility were related to social and economic circumstances and to religious and political commitments. Yet those circumstances and commitments in themselves fail to capture the novelty of the fertility transition.

The fertility transition was not an automatic reaction to any of the familiar sociological variables. Nowadays, choices about reproduction are popularly associated with levels of mortality, with economic circumstances, with the status of women, with religious authority, and with social constraints. Yet those associations are themselves historical constructs. Historians often render the unfamiliar familiar, but just as often they must do the reverse: clarify that what seems familiar in the past was actually radically different. Fertility is now responsive to infant deaths, to prosperity, to women's liberation, to piety, and to class; but this does not entail that such factors caused the original fertility decline. Quite the contrary, such responsiveness itself had to be made. Before a population can divide fifty-fifty in adjusting its fertility to social conditions, with half increasing births and half decreasing them, 100 % of the population has to be prepared to adjust.

For instance, the decline in births was not triggered by a decline in infant mortality. Rather, consciously adapting one's own fertility to mortality required a prior commitment to family limitation. Only after births were being prevented could a couple respond to a child's death by replacing him or her.[2] Those deaths might be no less frequent than before, and in fact in this area were growing *more* frequent. A typical couple's experience of deaths among their children might determine how much they limited fertility, but not whether they did. That prior decision or propensity was the starting point, from which other changes flowed.

In a related way, deliberately widening the spacing of births caught on only after contraception had proven its worth in stopping births altogether. Delaying the first birth within marriage is a still later development. At the time family limitation began, getting married meant starting a family. In the days when menopause terminated childbearing, family size was a function of age at marriage. Only those who could support a large family wed young. Here too, a move towards younger marriage was not the trigger that determined wives would cease getting pregnant younger as well. Rather the reverse: the prior possibility of stopping was a pre-requisite to make youthful marriage economically rational, to keep the prospective number of children within affordable limits.

Much the same reasoning applies to links between prosperity and fertility after marriage. A couple receiving a windfall could not act on it if the wife were already pregnant or infecund following a previous pregnancy. Only if the couple had already paused could they respond.

Other features associated with birth control late in the twentieth century were also not its sources. Contraception, even with males taking part, did not have to wait on new gender rôles.[3] Nor did it wait on the manufacture of devices. Contraception was possible without contraceptives. Indeed, mass demand for mechanical gadgets or pharmaceutical agents developed in populations who were already limiting fertility by natural means, such as withdrawal.[4]

Secularization bears a more complex relation to fertility, for antipathy to organized religion did predate contraception. Moreover, in late nineteenth-century Baden, defiance of the Church coloured politics and society right at the time family limitation was spreading rapidly. Yet their quarrels were not our quarrels.[5] Conflicts between State and Church turned on power and religion before sex and gender. Making the personal political awaited public discourse about sex as something problematic yet tractable, characteristics that arose from contraceptive practice itself.[6]

At first then, the fertility transition meant not escape from domination, but intensified control, self-control. Qualitative change in fertility came from within. These obscure rustics outpaced most towndwellers in contraception. Moreover, when change did come from outside, in the form of industrialization, it tended to boost fertility. Births nevertheless fell for many: this reflected not their passive integration into a new factory setting but rather their tenacious pursuit of their own interests. The impulse to limit family size was independent of urban or industrial environments.

Some of these points are logical truths, some lawlike regularities, others plausible speculations, and still others accidents of history. Yet all put family limitation first, disengaging thinking about fertility from its customary moorings. In so far as fertility itself has not always been bound to those moorings, a wider sense of possibilities captures the openness of the fertility transition. It was indeed a transition, a casting off of old controls on fertility and an articulation of new controls. Because those controls were new, contiguity hastened their adoption more than qualitative similarity did.

In short, the eternal categories of mortality, wealth, gender, religiosity, urbanism, industry, and occupation prove less important than the peculiar context in time and place. Historians are apt to suppose that where and when something happened make a difference to what kind of thing it is.[7] So it is with fertility. To predict fertility it turns out to be more useful to consider the time and place someone lived than to know what occupation he or she pursued. Rich peasants were, it is true, more apt to practise contraception than poor ones, but only at a time when their advantage in wealth was fading. Moreover, that time varied from municipality to municipality. Home village likewise outweighed religion or politics as a predictor of family limitation. Such patterns are characteristic of innovation, of successive sharp breaks in individual practice.

Differentiation is implicit in the spread of such innovations. To begin with, human beings bring varying material and psychological resources to their contests against natural, social, and personal obstacles. Perhaps even more interesting is that new controls open scope for further variation, as individuals exercise them for their own reasons.[8] How they reason and what they reason about depend on the setting, in particular on their relations with surrounding human beings. Because family limitation caught on in contingent ways for many different reasons, it cannot be traced to a single cause. Rather it brought masses of people together via their separate paths and prepared them to take common steps in future. That is what makes it a starting point.

Because family limitation is a starting point, its practitioners are agents, not puppets. They are not interchangeable products of the past, but themselves creative initiators of history. In distinguishing themselves from their neighbours and forebears, they made themselves historically interesting.

Likewise, the history of these three villages is important, not because they were microcosms of the entire continent, but precisely because of their diversity. It is the differences between villages and between villagers that matter. All suffered in war in the 1600s and all grew in peace in the 1700s. By the 1800s all faced the looming dilemma of accelerating population. Yet villagers met this massive challenge by making their own divergent histories. In particular, some resorted to family limitation.

I follow its onset in three Baden villages through the beginning of the twentieth century. The significance of this exercise is three-fold. First, genuine cases of family limitation in historical populations are considerably rarer than a cursory survey of the literature may suggest. Moreover, the Baden countryside exhibits the earliest reliably documented fertility transition in German history.[9] Already in the 1820s many couples were cutting down on the number of children they bore. That innovation put them half a century ahead of the rest of the country. They enjoyed the same lead over non-francophones in general, including the most modernized populations.

A second reason for focusing on this region is that the diversity of experiences within these three adjacent municipalities sharpens the testing of theories. This corner of the German lands constitutes a natural experiment, in which a variety of religions, sovereignties, nationalities, soils, inheritance customs, modes of production, and political tendencies nestled and jostled. Because the mix is so varied, it is possible to isolate specific factors while holding others constant.

Third and finally, the German sources permit especially detailed study of the social, economic, and political context of demographic change. The settled municipal framework and record keeping of high quality make it possible to treat the entire nineteenth century in the same terms as the eighteenth. There is no need to halt the story just when it gets interesting, as studies of British or French populations often do. Moreover, both eras can be treated thoroughly. Occupations are normally described. The wealth of most families can be traced in detail in tax records. Even the political allegiances of individuals are occasionally preserved. The abundant archival material allows one to analyse the precocious turn to contraception within a natural and social setting designed for comparison.[10]

That institutional setting lies at the heart of this project. What limited successes theories touting sociological factors in fertility decline can point to come largely because those factors were constructed historically on the framework of locality. Municipalities where contraception spread early and easily were also distinguished by a more equal distribution of wealth and by the political independence of their inhabitants. Individuals made their choices within differentiated local environments. Each municipality functioned as an incubator, or a cauldron, concocting an experimental amalgam of social relations whose distinctiveness endured even as it pursued its own peculiar evolution.

Let me turn to these incubators, in an attempt to site their peculiarities for the reader. Map 1.1 locates the villages of Grafenhausen bei Lahr, Kappel am Rhein, and Rust on the right bank of the Rhine river. They form part of the long Lotharingian fringe between France and Germany which has distinguished itself by innovation throughout European history. The links to the east and west

A Starting Point

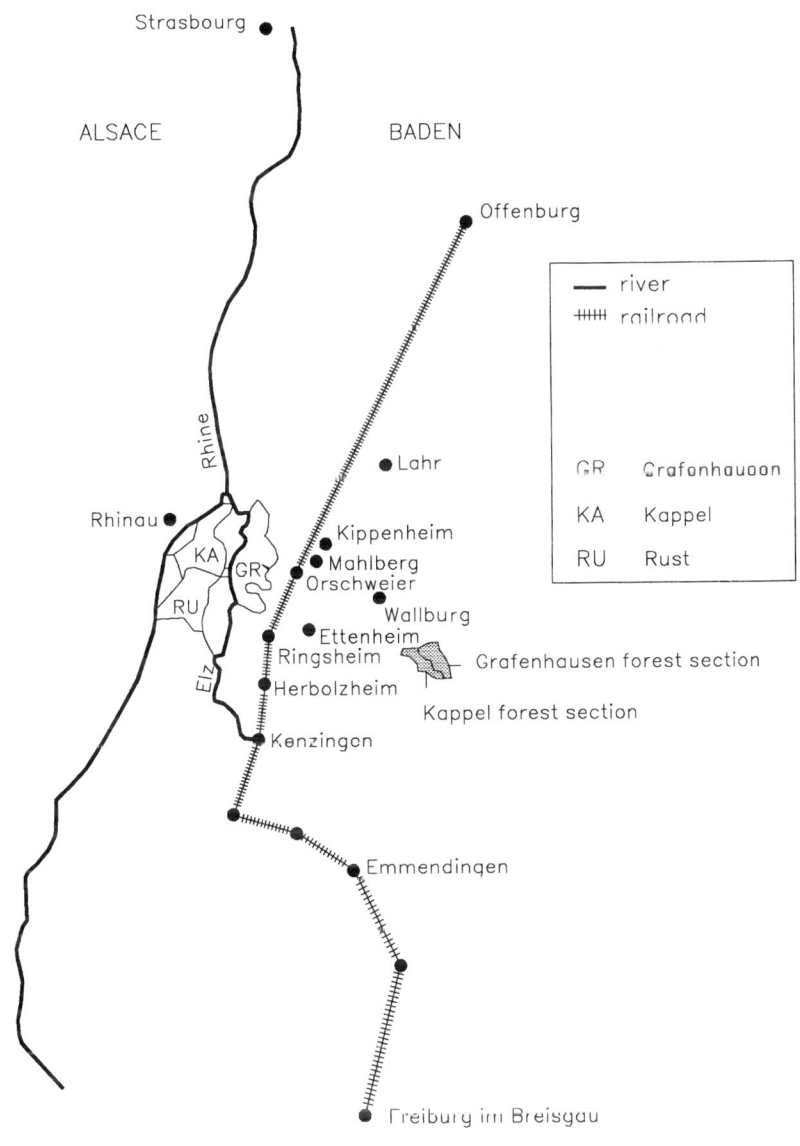

MAP 1.1 THE RHINE PLAIN

created by the Rhine crossing at Kappel supplemented the north-south waterway, and thereby rendered the position of these three municipalities doubly strategic.

Because of their proximity to one another, the villages enjoyed roughly equivalent climate and soil. To these similarities were added German language, Catholic religion, and rural custom. However, in the early modern period, and right through the eighteenth century, the political divisions that made this region the paradise of petty states came between the three communities. Grafenhausen and Kappel were directly subject to the bishops of Strasbourg in their guise as princes in Ettenheim.[11] Rust, on the other hand, was enfeoffed to nobles, and from 1441 remained under the control of the Böcklin family.[12]

All three villages were incorporated into the Grand Duchy of Baden in 1803, and from that point their political histories converged. They were initially subordinated to Baden's former outpost in Mahlberg, but its jurisdiction passed to Ettenheim county in 1810. That unit endured even after Baden became part of the German empire, and was superseded only in 1924. The new county Lahr survived Weimar and Nazi Germany, as well as the subsumption of Baden in Baden-Württemberg under the current Federal Republic. In the 1970s the seat of government was transferred even farther from the villages with the creation of the Ortenau district centred on Offenburg. That reorganization also saw the amalgamation of Grafenhausen and Kappel in the new municipality of Kappel-Grafenhausen.

From this summary, one might anticipate little contrast between the villages' histories. However, there were in fact striking differences, most notably with respect to fertility. Moreover, the greatest gap emerged between the experiences of Grafenhausen and Kappel. Strong family limitation emerged early in Grafenhausen, and spread widely and rapidly within that community in the nineteenth century. A fair number of Rusters were only somewhat slower to alter their fertility, but most Kapplers lagged generations behind. The book is devoted to exploring this divergence and the municipal environments that nurtured it.

An essential aid in that enterprise is the local genealogy or OSB.[13] An OSB is a book reconstituting family histories from the parish and civil registers of the community. Family reconstitution reassembles the separate entries recording family members' births and deaths, and links them to the wedding of the parents.[14] These full reproductive histories supply the basic data of demographic analysis. In arranging the disparate events noted in one locality in a collective family tree, each OSB makes accessible the experience of thousands of inhabitants, family by family.

Such works exist for each of Grafenhausen, Kappel, and Rust, and trace their populations from the second half of the seventeenth century until the 1960s.[15] Moreover, one can follow the peregrinations of mobile elements of the rural population through the OSBs for surrounding localities.[16] Because the OSBs record virtually every birth and wedding for three centuries, they furnish a firm foundation on which to reconstruct the three communities. By linking data on wealth, emigration, and political participation to the framework laid down by the OSB, one can recreate, layer by layer, the texture of the villagers' experiences.[17]

The value of this approach can scarcely be overemphasized. By breaking life into its component events, family reconstitution makes it possible to confront individuals directly. History can then be studied at ground level, in the presence of those who made it. Even when people are grouped for one analysis or another, the underlying structure of the data makes it possible to reclassify them to test alternative hypotheses or explore relations between the most diverse characteristics.

Building on the OSBs therefore offers the prospect of exploiting all the available sources to the fullest to do total history. In practice, that prospect is a bit premature. This book, for instance, largely limits itself to information on occupation, wealth, religion, and politics. These are important dimensions of life, but they by no means exhaust it. One can easily imagine other sorts of data that might be relevant to fertility, from women's educational attainments to men's military service. Yet even in the absence of such data, the available sources add ranges of colour seldom found in demographic histories.

The OSB backbone of this study consists of over six thousand couples wed before 1900. Of these, just over four thousand[18] have family histories of sufficient quality and detail to meet the exacting standards of historical demography.[19] I refer to these four thousand family histories as "documented" marriages.[20] Documented marriages are scarce in the earliest periods, as the marriages of women born before the records begin are by definition undocumented. In consequence, the families of just 42 % of all couples wed before 1800 are documented. That figure rises to 76 % in the nineteenth century, hitting a full 86 % in Grafenhausen between 1850 and 1874. Such a high figure places the completeness of the OSBs well above the sources used in most historical demography.[21]

That completeness is not limited to marital fertility. I collected data on all children born out of wedlock in Grafenhausen, Kappel, or Rust, or dying there before turning fifteen. To parallel the documented marriages, which include children born after 1900 to couples wed before 1900, I extend the study of illegitimacy into the first two decades of the twentieth century. This produces a collection of 1362 women with 2019 illegitimate children, again a larger and more comprehensive statistical base than historians customarily use.

The extent of OSB coverage makes it possible to give a detailed account of fertility both before and after the onset of family limitation. I close this introduction with an overview of that account. Chapter Two begins with a review of overall population trends, contrasting the steady growth of the eighteenth century with the erratic patterns of the nineteenth. I attribute this shift to heavy emigration, especially from Rust, in the face of population pressure. The remainder of Chapter Two refines this notion of population pressure and sets up Chapter Three's examination of the economic history of the three villages. That history shows Grafenhauseners repeatedly taking the lead in transforming agricultural organization and technique.

Examination of their fertility shows that they transformed themselves as well.

Chapters Four and Five look at the elements of the European marriage pattern, namely high celibacy rates and low illegitimacy rates. Births out of wedlock are tied to dislocation in the eighteenth century and to poverty in the nineteenth. The latter connection reinforces the conventional linking of inheritance and marriage. Because standard accounts of this link are blind to the property rights of women, I revise them to deal with this region of partible inheritance. Even the more intricate system I postulate broke down under the demographic, economic, and legal pressures of the nineteenth century. Those pressures and the switch to family limitation are traced through the rise and fall of ages at first marriage.

The general results of Chapter Five fix the parameters of marital fertility, but analysing its content directly requires developing technical concepts. Chapter Six reviews the historiographical background through a survey of definitions and indices of family limitation, thereby preparing readers for their practical application. These standard aggregate measures document the sharp differences in fertility between villages. I introduce the distribution of ages at second-last confinement to measure the percentage of the population practising family limitation. This criterion pinpoints twenty families from each cohort and village whose reproduction halted while they were still young, Their social, economic, and political characteristics provide clues about the spread of new patterns of fertility.

Subsequent chapters follow up each of those clues. Chapter Seven compares the fertility of groups defined by occupation or status, showing that innkeepers, landed proprietors, and notables led the turn to family limitation. Yet these gross social characteristics were overshadowed by locality, and so I move in Chapter Eight to a deeper investigation of relations between prosperity and fertility. In the course of that discussion, I present an analysis of economic structures that disentangles the contributions of demographic factors and contrasts in wealth. That analysis confirms the pattern that had emerged from the study of entry into marriage: Grafenhauseners were traditionally the richest and Rusters the poorest, on average. More important, however, was that property was distributed more evenly within the citizenries of those two villages, while Kappel presented greater extremes of wealth and poverty.

The significance of this finding becomes clear in Chapter Nine as I trace differences in fertility between rich and poor. In each village, solid proprietors made up the natural constituency for family limitation. As their influence varied from locality to locality, so too did the vigour with which family limitation arose and spread. The turn to the new fertility régime depended on a couple's relation to the rest of the population as well as on its absolute economic standing.

One interpretation of this phenomenon assigns an important part to popular psychology and relates it to locality. Different constellations of attitudes were fostered by variations in the experiences of each municipality and sustained by the municipal structure itself. The next three chapters bolster this speculation by exploring the extent to which the local patterns evident in the demographic and economic data also had a political dimension. Chapter Ten's treatment of public conflicts over power, from peasant uprisings to the revolution of 1848, confirms the existence of local traditions. Grafenhausen boasted a disproportionate number of restless minds who challenged authority of all kinds in pursuing their own goals. Many Rusters shared this restlessness, but they were considerably less successful in their endeavours. Kapplers, by contrast, were relatively quiescent.

By the end of the nineteenth century those traditions had merged into the general currents of Baden and German politics. Chapters Eleven and Twelve test theories linking anticlericalism and family limitation, and find them wanting, for the triumphs of ultramontanism and contraception coincided. Both federally and provincially, the Centre party rose to dominate the countryside wherever Catholics were in the majority. Yet even at that point, the specific tendencies that had coloured village life did not disappear. The consequence was an enduring local association between political independence and affinity for family limitation.

Chapter Thirteen reviews my major findings. In light of the mixed successes of theories reducing fertility to occupation, wealth, religion, and politics, it suggests that fertility be recognized as autonomous. In that sense, the conclusion returns the debate to its starting point.

Notes

1. Jacques Houdaille, "Fécondité des mariages dans le quart nord-est de la France de 1670 à 1829", *Annales de Démographie Historique*, 1976, 341–392. Alain Bideau and Jean-Pierre Bardet, "Fluctuations chronologiques ou début de la révolution contraceptive?", in Jacques Dupâquier and others, *Histoire de la population française* (Paris, 1991), vol. 2, 379–391.
2. Unless fertility is already (to be) curtailed, there is no room in the wife's fecund years to add extra children in response to the deaths of their older siblings. For evidence, interpreted differently, see John Knodel, *Demographic behavior in the past. A study of fourteen German village populations in the eighteenth and nineteenth centuries* (Cambridge, 1988), 393–442.
3. Compare Jane Schneider and Peter Schneider, "Going Forward in Reverse Gear: Culture, Economy, and Political Economy in the Demographic Transitions of a Rural Sicilian Town", in John Gillis, Louise Tilly, and David Levine (ed.), *The European Experience of Declining Fertility* (Cambridge, Massachusetts, 1992), 272–274.
4. Ernest Lewis-Faning, *Family Limitation and its influence on human fertility during the past fifty years* (London, 1949), 48–70.
5. Herbert Butterfield, *The Whig Interpretation of History* (Penguin, 1973—original 1931).
6. In that respect, contraception may ultimately give every love the daring to speak its name.
7. Compare Charles Tilly's contribution to "Review Symposium Ansley J. Coale and Susan Cotts Watkins (eds.) The Decline of Fertility in Europe", *Population and Development Review*, 12 (1986), 326.

8. David Levine, "'For Their Own Reasons': Individual Marriage Decisions and Family Life", *Journal of Family History*, 7 (1982), 255–264. Levine is of course not responsible for all that I read into his evocative phrase.
9. See the information on Herbolzheim, in addition to Grafenhausen, Kappel, and Rust, in Knodel, *fourteen*. Those data are from Albert Köbele, *Sippenbuch der Stadt Herbolzheim im Breisgau* (Grafenhausen, 1967). On country-wide trends, compare John Knodel, *The Decline of Fertility in Germany, 1871–1939* (Princeton, 1974).
10. My Ph.D. thesis ("Fertility in Three Baden Villages 1650–1900", University of Toronto 1988, cited as "Benz, Thesis") includes substantial technical information (on estimating the percentage limiting, discerning which marriages are mature, counting births out of wedlock, and so on) that has been omitted from this book. I hope to provide specialists an accounting on these points in other publications.
11. Johannes Ferdinand, "Ettenheim", *Badische Heimat*, 22 (1935), 308–321. Josef Rest, "Zustände in der südlichen Ortenau im Jahr 1802", *Die Ortenau*, 11 (1924), 17–18.
12. The previous lords made an unsuccessful attempt to regain control in the mid-sixteenth century. ADBR G 634 (5) (documents relating to court case, 1531–1556, including testimony from 1541).
13. From the initials of "Ortssippenbuch". For further information on the history of OSBs and the circumstances of their compilation, see John Knodel, "Ortssippenbücher als Daten für die historische Demographie", *Geschichte und Gesellschaft*, 1 (1975), 288–324, John Knodel and Edward Shorter, "The Reliability of Family Reconstitution Data in German Village Genealogies (Ortssippenbücher)", *Annales de Démographie Historique*, 1976, 115–153, Jacques Houdaille, "Quelques résultats sur la démographie de trois villages d'Allemagne de 1750 à 1879", *Population*, 20 (1970), 649–650, and John Knodel, "Two and a Half Centuries of Demographic History in a Bavarian Village", *Population Studies*, 24 (1970), 353–360. My own assessment of the registers and OSBs appears in appendix A of Benz, Thesis.
14. On the theory and practice of family reconstitution, see Michel Fleury and Louis Henry, *Nouveau manuel de dépouillement et d'exploitation de l'état civil ancien* (Paris, 1965), Anthony Wrigley, "Family Reconstitution", in Anthony Wrigley (ed.), *An Introduction to English Historical Demography* (New York, 1966), 96–159, and Manfred Hofmann, Albert Köbele, and Robert Wetekam, *Von der Kirchenbuchverkartung zum Ortssippenbuch* (Limburg a. d. Lahn, 1957).
15. Albert Köbele, *Ortssippenbuch Grafenhausen*, third edition (Grafenhausen, 1971). Albert Köbele, *Dorfsippenbuch Kappel am Rhein*, second edition (Grafenhausen, 1969). Albert Köbele, *Ortssippenbuch Rust* (Grafenhausen, 1969).
16. In addition to the OSBs for Altdorf, Altenheim, Dundenheim, Friesenheim, Herbolzheim, Kippenheim, Mahlberg-Orschweier, Münchweier, Nonnenweier, Rheinhausen (Niederhausen and Oberhausen combined), Ringsheim, and Schmieheim specifically footnoted in the text, I drew information from the OSBs for Binzen and Rümmingen, Broggingen, Efringen-Kirchen, Freiamt, Ichenheim, Istein and Huttingen, Kippenheimweiler, Meissenheim, Mietersheim, Ottoschwanden, Sexau, Wittenweier, and Wyhl. The OSBs for Egringen, Eimeldingen, Haltingen, Hüfingen, Müllen, Oberweier, Philippsburg, and Weingarten also yielded a few tidbits.
17. After considering other sources, Alan MacFarlane, *Reconstructing Historical Communities* (Cambridge, 1977) declares for a similar approach.
18. 1324 in Grafenhausen, 1068 in Kappel and 1673 in Rust, for a total of 4065 overall, including a few who reproduced in more than one village. 1367 couples wed before 1800, 577 wed 1800–1824, 724 wed 1825–1849, 698 wed 1850–1874, and 699 wed 1875–1899. Except where I specifically indicate otherwise, all statistics refer to these marriage cohorts.
19. That is, (1) the wedding is dated to the day, (2) the death date of at least one spouse is given, (3) the wife's birthdate is given (possibly only as an estimated year),

and (4) the birthdates of children, if there are any, are given to the day, or at worst the month. Families who emigrated out of observation are excluded.
20. In calculating the percentage of completed families practising family limitation, I limit the selection further to "well-documented" marriages, where in addition the wife's birth is specified to the day and there are death dates for both spouses (or there is a positive indication—independent of fertility—that the marriage endured until the wife was at least forty-five).
21. Compare Roger Schofield, "Representativeness and Family Reconstitution", *Annales de Démographie Historique*, 1972, 121–125, Poul Thestrup, "Methodological Problems of Family Reconstitution Study in a Danish Rural Parish before 1800", *Scandinavian Economic History Review*, 20 (1972), 1–26, David Levine, "The Reliability of Parochial Registration and the Representativeness of Family Reconstitution", *Population Studies*, 30 (1976), 107–122, and Susan Norton, "The Vital Question: Are Reconstituted Families Representative of the General Population?", in Bennett Dyke and Warren Morrill (ed.), *Genealogical Demography* (New York, 1980), 11–22, and the manuals referred to earlier.

2

Land and People

The key components of an agrarian economy are the resources it exploits and the population it supports. The relation between these two components is a dynamic one, for each varies qualitatively as well as quantitatively as they interact. For analytical purposes, I look first at the number of inhabitants of Grafenhausen, Kappel, and Rust at various points in the past four centuries, and then in Chapter Three at their means of livelihood. Despite this artificial separation, I stress that the source of changes in the economy and the population lay in their interaction, and more specifically in people's attempts to control both these crucial aspects of their lives.

Sustained population growth through the eighteenth century and the early part of the nineteenth came to threaten villagers' standards of living. They met this challenge by continuing to diversify their agricultural endeavours. When economic development proved insufficient to maintain their positions over the medium term, villagers resorted to manipulating the other side of the balance between resources and population. They did so in crude ways through emigration and in more sophisticated ways through family limitation. I reserve discussion of the latter development for subsequent chapters, since my focus here is on gross factors influencing the population in a direct way.

Figure 2.1 summarizes overall population trends.[1] In all three villages, a distinct pattern is associated with each century. The seventeenth century is characterized by sharp short-term fluctuations amid long-term stagnation, the eighteenth by an enduring rise, and the nineteenth by a resumption of erratic movements around a fairly constant mean. Each phase reflects a specific balance of forces.[2]

WAR AND PEACE

The seventeenth century is documented most fully for Rust, but in each village the population hit one or more low points at that time. These nadirs reflected the numerous wars fought in the region. The campaigns of the Thirty Years War and Louis XIV's attempts to extend French hegemony repeatedly devastated the Ortenau.[3] The religious and political patchwork spanning the Rhine focused interest on the strategic river crossing at Kappel. Incidental bloodshed and disease followed in the wake of early modern armies, but military operations affected the populations of small communities in a variety of

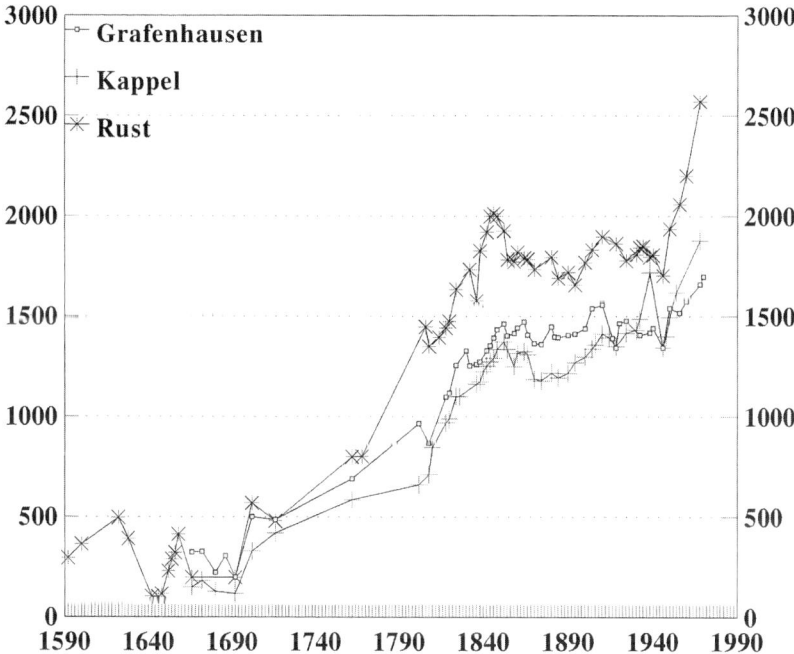

FIGURE 2.1   THE POPULATIONS OF GRAFENHAUSEN, KAPPEL, AND RUST 1593–1969

other ways. Haphazard plundering and more systematic taxation, together with accidental or deliberate destruction of crops, animals, and buildings, fostered economic insecurity.

The manner in which village life came to a standstill can be seen in the records of the renewal of municipal officials in Rust in the 1630s.[4] On several occasions, the annual ceremony had to be held in Strasbourg, where the Böcklin lord was then residing. In some years it could not take place at all. In 1640, when it was held in Bischeim bei Hönheim in Alsace, only a mayor, a treasurer, and three of the other five members of the court were appointed. This left vacant the positions of the six representatives of the citizens, the two overseers of the waterways, the two dispensers of wood, the two boundary watchers, the two advocates, the two trustees, the two meat inspectors, the two bread inspectors, the two collectors of the wine tax, the two roof inspectors, and the supervisor of the fields.[5] These gaps were filled only gradually over the following seven years.

The lists of citizens from this period, marked as they often are by marginal crosses and lines through names, leave an impression of increased mortality. However, it would be a mistake to assume that all losses that appear in Figure 2.1 during the years before 1715 were permanent. To begin with, the absences of conscripts were generally only temporary. More serious were the repeated marches and counter-marches, which produced floods of refugees. In emergencies, the village scattered, as institutions sent movable property to other centres for safekeeping and families took flight. For example, in the 1690s the registers of Rhinau, a left-bank parish where an army garrison was stationed, repeatedly mention the presence of refugees from the right bank.[6]

Entries that found their way into the registers of the three villages themselves bring out the dislocation attendant on the disorders of the late seventeenth century.[7] Typically, these laconically mention escape from war in explaining how births or deaths came to occur outside the parish. One is left to imagine the hardship of a birth and baptism amidst the shoals as a family fled across the Rhine.[8] While there is no encounter as dramatic as the later fatal beatings by French soldiers of a Ringsheim couple who vainly defended their last head of cattle against depredation,[9] the OSBs do note abuse of a member of Kappel's municipal council by French pillagers.[10] For most inhabitants, intermittent evacuation became a fact of life.

Many fugitives returned home as soon as the danger passed, and some even put in occasional appearances to keep up hope of raising a crop that year. Moreover, any significant drop in the ratio of labour to land drew immigrants from more populous areas who rapidly made up any shortfall. Just this process was at work in the early years of the eighteenth century.[11] Thus, it would be misleading to treat the troughs of Figure 2.1 as demonstrating a prolonged period of devastation.[12]

What the Figure does show is that villagers as a group had little need to restrict population growth at that point. War not only held down the absolute number of inhabitants, but also postponed the date at which that number could begin to rise. In the interim, whatever gradual progress was made in agriculture increased the average harvest that could be reaped from a fixed territory. Moreover, the troubled times forced a reduction in cultivated area, so that an even greater reserve for expansion lay stored up.

Grafenhauseners took notable advantage of this situation. A look at the village's borders on Map 2.2 reveals an outlying patch to the south which bears little relation to the rest of the municipality. This area had constituted the independent village of Reichenweier, which was abandoned at some point during these upheavals.[13] Grafenhausen annexed the vacant territory, claiming that its citizens had purchased the land from the last Reichenweilers.[14] They also possessed, this time as individuals rather than as a corporate body, much of the Rittmatten—the appendage belonging to Ettenheim that extends between the two parts of the municipality. Accumulation in time of depression served the villagers well when the economic tide turned.[15]

Turn it did, once a prolonged peace set in in the eighteenth century.[16] An initial jump eliminated the artificial depopulation of the preceding years.[17] Thereafter, the population of all three villages increased less dramatically but steadily. At first this growth impinged only slightly on the fields of the localities, in part because of the agricultural innovations discussed in Chapter Three.

Land and People 15

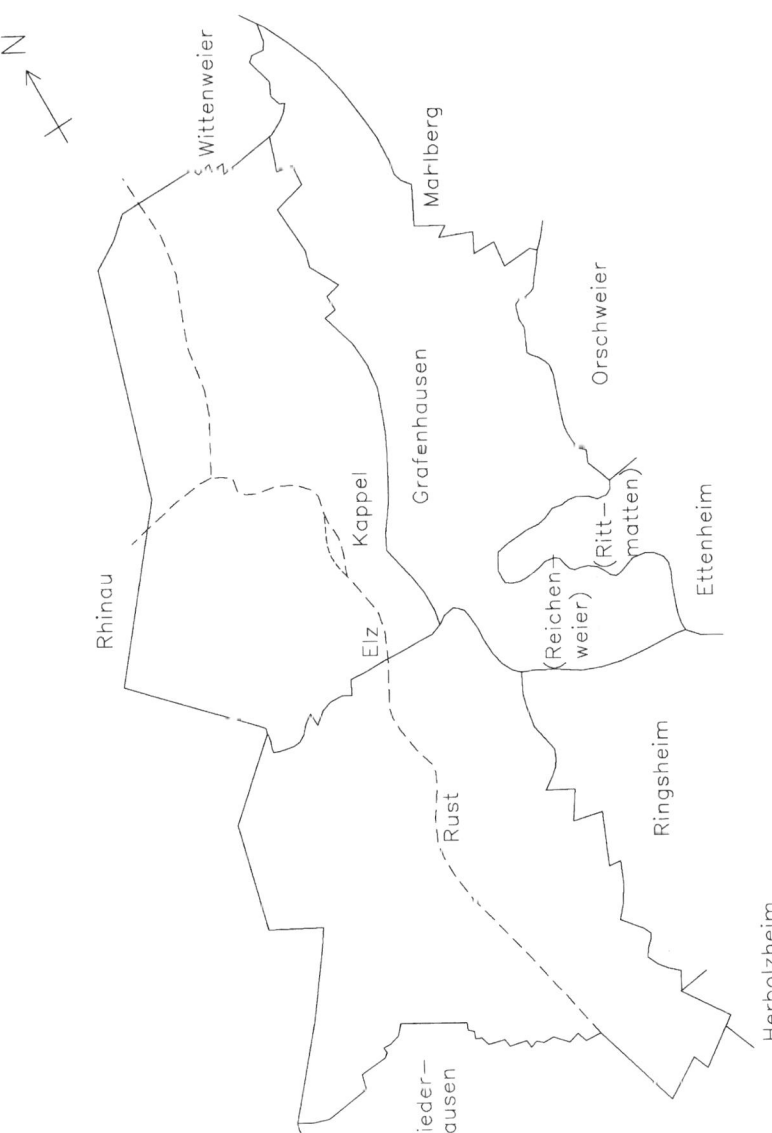

MAP 2.2 GRAFENHAUSEN, KAPPEL, AND RUST

Growing demand manifested itself more strongly in other spheres, where neither qualitative improvement nor quantitative expansion were possible. This limitation applied prominently to housing, which was restricted to the traditional area of settlement, and to the supply of wood. Because access to these goods[18] was limited to citizens of the municipality, the price of citizenship rights provides an index of population pressure. The entry fee charged outsiders marrying into Grafenhausen and Kappel remained at the low level established in the seventeenth century until at least 1737.[19] In 1763, in response to a petition from Grafenhausen complaining of crowding, the charge for women was set at twice the traditional level, and that for men at four times.[20] The complaints did not abate,[21] and in 1802 a further 50 % increase was imposed.[22]

These moves did not so much combat hardship as protect a favoured position. In practice, they turned immigration into a source of revenue, for the municipality split the proceeds 50–50 with the lordship. Indeed, when the newcomer was already a subject of the bishop of Strasbourg, the municipality got all of the fee.[23] Bilateral exemptions between many of the territories in the area extended these conditions so that they applied to the majority of solvent immigrants. Citizenship fees were a way of controlling immigration, not banning it.

The same strategy could not be implemented in Rust, where the presence of a secular lord altered the political balance. There too, charges increased over the centuries, but the lion's share went to the lord throughout.[24] Prices were also rather higher, as were the penalties for unauthorized movement.[25] The Böcklins encouraged immigration to generate revenue for their own coffers regardless of their subjects' interest in protecting their standards of living.

Despite the popular concern over immigration, the basic motor of the demographic expansion was natural increase. Individuals born locally constituted a majority of the population at all times, and a very substantial one most of the time.[26] A certain number of people moved to the homes of their brides or grooms at marriage, but such migration tended to even out across the countryside. Wandering families without citizenship rights became more numerous as the eighteenth century wore on, but their very mobility meant that they made little contribution to the growth of any single locality.[27]

This state of affairs altered in the early nineteenth century as the Baden government fixed such families in one of the places that their ancestors had passed through. This was resisted by the municipalities involved, who rightly feared they would end up footing heavier bills for poor relief.[28] Rusters in particular paid the price of the Böcklins' search for revenue, as the income the late eighteenth-century lords had derived from permitting strangers to wed was dwarfed by the costs the community incurred to support the descendants of those strangers.[29] To a certain extent the forced settlement of a previously transient group diluted the local character of each municipality. However, this effect was temporary, for it was precisely these families who were most apt to emigrate, thereby resuming their itinerant ways.[30]

Therefore, it was not immigration that drove the graphs in Figure 2.1 upward.

TABLE 2.3
Distribution of children's ages at death in documented marriages, by date of parents' wedding

	Died before age 1	Died between ages 1 and 15	Survived to age 15	Number of cases
pre-1800	23 %	17 %	59 %	2787
1800–1824	21 %	13 %	66 %	2527
1825–1849	22 %	11 %	67 %	3492
1850–1874	26 %	11 %	63 %	3537
1875–1899	26 %	8 %	66 %	3593

Notes
(1) *Source*: OSB *Grafenhausen*, OSB *Kappel*, and OSB *Rust*.
(2) The statistics are limited to periods when registration of infant deaths was judged relatively complete: in Grafenhausen after 1740, in Kappel after 1810 and in Rust after 1764. See Benz, Thesis, appendix A.
(3) Children for whom no fate is given in the OSBs are assumed to have survived to age fifteen.
(4) Deaths before age one include those the OSBs record as stillbirths, about 3 % of the total.

Nor was it a drop in infant mortality. Death rates before one year old were essentially constant at about 22 % until the middle of the nineteenth century, as Table 2.3 shows. Thereafter, they rose to 26 %, remaining at that level into the twentieth century. I emphasize this *increase* in infant mortality to dispel any attachment readers may feel to traditional accounts of the demographic transition, according to which a reduction in deaths among offspring precipitated a decline in fertility, together producing the demographic régime typical of the industrialized world in the twentieth century.[31] That simply did not happen in these villages.[32]

Diehard partisans of the demographic transition may take more comfort from the lessening in death rates among children who had survived infancy (in the second column of Table 2.3), but only by revising their theory.[33] For my part, I prefer to emphasize that this improvement extended to adults, so that the lifespans of married couples lengthened by about five years between the eighteenth century and the end of the nineteenth. Adult survival may have increased birth rates slightly by allowing women to bear children over a larger part of their fecund years. More important, it meant that population growth created pressure on adults. The world of the citizen became increasingly crowded. Because the older generation survived past its customary time, its children inherited later. This postponement attenuated their entry into full adulthood economically and demographically.[34]

These developments can be interpreted within the conventional framework of a decline in the frequency of demographic crises.[35] In the seventeenth century, war, disease, and harvest failure had produced periodic peaks of mortality for both children and adults. This Malthusian ceiling on the population operated statistically rather than absolutely. Thus, even as agricultural innovations raised the average height of the ceiling, an increase in the variability of that ceiling prevented sustained population growth in the 1600s. Peace did not in itself increase the average number of people who could be supported at particular standards of living by the use of specific technology, but it did provide the opportunity for annual surpluses of births over deaths to build up over longer periods.

Emigration

Following a brief check during the Napoleonic wars,[36] population accelerated until the 1830s. Thereafter, waves of emigration were interspersed with spurts of growth, producing in Figure 2.1 the jagged curves typical of the mid-nineteenth century. Substantial numbers departed the villages for longer or shorter periods, legally or illegally, on their own or with financial assistance, as individuals or as families.[37] This was a novel phenomenon, for despite the movement between localities at marriage, in the eighteenth century families of citizens had emigrated less often.[38]

The OSB data, although incomplete, show an upsurge in emigration overseas—to Algeria, Brazil, Venezuela, and above all the United States of America—just as the population hit its peak. 9 % of families formed in the 1820s left Baden, and the tide did not slacken until after the 1850s.[39] The cohort wed in the 1840s was most depleted, as 14 % emigrated. Trends in the movements of lone individuals were similar.[40] The flow overseas fell off after the creation of the German empire opened new outlets within Europe. Emigration by families grew less significant towards the end of the nineteenth century, for it was adolescents whom the urban centres enticed away from their birthplaces.[41]

Reasons for leaving the villages varied, but emigration was linked to poverty, and more generally to marginality. Sudden reversals of personal fortune, such as bankruptcy or conscription, prompted some individuals to make fresh starts in the New World.[42] More general disappointments, from the harvest failure of 1817[43] to the suppression of the revolutions of 1848–1849, moved larger numbers to flight. Over the long haul, however, mass emigration was a function of population pressure, manifested on the one hand in the conviction of the authorities that there were too many people in the villages and on the other hand in the willingness of the poor to restructure their lives.

The scope of these undertakings can be seen from one episode in the history of Rust. Between 1831 and 1834, thirty-three families emigrated, a loss of about 7 % of the village's population. The municipality itself paid the cost of passage for 122 people. Such an expenditure was fiscally sound, in that those leaving, together with their dependants and descendants, ceased to drain the treasury for relief.

Rust continued to be the leading source of emigrants in subsequent years. Kappel was only slightly behind in absolute terms, and because it was much smaller Kappel's losses were proportionately the most severe. However, almost all Kapplers paid their own way overseas. Grafenhausen subsidized more departures than Kappel, but lost only half as many people. The emigration statistics therefore leave the impression that Rusters were poor, Kapplers numerous, and Grafenhauseners stable.[44]

The stealth many employed in setting out reinforces the link between poverty and emigration. Departing without State permission risked forfeiting all assets left behind.[45] Such a course made sense only for those whose property was already encumbered with debts. Others tried their fortunes abroad while awaiting their inheritances. Still others had no patrimony to look forward to, and illegitimate children, together with their mothers, joined the stream headed for the United States.

Once initiated, emigration acquired momentum of its own. Lone family members often built up a nest-egg abroad to support bringing over their relatives. Such arrangements, together with letters from the departed, meant that information about life overseas was readily available.[46] Moreover, many kept a foot in each world, leasing out their lands in the home village, but retaining their rights as citizens—or children of citizens—even while living overseas. This facilitated the movement of population in both directions.[47]

The history of the Jewish community in Rust corroborates my interpretation of population movements. Although subject to more social constraints, Jews responded to opportunities and challenges much as the rest of the population did. They came when places were open, and left when alternatives to a crowded home beckoned.

A Jewish community first settled in Rust as part of the influx following the seventeenth-century wars.[48] In nearby Nonnenweier, where the Böcklins shared the lordship, the first mention of a resident Jew comes from the municipal accounts for 1708.[49] In a letter of January 1732 from Rust, the lord's brother complained of an attempt by the priest to force Catholic houseowners to evict Jewish renters. The secular authority rebuffed this initiative.[50] In extending protection over the Jews, the Protestant lords served their own interests as well. Because Jews were a persecuted minority with few other places to turn, the lordship could and did levy unusually high dues from them.[51]

For much of the eighteenth century, the Jewish community was limited to twelve families,[52] but their numbers had tripled by the second decade of the nineteenth century.[53] Nevertheless, the community was never large, and marriage partners were frequently brought in from elsewhere. Moreover, because Jews were often on the road as pedlars, traders, and brokers, they kept in touch with distant locations, including many in France. Their ties to the locality were thus relatively weak.

Natural increase among Jews and disproportionate emigration among Catholics left the Jewish community of 245 with an eighth of Rust's population at the middle of the nineteenth century. However, after 1862, when recognition of full civil equality bestowed freedom of movement, the Jewish population was rapidly reduced by a drift to the towns.[54] It was halved between 1852 and 1890, and halved again in the succeeding fifteen years.[55] By the early twentieth century, emigration by the young and natural attrition among the old left only a few Jewish residents. The number fell even further in the years after the National Socialists seized power, so that just nine remained to be deported to camps in October 1940.[56] However, many Jews originally from Rust found themselves caught in the same extermination campaign.[57]

This overview reveals that the Jewish community constituted a sub-population within which factors promoting emigration were particularly strong. The ties Jews had always maintained with the wider world made them less sedentary and more aware of prospects elsewhere. As a marginalized part of the rural community, they had little to lose by relocating.[58] Cultural considerations, from educational opportunities to the levelling anonymity of urban life, also played a rôle. With the significant exception of its dénouement, the story of Rust's Jews therefore confirms the mechanisms implicated in the general movement.

Emigration, by Jews or Catholics, transformed those left behind but little. At all times there existed a core of sedentary families surrounded by loose individuals without the economic resources or psychological commitments to tie them to a single locale. Villagers took advantage of improved transportation facilities to preserve these social rôles, simply playing them out on a larger stage.[59] By limiting the impact of population growth, emigration met their objectives.

THE LOGIC OF POPULATION PRESSURE

On the basis of the information I have presented thus far, a straightforward—if ultimately unsatisfactory—account of the history of all three villages can be offered. Following an extended demographic downturn in the seventeenth century, population growth resumed in the eighteenth and eventually came to press on the available resources. Once a saturation point was reached in the nineteenth century, the population fluctuated about that level, repeatedly growing somewhat above it until a burst of emigration reduced it below the ceiling, allowing a fresh rise. At the level of aggregates, there is little reason to quarrel with this interpretation.[60]

However, investigation of the fertility of individual couples shows that more was going on than a simple reassignment of people to a wider range of geographic locations. In particular, some couples responded to population pressure not by leaving or forcing others to leave, but by cutting down on the number of children they themselves bore within marriage. Understanding this development requires (1) refining the notion of population pressure, (2) looking more closely at economic trends, and (3) exploring how population growth and economic change had modified marriage patterns. The first task will be taken up in the remainder of this chapter, while the second and third are left for Chapters Three and Five respectively. Only after this background is in place will it be profitable to examine directly marital fertility and the factors influencing it.

In the foregoing, I have written rather generally of population pressure, and left to readers' imaginations a detailed account of the impact of population growth on economic and social structures. The time has come to define the concept more narrowly. I draw attention first to a near-universal consequence of an abundance of population, and then explore how differentiation mediated its impact.

There is an important technical sense in which Grafenhausen, Kappel, and Rust were under population pressure at virtually all times, in that marginal returns fell off sharply with increased labour. In other words, each additional effort—in the form of more time worked or more people working—produced much less on average than the effort preceding it. Only by acquiring substantial new natural resources could someone hope to reap as much benefit from further labour as from previous work. Every individual and household therefore spent some time in activities of relatively little value. Readers may find it more intuitive to think of this as underemployment rather than overpopulation, but my point is that the two are opposite sides of the same coin.

This economic logic underlies several characteristics notoriously associated with peasant societies. The most prominent is land hunger: attaching to real estate a value greater than that assigned to it by outsiders—whose evaluations were formed under a different balance of economic circumstances. Unlike such observers, rural householders could make effective use of additional land, because the labour required to exploit it was both available and free.[61] Conversely, labour held little value, for most households possessed more than they knew what to do with. Accordingly, villagers looked eagerly for opportunities to use their superabundant workforce more efficiently. Intensive agriculture and the proliferation of by-employments were natural results.[62]

Economic differentiation meant that the need for such opportunities and the ability to take advantage of them varied widely. Some families had accumulated resources so extensive that they could live comfortable and even luxurious lives heedless of any overall shortages.[63] This relative immunity to economic pressure at one end of the scale was more than balanced at the other by large numbers of families with insufficient resources to guarantee a livelihood—at least one on the same level with the wealthy.

This last reflection serves as a reminder that psychological differences complicated the patterns produced by social and economic differentiation. Strictly, individuals responded less to population pressure than to a sense of population pressure. That sense in turn rested on some notion of what constituted an acceptable standard of living for a person of their station, a standard which increasing population might then undermine. Because long-term poverty lowered expectations, consciousness of an overabundance of people relative to resources did not appear first among those enduring the worst conditions. Instead, the threat of being squeezed out by growing numbers was perceived most acutely by those with more to lose. Moreover, because power was distributed unevenly, the idea occurring to the powerful that there were too many people about first led them to modify not their own behaviour, but the behaviour of the weaker.[64]

This state of affairs had obtained on the Rhine plain long before the rise of population in the eighteenth century. What that expansion did was accentuate all aspects of the problem and prompt wider sectors of the community to respond to it. The supply of labour rose at the same time as the demand for agricultural products grew, thereby increasing still further the leverage exerted by land over labour. More important, the division of resources among more and more hands made that leverage work against a larger and larger percentage of the population. This intensified the urgency of the situation and accounts for the vigour with which it was tackled.

The full range of responses to population growth was even more diverse, for there was a further level of distinctions within the community. Thus far, I have written of a general pressure of population upon resources, taking for granted that increasing numbers weighed equally upon all kinds of resources. That is implausible,[65] and indeed false in the case of these three villages. In so far as individuals and families depended on different balances of resources or even on completely disparate ones, their responses to population growth were far from uniform. Moreover, there is no need to take a static view of the resources present in a locality, nor to assume that villagers took them to be fixed. More generally, there is no reason to suppose that villagers preferred manipulating population to transforming resources in ways that permitted them to support more people. Indeed, in the next chapter, I look at how some villagers did just that.

Notes

1. The points on the graphs are connected purely as an aid to the viewer. It is by no means claimed that trends were linear during the periods for which there is no direct evidence. Some totals up to 1762 are estimates based on four times the number of citizens or 1.5 times the number of communicants. See Benz, Thesis for details.
2. The renewed growth of the twentieth century lies outside the scope of this book.
3. The impact of the wars on the three villages is described in *OSB Grafenhausen* pages 129–136, *OSB Kappel* pages 47–51, and *OSB Rust* pages 53–57. The general situation is discussed in Manfred Krebs, "Politische und kirchliche Geschichte der Ortenau", supplemented by L. Lauppe, *Die Ortenau*, 40 (1960), 178–219, Eberhard Gothein, "Die oberrheinischen Lande vor und nach dem dreissigjährigen Kriege", *Zeitschrift für die Geschichte des Oberrheins*, N.F. 1 (1886), 21–39, and Otto Ifele, "Die Bevölkerung der Ortenau im 17. Jahrhundert", *Die Ortenau*, 19 (1932), 7–8.
4. BvB A U. 372.
5. The duties associated with these positions are described in detail in *OSB Rust* pages 62–69, which incorporates Benedikt Schwarz's 1902 article in *Breisgauer Erzähler*, "Eine Dorfrecht vor 300 Jahren".
6. 19 September 1690, 30 September 1691, 5 October 1693, and 10 October 1693 saw baptisms of children born to citizens of Grafenhausen "currently dwelling here in refuge from the war". Other entries from the same years refer to couples from Kappel, Altdorf, Mahlberg, and Kippenheim. ADBR 3E 397 2. *OSB Rust* page 54 mentions islands in the Rhine as another hiding place (in 1624).
7. There are references to flight, exile, or plundering from the years 1677 (*OSB Grafenhausen* entry 701, *OSB Rust* entry 562), 1678 (*OSB Rust* entries 1065, 2874, and 3686), 1690 (*OSB Grafenhausen* entries 1166, 1873, and 2902), 1691 (*OSB Grafenhausen* entry 3173, *OSB Rust* entry 3681), 1703 (*OSB Rust* entry 99), and 1713 (*OSB Kappel* entry 2478, *OSB Rust* entries 1068, 1897, and 4110).

8. 14 May 1704. *OSB Rust* entry 97.
9. July 1796. Albert Köbele, *Dorfsippenbuch Ringsheim* (Grafenhausen, 1956) entry 2211.
10. September 1691. *OSB Kappel* entry 273.
11. Michael Hennig (*Chronik der Pfarrei Kappel am Rhein*, 155–159, in Pf A Kappel) lists ten old families and fifty-nine new ones in the eighteenth century. See also *OSB Rust* page 56 (referring to 1650).
12. As Hennig (*Chronik*, 5, 155–156) does in asserting that 1692 marked the first time since Kappel had been laid waste in 1638 that it contained even 118 people.
13. The last references to Reichenweier as a going concern date from the sixteenth century. *OSB Grafenhausen* pages 220–222.
14. Gem A Grafenhausen A U. 24 (unilateral declaration of 29 March 1715). They adduced a copy of dues from 1621 (GLA 66/2964) in support.
15. Subsequent chapters discuss economic and political ramifications of these acquisitions.
16. The OSBs refer to the War of Polish Succession, 1733–1735, as the only notable exception. *OSB Grafenhausen* page 138. *OSB Rust* page 58. Again refugees fled to Rhinau. *OSB Kappel* entry 628. *OSB Rust* entries 1514 and 4799.
17. This observation clears up the discrepancy between the population estimates in the 1692 visitation reports (Karl Reinfried, "Visitationsberichte aus der zweiten Hälfte des 17. Jahrhunderts über die Pfarreien des Landkapitels Lahr (Schluss)", *Freiburger Diözesan-Archiv*, 31 (N.F. 4, 1903), 283, 285, 288) and the count of weddings (and inferred weddings) in the OSBs (which puzzles John Knodel, "Demographic Transitions in German Villages", in Ansley Coale and Susan Watkins (ed.), *The Decline of Fertility in Europe* (Princeton, 1986), 342).
18. Like access to allotments of pasture and to poor relief.
19. Hennig, *Chronik*, 69. GLA 138/9 (letter of 7 April 1803 from Ettenheim setting out the rights then passing to Baden).
20. Ibid. Gem A Grafenhausen A U. 36 (1 February 1763). See also *OSB Grafenhausen* page 33.
21. Gem A Kappel A U. 82 (shortage of wood in 1782) and Gem A Kappel A U. 91 (attempt to refuse immigrants in 1790). See also *OSB Kappel* page 65.
22. GLA 138/9 (letter of 8 August 1803 from Ettenheim). In 1815 and in 1826–1829, Grafenhausen again sought a substantial increase in entry fees, but the request was rejected on each occasion. GLA 239/1608.
23. Reduced to one-quarter its standard size. GLA 138/9.
24. Compare BvB A U. 372 (records of admission of new citizens 1595–1646 with occasional references to fees) and GLA 314/2256 (excerpt from 1801 regulations).
25. Ibid. BvB A U. 887 (August 1751 agreement that those leaving for unrecognized territories forfeit one-tenth of their property).
26. The exceptions occurred in the years immediately following a major crisis, as discussed above. 87 % of the lord's Catholic subjects recorded in a Rust census of 1769 (BvB A U. 965) had been born in the village. (I have assumed that none of the unnamed servants was born locally.) In Grafenhausen in 1839 (Gem A Grafenhausen B XV/809), the corresponding figure was 85 %.
27. They thus constituted a mere symptom of population growth.
28. GLA 239/1648 through GLA 239/1664 (correspondence surrounding cases in Rust from 1826 to 1847). GLA 239/1607 (Grafenhausen in 1828–1829), Gl A 239/5457 (Grafenhausen in 1842–1843). GLA 239/1610 and GLA 239/1612 (Kappel in 1828 and 1833–1835). On the general struggle between municipal leaders and State bureaucrats, see Mack Walker, "Home Towns and State Administrators: South German Politics, 1815–30", *Political Science Quarterly*, 82 (1967), 35–60, and Loyd Lee, *The Politics of Harmony Civil Service, Liberalism, and Social Reform in Baden 1800–1850* (Newark, 1980).

29. GLA 239/1607 (letter of 23 March 1828 from county prefect).
30. Chapter Five traces the fates of each generation of non-citizens in connection with their contributions to illegitimacy rates.
31. Compare Peter Marschalck, *Bevölkerungsgeschichte Deutschlands im 19. und 20. Jahrhundert* (Frankfurt, 1984), 59–61.
32. Or elsewhere. Francine van de Walle, "Infant Mortality and the European Demographic Transition", in Coale and Watkins, *Europe*, 201–233.
33. On the potential significance of such developments, see Poul Matthiessen and James McCann, "The Role of Mortality in the European Fertility Transition: Aggregate-Level Relations", in Samuel Preston (ed.), *The Effects of Infant and Child Mortality on Fertility* (New York, 1978), 47–68.
34. In Chapter Four, I give conventional ideas of these processes a twist or two, but the relationships in the text still hold.
35. See Karl Helleiner, "The Vital Revolution Reconsidered", in David Glass and David Eversley (ed.), *Population in History* (London, 1968), 79–86, and Jacques Dupâquier, "De l'animal à l'homme: le mécanisme autorégulateur des populations traditionelles", *Revue de l'Institut de Sociologie* (Free University of Brussels), 45 (1972), 199–208.
36. There is evidence of renewed economic burdens. *OSB Rust* between pages 58 and 59 reprints an article entitled "Kriegslasten gab es auch schon früher" from the *Ettenheimer Heimatbote* dealing with billeting and quartering. Again, some people were drawn into the military. *OSB Kappel* page 53, *OSB Rust* page 59, and *OSB Grafenhausen* pages 145, 295–296 name veterans of campaigns as far afield as Russia and Spain. Compare Hennig, *Chronik*, 5–6.
37. My account of emigration draws on anecdotes from *OSB Grafenhausen*, pages 231–237 and *OSB Rust* pages 91–98 (reprinting a 1957 article by Albert Köbele in *Altvater*, supplement to the *Lahrer Zeitung*), as well as on archival sources such as Gem A Grafenhausen B XIV/801 and Gem A Grafenhausen B XV/809. In their reports on county Ettenheim the prefects commented on emigration in some detail from 1865 to 1874 (GLA 236/10289 and GLA 236/10290) and more perfunctorily thereafter (GLA 236/10291).
38. There are occasional references to departures for Hungary (or returns from there): *OSB Grafenhausen* entry 2134 (after 1777), *OSB Kappel* entry 2364 (before 1769), and GLA 229/90576 (1762 questioning of Rust's mayor about the goods of an emigrant). More generally, see Theodor Ludwig, *Der badische Bauer im achtzehnten Jahrhundert* (Strasbourg, 1896), 89–90.
39. In no decade of marriage before 1820 or after 1860 were more than 4 % of families recorded emigrating.
40. General statistics confirm these patterns. Ettenheim county lost 9 % of its population between 1850 and 1855. 70 % of those emigrating did so as part of a family. *Beiträge zur Statistik der inneren Verwaltung des Grossherzogthums Baden*, 5 (1857), 8. Compare Josef Griesmeier, "Die Entwicklung der Wirtschaft und der Bevölkerung von Baden und Württemberg im 19. und 20. Jahrhundert", *Jahrbücher für Statistik und Landeskunde von Baden-Württemberg*, 1 (1954), 132, 142, 154–155.
41. The towns promised higher earnings, steadier work, and more pleasures. GLA 236/10290 (reports on county Ettenheim for 1870 and 1874).
42. The prefect cited evasion of military service as a motive in the reports on county Ettenheim for 1866, 1867, 1868, 1869, 1872, and 1874 (GLA 236/10289 and GLA 236/10290). Gem A Rust B XX/429 lists the local cases from 1865 through 1877.
43. Most people in this first wave of departures came back. Hermann Baier, "Die Ortenau als Auswanderungsgebiet", *Badische Heimat*, 22 (1935), 147. *OSB Rust* page 98. In Rust, 28 returning emigrants to America were listed separately from 197 other Christian citizens and subjects at the ceremonial swearing of allegiance to Baden's new grand duke on 6 January 1819. GLA 236/1758.

Land and People

44. 35 % of the 392 people who left Rust in the twenty years before 1852 were supported from municipal coffers. (Report on 1852 inspection tour of Rust in GLA 360/1935-11/1164.) Only 1 % of 378 emigrants from Kappel over the same period were subsidized. (Report on 1852 inspection tour of Kappel in GLA 360/1935-11/822.) In Grafenhausen, 19 % of 191 emigrants won partial support from the municipality. (Report on 1852 inspection tour of Grafenhausen in GLA 360/1935-11/778.) For emigrants' attempts to secure assistance from Grafenhausen, see Gem A Grafenhausen B XIV/802. On general practice, see Baier, "Auswanderungsgebiet", 147–148.
45. In his 1866 report, the county prefect estimated that as many people left without authorization as with it. GLA 236/10290.
46. The prefects singled out letters from North America as the proximate cause of the majority of departures in 1865, 1868, 1869, and 1870. (GLA 236/10289 and GLA 236/10290.) One such letter is reprinted in OSB Grafenhausen pages 231–234.
47. The OSBs include numerous entries indicating the return of emigrants to marry or remarry in their old homes, for example OSB Grafenhausen entry 257, OSB Rust entries 588 and 3464. On connections between the two worlds generally, see OSB Rust page 97.
48. Here, I depart from the view of Franz Hundsnurscher and Gerhard Taddey (Die jüdischen Gemeinden in Baden (Stuttgart, 1968), 249–250), who state that Jews lived in Rust as early as the Thirty Years War. The regulation of 1566 to which they refer (see footnote 5 above) speaks only of Jews in the vicinity. Other mentions of Jews (Otto Kähni, "Geschichte der Offenburger Judengemeinde", Die Ortenau, 49 (1969), 84–87, and possibly GLA 66/2964 for Grafenhausen in 1621) refer to isolated individuals.
49. Karl Ludwig Bender, Joachim Krämer, and Eugen Eble, Ortssippenbuch Nonnenweier (Grafenhausen, 1971), page 152. The discussion of the Jewish community there (pages 151–168) is considerably more extensive than that in OSB Rust pages 101–102. For more information on Nonnenweier's Jews, see Elfie Labisch-Benz, Die jüdische Gemeinde Nonnenweier (Freiburg, 1981) and Alice Goldstein, "Some Demographic Characteristics of Village Jews in Germany: Nonnenweier, 1800–1931", in Paul Ritterband (ed.), Modern Jewish Fertility (Leiden, 1981), 112–143.
50. BvB A U. 850. He opined that Jews had lived in Rust for at least forty years, but this is apparently the earliest document in the family archive in which Jews in Rust are mentioned. (Benedikt Schwarz, "Freiherrlich Böcklin von Böcklinsauisches Archiv in Rust, Bezirksamt Ettenheim", Zeitschrift für die Geschichte des Oberrheins, N.F. 25 (1910), m14–m121.) In October 1737 the lord wrote to the abbot of the monastery Ettenheimmünster seeking a loan to erect houses to bring Jews to Rust. (GLA 229/90547.) In the previous century, the Böcklins had tolerated heterodox Protestants. (1659 dispute in BvB A U. 682.)
51. For examples, see BvB A U. 885 (1751 dues), BvB A DEPOSITA 356 (1763 accounts) and GLA 314/2256 (redemption based on 1803–1814 income). Obligations and rights of Rust's Jews are set out in BvB A U. 949 (1768 regulation, reprinted in Karl-Heinz Debacher, "Geschichte der jüdischen Gemeinde Rust", in Bernhard Uttenweiler (ed.), Schicksal und Geschichte der jüdischen Gemeinden Ettenheim Altdorf Kippenheim Schmieheim Rust Orschweier (Ettenheim, 1988), 400–405).
52. BvB A U. 887 codified this arrangement in 1751.
53. There are lists of about 150 Jewish residents in 1809 (GLA 353/1908–105/43), 1814 (GLA 353/1908–105/36), and 1817 (Ibid. and draft in Gem A Rust A U. 23).
54. On the general situation, see Steven Lowenstein, "The Rural Community and the Urbanization of German Jewry", Central European History, 13 (1980), 218–326, and for nearby locations Alice Goldstein, "Urbanization in Baden, Germany Focus on the Jews, 1825–1925", Social Science History, 8 (1984), 43–66.

55. Census figures for 1852, 1890, and 1905 in *Beiträge zur Statistik der inneren Verwaltung des Grossherzogthums Baden*, 1 (1855), 68, *Beiträge zur Statistik des Grossherzogthums Baden* N.F. 6 (1893), 26–27, 112–113, 198–199, and Gem A Kappel B XV/713.
56. St A LA Lahr 1308 (list by name and address).
57. Although *OSB Rust* (page 102) asserts, presumably truthfully as far as it goes, that no one in 1968 was aware of the fates of individual Jews, OSBs published later incorporate material from Gurs (the camp in the Pyrenees to which Baden's Jews were first sent) and the killing centres of eastern Europe. In addition, several families can be traced through Hildegard Katterman, *Geschichte und Schicksale der Lahrer Juden* (Lahr, 1976) and Kähni, "Offenburger". Now see in addition, Uttenweiler, *Schicksal*, 19–31.
58. Chapter Three covers their places in the economy.
59. Compare David Galenson, *White Servitude in Colonial America* (Cambridge, 1981), 9: "Instead of moving from one village to another to enter service, after 1607 English youths frequently moved to another continent." David Levine called my attention to this parallel.
60. Events in nearby Altdorf have been summarized in just such terms by Alice Goldstein, "Aspects of Change in a Nineteenth-Century German Village", *Journal of Family History*, 9 (1984), 145–157. See also the fuller *Determinants of Change and Response among Jews and Catholics in a nineteenth century German village* (New York, 1992). Her account appears to do justice to the facts of that case.
61. The relations within households which made this possible are of less interest to me here, and are therefore taken for granted. Those who are interested may profitably consult David Sabean, *Property, production, and family in Neckarhausen 1700–1870* (Cambridge, 1990).
62. For a positive evaluation of the impact of population growth on development, see Ester Boserup, *The Conditions of Agricultural Growth* (Chicago, 1965).
63. A few families even took on additional labour. In such cases, the marginal return generated for them by another farmhand—even one whose productivity was lower than their own—exceeded the direct contribution that individual could make to his or her household of birth.
64. Compare Ron Lesthaeghe, "On the Social Control of Human Reproduction", *Population and Development Review*, 6 (1980), 531–532, which exaggerates the stakes involved.
65. Except over the very long run, which is less important in human history. Compare Pierre Vilar, "Réflexions sur la «crise de l'ancien type», «inégalité des récoltes» et «sous-developpement»", in *Conjoncture économique, structures sociales* (Paris, 1974), 48.

3

Agriculture and Industry

The previous chapter closed with theoretical reflections on differentiation within rural populations. This chapter renders those remarks more concrete by examining in detail the occupations pursued in Grafenhausen, Kappel, and Rust. In fleshing out the economic history of the area by showing how resources were augmented and transformed, it complements Chapter Two's discussion of changes in population. At the same time, the present chapter familiarizes readers with developments that will be drawn on later when I deal more directly with demographic matters. The most prominent of those developments is the pattern of successful innovation by Grafenhauseners. Control over the environment engendered assets and attitudes that coloured all aspects of their lives.

For the moment, my focus is on overall variety rather than on differences between localities. Table 3.1 shows that that variety was extensive indeed. Villagers' occupations fell into clusters of varying significance. The most prominent cluster, including almost half the designations in the OSBs, refers to agriculture, carried out either for one's own benefit or at the behest of others. Artisanal pursuits were almost as frequent, totalling 37 %. The remainder were a mixed bag of supplementary positions, marginal occupations, and mobile services. Because villagers drew livelihoods from so many different sources, they experienced economic and demographic changes in myriad ways. To make sense of this diversity, I examine each occupational category and the transformations it underwent over the centuries. This review underlines the flexibility and dynamism of the rural economy.

Farming and Labour[1]

I consider landed proprietors and day labourers together because economic logic united their fortunes in perpetual tension. The former typically hired the latter to assist in exploiting their landholdings.[2] As co-workers, they shared an interest in the success of the enterprise, but as employer and employee their shares of the reward were mutually exclusive. They worked within the same natural constraints: weather, soil, floods, animal physiology. On the other hand, wealth and standing distinguished proprietors from labourers. Free peasants able to make a living from their own holdings had no reason to work for others,

TABLE 3.1
Distribution of occupations in Grafenhausen, Kappel, and Rust combined

Category	Percentage
Farming	29 %
Labour	15 %
Craft	17 %
Weaving	5 %
Fishing	5 %
Substantial	6 %
Affluent	4 %
Menial	0 %
Petty	1 %
Order	3 %
Itinerant	2 %
Commerce	4 %
Profession	4 %
Local Position	3 %
Industry	2 %
Absolute total	4806

Notes
(1) The distribution covers the first two occupations assigned to each husband wed before 1900 in his first OSB marriage, documented or not. Singleton occupations are weighted double. 816 cases in which no occupation was assigned to the husband are omitted.
(2) The construction of the occupational classification is described in detail in appendix C of Benz, Thesis.

while the less endowed had no alternative but to sell their labour in a marketplace weighted against them.[3]

That contrast carried over into their family lives. Landed proprietors enjoyed greater freedom of action and ultimately extended that freedom by exerting control over themselves through family limitation. The fertility of day labourers, like their work, was more often controlled by others. A look at these two categories thus provides a sense of the range of experience within the villages, in so far as it was a function of occupation.

The centrality of agriculture in a peasant community is a commonplace. However, since much of this chapter focuses on the other activities in which villagers engaged, the near-universality of farming merits emphasis. Virtually every man owned or controlled land, often through a claim based on a wife. For that matter, many children, both female and male, possessed parcels on paper. Not every holding was sufficient to support a family, but the psychological significance of property was not determined by its economic viability.

That artisans, and even so-called landless labourers, were actually half-peasants was proverbial in the Ortenau.[4] These villagers were no exceptions. In the report of his 1863 inspection tour of Grafenhausen, the county prefect noted that "they are all landed proprietors, although they also pursue the usual lesser trades [niederen Gewerbe]".[5] Farming occupations were more widespread in Grafenhausen than in the other two villages,[6] but similar assessments were made there. In Kappel in 1852, "the chief sources of livelihood [were] cultivation and cattle raising".[7] Even in Rust the prefect observed (in 1872) that "agriculture, particularly cattle raising, constitutes almost the sole and exclusive source of livelihood".[8] Occupational censuses from the end of the nineteenth century confirm that practically every household engaged in agriculture.[9] Thus, villagers assigned occupations in the Farming category were merely those whose agricultural activities were particularly noteworthy.

Those activities were carried on within certain basic physical limits. The three municipalities were roughly equal in size, and each devoted significant space to arable, woods, meadows, and gardens. Nevertheless, detailed statistics from 1852 reveal some differences.[10] At that point, more arable land was available to the average resident of Grafenhausen.[11] This fit the greater frequency of Farming occupations in Grafenhausen. Its extra land was partly counterbalanced by the presence in Kappel and Rust of rivers such as the Elz which supported fishing rather than farming.[12]

Even so, the advantage in the land to hand ratio is insufficient to explain the high frequency of landed proprietors in Grafenhausen. In fact, weighting the ratio by the percentage Farming completely reverses the picture. Quantitatively, Grafenhauseners now appear worst off, with Kapplers a third better, and Rusters a full 73 % ahead. Overall then, Grafenhausen boasted a higher percentage Farming, but the average landed proprietor there farmed less land in 1852.

Gross differences in resources mattered less than the use villagers made of them.[13] Moreover, both the resources and their uses were transformed in the course of the eighteenth and nineteenth centuries. The agrarian history of the area time and again reveals Grafenhauseners at the forefront of change.

In the early modern era the communities followed three-field systems of crop rotation.[14] In the late seventeenth century two fields were sown with winter rye and wheat (or half-wheat), and summer barley and oats respectively.[15] In the third, "fallow", field, beans, peas, lentils, rapeseed, poppyseeds, and maize were grown.[16] Hemp was also cultivated and sold.[17]

Towards the middle of the eighteenth century, potatoes were integrated into this system.[18] Flax also appeared around this time.[19] These innovations, together with the flurry of eighteenth-century court cases over tithes from crops or areas which had not previously been cultivated, indicate a flexibility and growth at odds with the stereotype of traditional agriculture as sterile and backward.[20]

A still more dramatic transformation occurred in the second half of the eighteenth century. The key change involved the more efficient integration of animal husbandry into the farming operations of individual peasants.[21] The use of waste or scrub brush for common pasture[22] was discontinued. Instead, livestock were quartered and fed in their stalls. Much of their fodder was imported from the marshlands of Rhinau.[23] Oilseeds and clover were grown locally in increasing quantities. The old commons were broken into individual holdings to be divided amongst the citizenry as arable or meadow. Only tiny plots were left as forage for geese, although the surviving true woodlands remained available to the villagers' pigs. The keeping of cattle and horses at home, as poultry had always been, permitted more efficient collection and use of manure. The most obvious result of all these developments was that winter grains were no longer limited to one year in three on any particular field. Average yields therefore increased substantially.

Many of these changes in agricultural organization formed part of the programme of physiocratic agronomists such as Franz Böcklin, lord in Rust from 1762 to 1813.[24] However, innovation did not come from above. For example, the centrepiece of textbook agrarian reform was consolidation of holdings, yet farms remained dispersed until after World War II. Franz Böcklin did try out new crops on his own land, but his subjects had smaller margins for experiment on their scattered strips. Perhaps the most significant change made by Rust's lords was to cease leasing their own holdings to groups of villagers for nine-year periods.[25]

The significant changes in agricultural practices reflected villagers' responsiveness to the economic opportunities they did enjoy. Peasants in this region had always been personally free.[26] Feudal dues had long been fixed.[27] Thus, they functioned as license fees or nominal taxes. The Rohan prince-bishops and the Böcklins resided in Alsace for much of the eighteenth century, and therefore exerted only indirect control over their subjects' daily lives. The villagers resisted attempts to increase lordly revenues in the eighteenth century, and frequently resorted to legal proceedings to enforce their claims against their overlords.[28] Such self-conscious and assertive individuals were fully capable of introducing new crops and techniques on their own.

A further factor in the agricultural transformation was the dislocation attendant on the revolutionary wars. Part of the incentive to convert commons into individual holdings came from the municipalities' need for revenue to offset the taxes and costs associated with military occupation and provisioning.[29] This was a consideration in Kappel in 1796, 1801, 1806, and 1815–1817.[30] Indeed, the need to pay off lingering war debts was a reason to undertake agricultural improvements in Grafenhausen as late as 1827.[31]

The administrative reorganization as Baden incorporated the villages between 1803 and 1810 provided additional occasions for reform. For example, purely feudal dues were abolished. However, most payments carried over into the new State, which assumed the powers of the deposed lords. In the 1820s, the lords, including the Böcklins, were even compensated for lost feudal exactions.[32] Not until the 1840s could villagers begin paying off tithes once and for all.[33]

By that time, wider commercial networks had brought them new opportunities. Responding initially to the disruptions of the Napoleonic wars, traders and manufacturers in the town of Lahr sought to guarantee a nearby source of cheap raw materials. Under their influence, chicory cultivation began around 1798. It won a lasting position as a cash crop, as did sugar-beet.[34]

Of even more significance was tobacco, another product that spread under the influence of urban manufacturers.[35] It may have been introduced experimentally in the 1790s,[36] but as late as 1805 very little was grown in this area. At that point the Lotzbeck firm in Lahr began to promote tobacco in a more systematic way, distributing instructional material and free seed. These moves met with a lively response, especially in Grafenhausen. By 1809 tobacco was to be found in all three villages, although the total area under cultivation was dwarfed by that devoted to hemp, the traditional cash crop. Two years later, the acreage under tobacco had more than quintupled. Grafenhausen alone was producing two and a half times the 1809 output of the entire county.[37]

Improvements in transportation during the first half of the nineteenth century only intensified villagers' capacity for innovation. By 1850 the established repertoire of crops ran: wheat, barley, potatoes, tobacco, half-wheat, hemp, rye, clover, maize, beet-root, oats, lucerne, rapeseed, and chicory.[38] Grain, cattle, and yarn traded informally at the local level and at periodic retail markets held in Rust and in the nearby communities of Ettenheim, Kippenheim, Münsterthal, and Wallburg. (See Map 3.2.) Cash crops sold on more distant urban markets: Emmendingen, Lahr, Offenburg, Freiburg, and Strasbourg.[39] (See Map 1.1.)

These years also saw further changes in agricultural organization. Starting in the 1820s, Grafenhausen became the first municipality in the region to carry through a complete field clearance.[40] Patches of scrub and wood that remained among the cultivated fields were burnt down or sold off. At the same time pathways and field boundaries were rationalized. Upgrading of land through the creation of water meadows proceeded apace. Indeed, the failure of neighbouring Ettenheim to implement similar improvements in the Rittmatten (shown on Map 2.2) constituted a perennial grievance.[41]

In Kappel and Rust similar changes waited on the Rhine correction, which allowed the draining of low-lying marshes, and on more enterprising municipal leadership. The area west of the Elz in Kappel was not cultivated before the second half of the nineteenth century. (See Map 2.2.) Then, between 1852 and 1871, Kappel's arable land increased by 12 % and its meadowland by 44 %.[42] Much of this expansion depended on a single large irrigation project carried out between 1866 and 1871. Small ventures of this kind were initiated in Rust in the 1850s and 1860s, but as late as 1884 extensive improvements remained to be made.[43]

The close of the nineteenth century saw the proliferation of associations and cooperatives.[44] Grafenhausen led the way, beginning in 1881 with a rudimentary cattle insurance scheme.[45] Following the example set in the early 1880s by Ludwig Häfele, a future mayor, Grafenhauseners enthusiastically took up artificial fertilizer.[46] A thriving credit union emerged around the same time. In 1883, over the opposition of dealers and merchants, 98 Grafenhauseners created the first consumers' cooperative in Ettenheim county.[47] When a horsebreeders' association was set up for the whole county around 1890, Grafenhausen played a leading rôle and contributed a full sixth of the membership.[48] The community's

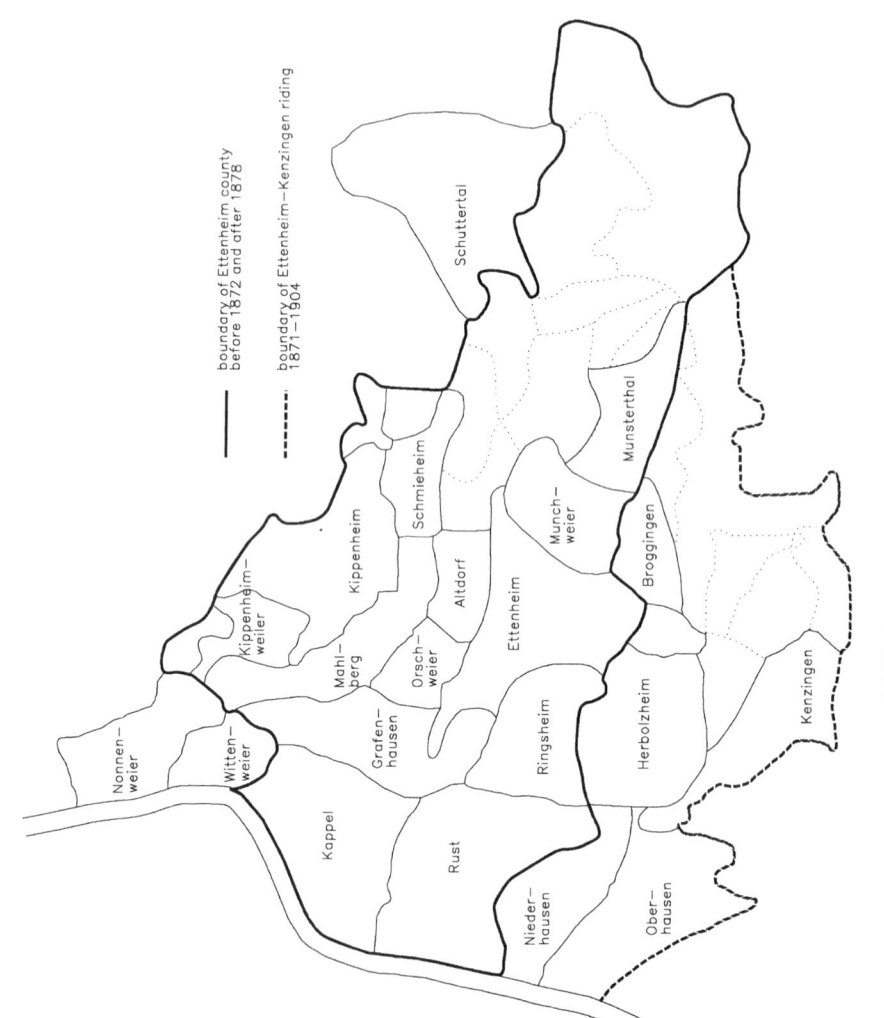

MAP 3.2 ETTENHEIM COUNTY

most striking success followed the establishment in 1893 of a dairy cooperative. The purchase of a mechanical separator enabled cattleowners to profit from selling sweet butter, cream, and delicacies made with it, while getting back the skim milk for their own use.[49]

In 1895 the cooperative craze even spread to the auctioning and curing of tobacco. Dissatisfied with prices in the range from twelve to eighteen Marks per half-hectoliter, Grafenhauseners refused to sell their crop to the usual dealers. Led by Häfele, the villagers maintained a solid front, holding out for a minimum of twenty to twenty-one Marks. The cooperative's members were able to dispose of only five-sixths of their stock at that price, but they had prepared for this eventuality. Rather than dump the remainder on the market, they cured it themselves and held it until later in the fall. At that point they sold it at a price corresponding to the twenty-four Mark level for uncured tobacco. This demonstration had a lasting impact, for in 1896 dealers offered Grafenhauseners thirty Marks, while paying only twenty-six to twenty-eight Marks in other municipalities.[50]

The interlocking organizations enjoyed widespread participation. In 1898 the dairy cooperative, whose space and membership were limited, had 100 members. In the same year the consumers' cooperative boasted 139 members, and the credit union 294. The cattle insurance plan had 277 subscribers and a horse insurance plan 90.[51] Since Grafenhausen's population in 1900 was divided into 356 households living in 283 homes,[52] these voluntary combinations encompassed practically all families. By 1903 new cooperatives to market poultry and eggs had been added.[53]

Nothing on a similar scale took place in the other villages. Kappel's credit union was established in 1880, but the one that opened two years later in Grafenhausen began with more than twice as many members (153 vs. 70). Grafenhausen's also proved more vigorous, reaching 325 members in 1908. The 42-member consumer cooperative founded around 1886 in Kappel also suffered from comparison with its counterpart in Grafenhausen. In 1908 the absence of dairy and marketing cooperatives struck the prefect, who had passed through Grafenhausen on his way to Kappel.[54]

Government officials found the situation in Rust, where there was no credit union at all until 1896, even more disheartening. Prefects searched Rust in vain for the solidity and industry they detected in some inhabitants of Grafenhausen and Kappel. The failure of a self-conscious progressive ["vorwärtsstrebenden"] peasantry[55] to emerge in Rust was attributed to the debilitating practice of leasing. Credit for the overall difference between the villages went to Grafenhausen's more energetic municipal leaders. None the less, these contrasts convey something of the atmospheres in the communities as a whole.

The late nineteenth century saw further evolution in the selection of crops. Orchards of fruit trees were introduced,[56] while hemp, chicory, and sugar-beet largely disappeared. Hops enjoyed a brief vogue at the turn of the century. In the end, tobacco, maize, potatoes, and beet-root persisted alongside the staple grain and fodder crops.[57]

The rearing of livestock, particularly cattle and horses, also remained important. At one point Grafenhausen possessed the largest population of these animals in the county.[58] In the early years of the twentieth century, Grafenhausen was distinguished by the electrification of stalls. In addition, a few individuals there acquired machines for threshing grain and feeding livestock.[59] This new technology continued the pattern of innovation that had characterized the agricultural practices of the leading sectors of the peasantry for two centuries.

This account provides some idea of the aggregate experience of agriculturalists. The peculiar fortunes of day labourers require additional attention. Their numbers dropped slightly in the course of the economic changes I have been describing. As increasing productivity made it possible for the number of landed proprietors to rise, the ratio of labouring families to potential employers fell sharply.[60] In part this decline reflected greater emigration by those with little land and uncertain prospects, but a more important development was the emergence of new unskilled occupations in industry.[61]

Both emigration and the availability of alternative employment increased the minimal bargaining power of the remaining day labourers. As a result, they shared to a limited extent in the benefits of more efficient agriculture. A series of daily wage rates in Grafenhausen shows little change from 1874 to 1898.[62] Since prices were falling, the ability of day labourers to maintain customary nominal rates, and even improve them slightly, meant that their real wages were increasing.

Rates varied with the season, with the sex of the labourer, and with the proportion of the employee's upkeep borne by the employer. In the late nineteenth century the wages of a man working in the summer were more than double those of a woman working in winter. Labourers who received board obtained even less money.[63] In general, long-term employment was more important than the nominal wage rates set under these competitive pressures. Regardless of the success of individuals in securing such employment, day labourers as a group enjoyed far less comfortable lives than neighbours who tilled their own land.

The Artisanate

The third major component of the sedentary village population was the artisanate, comprising five of the occupational categories of Table 3.1: Crafts, Weaving, Fishing, Substantial,[64] and Affluent.[65] All but the affluent belonged to guilds of one sort or another. Thus, almost all the artisans described in this section were master[66] craftsmen.[67]

The nature and techniques of most crafts changed little in the eighteenth and nineteenth centuries. Throughout, large numbers of villagers, especially in Rust, spent part of their time making items of apparel, such as shoes, coats, and hats. Others worked in metal, wood, and stone, especially in the construction of houses. Ploughshares, horseshoes, barrels, pots, and rope were produced for the local market. A few villagers supplied more unusual goods such as windows, candles, and books, or provided cleaning and decorating services. As a rule, exotic occupations carried more prestige and income, while the numerous masons and tailors were scarcely better off than day labourers.

Those pursuing the two most common artisan trades, weaving and fishing, belonged to separate guilds. Moreover, their fortunes diverged from those of other artisans in that both fields entered prolonged declines in the nineteenth century from which they did not recover. I therefore examine each of them in rather more detail.

The position of weavers had never been too secure. Households produced much of their clothing and bedding themselves, reducing demand for woven goods. Moreover, this work was done by women, and so less prestige attached to spinning and weaving in general. High-quality luxury cloths, on the other hand, were generally imported. Weavers were left with a narrow range of products and markets.

For the most part weavers worked with locally grown flax and hemp, which was prepared for spinning on special plots of land.[68] The yarn, linen, and cord they turned out were sold for cash in the immediate vicinity. A few supplemented their operations by bleaching the linen before sale.[69] Other occupations linked to weaving included flax-combing, hemp-working, sack-making, embroidery, and the manufacture of sails and rigging.

After 1800, flax cultivation retreated in the face of the more attractive opportunities in tobacco, and weaving retreated with it. Improved transportation brought in machine-made goods, undercutting older techniques. The number of weavers declined dramatically. At its peak in the early nineteenth century, Weaving occupied 8 % of documented families; by the final quarter of the century, the figure was down to 1 %. The few who did persist concentrated on rugs or other specialized goods.[70]

Fishing was rather more exalted. Its traditional importance can be gauged from the fact that fish appear in the coats of arms of Kappel and Rust.[71] The identification of village and fishing in legend went back to the sixth century when Fridolin converted the fishers of Kappel as he crossed the Rhine.[72] More reliable documentation of fisher guilds can be found as early as the fifteenth century. In the early modern era, the guild hierarchy often overlapped the village government. Partly as a result, fishing rights within the municipal boundaries were jealously guarded and became a constant source of tension between the villages.[73] Guild members enjoyed considerable prestige and took an active part in the social life of the villages, particularly during ceremonies with religious connotations.

On a more mundane level, fisher guilds functioned much as more conventional guilds did. They enforced uniform regulations governing fishing methods, seasons, the placement of nets, and the size of the catch. The substantial entry fees required of outsiders rendered membership by and large hereditary. Externally, the guilds formed part of a network of river villages centred on Strasbourg.[74]

The social prominence of fishers persisted to a certain extent even when the economic significance of fishing began to decline. The traditional catch of pike, carp, trout, salmon, and dace fell off as a result of overfishing and pollution. The corrections of the Rhine and the Elz eliminated many inland waterways. Fishers were driven to emigrate or forced into other occupations. By the end of the nineteenth century, only 2 % of documented families engaged in Fishing, although it had once occupied 11 %. The appellation "fisher" persisted, but its use became increasingly honorific.[75] Although fisher guilds outlived the other guilds, they became primarily social organizations.[76]

The lowly condition of weavers and fishers towards 1900 should not be read back into earlier centuries. Both categories were represented among the notability.[77] Moreover, the families who stuck with these trades in the face of diminishing returns at home and increasing opportunities abroad tended to have the greatest local resources.[78] For instance, some fishers made the transition to shipping goods along the Rhine, and earned a comfortable living thereby.[79]

Substantial artisans were considerably more mobile than the local fishers. In acquiring raw materials and distributing products, they maintained extensive ties with surrounding communities.[80] They were exposed to a wider range of ideas and practices. Despite the variety of their backgrounds and the changes technology wrought in their trades, the scale of this category's operations distinguished it throughout the eighteenth and nineteenth centuries.

Millers were particularly apt to move about, because rights to thresh or grind grain were typically auctioned off for nine-year periods. In Rust and Kappel, the municipality owned the grain mills themselves. The one in Kappel also used its water power to run a sawmill. There were no such mills in Grafenhausen, which relied on one located on the Ettenbach stream in the Rittmatten. (See Map 2.2.)[81] By contrast, the seed-crushing mills of the oil-pressers were private family enterprises. They became especially prominent after the new animal husbandry created a market for oilseed cakes for fodder.[82]

Brewers were less apt to migrate, but their operations were even more variable. Like millers, brewers purchased much of their raw material, including barley or potatoes and sugar-beet, directly from agricultural producers. Other commodities were obtained through wine merchants and the like. Demand fluctuated, as beer brewers shifted into distilling brandy or whisky and back. At the end of the nineteenth century, some even diversified into coffee. These shifts and commercial dealings required large outlays of capital. Moreover, the sheer size of breweries represented a considerable asset, for few other village buildings were suitable for large-scale production.

This applied on a lesser scale to the extensive workshops of cartwrights. They possessed, moreover, an affinity for transport, and were natural choices when it came time to move goods to market. They also benefitted from the general prestige attaching to occupations having to do with horses. This was even more true of saddlers. In serving horseowners, who were typically rich proprietors, they added to their own assets. In addition to providing harnesses and other specialized equipment, saddlers sometimes opened feed or livery stores.

Bakeries and butcher shops were less extensive, and also less subject to technological change. Bakers and butchers enjoyed lower incomes than other substantial artisans, but they were exposed to less risk and their social positions were secure. As with the fishers, the exotic dues they paid illustrated their standing.[83]

Virtually the entire Substantial category linked to the Affluent. Purveyors of food or drink had some affinity with merchants. They also dealt on a regular basis, directly or indirectly, with managers of breweries and similar enterprises. Capital acquired in one endeavour was sometimes applied to another. Moreover, many substantial artisans integrated their operations with a tavern or inn. Because taxes, especially those on alcoholic beverages and salt, were collected through the proprietors of such establishments, they integrated themselves into governments' financial networks.

The prosperity of the affluent was based on access to cash. Publicans of both kinds, that is innkeepers and tax-collectors, had money on hand for emergency loans, and so took advantage of auctions, bankruptcies, and credit squeezes. Much the same was true of merchants, manufacturers, and those who managed an estate or business on behalf of an absentee owner. The affluent maintained contact with suppliers and government officials, and these connections kept them abreast of opportunities outside the village.

Almost all the operations being considered, whether strictly artisanal or not, were small-scale family enterprises.[84] Since space was at a premium in the villages, especially within the areas of settlement, they were typically located in the homes of the artisans, who paid a nominal tax for the right to maintain a shop.[85] The longstanding practice of admitting masters' sons to the guilds at reduced rates reflected and reinforced the familial nature of these crafts.[86] Moreover, while most parents were forbidden to employ their children, artisans were allowed to pay their offspring in the course of their training.[87] These advantages led many craftsmen to preserve their connection with the local guild even after their families had migrated to other municipalities.[88]

The guild structure was closely integrated into the social and political hierarchy. To practise, each new master had to win recognition from both sovereign and guild. This arrangement promoted social control and protectionism. Discouraging the admission of outsiders and restricting entry to journeymen who had undergone extensive training limited the number of masters. This protected the incumbents against competition and rather mechanically preserved social structures.

Artisanal behaviour patterns survived right to the end of the nineteenth century. Baden abolished all guilds as it turned to free trade in 1862, but contemporary observers noted little effect in this area.[89] Craftsmen continued to apprentice their sons to their erstwhile brethren, who trained them in the old ways. Shops still changed hands through inheritance more often than through sale. Few outsiders took advantage of the legal opportunities to enter previously closed fields, and those who did generally took up citizenship and adopted local ways.

This inertia arose from the dual status of village artisans. For most peasants, a craft was a mere by-occupation, both economically and psychologically. It might provide a cushion in time of crisis, but few artisans got rich through small-scale production for the local market. Lack of interest and lack of competition led to a low level of skill, which became self-perpetuating. Brief exposure to other localities, where conditions were essentially similar, did not improve journeymen's techniques or broaden their horizons. In any case, more ambitious endeavours required capital in amounts that few could raise. Those who could, preferred to invest it in agriculture, which they found less risky and more lucrative.

The few respects in which laissez-faire did make an impact bear out this analysis. The lifting of government controls on products and prices granted greater scope to sharp practices, including adulteration, short-weighting, and price-fixing. Apprentices and journeymen had even less incentive than before to wander or to postpone setting up shop. The opposition of local artisans to public institutions designed to improve skills suggested a fine understanding of how to exploit the principles of free trade to prevent competition.

There was little scope for true competition in any case. Close-knit communities frowned upon cut-throat business practices. In addition, most artisans fell back happily to farming to ride out temporary reverses. With most fields overcrowded, there was little incentive for newcomers to break longstanding oligopolies. Transportation costs were high and local markets were limited. Moreover, those markets were stratified, in that certain goods were within the budgets of only a few villagers. In such an environment, it made sense to compete on the basis of quality rather than price. Such considerations were quite reminiscent of the ones that had dominated the closed world of the guilds. Their regulations were as much the product of social stability as its cause.

Outsiders

The circulation of resources and ideas within the countryside depended upon more mobile categories than those considered thus far. The marginal categories listed towards the bottom of Table 3.1 formed a layer of insulation around the more sedentary elements of the population. Menials and petty tradespeople fostered interchange across municipal and even international boundaries, but their impact was transitory and their contributions were limited. This was even more true of the extremely mobile forces of order and the itinerant. Traders functioned as ambassadors from the villages to the wider world. In this they mirrored the rôle of professionals, who were generally outsiders who took up residence in the village for shorter or longer periods.

Brevity was built into some occupations. Many adolescents spent time in domestic service or working as helpers in fields or shops in their own or other villages.[90] Unlike apprenticeship, menial service offered no prospect of direct advancement. Its importance lay in the opportunities it afforded to reassign labour between households and to establish networks of clientage across the countryside.

The occupations classified under Order were far less integrated into rural society. In the eighteenth century, this category consisted primarily of soldiers in the garrisons watching the Rhine in time of war. In the nineteenth century, gendarmes and border guards served brief tours of duty in the area and moved on. As agents of external authority, they were mistrusted by the local inhabitants.

Among the people the forces of order strove to suppress were wandering troupers, pedlars, and vagrants. These marginal elements lacked the fixed addresses and assets of more respectable citizens. Indeed, many of them did not possess citizenship rights anywhere. Their numbers multiplied during periods of social upheaval, and were particularly high in the years around 1800.

Some of the itinerant settled in this area, often over the objections of their hosts. To alleviate the burdens they imposed on the community's purse, local councils obtained licenses enabling them to ply petty non-guild trades. Male and female tinkers, basket-weavers, and knife-grinders travelled from place to place, offering their minimal skills to the inhabitants and moving on under pressure from local authorities. Goods like rakes, tubs, and brushes were common, and many households produced them for themselves.[91] Selling them therefore provided little income, and eventually the search for greener pastures took the remaining itinerant and petty families to the United States.

COMMERCE

The economic position of commercial families was ambiguous.[92] Although I have excluded from this category both pedlars whose activities amounted to door-to-door begging and merchants who laid out great amounts of capital to finance long-distance trade, considerable diversity remains. The proprietors of fixed retail outlets selling imported goods, such as tea, coffee, and sugar, were only somewhat less wealthy than merchants, as were those engaged in water transport. In boats built by Rust's woodworkers, bargees carried bulk lumber and stone for construction projects and house-building.[93] Horses transported much the same goods more expensively overland, along with agricultural produce.[94]

The remaining traders, dealers, and brokers purveyed a wide variety of goods, generally with less success. Those transporting and selling textiles in outside markets enjoyed the greatest incomes.[95] Retailers of iron, leather, and spices were relatively well off, while hawkers of second-hand goods and trinkets found the going tough. Go-betweens and cattle brokers were seen as parasites, for the manner in which they eased the strains of the rural economy was little appreciated.

Rust had the most varied occupational distribution of the three villages, with particularly high numbers engaged in artisanal production and small-scale commerce. In part, this variety was a function of Rust's size, which meant that there was a larger market for such goods and a larger population outside Farming to produce them. Moreover, the lords directly fostered local business. In 1756 Rust was declared an imperial market, and from 1783 held three fairs annually. By all accounts these events had no far-reaching effects, and the local traders rejoiced at their recession in the nineteenth century.[96]

Commercial occupations were less numerous in Grafenhausen and Kappel, but this did not mean that entrepreneurship was unknown in either village. Grafenhauseners, in particular, acquired reputations as canny bargainers. In their management of animal stocks and in their negotiations with outside dealers, they displayed an acute understanding of market forces. In 1867, the county prefect reported that formal commerce was insignificant there, but also noted a thriving trade in livestock that meshed the animals' life cycles with swings in prices.[97] A later prefect alternately marvelled and rejoiced in 1895 as Grafenhausen's tobacco cooperative drove prices up in the manner described earlier. Disregard of State prohibitions on economic activity was another enduring characteristic of this village.[98]

What held dealers proper together was the fact that many of them were Jewish. Because Jews were barred from owning land or entering guilds until the nineteenth century, most were left with marginal rôles in local commerce. Even those activities were licensed and controlled by the sovereigns for the eighteenth and much of the nineteenth century.[99]

Economic and social obstacles endured long after legal barriers lifted. In an environment in which land, capital, and status generally accumulated through inheritance, Jews remained shut out of the rôles long occupied by Christians.[100] The customs that led children to learn their parents' trades defied all the efforts of the Baden government to encourage crafts among Jewish adolescents in the early nineteenth century.[101] The sharply defined confessional lines did blur somewhat as Jews moved towards full civil equality. Markets were moved from saints' days to avoid conflicts with the Jewish sabbath,[102] kosher butchers were admitted to the general guild, some traders acquired small plots of land, and a rare few wed Catholics. However, the attitudes that lay behind the concept of a "trading Jew" (Handelsjude) persisted well after the term itself was no longer employed in polite discourse.

On the other hand, the close association of economics with religion, and the political status attaching to it, did have some advantages for dealers. At the close of the nineteenth century, matzoths produced in Rust supplied the entire region. Most Jewish traders did not operate from an established store, and so spent much of the year on the road. The ties they maintained with co-religionists in other municipalities on both sides of the Rhine provided way stations for long-distance sales trips.[103] That managers attending to business interests died as far afield as Prague and Paris illustrates the scope of successful mercantile operations.[104] Humble pedlars who suffered when the market for their own obscure products dried up could count on aid from others who had anticipated the latest fashion. Philanthropists advanced rapidly in the synagogue council.[105]

Professions

Professionals remained outside the mainstream of village life. The education and interests of teachers and doctors set them apart from the masses, and the respect due their families intensified the gulf. The expertise of lawyers and clerks was valued, but its arcane nature raised perpetual suspicions of trickery. Even clerics, who were sometimes posted to a parish for only a few years, found it hard to win acceptance. The push by external bureaucracies for uniformity and efficiency was resisted by villagers all too conscious of their own peculiar needs and interests.

At times these conflicts were muted because professionals functioned as municipal civil servants, albeit with more prestige than those holding strictly local positions. For centuries, schoolmasters had been chosen by the municipality, which provided them with lodging and gardens. The municipality collected fees from the family of each pupil, and was usually also responsible for pensions. These conditions ensured that some teachers remained in a single location for most of their lives. By acting as sextons and organists, schoolmasters became more closely integrated into the life of the community, while supplementing their salaries. From this point of view, the teacher's special rights to grazing land and firewood were not so different from those enjoyed by the midwife or the overseer of the forest.

Other professionals also led double lives. Surgeons functioned as undertakers, and veterinarians inspected meat. By entering into contracts to treat the poor at municipal expense, doctors too became part of the local infrastructure. Such moves allowed outsiders to win a measure of acceptance from the citizenry.

As time passed, professionals became more clearly aligned with external authority. Public functionaries, such as surveyors, assessors, and tax clerks, served at the pleasure of the county office. In enforcing regulations and collecting fees set by the central government, they easily estranged themselves from the local population. Because the public service was predominantly Protestant and urban, it was hard for Catholic villagers to identify with its aims and procedures. In the second half of the nineteenth century, teachers acted as agents of the anticlerical government, fomenting cultural revolution in the countryside. Their numbers increased more rapidly than the population, as the State made increasing demands of the educational system. Terms became shorter, and professionals were ever more apt to be strangers.

Local Positions

Local positions and industry essentially provided alternative means of livelihood for people who lacked land, skill, and capital. The principal difference between these two categories of occupations lay in their nature. Those classified under Industry involved goods, services, or processes that became common only in the second half of the nineteenth century; local positions boasted a longer history. Following chronology, I discuss local positions first.

The typical local position involved minor services for the municipality or the lord. Throughout the eighteenth and nineteenth centuries, each village employed a messenger or errand runner to transmit official communications from Ettenheim and to perform odd jobs around the municipal buildings. In addition, at any one time several individuals were charged with maintaining order and cleanliness on village streets and byways.[106] Where appropriate, they also collected local tolls.

A more serious task, if not always an onerous one, was the protection of the municipal fields and forests. In addition to controlling petty trespasses by villagers against one another, field-wardens combatted the ravages of mice and rabbits. Foresters defended the diminishing stock of game—rabbit, deer, partridge, fox, badger, otter, ducks, and geese—against poachers.[107] Their protection extended to the woods themselves, a valuable resource in the densely populated Rhine plain. Grafenhausen and Kappel held sections of the Ettenheim forest from which Rust had been excluded for a millennium.[108] This asset provided significant revenue to those two municipalities, and enhanced the value of citizenship in them. Because the forest was on the other side of the county, municipal foresters lived well away from the rest of the villagers, and their families often developed closer ties with the communities that bordered the woods.

The third major type of local position, herding, was part of the three-field system. In the days when livestock grazed indiscriminately on common pastures, the municipality supplied someone to tend them. These jobs disappeared when all animals but geese and swine ceased to be handled in common.[109] Thereafter herdsmen were paid by the owners of the animals themselves.[110] The remaining positions, like other civil service jobs involving minimal skill, responsibility, and remuneration, were filled by women, the elderly, or the sick, or by underemployed day labourers.[111]

Modernization continued to threaten local positions as the years passed. Field clearances eliminated much of the local game, especially in Rust. They also cut down the animals who had preyed on the crops. The central State took over many policing functions that had previously been the preserve of local governments. New technology, in the form of gas and electric lighting, eliminated the need for night patrols, first in Grafenhausen (1903) and later in Kappel.[112]

Most local positions provided a meagre income, but one that often proved a valuable supplement to the resources of a poor family. Their need for such support forced them to curry the favour of the officials who dispensed these jobs.[113]

INDUSTRY

At the same time as economic change was reducing the number and significance of local positions, other transformations were creating entirely new occupations for villagers. In the late nineteenth century, job openings multiplied as the correction of rivers and the construction of the Rhine dam provided temporary employment.[114] After the annexation of Alsace in 1871, plans to promote trans-Rhine traffic intensified, and in 1873 a crossing between Kappel and Rhinau opened. As east-west trade increased in the 1890s, a new bridge across the Elz was constructed in Kappel and the one in Rust was repaired.[115]

Still more important in linking nineteenth-century villagers to the wider world was the railroad. The north-south line running through nearby Orschweier, Ringsheim, and Herbolzheim was constructed in 1845.[116] After that, increasing numbers of villagers found work on trains or in stations. This trend intensified in 1893 with the inauguration of a spur line from Münsterthal towards Rhinau which ran through Grafenhausen and Kappel.[117] By 1922, this line was abandoned and broken up for farmland, but in the intervening years it brought villagers into closer touch with industrial suppliers and markets.

Another new feature of the late nineteenth-century economy provided more evidence of ingenuity than dynamism. Beginning in 1863, Rusters with holdings too small to sustain agriculture resorted to converting the land into bricks.[118] The stone they produced found a certain market outside the village, but the hot and heavy work with the kiln did not provide a comfortable living. Ordinary brickmakers generally pursued another occupation or two, most typically in Farming or Labour.[119]

Even more significant for the occupational distributions of the villages was the establishment of manufacturing plants towards the end of the nineteenth century. Lured by the low wage rates sought by surplus agricultural workers, urban entrepreneurs transferred their operations to the countryside.[120] Poor villagers welcomed these new outlets for their labour. Earnings were lower than in crafts, but to men outside such occupations, steady employment was the main consideration, and this industry provided.[121]

Many enterprises were short-lived. Two Kappel merchants dabbled in gunpowder production briefly in 1866.[122] In 1874 a silk-spinning mill with thirty-two female employees was established on the premises of a former brewery in Kappel. The work force peaked at over 100, still virtually all women, in 1879, but the business collapsed the following year.[123] Plans for a sugar-processing plant in Rust fell through in 1880–1881.[124] A much more modest establishment converting rags into paper did spring up there in 1881. Later, various small plants turned out other goods, including cement.[125]

Far and away the most important enterprises were tobacco-processing and cigar-manufacturing plants.[126] The tobacco trade had fostered ties to manufacturers in Lahr and other nearby towns, and so factory owners looked to this area when they considered how to expand their operations and cut costs. In 1871, Rust became the first of the three villages to acquire a cigar factory.[127] Individual enterprises led precarious existences, but the industry became a fixture in all three villages.

The labour force in the plants was two-thirds female. Indeed, factory work became almost universal among adolescent women at the end of the nineteenth century.[128] They stemmed, rolled, shaped, cut, and wrapped tobacco leaves as they assembled filler, binder, and wrapper into finished cigars. The young men who worked at their sides generally did so only for brief periods. At that stage, industrial employment was not a career for married men. A few husbands stayed on to oversee their younger colleagues or continued to work in the factories in tandem with a more traditional pursuit such as agricultural labour. It was less unusual for women to remain in the factories after marriage, especially in Rust.[129] Choosing factory life was an indication that there were few profitable outlets for one's labour. Families where both parents did so were therefore among the neediest in the villages.

Wage rates confirm this reasoning. Because the factories drew on the surplus labour of women and adolescents, pay was low. Around the turn of the twentieth century, wages for a twelve-and-a-half-hour day ran at about half the remuneration of a male day labourer.[130] However, the effects of those wages on the fortunes of the lower echelons of village society were complex.[131] On the one hand, some landed proprietors complained that soft factory work was too attractive, and that the competition was driving up the cost of agricultural labour. In their view only the availability of soldiers on leave kept wages under control. On the other hand, the influx of women into factory work was said to have displaced men and so depressed the wages of day labourers.

In reality, as I maintained earlier, male labourers' nominal rates held constant. However, there was some upward movement in the lower wages paid for women and for winter work. Salaries for domestic servants of both sexes climbed even more rapidly in the late nineteenth century.[132] It was the marginal age-group previously sent into service that was most attracted to factory work—and most attractive to factory owners. That both parties saw such employment as a windfall is borne out by the attempts of parents and manufacturers to circumvent the child labour laws. For those who were entitled to work, the plants offered a taste of freedom and spending money. These qualities were most appreciated by adolescents still living at home who saw factory work as a brief phase in their lives before marriage. Naturally, wage rates set in accordance with their desires were hardly sufficient to support an adult with a family.

These circumstances meant that industry assumed a different place in each village. Right from the start, Grafenhauseners lagged behind Kapplers and Rusters in flocking to the plants.[133] This reflected the more lucrative opportunities in established fields in Grafenhausen and the correspondingly smaller labour surplus there. None the less, by the early twentieth century, about 300 factory workers were found in Grafenhausen in any given year, joining about as many Kapplers and over 400 Rusters.[134] Even at that point, industry had penetrated the economies of Kappel and Rust more deeply, claiming young men twice as often as it did in Grafenhausen.[135] Indeed, Rust was well on the way to earning its later designation as a veritable "cigar village".[136]

That epithet was prompted by the discovery that in 1925 cigar manufacturing had come to employ 32 % of all Rusters, men, women, and children—and 48 % of the adult population. The reception accorded industry in Rust, and to a lesser extent in Kappel, parallels the welcome they earlier granted weaving and crafts. From that perspective, factory work constituted just one more by-employment. Occupations outside Farming had always been less significant in Grafenhausen, whose inhabitants preserved a favoured position by keeping abreast of the latest innovations in agricultural organization and technique. In

Agriculture and Industry 45

all three localities, economics created constraints and opportunities which villagers transformed even as they lived within them. Patterns of choice and endurance also characterized their fertility, to which I now turn.

Notes

1. Farming is defined by the occupational labels peasant or landed proprietor. Labour essentially comprises only the term day labourer. A very few rare synonymous labels are included in each case.
2. The two categories overlapped. 17 % of day labourers were also described as landed proprietors.
3. For the reasons explained in Chapter Two.
4. A literary example: "like all craftsmen [Handwerker] in villages and small towns in those days, [he was] half peasant and half potter". Heinrich Hansjakob, *Bauernblut* (Stuttgart, 1922), 18.
5. GLA 360/1935–11/778.
6. 42 % of Grafenhauseners' occupations were in Farming according to the OSBs. The corresponding figures for Kappel and Rust were 27 % and 19 % respectively.
7. GLA 360/1935–11/822.
8. GLA 360/1935–11/1164. Reports in 1852 and 1861 had also mentioned commerce, especially by Jews, and some transport. Ibid. GLA 360/1935–11/1163.
9. 98 % in Grafenhausen in 1882. Gem A Grafenhausen B XV/811.
10. GLA 360/1935–11/778 (Grafenhausen), GLA 360/1935–11/822 (Kappel), and GLA 360/1935–11/1164 (Rust).
11. By 17 % over the average Kappler and by 29 % over the average Ruster.
12. See Map 2.2. Fishing is discussed in detail below.
13. This rough comparison also ignores the distribution of landholding within the peasantry, variations in the age-structure of the populations, land held outside the municipality, territory belonging to lords or churches, and so on. In so far as they are relevant to my argument, those topics are taken up in Chapter Eight.
14. Even then village practice was less tidy than textbook agrarian history allows. The record of hail damage in Kappel in 1797 (GLA 229/51133a) shows that one of the three fields actually consisted of two agglomerations of land at opposite ends of the municipality.
15. Wheat had been grown in Kappel in addition to rye as early as 1314. ADBR G 4272 (3). Although Kappel rents in 1536 were calculated in rye and oats only (GLA 33/30 1536 U. 603), tithes in 1654 included wheat, corn (meaning rye), barley, and oats (GLA 229/51133).
16. GLA 229/33749 (Grafenhausen in 1692–1714). GLA 229/51131a (Kappel in 1718–1719).
17. OSB *Grafenhausen* page 262 (hempland in Grafenhausen in 1574). BvB A U. 586 (hempland in Rust in 1633). GLA 229/51131a (hemp in Kappel in 1718). Grafenhausen's hemp tithe was collected in money from the 1690s through the 1740s. GLA 229/33749.
18. Potatoes were mentioned in 1742 in Rust (BvB A U. 867). Grafenhausen paid a potato tithe that year, but not from 1692 through 1740 (GLA 229/33749). 1742 also marked the first appearance of elderberries.
19. In 1759 the mayor of Kappel reported that flax had first been grown twenty years earlier in very small quantities. However, it had been mentioned as early as 1719. GLA 229/51131a.

20. For the stereotype, see *OSB Grafenhausen* page 59, and especially *OSB Kappel* page 67 and *OSB Rust* page 103. In the same vein is Ludwig, *badische*, 102–120. More generally, contrast my account with Gérard Bouchard, *Le village immobile Sennely-en-Sologne au XVIIIe siècle* (Paris, 1972) or Emmanuel Le Roy Ladurie, "L'histoire immobile", in *Le territoire de l'historien*, vol. 2 (Paris, 1978), 16, 32.
21. *OSB Grafenhausen* pages 59–60.
22. GLA 229/33747 (Grafenhausen in 1717).
23. The 1778 conversion of the Auli field in Kappel from common grazing land into individual meadows was justified by reference to a shortage of fodder and to the advantages that would accrue from having the owners of livestock keep them themselves. The major opponent of this move had cornered the Rhinau fodder supply. GLA 229/51100.
24. Albert Köbele, "Freiherr Franz von Böcklin, Bannbrecher für die Landwirtschaft schon vor der französischen Revolution", *Geroldseckerland*, 8 (1965–1966), 174–177 (also in *OSB Rust* pages 35–38).
25. *OSB Rust* pages 103–104. The last such leases noted in the Böcklin family archive are dated 1795 (BvB A U. 1025) and 1797 (BvB A U. 1018). This move was resented and has passed into folklore as an explanation for the poverty of Rust's inhabitants. The disadvantages of a shift from renter to labourer, even on the same piece of land, follow from the economic logic elucidated towards the end of Chapter Two.
26. GLA 138/78 (question 39 of 1802 return).
27. BvB A U. 664 covers the 1654 commutation of remaining corvée duties. Five years later Rusters petitioned for a reduction in these fees (BvB A U. 685).
28. A 1759 memoir (in GLA 229/51131a) describes the difficulty of collecting a tithe that came to a full tenth of the harvest in Kappel. For the more numerous and better organized upheavals in Rust and Grafenhausen, see Chapter Ten.
29. In 1800, for example, Grafenhausen's special collection for military costs took in more than the municipality's regular taxes did. Gem A Grafenhausen C IX/1 (municipal accounts).
30. GLA 229/51101, GLA 229/51102, and GLA 229/51103. The timing of similar transactions there and in Grafenhausen suggests that it may have played a part in those cases as well: GLA 229/33726 (Grafenhausen in 1798), GLA 229/51101 (Kappel in 1802), and GLA 229/33727 (Grafenhausen in 1807).
31. *OSB Grafenhausen* pages 47–48.
32. GLA 314/2246 through GLA 314/2256.
33. Adolf Kopp, *Zehentwesen und Zehentablösung in Baden* (Freiburg, 1899), 17–30, 102–123.
34. Hermann Baier, "Wirtschaftsgeschichte der Ortenau", *Die Ortenau*, 16 (1929), 249.
35. For this and other points concerning tobacco cultivation, see Heinrich Hassinger, *Der oberbadische Tabakbau und seine wirtschaftliche Bedeutung* (Karlsruhe, 1911), Albert Straus, *Der Tabakbau im Grossherzogtum Baden und seine natürlichen Vorbedingungen* (Halle a. S., 1909), Franz Meisner, "Der Tabakbau in der Ortenau", *Badische Heimat*, 22 (1935), 547–557, Baier, "Wirtschaftsgeschichte", 251–252, and Hans Georg Zier, "Die Wirtschaft der Ortenau im 19. und 20. Jahrhundert", *Die Ortenau*, 40 (1960), 253–259 and 285–294.
36. *OSB Grafenhausen* page 62. *OSB Kappel* page 67. *OSB Rust* page 106.
37. The statistics are based on Hassinger, *Tabakbau*, 7–9.
38. They are ordered by the acreage devoted to them in Kappel. Gem A Kappel B VII/379.
39. Data on marketing from the harvest report of 1849 for Kappel (ibid.), reports on 1852 and 1855 inspection tours of Grafenhausen (GLA 360/1935–11 778), Kappel (GLA 360/1935–11/822 and GLA 360/1935–11/821), and Rust (GLA 360/1935–11/1164 and GLA 360/1935–11/1163), and the report on county Ettenheim for 1865 (GLA 236/10289).

40. OSB Grafenhausen pages 45–48.
41. Complaints came up during inspection tours of Grafenhausen in 1857, 1859, 1867, 1879, and 1883 (GLA 360/1935-11/778). See also reports on county Ettenheim for 1885–1886 (GLA 236/10229) and 1894–1895 (GLA 236/10491). Plans had existed since 1813 and were renewed in 1856. The project was finally put through between 1898 and 1910. The brief account of this matter in OSB Grafenhausen (pages 193–195) draws on Wilhelm Schneider, *Bewässerung und Bereinigung der Rittmatten Ein genossenschaftliches Kulturunternehmen* (Karlsruhe, 1911), which I have not consulted.
42. Calculations based on GLA 360/1935-11/822 (for 1852) and Gem A Kappel B VII/379 (for 1871).
43. Reports on 1852, 1865, and 1884 inspection tours of Rust in GLA 360/1935-11/1164. Compare reports on county Ettenheim for 1865 (GLA 236/10289) and 1868 through 1871 (GLA 236/10290).
44. The Agricultural Union and the Peasants Union acquired members in each village, but since they were as much political fronts as educational organizations, they are dealt with in Chapter Twelve.
45. Report on county Ettenheim for 1881 (GLA 236/10427). See also St A LA Lahr 2173.
46. Report on 1892 inspection tour of Grafenhausen in St A LA Lahr 2130. See also report on county Ettenheim for 1889–1892 in GLA 236/10490.
47. Report on county Ettenheim for 1882–1883 (GLA 236/10293). Compare the 1889–1892 report in GLA 236/10490.
48. Ibid. Grafenhausen then represented 8 % of the county's human population. *Beiträge zur Statistik des Grossherzogthums Baden*, N.F. 6 (1893), 272.
49. Report on 1894 inspection tour of Grafenhausen in St A LA Lahr 2130. Report on county Ettenheim for 1894–1895 in GLA 236/10491. The cooperative survived until World War I and later revived. See OSB Grafenhausen page 85.
50. Report on county Ettenheim for 1894–1895 (GLA 236/10491).
51. Gem A Grafenhausen B XV/812.
52. Gem A Grafenhausen B XV/810. The total population was 1438.
53. Selling directly to consumers through the egg co-op, some 260 Grafenhauseners got six to twelve Pfennigs per egg (averaging 8.5 Pfennigs in 1910), while Kapplers settled for the four to seven Pfennigs egg dealers offered them as individuals. Rust did not export eggs. (Reports on 1903, 1908, and 1910 inspection tours of Grafenhausen in St A LA Lahr 2130 and St A LA Lahr 2131. Report on 1908 inspection tour of Kappel in St A LA Lahr 2291.)
54. Reports on county Ettenheim for 1880, 1882–1883 (both in GLA 236/10293), 1886–1887 (GLA 236/10229), and 1894–1895 (GLA 236/10491). Reports on 1908 inspection tours of Grafenhausen (St A LA Lahr 2131) and Kappel (St A LA Lahr 2291).
55. Report on 1914 inspection tour of Rust in St A LA Lahr 3454.
56. On fruit, see Baier, "Wirtschaftsgeschichte", 252–253 and Zier, "Wirtschaft", 264–269.
57. Reports on 1905, 1908, and 1913 inspection tours of Kappel (St A LA Lahr 2291). Report on 1910 inspection tour of Grafenhausen (St A LA Lahr 2131). Report on 1914 inspection tour of Rust (St A LA Lahr 3454). On turn-of-the-century agriculture in general, see Moritz Hecht, *Die Badische Landwirtschaft am Anfang des XX. Jahrhunderts* (Karlsruhe, 1903).
58. Report on 1911 inspection tour of Kappel (St A LA Lahr 2291).
59. Report on 1910 inspection tour of Grafenhausen (St A LA Lahr 2131).
60. From .7 : 1 in the eighteenth century to .2 : 1 by the last quarter of the nineteenth century. The change relative to the population as a whole was less marked. Labour engaged 21 % of documented families in the eighteenth century, but fell to 10 % over the nineteenth century.

48 CHAPTER THREE

61. Such activities were virtually non-existent in the 1700s, but came to occupy 8 % of the population in the final quarter of the nineteenth century. See below for more details on this category.
62. Gem A Grafenhausen B XV/812. The figures are not out of line with the rates in the reports on county Ettenheim for 1865 (GLA 236/10289) and 1880 (GLA 236/10293). For that matter, wages in the last quarter of the nineteenth century were only slightly above those reported for Rust in 1815–1827. (GLA 314/2251.) The level of the 1860s and 1870s had been reached as early as 1833. (Ibid.)
63. Gem A Grafenhausen B XV/812.
64. Defined as the occupations: baker, brewer, butcher, cartwright, miller, and saddler. All other guild occupations but fisher and weaver are Crafts. The name "Substantial" evokes their large premises.
65. Defined as the occupations: innkeeper, merchant, manufacturer, tax collector, postmaster, independent (Rentier), steward, and manager of dairy or granary or kiln or factory. The designation "Affluent" alludes not to wealth directly but to liquid assets.
66. The designations in the OSBs often do not make this clear. *OSB Rust* explicitly described as masters only 29 % of the 120 guild masters mentioned in Rust between 1835 and 1862 (Gem A Rust C VIII/30).
67. On the occupations of women, see Benz, Thesis, appendix C.
68. Karl-Heinz Debacher, "Hanfbereitung in Rust—Eine Pflanze in der Geschichte der Gemeinde", *Die Ortenau*, 71 (1991), 397–401.
69. All bleachers in the OSBs were also weavers.
70. *OSB Grafenhausen* pages 61–62. St A LA Lahr 2131 (1935 inspection tour of Grafenhausen). *OSB Rust* page 106.
71. The two solitary fishers in *OSB Grafenhausen* are also found in other OSBs. The following discussion draws on *OSB Rust* pages 84–90 and *OSB Kappel* pages 42–46, as well as on Baier, "Wirtschaftsgeschichte", 269–271.
72. On Fridolin, see *OSB Kappel* pages 30–31.
73. In a running legal and extra-legal battle, the fishers of Rust established their right to fish in Kappel's waters. The converse did not hold. *OSB Rust* page 89.
74. GLA 229/51096 (fishing regulations and treaties from about 1500 to 1698).
75. Reports on 1852, 1865, and 1890 inspection tours of Rust in GLA 360/1935-11/1164.
76. A copy of the 1864 ruling that the fishers' guilds were mere associations of members with exclusive fishing rights, and therefore entitled to continue functioning, may be found at the front of Gem A Rust C VIII/30.
77. In the eighteenth century, fishers took office in local government in proportion to their numbers, but they became less prominent thereafter. Weavers were under-represented throughout, but never non-existent.
78. These considerations undercut the link the OSBs make between fishing and poverty. For example, *OSB Rust* (pages 104–105) emphasizes the social contrasts between peasant and fisher, and claims that this was manifested in their dwellings. (See also *OSB Kappel* page 46.) However true this may have been at the beginning of the twentieth century as Albert Köbele was growing up, it was not so in earlier times. In 1855, for example, the houses owned by fishers were worth 83 % of the average house, putting them ahead of labourers and weavers, and in line with many crafts. (Occupations from *OSB Rust*. House assessments from Gem A Rust A U. 32.) Likewise, in eighteenth-century Kappel, fishers' houses were taxed at 88 % of the average. (*OSB Kappel*, Gem A Kappel B IV/187, Gem A Kappel B IV/189, and Gem A Kappel B IV/191.)
79. As bargees, they appear below under Commerce.
80. They therefore drew on a geographically wider range of marriage partners. Indeed,

it was sometimes marriage that brought them into a village in the first place. Such movement meant that their families were less frequently documented.
81. GLA 138/78 (question 59 of 1802 return). OSB *Rust* pages 111–114. OSB *Kappel* pages 69–70. OSB *Grafenhausen* pages 260–262.
82. Mixed with honey and nuts, such cakes were also consumed by humans. OSB *Rust* page 105.
83. For example, Rust's kosher butchers had to deliver the tongues of slaughtered animals to the lord. GLA 314/2250.
84. In 1882, only 4 % of Grafenhausen's households had establishments employing helpers, apprentices, or other workers, or run by active partners. Gem A Grafenhausen B XV/811. Interpretation from GLA 233/4268.
85. Noted, for example, in the 1739 tax register in Gem A Kappel B IV/187. For more information on taxes, see Benz, Thesis, appendix D.
86. In Rust masters' sons were charged 15 % of what sons of other citizens were, and 7.5 % of what outsiders paid. The preferential rates themselves were allegedly fixed from at least the 1780s until 1862. GLA 314/2255 and Gem A Rust C VIII/30.
87. BvB A U. 955 (Rust in 1769).
88. 38 % of 157 apprentices in Rust between 1836 and 1862 were from outside the village, according to Gem A Rust C VIII/30. The same was true of 26 % of the 120 masters mentioned there. Kappel and Grafenhausen were the most frequent outside sources, followed by Rheinhausen and Ringsheim, which also border Rust.
89. Each of the prefects' reports on county Ettenheim from 1864 to 1872 (GLA 236/10289 and GLA 236/10290) dealt with the impact of free trade, and the nature of handicraft production came up from 1878 through 1884–1885 (GLA 236/10291, GLA 236/10293, and GLA 236/10463). The following discussion draws on those reports and on remarks in the reports on the 1865 inspection tour of Rust (GLA 360/1935–11/1164) and the 1866 inspection tour of Grafenhausen (GLA 360/1935–11/778).
90. Most menials were unmarried, and to that extent were life-cycle servants. None the less, at any given point the great majority of unmarried children over fifteen resided with their parents. In addition, most families who took on servants did not lack children of their own, unlike those studied by Martine Segalen, "The Family Cycle and Household Structure: Five Generations in a French Village", in Robert Wheaton and Tamara Hareven (ed.), *Family and Sexuality in French History* (Philadelphia, 1980). Rather they were simply rich. (For instance, one third of couples with servants in Rust in 1769 were notables. BvB A U. 965.)
91. For more information on these occupations, see Franz Kistler, *Die wirtschaftlichen und sozialen Verhältnisse in Baden, 1849–1870* (Freiburg, 1954), 68–79.
92. Information on various commercial activities can be found ibid., 42, 51, 140–153, and 282.
93. Report on 1903 inspection tour of Rust in St A LA Lahr 3454. Report on county Ettenheim for 1877 in GLA 236/10291. On shipping more generally, see Zier, "Wirtschaft", 306–314 and the less relevant section in Baier, "Wirtschaftsgeschichte", 264–267.
94. Report on county Ettenheim for 1873 in GLA 236/10290.
95. Report on 1855 inspection tour of Rust (GLA 360/1935–11/1163).
96. Ibid. BvB A U. 998 (1783 declaration). BvB A U. 999 (preparations for fair in 1783). Report on 1852 inspection tour of Rust in GLA 360/1935–11/1164.
97. Report on 1867 inspection tour of Grafenhausen in GLA 360/1935–11/778. Such cycling of pigs, selling them young and buying them old, is described in Robert Moeller, "Peasants and Tariffs in the *Kaiserreich*: How Backward Were the *Bauern*?", *Agricultural History*, 55 (1981), 379. Jim Retallack directed me to this article.

98. "Grafenhausen had already acquired notoriety during the war as a "nest of hamsters", possibly because of the entrepreneurship [Handelsgeist] of the inhabitants." Report of 1922 inspection tour of Grafenhausen in St A LA Lahr 2131.
99. The 1758 trader's permit in BvB A U. 922 notes that foreign retailers were not allowed to do business in Rust.
100. For many, exclusion meant a life of want. An 1817 list of Rust's Jews (Gem A Rust A U. 23) describes half the families as "poor", "beggar poor", "needy", "notoriously poor", "destitute", "barely [kümmerlich] getting by", or "suffering due to intense poverty".
101. Gem A Rust A U. 23 (1825 listing of the training of young Jewish men).
102. St A LA Lahr 3467 (1841, 1842, 1867, but not 1872).
103. Other Jewish communities in the immediate vicinity were found in Nonnenweier, Kippenheim, Schmieheim, Altdorf, Ettenheim, and Orschweier. See Map 3.2.
104. GLA 353/1908–105/4 (1861 death in Prague of manufacturer from Rust). OSB Rust family entries 5292 and 5295, and 5298 (1864 deaths in Paris of unmarried adult children).
105. OSB Rust page 105. Report on 1890 inspection tour of Rust in GLA 360/1935–11/1164.
106. This was found more convenient than having all citizens take turns. BvB A U. 966 (institution of night patrols in Rust in 1770).
107. Report on 1852 inspection tour of Rust (GLA 360/1935–11/1164). Report on 1909 inspection tour of Kappel (St A LA Lahr 2291).
108. OSB Rust pages 14–17. August Fessler, "Mark- und Waldgenossenschaften der Ortenau", Badische Heimat, 22 (1935), 96. The forest sections are shown on Map 1.1.
109. GLA 229/90539 (Rust paying swineherd in 1790). In Kappel, herders were appointed from at least 1739 to 1807. Gem A Kappel B IV/187 and Gem A Kappel B IV/191 (lists in tax rolls).
110. Reports on the 1852 inspection tour of Grafenhausen (GLA 360/1935–11/778) and the 1855 inspection tour of Rust (GLA 360/1935–11/1163).
111. In the report of his 1873 inspection tour of Grafenhausen, the prefect explicitly stated that boundary-stone setters and streetsweepers were supposed to be day labourers. GLA 360/1935–11/778.
112. Reports of 1903 inspection tour of Grafenhausen (St A LA Lahr 2130) and 1907 inspection tour of Kappel (St A LA Lahr 2291).
113. The significance of local positions thus lay less in the economic insecurity attaching to them in isolation than in the social connections required to get and hold them.
114. Report on 1878 inspection tour of Rust in GLA 360/1935–11/1164. Report on county Ettenheim for 1872 (GLA 236/10290).
115. On the plans, see Karlsruhe Zeitung 2 November 1871 and Breisgauer Zeitung 25 and 31 October 1871. On their implementation, see reports on county Ettenheim for 1872 and 1874 (GLA 236/10290), 1877 (GLA 236/10291), and 1894–1895 (GLA 236/10491). Neither the Rhine link nor the trade survived the First World War.
116. See Map 1.1. On the railroad, see Zier, "Wirtschaft", 314–317, Albert Kuntzemüller, "Achtzig Jahre Eisenbahnen in der Ortenau", Die Ortenau, 13 (1926), 21–40, report on county Ettenheim for 1894–1895 (GLA 236/10491), Breisgauer Zeitung 20 September and 20 October 1893, and report on 1935 inspection tour of Grafenhausen in St A LA Lahr 2131.
117. Bernhard Uttenweiler, 's Ettenheimer Bähnle (Ettenheim, 1992).
118. The citizens of Kappel who later entered this field generally did so as employers rather than as workers.

119. *OSB Rust* page 107. Reports of 1890 and 1909 inspection tours of Rust in GLA 360/1935-11/1164 and St A LA Lahr 3454 respectively. Gem A Rust B XVIII/360.
120. Report of 1910 inspection tour of Grafenhausen (St A LA Lahr 2131) and 1903 tour of Rust (St A LA Lahr 3454). See also Zier, "Wirtschaft", 288.
121. Gem A Kappel B XVIII/771 reports that in 1914 a cement worker was employed twice as many days per year as a carpenter, and one-and-a-half times as many as a mason.
122. Report on county Ettenheim for 1866 in GLA 236/10290.
123. Report on 1879 inspection tour of Kappel (GLA 360/1935-11/822. Reports on county Ettenheim for 1873 and 1878 through 1880 (GLA 236/10290 through GLA 236/10293).
124. Ibid. Report on county Ettenheim for 1881 (GLA 236/10425).
125. Report on 1911 inspection tour of Kappel (St A LA Lahr 2291).
126. Tobacco and cigar plants are described in *OSB Grafenhausen* pages 62–63, *OSB Kappel* pages 67–68, and *OSB Rust* pages 106–107. On the industry more generally, see Dagmar Burgdorf, *Blauer Dunst und Rote Fahnen* (Bremen, 1984) and Patricia Cooper, *Once a Cigar Maker* (Urbana, 1987). The village workers resembled the rural women of southeastern Pennsylvania (ibid., 159–179, 198–270) more closely than the men who wandered the United States or staffed the workshops of Bremen.
127. The firm had been based in neighbouring Ringsheim. (Report on county Ettenheim for 1871 in GLA 236/10290.) Plants had existed since 1864 in the nearby towns of Mahlberg and Ettenheim. (Reports on county Ettenheim for 1864 and 1865 in GLA 236/10289.)
128. Gem A Kappel B V/283 (work permits issued 1892–1894 in Kappel). The distribution of workers' fathers' occupations matched that of the whole village fairly closely, although Local Positions, Labour, and Crafts were over-represented, while the Farming, Affluent, and Substantial categories were under-represented.
129. In 1909 the work force in its five cigar-manufacturing plants comprised 159 married women, 135 unmarried women, and 130 men, according to the report on the 1909 inspection tour of Rust in St A LA Lahr 3454.
130. Factory wages from reports on county Ettenheim for 1880 and 1881 in GLA 236/10293 and GLA 236/10425 respectively. Hours of work from Gem A Grafenhausen B V/309. Day labourers' wages from Gem A Grafenhausen B XV/812.
131. The following discussion draws on the reports on county Ettenheim for 1872 through 1877 (GLA 236/10290 and GLA 236/10291) and 1884–1885 (GLA 236/10463).
132. The daily wage of a female labouring in winter with board doubled in Grafenhausen between 1883 and 1898. Over the same period the salary of a male servant rose 50 %. Gem A Grafenhausen B XV/812. See also the more sporadic figures in Gem A Kappel B XVIII/771, which extend into the inflation of the twentieth century.
133. At the end of 1887 there were only 46 factory workers in Grafenhausen, while there were 103 in Kappel and Rust already boasted 190. GLA 236/15840 (county health officer's report for 1886–1887).
134. For Grafenhausen, see reports on inspection tours of 1908, 1910, and 1935 in St A LA Lahr 2131. For Kappel, see reports on 1909, 1911, and 1922 inspection tours in St A LA Lahr 2291. For Rust, see reports on 1908 and 1909 inspection tours in St A LA Lahr 3454.
135. The proportion of men aged twenty-five to thirty-four assigned Industrial occupations on voters' lists for federal elections from 1898 to 1912 was 11 % in Grafenhausen, 24 % in Kappel, and 22 % in Rust. Gem A Grafenhausen B XIII/743. Gem A Kappel B XIII/658. Gem A Rust B XIII/294.
136. "Zigarrendorf". Zier, "Wirtschaft", 288.

4

Heirs and Heiresses

Early modern villagers controlled fertility by restricting entry into marriage and curbing childbearing outside it. For a time, these measures preserved accepted ways of life by maintaining a rough balance between population and resources. By the early nineteenth century, they were clearly failing. From that point, a growing number of inhabitants of Grafenhausen, Kappel, and Rust extended control over reproduction into marriage. Later chapters document their efforts in detail, but here I examine the framework within which they operated.

Malthus and Oedipus

My approach reflects the manner in which villagers themselves proceeded from Malthusian to neo-Malthusian fertility control.[1] A Malthusian population is one in which the "'preventive checks of moral restraint' ... 'principally delay of the marriage union'" produce the west European marriage pattern of low illegitimacy rates and high celibacy rates.[2] These restrictions are enforced through personal prudence, political power, parental prerogative, and popular pressure. In contrast, neo-Malthusian populations are characterized by control of fertility within marriage by the couple itself.[3] Where contraception is understood, compressing women's married years becomes less important and Malthusian practices gradually decay. Just such a process took place in these three villages.

Because much of this book documents failings of the old demographic régime, I begin by stressing the degree of success it did enjoy. The impact of Malthusian control is best appreciated by considering what uncontrolled fertility might have meant. Studies from both sides of the Rhine indicate that women were fecund over a much wider range of ages than those during which they actually bore children. The investigations most relevant to this area come from Strasbourg in 1861.[4] They report average ages at menarche of fifteen to sixteen for women born in the countryside and for women working in the tobacco-processing industry. The average woman could then have borne children over three decades.[5]

However, women spent much of that period unmarried. The ages during which childbearing was forgone were not always the most fecund, but even taking that into account, postponement of marriage—and with it reproduction— reduced fertility considerably. Combining census data on women's ages with

OSB information on their marital statuses, one can estimate the extent to which late marriage cut into childbearing. The results suggest that marriage was only half as prevalent as would have been required to maximize childbearing.[6]

This finding is in line with other studies, including broader analyses of census data.[7] In these villages, as elsewhere in western Europe, a substantial proportion of fecund men and women were unmarried at any given point, and many remained celibate throughout their lives.[8] Demographers attach considerable significance to such high celibacy rates, and there is a popular account of how they were maintained.[9] For reasons that will become clearer shortly, I have dubbed this account the Oedipal model.[10] In the paragraphs that follow, I present that model without comment and then outline where I dissent from it, before proceeding to my reasons for doing so.

A network of formal and informal controls prevented men from marrying until they were capable of supporting an independent household. Blocks of land or status as a guild master constituted economic niches from which a man could maintain a family, but the number of such niches was limited. Moreover, most were already occupied. Commencement of reproduction by one generation therefore had to wait on the death or retirement of its predecessor. The feedback between mortality and fertility tended towards demographic equilibrium. Increasing mortality opened more niches to the young, who wed earlier and made up the losses. Conversely, population growth choked at the point of entry into niches, curtailing reproduction by those without opportunities.[11]

Long-term stability was built on a flexible response to economic conditions. For example, in an expanding economy where new livelihoods emerged or the productivity of old ones increased, the newly created positions were taken up with alacrity and the population grew. Conversely, during depressions new opportunities to earn a living, and hence to marry, were limited, and so the population fell back. Such systems operated both on an annual level, where the extent of the harvest determined the number of weddings and conceptions, and on a secular one, where long waves of inflation and deflation coincided with centuries of demographic growth or stagnation.[12]

Even where the economy was static, dynamic tensions arose within the family. Niches were not equally accessible to everyone. Mortality in the older generation freed up resources to support new households, but this was of no benefit to a man whose father survived. It was not resources in general, but the specific resources belonging to the family holding or business that would provide the basis for the son's future household. Malthusian controls therefore prolonged the extended childhood that characterizes human beings as a species. Adolescents fell into holding patterns, as domestic servants, farmhands, apprentices, soldiers, students, and the like, and waited for their time to come.

The lock-step replacement of one man by another did not require that a father die before his son succeeded him. A groom might, for instance, take over the family property, and consign his father to an upstairs apartment or a small cottage. Resisting being shunted aside in this fashion, a father prevented his son from marrying until he was forced to stand down. From the son's point of view, access to wealth and sex depended on removing the father from the scene. This Oedipal dynamic lay behind the European marriage pattern.[13]

However neat such simple models may be, in three key respects they fail to do justice to the realities of rural life. My central disagreement hinges on inheritance, the mechanism that moves the model. Oedipal theory is androcentric, in that it treats controlling property and marrying as rôles of males exclusively. However, the inhabitants of this region practised partible inheritance, with daughters sharing equally with sons.[14] Once free of the straitjacket imposed by thinking in terms of one father and one son, the researcher can come to grips with the complexities of the concrete situations facing unmarried women and men.

The second major shortcoming of Oedipal thinking is its assumption that the bulk of property was passed on at the time a child wed. Fathers did not retire so that their sons could marry. Rather, the resources to establish new families came from any of four parents, the groom's mother, the bride's father, and the bride's mother being just as important as the groom's father. In part, this point is a corollary of the preceding one, for it relies on the fact that property did not come in unbreakable blocks.

Finally, standard accounts are far too sanguine about the ability of such systems to function over the long term. Even with homeostatic adjustments to mortality and economic conditions, even taking into account the rôles of women and the possibilities for redistributing property,[15] there was no guarantee of equilibrium. In Grafenhausen, Kappel, and Rust, a century of sustained population growth placed the system under such stress that it came apart. Before I proceed to that crisis in Chapter Five, I pause to acquaint readers with the concrete workings of the inheritance system.

Inheritance

Customary regulations concerning property were identical in Grafenhausen and Kappel, and practices in Rust varied only slightly.[16] The assets of a husband and wife were treated as a unit regardless of when they had been acquired.[17] Each surviving child, male or female, was to receive an equal share of the parent's wealth. The youngest son, and following him the eldest daughter, had a preferential right to include the family dwelling in his share.

Children did not accede to these claims all at once. At the death of his wife, a widower retained two-thirds of their holding, with just one-third assigned immediately—if only on paper—to the children. When it was the husband who died first, the widow kept one-third of the holding and two-thirds passed to their children. The shares of children who died unmarried reverted first to their parents and eventually to their siblings. These terms could be amended only slightly through a marriage contract. Typical provisions dealt with the disposition of the marriage bed—or the right to use the premises where it was located—or specified that new assets were to be split fifty-fifty regardless of the sex of the surviving spouse. In any case, only when the second parent died did the next generation acquire title to the remainder of the holding.

The fact that each married villager stood to inherit from four parents, more if he or she remarried, profoundly affected marriage strategies. Because the resources required to maintain a new family came from either side of the family following the death or incapacity of any member of the older generation, barriers to marriage were lower than in regions of impartible inheritance. The wide distribution of property within families contributed to a more egalitarian social structure, as each family member had a concrete stake in the community. It further promoted cooperation, and of course particular sorts of rivalries. Resources were often shared within a single generation,[18] and more important across generations in anticipation of inheritance.

Close economic ties between in-laws contributed to the united front villagers presented to the outside world. Coming into one's inheritance gradually as the older generation died off further promoted solidarity. Nearly all adults spent many years in control of fewer assets than most other villagers. Even if they ultimately outstripped their neighbours, an event that might come later for the rich, whose parents tended to live longer, they retained a sense of identification with their less fortunate fellow citizens. In addition, direct acquaintance with social mobility engendered a more confident outlook on the world. Like other facets of village life, inheritance customs acted dynamically to maintain social cohesion. Amid the variety of individual experiences, the ordered pattern of relations within the community reproduced itself.

The fact that a family's assets were as apt to derive from the female line as from the male one had important consequences for the choice of spouse and for the status of women. Marrying a member of a family poorer than one's own virtually ensured one's children a worse start in life. More immediately, such a match guaranteed that one would be poorer than one's parents had been.[19] On the other hand, a man whose bride brought substantial resources with her was apt to find his social and economic position determined by his wife's family. In such a situation, her influence on decision-making might well increase.[20]

Because these reflections applied at all levels of village society, marriage circles formed in which ties were established between couples of roughly equal wealth. For the most part, this fostered endogamy, but at the extremes the effect was the reverse. Rich families often had to look beyond the municipal boundaries to locate suitable mates, while marginal elements had nothing economic to entice local partners.

Economic considerations based on inheritance customs also underlay high rates of remarriage.[21] Those without a spouse enjoyed a lower standard of living to begin with. Loss of a partner removed a major contribution to the family enterprise in the form of sex-segregated labour for which there was generally no ready substitute. Moreover, it threatened to reduce the survivor's holdings substantially. If any of the children were already of age, they could take over their shares of the deceased spouse's lands. Sons and daughters who had not yet wed were encouraged to finalize commitments as they were now in a position to set up on their own. Minors were not able to claim their inheritances at once,

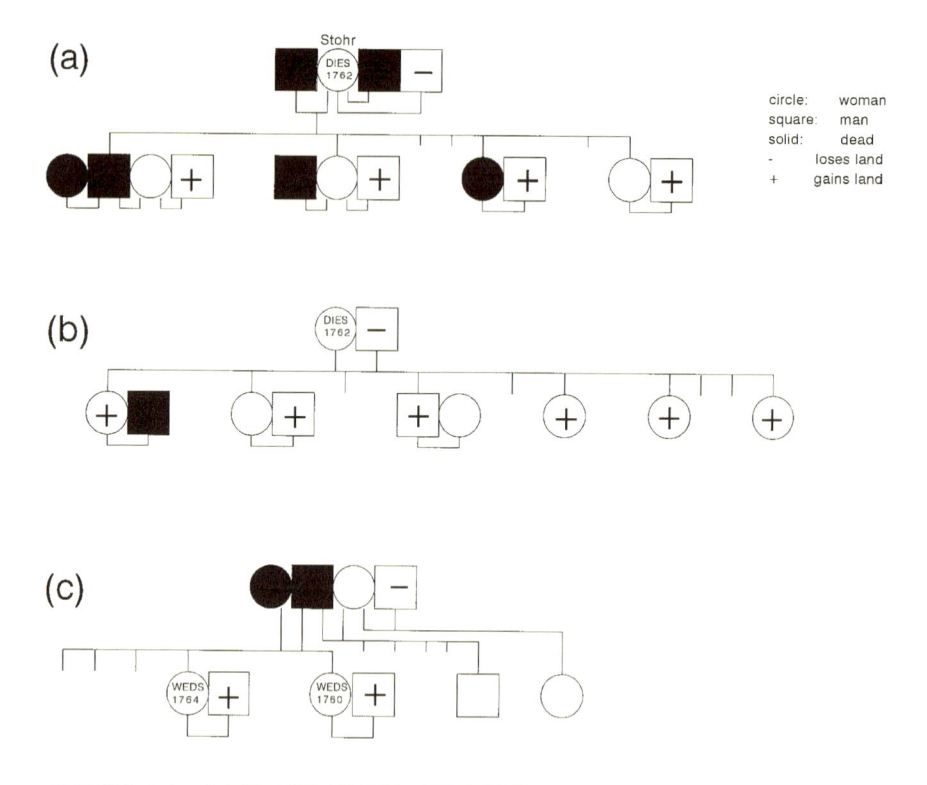

FIGURE 4.1 CASE HISTORIES OF THREE INHERITANCES IN RUST IN THE 1760S

but they constituted a looming menace to a young widow or widower who faced the prospect of living from a much smaller holding for an extended period.

In the circumstances, it made eminent economic sense to enter into a new union to replace the lost or threatened assets. Matches with a widow or widower were also attractive to potential partners. From their point of view, even the diminished holdings of a survivor might outweigh the as yet undelivered inheritance of a bachelor or spinster. Thus, the calculations of both parties encouraged remarriage.[22]

In practice, these considerations lent themselves to complications of which contemporaries were only too aware. Figure 4.1 summarizes three examples from Rust's tax rolls, which were renewed in 1759 and updated through 1765.[23] I have chosen them to illustrate the distinctive patterns produced by the timing of deaths and weddings. In the first case, all the heirs had been married before their mother died, in the second some were married and some unmarried, and in the third all were unmarried. The logic of the system I have been describing shows through clearly right across the range of wealth.

The first case (a) traces the repercussions of the death of Catharina Stöhr, who had wed three times. The extensive assets she accumulated in the first two unions had been credited to her third husband. His origin is not given in the OSB, but he may have come from the nearby village of Oberhausen. His lands in Rust, 5.62 hectares plus a complex of buildings occupying a further .72 hectares, were therefore acquired almost entirely through marriage—or purchase. His wife's death removed much of that land from his hands. His loss was the gain of the children from her first marriage, the last two having been childless.

The conflict of economic interests between parent and step-child had a number of aspects.[24] All four children had long been married, but until their mother passed away, they had no right to their full inheritances. As long as Stöhr kept marrying, her husbands controlled the holding and resisted sharing. Moreover, even the timing of her death affected the division of the family's assets. Because the third husband had no children of his own, if he had died first, her children would in time have inherited still more. In the event, their mother died first, and the holding was split accordingly.

Not one of the children themselves was credited with the land they had inherited. The assets of the two surviving married daughters, on the far right and in the centre of the Figure, were recorded under their current husbands' names. The other daughter and the son had predeceased their mother. All their land was assigned to their erstwhile spouses, since none of the grandchildren was yet of age. The widowed son-in-law even acquired the large family homestead as those with better claims already had houses. Because the widowed daughter-in-law had remarried in the interim, her first husband's share appeared among her new husband's holdings.[25]

Bands of reproduction and marriage thus stretched right across the village. I have just described how land passed from Stöhr's third husband to the husband of the widow, once second wife, of the eldest son from Stöhr's first marriage. Other economic ties followed the lines of inheritance. Here, for instance, the heirs were the preferred buyers when the widower sold off his share of the inheritance in 1763 and severed his tenuous links with Rust for good.

The results in case (b) were not that different, although it varied from (a) in two respects. Both husband and wife had wed only once, and three of their children were as yet unmarried at the time the mother died. Nevertheless, all the children shared in the division of 4.70 hectares and a modest house that was recorded twelve days later. The eldest daughter was between marriages in Grafenhausen, and her share cannot be traced. The husband of the second-eldest daughter received her inheritance over two years from his father-in-law. The only son took a full share at once, and in 1763 purchased from his father further land as well as the family dwelling. The shares of the other three daughters, who did not wed until 1764, 1765, and 1771 respectively, are not specified, but the first of them did bring real estate to her marriage. Having lost more than half the holding, the sixty-two-year-old widower surrendered his remaining rights the next year and retired to Grafenhausen, his wife's birthplace, where he died in 1771.[26]

Case (c) illustrates a rarer event in which accession to property coincided with marriage. As in (a), a surviving spouse acted as the carrier of assets from one union to the next. The connections to the heirs were even more tenuous, as neither husband nor wife was a biological parent of the children who wed. Following their mother's death in 1740, their father had remarried. His death in 1752 left the step-mother in control of the full inheritance of both families, for all three children were still minors. The man who wed the widowed stepmother therefore gained control of all these small holdings, including three houses and 1.28 hectares, at one stroke.

However, the daughters' marriages began to unravel this knot of property. Their weddings triggered the transfer of their inheritances, including one house, to their grooms. The widow's husband could look forward to more of the same, for in a few years the son his wife had brought to the marriage would claim his inheritance through his natural father. That loss would complete the disintegration of a holding that was small to begin with, thereby illustrating one of the perils of marrying for short-term economic gain.

In addition to highlighting themes I brought out in the abstract discussion earlier, these three examples direct attention to the basic feature of the inheritance system: death determined property transfers. Other events, such as the weddings of case (c), acquired significance only through earlier deaths. Even the retirement of the husband in case (b) was prompted by his wife's death. All the informal arrangements, plans, and hopes of the living were constrained by the framework created by the dead.[27] The foregoing examples therefore illustrate how demographic realities structured the economy and thereby influenced thinking about marriage.

Because the lag between marriage and acquisition of one's full inheritance is often neglected in treatments of economic and demographic history,[28] the phenomenon merits additional attention. As it happens, the argument that children generally received no property from their living parents at marriage can be traced in detail for two of the villages towards the end of the nineteenth century. Property slips recording the assessed value of holdings from 1876 to 1902 are available for all of Kappel's landowners and for many of Rust's. Here I limit my attention to married male proprietors who died in those years. These men are therefore being observed towards the end of the cycle of accumulation that typified villagers' lives.[29] Since the slips were updated each year it is possible to check whether the weddings of their offspring made any dent in that accumulation.

Table 4.2 indicates that they did not. Although average assets dropped 9 % following a child's marriage, most of that drop reflected coincidences between his or her wedding and the death of one or the other parent. Since the death of the proprietor reduced his holding to zero independent of any action by his

TABLE 4.2
Average change in the Land tax assessment of a married man, At the wedding of a child, At the wedding of a son, At the wedding of a daughter, At the wedding of a youngest son, and At the death of a wife, in late nineteenth-century Kappel and Rust

	Change overall	Excluding events coinciding with death of husband	Excluding events coinciding with death of husband or wife	Number in last case
Wedding of				
Child	–9 %	–6 %	–3 %	183
Son	–10 %	–6 %	–2 %	88
Daughter	–8 %	–5 %	–3 %	95
Youngest son	–7 %	–5 %	+2 %	42
Death of				
Wife	–27 %	–25 %	—	37

Notes
(1) *Source*: Gem A Kappel B IV/198 and Gem A Kappel B IV/199 (property slips for 1876–1902), Gem A Rust (property slips written off 1878–1899), OSB Kappel, and OSB Rust.
(2) The Table covers only husbands who died in the indicated years, and of that group just those who had at least one child wed then or who became widowers in that period. Only slips written off during the proprietor's lifetime or within one year of his death were considered. 113 cases met all these restrictions.
(3) Because in about half of cases deaths were not noted until the following year, all of the figures represent changes between the year of the event and two years afterwards.

children, it is appropriate to exclude such coincidences from consideration. When this is done, the loss of land at a child's marriage becomes less significant. As the succeeding rows of the Table show, this minimal drop was true of sons and daughters alike[30] and even applied to the wedding of the youngest son. Despite the special position of that child and despite the fact that he was usually the last to wed, fathers showed no more inclination to divide their holdings on that occasion than on any other.

The bottom row of Table 4.2 reveals that the lone exception to this pattern was the death of the mother. Fathers' holdings fell more than 10 % three times as often following the death of a spouse as following a child's wedding, and usually by a considerably greater margin. The average holding dropped 25 % (where the widower did not expire right after his wife). This contrast reinforces my argument. Only the mother's death gave the children a lever to pry loose their inheritances, previously controlled by the father in his wife's name.

That holdings did not immediately tumble by a full third might reflect, among other things, some fathers' residual ability to hold off any children who had not yet wed. Only in such a case could the child's subsequent marriage result in a transfer of assets and reduce the father's holding.[31] That this was a rare event, especially after remarriage became less common, is borne out once again

60 CHAPTER FOUR

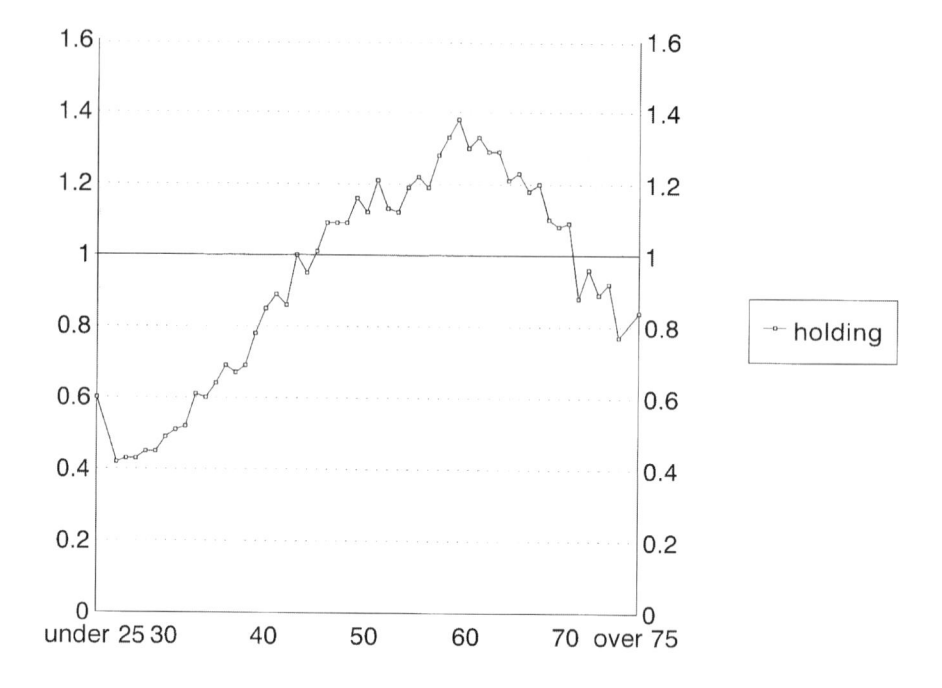

FIGURE 4.3 AVERAGE HOLDINGS OF MARRIED COUPLES AS A FRACTION OF THE VILLAGE AVERAGE, BY THE AGE OF THE HUSBAND

when weddings that were confounded with the mother's death are excluded (second-last column). Under those circumstances, the net effect of children's marriages was negligible. Indeed, in a majority of cases, the father's holding two years following a child's wedding was exactly what it had been before it.

The patterns of Table 4.2 hold good in both villages, among rich and poor, and for all sizable occupational groups.[32] In broader perspective, what this means is that the link between children's weddings and fathers' retirement, from farming at least, was even weaker than that between fathers' deaths and children's marriages. Fathers retained their holdings till their children were wed, and even after.

This arrangement produced a distinctive lifetime curve of landholding, displayed in Figure 4.3. The Figure summarizes some sixteen thousand measurements of the landed wealth of married couples in Grafenhausen,[33] Kappel,[34] and Rust[35] over the eighteenth and nineteenth centuries.[36] There are small random fluctuations, but an overall pattern is easily discernible in which holdings remain below average until well into middle age, exceed the average for almost three decades, and then fall below it once more.[37]

Clearly the bulk of a couple's property accumulated well after the wedding. Some extremely young grooms were relatively well off, but once a large number of cases is available, men in their twenties can be seen to control less than half as much land as the average husband. Their holdings increase year by year in their thirties, and by their mid-forties have reached the village mean. The gradual rise continues unabated, and a plateau in the early fifties gives way to an overall peak around sixty. Holdings begin to decline thereafter as the conventional retirement age of sixty-five is passed. However, not until the average man was in his seventies did he again enjoy less wealth than the village average. Indeed, even at advanced ages, by which point all of their children had wed, some villagers continued to control substantial expanses of land.

Figure 4.3 deals with a couple's landed wealth as a unit. Although its age-patterns can plausibly be described in non-Oedipal terms, the Figure gives no direct indication of the sources of a couple's wealth. A sharper examination of those sources comes from a cross-section through the population of Grafenhausen in 1877.[38] There was no significant correlation between a groom's age at marriage and his age at his father's death—or his mother's, for that matter. There was, however, a significant relationship with the groom's age at the death of his bride's father. Patricidal usurpation might be a necessary prelude to sex in Oedipus's Thebes, but in Grafenhausen sex was itself the means to a niche. Moreover, sizes of landholdings correlated most strongly (negatively) with husbands' ages at the death of their wives' mothers. Thus, when a woman's parents survived to old age, her groom had to wait longer to wed, and when they died young, her new family was richer. These findings show that the resources required to establish a new household passed at least as easily through the female line as from father to son.

My examples thus far have dealt with landed property. That effectively covers all forms of wealth in a peasant community subject to the logic set out in Chapter Two.[39] For the sake of empirical completeness, I look at another basis of livelihood, namely status as a guild master. Because this asset fits the concept of a unitary niche, and because such positions were invariably filled by men, artisanal marriage patterns provide a sharp test of my views. It turns out that the Oedipal model fits their behaviour no better than it did the landed proprietors'.

This does not mean that there is no evidence for sons succeeding their fathers. Occupations ran in families through the centuries.[40] In addition, well-placed observers took Malthusianism for granted in relating their impressions of villagers.[41] Moreover, by limiting the number of masters in each trade and by prescribing tools and standards, guild regulations put a ceiling on livelihoods even more rigorous than the one physical conditions imposed on agricultural pursuits.[42] Mandatory apprenticeship, together with the preferential treatment accorded sons of guild members, kept the younger generation in line, in every sense. If this Oedipal outline is correct, after an extended period as a journeyman, father's death, acquisition of master status, and marriage should follow in rapid succession.

Some artisans' lives did take that course. Alois Engelmann, a twenty-eight-year-old journeyman in Rust, lost his father in February 1840, was accepted as a master baker by the general guild in January 1841, and wed eight days later.[43] The full records of Rust's general guild, covering the Craft and Substantial categories from 1835 to 1862, provide an opportunity to see how typical his experience was.[44]

The guild minutes show that men did indeed wait years before becoming masters. After an apprenticeship of one and a half to two years in their late teens, journeymen spent seven or eight years in the service of local or outside masters. Their accession to master status and their first weddings both came at age 28.5, on average. That coincidence was no statistical artefact. In 57 % of cases marriage followed within a year of entry into full guild membership. Indeed, as in Engelmann's case, there was often only a few days' difference. The isolated instances in which someone wed before becoming a master reflected legal anomalies, such as the acquisition of rights by Jews who had been plying their trades for years, or incompleteness in the records.[45] Acceptance as a master was a customary preliminary to the wedding ceremony, like reading the banns or drawing up a marriage contract. Thus, postponed entry into the guild coincided with delayed marriage.[46]

The empirical connection between marriage—or master status—and the father's death, on the other hand, is far from clear. Son's ages at their fathers' deaths were distributed fairly uniformly from zero to almost sixty. Mean and modal ages at father's death exceeded those for marriage by a couple of years. Sons who lost their fathers while still quite young actually acceded to master status later than those whose fathers were still alive. The idea that being orphaned hindered accumulation of the capital necessary to set up shop is not that surprising, but theories that assume a father's establishment would be there waiting for the son cannot account for this delay.

Moreover, there is a strong correlation between age at first marriage and age at entry into the guild, but no relationship whatsoever between age at father's death and the other two variables. This holds even when attention is restricted to men who wed, became masters, and lost their fathers all in their twenties and thirties. Indeed, even among sons who followed their fathers' crafts, age at father's death was not significantly related to age at entry into marriage or the guild. Thus, there is no real evidence that a father's death was what brought into operation the customary mechanisms leading to master status and marriage.

In fact, taken at face value, the evidence suggests a decidedly different hypothesis. The one significant correlation between deaths in one generation and entry into the guild by the next concerned the bride's father. That is, when a woman's father died young, her sweetheart entered the guild earlier and wed younger. When her father survived, her sweetheart had to wait to become a full adult economically and socially. That this same pattern emerged in the 1877 cross-section of landholdings in Grafenhausen described earlier is suggestive. It may well be that the female line more frequently transmitted the crucial assets that allowed a couple to set up a household of its own. Again, Oedipus would have gone about it backwards.

CAN THE OEDIPAL MODEL BE SAVED?

These reflections stimulate a modification of the Oedipal model. A more sophisticated variant of Oedipal theory would link setting up a household to general mortality in the previous generation, and not to a death within the same family.[47] In this context, the argument might run that it was the death of another shoemaker or butcher, not necessarily the journeyman's father, that opened a place and prompted the guild to admit him. Indeed, on this approach the occupation itself becomes almost irrelevant. Niches in the village economy would open and be taken up in order as the previous generation departed. In such a model the average villager could marry at twenty-eight, produce an heir at thirty-two, and die at sixty for centuries.[48] Demographic stability would endure independent of social and economic turnover.

In this generalized Oedipal model, the aspirations of the young for sex and wealth are stymied by the older generation as a whole, not by their fathers alone. Moreover, when gratified, they are likewise gratified by the older generation as a whole.[49] Within the framework of Oedipal theory, such a generalization is open to serious objections from proponents of the more basic interpretation. It is hard to see what mechanism would make the space that opened available to a particular journeyman. How would his family link up with the one that had suffered the loss?[50] If the journeyman's father still ran the family shop, where would the funds to acquire another one come from?[51] If the capital were available, why wait for a death?

Furthermore, this theory requires that ages at marriage be, if anything, higher among the prosperous, who tended to live longer. Actually, they were the first to wed.[52] Finally, there were only a handful of positions in most village trades. It is simply implausible to imagine that masterships would come open at about the time journeymen were prepared to wed unless there corresponded to each journeyman a master about one generation older. The natural corresponding master is the journeyman's father, as the simple Oedipal model claimed all along. Under such conditions, Oedipal theory has to be established in its strong form, in which son succeeds father in lock-step, if it is to be established at all.

In villages where partible inheritance was practised, the generalized model enjoys a line of defence to these objections. Rather than concede defeat in the face of the empirically evident importance of the female line, a proponent of a generalized Oedipal theory can instead turn that importance to advantage. In particular, it might be claimed that partible inheritance provides the missing link between generations, the plausible mechanism by which a niche opening in one generation became accessible to an adolescent in the next. As I indicated in discussing Figure 4.1, under partible inheritance a death transferred assets to many heirs along intricate routes. In such an environment the chances are greatly enhanced that a death would accommodate some couple waiting for an opportunity to wed.[53]

Because the past few pages may have left readers wondering just which aspects of the Oedipal model I am attacking and which ones I am endorsing,

I pause at this point to clarify the situation. All three of its distinctive legs have been wounded. First, the population equilibrium the model purports to explain did not exist. Second, the idea that livelihoods came in permanent packets held from wedding till death is clearly untenable. So too is the idea that economic structure can be analysed without taking account of women. Both as heirs and as benefactors, their contributions were crucial to the functioning of this partible inheritance system. With these underpinnings cut away, the Oedipal theory must be rejected as a universal explanation.

In what follows, I summarize a revised understanding of European marriages, and then extend that understanding by examining sources of flexibility within the system. The basic Malthusian insight, that controlling entry into marriage controlled fertility, remains sound. In these villages, marriage did coincide with the creation of a new household. However, that creation did not require the complete destruction of an existing economic unit. Partible inheritance meant that the death of a groom's father was no more necessary than the death of any of a couple's other three parents. In addition, property could be sold, leased, or loaned in parts.[54] Such partial transfers could take place at any time, not just at weddings. Moreover, assets could be shared without any legal transfer. As long as one parent or another was willing to stand behind the new couple, they could create a new family without producing a fully independent household. Finally, additional households could be supported from the new resources created by economic expansion.

This broader understanding of the ways in which resources accumulated makes it possible to sketch how marriages were made. Popular psychology determined what constituted an appropriate standard of living within a social stratum. Once the critical mass of resources was available, whether lying fallow or as a disposable portion of the assets making up a larger holding or merely in prospect, it constituted a marriage waiting to happen. In a close-knit community, that potential place drew suitors,[55] one of whom eventually proved acceptable from social and affectional points of view. Those who were rebuffed, or who knew better than to try, waited for subsequent opportunities and were therefore older by the time they wed. Positions opened more easily in wealthy families and opened more easily for prestigious families, and so their children married younger on average.

On the Rhine plain, where land was at a premium, this system was as much a response to populousness as an attempt to forestall it. By restricting the range of ages during which people enjoyed full control over property, the system permitted more villagers to hold land, and to hold larger amounts of it. Tying marriage to access to resources sufficient to support a family offered hope of keeping both demographic and economic units viable. In the next chapter, I show how that mechanism functioned even at a time when too much was being demanded of it.

Notes

1. My usage follows Ansley Coale, "Factors associated with the development of low fertility: an historical summary", *Proceedings of the World Population Conference* (Belgrade, 1965), II, 205–207.
2. John Hajnal, "European Marriage Patterns in Perspective", in Glass and Eversley, *Population*, 101–143. (Quotation from page 130.) If successful, such measures obviate the need for the more notorious positive checks to cut back overpopulation.
3. Anthony Wrigley, "Fertility Strategy for the Individual and the Group", in Charles Tilly (ed.), *Historical Studies of Changing Fertility* (Princeton, 1978), 148–152. See also Anthony Wrigley, *Population in History* (New York, 1969), 111–119, 147–149, 191, 231–234. Replacing open coercion by local government and neighbours with the more pervasive and less tractable forces of the global market need not increase people's effective control over their own destinies. Much the same caveat applies to relations within the family, for conveying responsibility from the community to the couple might not improve the position of women. When I refer to couples making decisions, I describe the locus of decision not the process. In particular, I am not endorsing the vision presented in Edward Shorter, "Female Emancipation, Birth Control, and Fertility in European History", *American Historical Review*, 78 (1978), 631–632. For examples of other modes of decision, see Germaine Greer, *Sex and Destiny* (New York, 1984), 134–137.
4. The work of Stoltz and Levy was reported by V. Stoeber and G. Tourdes, *Topographie et histoire médicale de Strasbourg et du Département Bas-Rhin* (Paris, 1862), which has been cited in G. Lagneau, "Recherches comparatives sur la menstruation en France", *Bulletins de la Société d'Anthropologie de Paris*, 6 (1865), 724–743, in Gaston Backmann, "Die beschleunigte Entwicklung der Jugend", *Acta Anatomica*, 4 (1948), 421–480, and in Edward Shorter, "L'âge des premières règles en France, 1750–1950", *Annales Economies Sociétés Civilisations*, 36 (1981), 495–511.
5. Inquiries about menopausal ages are less reliable because of the proximity of age fifty, a round number which dominates retrospective surveys. Backmann, "Entwicklung", 454–455. D. Hofmann and T. Soergel, "Untersuchungen über das Menarchen- und Menopausenalter", *Geburtshilfe und Frauenheilkunde*, 32 (1972), 969–973.
6. This claim is based on the Princeton Im index (defined in Ansley Coale, "The Decline of Fertility in Europe from the French Revolution to World War II", in Samuel Behrman, Leslie Corsa, and Ronald Freedman (ed.), *Fertility and Family Planning* (Ann Arbor, 1969), 5–6). For Rust in 1769, Im = .55 and Im* = .50. (Data from BvB A U. 965 and *OSB Rust*.) For Grafenhausen in 1839, Im = .52 and Im* = .49. (Data from Gem A Grafenhausen B XV/809 and *OSB Grafenhausen*.) In each case I omit domestic servants, to whom the censuses did not assign names or ages. The values are therefore over-estimates.
7. Knodel, *Germany*, 35–39.
8. In Grafenhausen in 1839, about one-tenth of men and women aged forty-five or more had never been married. This calculation again omits domestic servants. On the general situation, including the prevalence of celibacy among menials, see John Knodel and Mary Jo Maynes, "Urban and Rural Marriage Patterns in Imperial Germany", *Journal of Family History*, 1 (1976), 129–168.
9. This account is distinct from the European marriage pattern, and purports to explain it.
10. In calling it a model, I do not mean to imply that Oedipal thinking is conscious or clear. Rather, it constitutes a widespread set of assumptions about European populations. Precisely because these beliefs are taken for granted, their lack of justification has gone generally unnoticed. For two of many examples, see Robert Lerner

and others, *Western Civilizations* (New York, 1988), vol. two, 581, and John McKay and others, *A History of Western Society* (Boston, 1991), 629.
11. G. Ohlin, "Mortality, Marriage, and Growth in Pre-Industrial Populations", *Population Studies*, 14 (1961), 190–197. Ronald Lee, "Introduction", in Ronald Lee (ed.), *Population Patterns in the Past* (New York, 1977), 4–6. Daniel Smith, "A Homeostatic Demographic Regime: Patterns in West European Family Reconstitution Studies", ibid., 21, 37. Dupâquier, "animal", 177–211.
12. For examples of this interpretation, see Pierre Goubert, *Louis XIV and Twenty Million Frenchmen* (New York, 1970), 308–310, Wilhelm Abel, *Agrarkrisen und Agrarkonjunktur* (Hamburg, 1966), H. J. Habakkuk, "The Economic History of Modern Britain", in Glass and Eversley, *Population*, 147–151, Anthony Wrigley and Roger Schofield, *The Population History of England 1541–1871* (London, 1981), 402–484, and Ronald Lee, "Short-term variation: vital rates, prices, and weather", ibid., 356–401.
13. Explicitly Oedipal interpretations can be found in such otherwise diverse works as Lutz Berkner, "The Stem Family and the Developmental Cycle of the Peasant Household: an Eighteenth-Century Austrian Example", *American Historical Review*, 77 (1972), 398–418 (compare Lutz Berkner, "Peasant Household Organization and Demographic Change in Lower Saxony (1689–1766)", in Lee, *Patterns*, 59, 67), Edward Shorter, *The Making of the Modern Family* (New York, 1975), 31–35, Daniel Smith, "Parental Power and Marriage Patterns: An Analysis of Historical Trends in Hingham, Massachusetts", *Journal of Marriage and the Family*, 35 (1973), 419–428, and Richard Wall, "Real property, marriage and children: the evidence from four pre-industrial communities", in Richard Smith (ed.), *Land, Kinship and Life-Cycle* (Cambridge, 1984), 445.
14. In fairness, I point out that in his seminal article ("Patterns", 133–134), Hajnal carefully links such explanations to impartible inheritance. Later, ("Two Kinds of Pre-industrial Household Formation System", *Population and Development Review*, 8 (1982), 449–494), he focuses instead on the prevalence of domestic service.
15. These possibilities are stressed by Sabean, *Property*.
16. The following exposition is based on GLA 138/74 and GLA 138/78 (questions 31, 32, and 51, and answers, respectively, for the 1802 return covering Grafenhausen and Kappel—used previously by Rest, "Zustände", 29) and on GLA 61/10492, GLA 61/10493, and GLA 61/10494 (Rust marriage contracts from 1752–1763, 1795–1809, and 1810–1813, respectively). GLA 229/33716, detailing the splitting of one Grafenhausen inheritance in accordance with a marriage contract, was also helpful. Sabean, *Property*, explains the mechanics of a similar inheritance system in Württemberg.
17. These assets were the property of the husband, but his rights over them were not unlimited. Instead, he functioned as a trustee for the vested interests of the wife and the children. To forestall disputes, the Böcklins in 1786 required women and their counsellors to be present at any negotiation involving housing. BvB A U. 967.
18. On sibling bonds, see David Sabean, "Young bees in an empty hive: relations between brothers-in-law in a south German village around 1800", in Hans Medick and David Sabean (ed.), *Interest and Emotion* (Cambridge, 1984), 171–186.
19. Strictly, this assumes that each spouse had a surviving sibling.
20. For other thoughts along these lines, see Jack Goody, "Inheritance, property and women: some comparative considerations", in Jack Goody, Joan Thirsk, and Edward Thompson (ed.), *Family and Inheritance* (Cambridge, 1976), 10–12.
21. 24 % of 1367 documented marriages beginning before 1800 involved a widower and 17 % a widow. By 1875–1899 the figures had fallen to 13 % and 4 % (of 699), respectively.
22. This logic especially favoured widowers, who were twice as well off as widows from

an equivalent background. On remarriage strategies, see B. A. Holderness, "Widows in pre-industrial society: an essay upon their economic functions", in Smith, *Life-Cycle*, 428–435.
23. The information comes from Gem A Rust C I/6 (tax rolls 1759–1765) and OSB Rust entries 3650, 3939, and 389 in particular. Both the nature of these sources and my heuristic purposes limit consideration to inheritances from women.
24. Like Martine Segalen ("Mentalité populaire et remariage en Europe occidental", in Jacques Dupâquier and others (ed.), *Marriage and Remarriage in Populations of the Past* (London, 1981), 70, 75), I attribute the stereotype of the evil stepmother to this conflict.
25. This set up a situation similar to case (c).
26. Perhaps he dwelt with his daughter, who brought a new husband to her bakery in 1763 as well.
27. Compare the old French legal maxim "the dead distrain the living", cited in Jack Lively (ed.), *The Works of Joseph de Maistre* (New York, 1965), 275.
28. The only significant exceptions of which I am aware are Hervé Le Bras, "Parents, Grands-parents, Bisaieux", *Population*, 28 (1973), 1–38, and more recently Sabean, *Property*.
29. See Figure 4.3, upcoming.
30. In this respect, dowries were treated like other inheritances.
31. As in case (c) of Figure 4.1.
32. Details not shown.
33. Extent of land from 1727 survey, from 1860 property slips, and from 1877 survey (Gem A Grafenhausen C VII/1, Gem A Grafenhausen C IV 4/16, and Gem A Grafenhausen C VII/3). Land assessment from 1842–1843 tithe register (Gem A Grafenhausen C I/10). Municipal tax paid from 1800 roll (Gem A Grafenhausen C IX/1). Tax assessment from 1819 rolls and from 1855, 1856, and 1859 voters' lists (Gem A Grafenhausen C IX/1 for 1820 and Gem A Grafenhausen B IV/166).
34. Extent of land from 1728 survey, from 1739, 1741, 1745, 1750, 1771, 1775, 1779, 1785, 1786, 1787, 1800, and 1807 tax rolls, and from 1877 survey (Gem A Kappel C VII/2 ii, Gem A Kappel B IV/187, Gem A Kappel B IV/189, Gem A Kappel B IV/191, and Gem A Kappel C VII/3). Land assessment from 1846 tithe register, from 1849, 1862, 1875, 1882, 1888, and 1901 cadastres, and from 1876–1902 property slips (Gem A Kappel Tithe register, Gem A Kappel B IV/195, Gem A Kappel B IV/196, Gem A Kappel B IV/201 through Gem A Kappel B IV/203, Gem A Kappel B IV/198, and Gem A Kappel B IV/199). Land and building assessment from 1912 cadastre (Gem A Kappel B IV/204).
35. Extent of land from 1759–1765 tax rolls, from 1827 land register, and from 1877, 1878, 1880, 1882, 1883 property slips (Gem A Rust C I/6, Gem A Rust C IV/46 through Gem A Rust C IV/50, and Gem A Rust B XIII/311). Land assessment from 1876–1899 property slips written off in those years (bundled in Gem A Rust). Tax assessment from 1870–1872 record of quartering (Gem A Rust C XII/47). Tax paid from 1890, 1893, and 1896 voters' lists, and from 1907 and 1913 cadastres (Gem A Rust B IV/80 and Gem A Rust B IV/94).
36. Because a family's assets were recorded under the husband's name, I describe the Figure as if the property were entirely his own. At each point landholdings are compared against the average for all married male villagers included in the source. Because my major concern is the timing of movements with respect to that average, I have added to the Figure a horizontal line at that level.
37. A smoother pattern, with sharper extremes, can be obtained by graphing holdings against years since first wedding instead of raw age.
38. Gem A Grafenhausen C VII/3 (1877 land survey) and *OSB Grafenhausen*.
39. This claim is empirically substantiated in Benz, Thesis, appendix D.

40. Although they devolved through the female as well as the male line.
41. In his 1878 report on county Ettenheim (GLA 236/10291), the prefect explained the fall in the number of weddings that year by a decline in real wages. The following year (ibid.), he criticized young artisans for hastening to set up as masters and beginning families without considering how they might be supported.
42. This applied as much to fishing and innkeeping as to ordinary crafts.
43. *OSB Rust* entries 845 and 850. Gem A Rust C VIII/30 (guild records).
44. The following discussion is based on 74 apprentices, 103 journeymen, and 85 masters whose careers could be traced ibid. and in *OSB Rust*.
45. Writing up the account of an acceptance in Rust often followed governmental recognition as a master by a couple of weeks, and some individuals wed in the interim.
46. Possibly because delay of marriage postponed acquisition of master status.
47. The parameters of such a theory are explored in Wrigley, "Strategy". He calls attention to the significant number of couples without a direct heir, and to the larger number without an adult son. See also Richard Smith, "Some Reflections on the Evidence for the Origins of the 'European Marriage Pattern' in England", in Chris Harris (ed.), *The Sociology of the Family: New Directions for Britain* (Keele, 1979), 90–91.
48. David Levine, *Family Formation in an Age of Nascent Capitalism* (New York, 1977), 108–109 states the general principle of which this is a corollary. See also ibid., 11, 45.
49. "Therefore, from a young man's viewpoint, it was not necessarily death or retirement of his own father that determined access to property and thus the economic wherewithal to marry, but in addition any heirless man's death or retirement, or indeed sale or lease, within the community could make available a 'niche' to be 'colonized'." L. R. Poos and R. M. Smith, "'Legal Windows Onto Historical Populations'? Recent Research on Demography and the Manor Court in Medieval England", *Law and History Review*, 2 (1984), 143.
50. One way to make the connection was to have the journeyman marry the widow or a daughter, if one were available. However, that sort of thinking requires moving outside the Oedipal model.
51. Jews urged to assimilate by setting their sons up in workshops and farms posed virtually the same question: "from what sources then is the wherewithal [Mitteln] to be obtained?". GLA 231/1423 (petition to parliament from area leaders, not including Rust's, 16 March 1831).
52. See Chapters Seven and Eight.
53. This could boost population. Offspring might begin reproducing, not when the father died or retired, but rather younger, when any parent died or retired.
54. Compare Sabean, *Property*, Lloyd Bonfield, "Normative Rules and Property Transmission: Reflections on the Link between Marriage and Inheritance in Early Modern England", in Lloyd Bonfield, Richard Smith, and Keith Wrightson (ed.), *The World We Have Gained* (Oxford, 1986), 155–176, and Zvi Razi, *Life, Marriage and Death in a Medieval Parish* (Cambridge, 1980), 50–64.
55. Younger marriage depended on being sought after, not on how strongly one sought. It was precisely those most in need of a partner for economic reasons who were least able to obtain one.

5
Malthusians and Neomalthusians

The nineteenth century saw the death agonies of the Malthusian system and the advent of neo-Malthusianism. Within the framework of the old demographic régime, the only way to forestall immiseration was to restrict marriage ever more tightly. When ages at marriage reached heights villagers refused to accept, the conventional ties uniting marriage and sex and childbearing were broken, but along two radically different lines. To begin with, sex became more frequent outside marriage, but because sex was still tied to childbearing, births out of wedlock rose dramatically. Later, and usually in different groups, married couples practised contraception, and family limitation began. For them, the link between sex and childbearing was broken, but within marriage. The neo-Malthusian possibility of stopping births inside marriage made it less imperative to control marital fertility from the outside in the old Malthusian ways.

Thus, movements in age at marriage track the changing prospects of villagers. For the first half of the 1800s it became more difficult to wed; Malthusian brides and grooms grew older. Later in the nineteenth century, marriage became more accessible, but only to neo-Malthusians. In this perspective, the evolving distributions of ages at first marriage call attention to the distinct economic structure of each village. Rust was characterized by widespread poverty, Grafenhausen by widespread ease, and Kappel by sharply opposed extremes of wealth. These differences play key rôles in my interpretations of villagers' non-marital and marital fertility.

ILLEGITIMACY[1]

In Malthusian societies, networks of control conditioned individuals to abstain from intercourse outside marriage, and those who strayed were brought back into conformity through renewed pressure from legal, familial, religious, and popular authorities. Such a system could break down as sexual desires strengthened or as social restraints weakened. Controversy among historians of illegitimacy turns on the relative weight assigned to those two processes.[2] Because I am interested in illegitimacy primarily for the light it sheds on marital fertility,

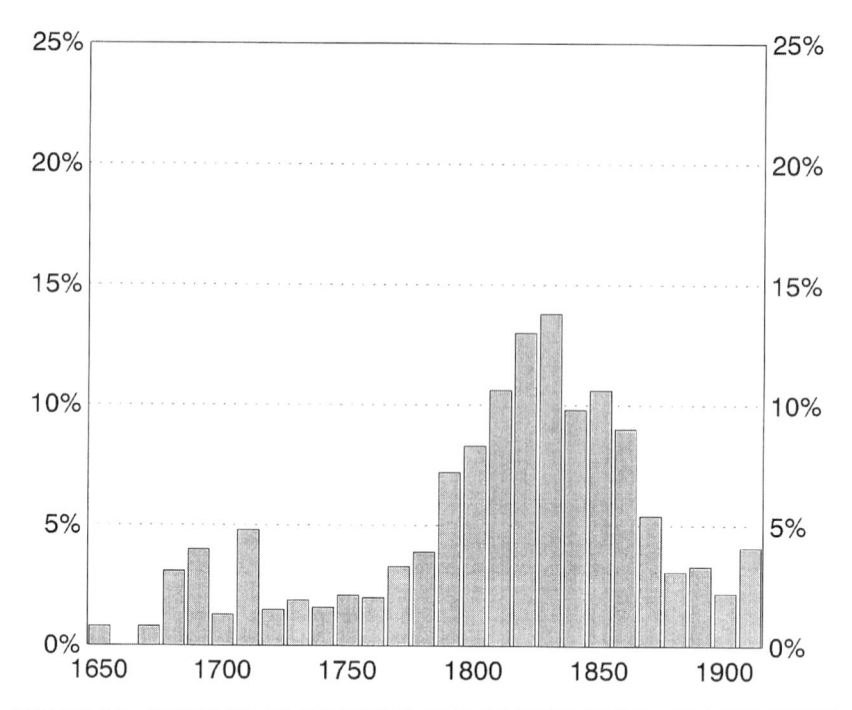

FIGURE 5.1 PERCENTAGE OF BIRTHS OUT OF WEDLOCK IN GRAFENHAUSEN, KAPPEL, AND RUST COMBINED, BY DECADE OF BIRTH FROM 1650–9 TO 1910–9

I bypass that controversy. Instead, my presentation focuses on variations in non-marital fertility over time and across social groups. These data are supplemented by more general anecdotes and impressions, but my concern throughout is with specific differences rather than overall similarities.

Even researchers who begin with larger ambitions rapidly find themselves distinguishing types of illegitimacy.[3] That approach is also in order here, for Figure 5.1 reveals several distinct periods in the history of illegitimacy in Grafenhausen, Kappel, and Rust. Following spikes as high as 5 % around 1700, the illegitimacy ratio[4] fell to about 2 % for much of the eighteenth century. It began to climb again in the 1770s, scaling new heights each decade from the 1790s to the 1830s when an all-time peak of 14 % was achieved. The rate hung close to a high 10 % for the next thirty years. Beginning with the 1860s, it fell back precipitously to levels only somewhat above the eighteenth-century trough.

Each phase corresponded to a different mix of situations contributing to nonmarital fertility. There was a low background level representing intermittent seductions of vulnerable women by strategically placed men.[5] Added to these were more stable adulterous affairs, involving people separated from their spouses.[6] Such events made fairly uniform contributions to the illegitimacy ratio in all periods.

The peaks above this background level came about through dramatic swings

TABLE 5.2
Distributions of occupations of Lovers of unwed mothers, Fathers of unwed mothers, and Future husbands of unwed mothers, compared to the Overall occupational distribution

Categories	Unwed mothers' Lovers	Unwed mothers' Fathers	Unwed mothers' Husbands	Married women's husbands
Order	11 %	1 %	3 %	3 %
Industry, Menial	7 %	1 %	6 %	3 %
Petty	2 %	2 %	2 %	1 %
Labour, Local Position	21 %	23 %	28 %	18 %
Craft, Fishing, Weaving	28 %	39 %	31 %	27 %
Itinerant	1 %	1 %	1 %	2 %
Farming, Affluent, Substantial, Commerce, Profession	28 %	33 %	29 %	46 %
Absolute total	697	1067	767	

Notes
(1) Source: OSB Grafenhausen, OSB Kappel, and OSB Rust.
(2) The unit of analysis is the woman, not the child. That is, all unwed mothers are weighted equally, regardless of the number of children they had.
(3) The occupations used are those of the first lover or future husband asigned an occupation in the OSBs.
(4) 539 cases where no lover was indicated, and a further 126 cases where a lover was given but without an occupation, are omitted from column 1.
(5) 137 cases where the mother's father was not indicated are omitted from column 2, as were 74 cases where he was named but assigned no occupation and 84 cases where the mother's parents were themselves unmarried.
(6) 547 unwed mothers for whom no marriage was included in the OSBs are omitted from column 3, as were a further 48 for whom the OSBs indicate a marriage, but without assigning an occupation to the husband.

in mass behaviour. At the beginning and at the end of the eighteenth century, wars brought into the region large numbers of troops, who made their presence felt in an escalating illegitimacy ratio. The second wave of births out of wedlock did not recede as wartime dislocation subsided, for it had stirred up both social groups predisposed to illegitimacy and a legal framework that pushed ever more couples into that position. Moreover, they were held there, producing broods of illegitimate children rather than the lone offspring typical of earlier eras.[7] Under these conditions, the ratio remained high until emigration removed the most prolific unwed mothers and legal reform ensured that their ranks were not replenished.

Table 5.2 substantiates each of these claims and provides a base from which to analyse them more deeply. The Table orders occupational categories by their degree of over-representation among the fathers of illegitimate children.[8] For instance, men charged with maintaining order appeared as unwed fathers three and a half times as often as they did as husbands, while only six landed proprietors were encountered as lovers for every ten who were husbands. The categories Industry, Menial, and Petty occurred about twice as often among unwed fathers as among married men.[9] Labour, Local Positions, Crafts, Fishing, and Weaving were just slightly over-represented. The other categories occurred less often among the unwed than among the wed.[10] Because these different frequencies illuminate the circumstances surrounding non-marital fertility, I discuss each significant category in turn.

The over-representation of the forces of order was due entirely to the soldiers amongst them,[11] and that almost exclusively in the eighteenth century. In the years before 1800, more than a fifth of unwed mothers identified soldiers as their lovers.

The contribution troops made to births out of wedlock has been noted occasionally in the historical literature,[12] but seldom stressed or analysed. This is unfortunate, for throughout the eighteenth century the illegitimacy ratio varied in cadence with military manoeuvres great and small. The heights scaled during Louis XIV's expansionist wars were not regained until the French Revolution made the Rhine plain a battlefield and campground once more. Weaker effects, such as the bifurcation in the summit around 1700 and a brief rise in the mid-1730s, also corresponded to outbreaks of conflict. Finally, the years in which soldiers were alleged to have fathered children were also the ones in which they appeared most often as husbands.

However, not all unions involving soldiers were consensual.[13] Unlike other genealogies from this area,[14] the Grafenhausen, Kappel, and Rust OSBs include no explicit references to rape. Nevertheless, the circumstances of some pregnancies do suggest compulsion.[15] Even where some consent was present, the sheer force associated with the troops enabled them to operate outside the local power structure. Soldiers far away from home were not subject to communal pressures or familial oversight, and were able to bypass restraints still hanging over the local women.

The strong representation in the first column of Table 5.2 from industrial and menial occupations was of less social significance. Most factory workers and servants were young and unmarried. Those who entered into liaisons tended to find partners with similar characteristics. Work in either field threw the sexes together, fostering such choices by both parties.[16] The result was "premature and lengthy acquaintanceships", some of which culminated in pregnancy.[17]

This did not mean that cigar makers or domestics had any special affinity for pre-marital sex. Rather it was simply that people who did were apt to have that fact recorded while passing through these stations. The larger number of their colleagues experienced no vital events during their time in the plants or in service. Those occupations therefore do not appear in their OSB entries, which instead record whatever careers they pursued while married. In consequence the figures for the Industrial and Menial categories are inflated in a largely artefactual way.[18]

The bulk of illegitimate children were born after peace had banished the military[19] and before the rise of the cigar plants. Those years also saw the wan-

Malthusians and Neomalthusians 73

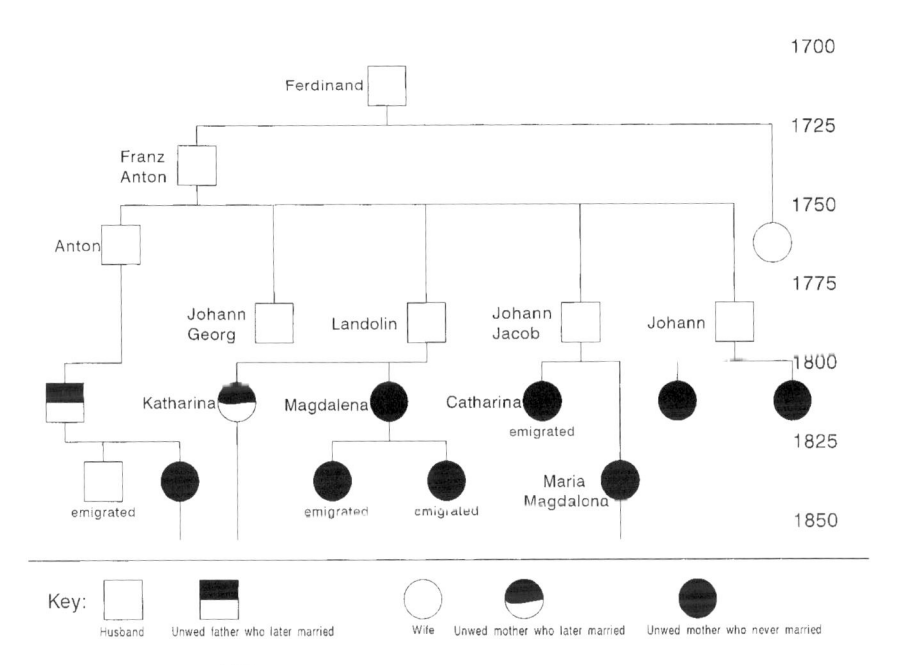

FIGURE 5.3   THE SARTORI FAMILY TREE

ing of old centres of power and the imposition of new forms of authority. Paradoxically, each development promoted illegitimacy. Examining the disproportionate rôle played by petty tradesmen in Table 5.2 reveals both sides of the process at work.

The Petty category possesses added significance because it resembled most closely the "bastardy-prone sub-society" some researchers have postulated as a significant source of illegitimate births.[20] Its members pursued a distinct range of occupations characterized by low skill and high mobility. Similar trades were often attributed to mothers of illegitimate children. Common occupations created a certain camaraderie within the wandering population. Their cohesiveness was reinforced by the harsh treatment they received at the hands of the sedentary population, who excluded them from local citizenship and guild membership. With social lines drawn so clearly, a sub-culture with its own mores emerged.

The Sartoris

Perhaps the most effective way to illustrate the petty way of life is to consider a concrete example.[21] Figure 5.3 displays the lineage of Ferdinand Sartori, a tramp, tinsmith, and vagabond of the first half of the eighteenth century, who spread his three marriages over the municipalities of Rust, Ringsheim, and Herbolzheim.[22] His son Franz Anton pursued an even more varied career, beginning his marriage in Rust, but producing children in Orschweier, Ringsheim,

Münchweier, Ringsheim again, and Grafenhausen, as well as in other locations as far afield as Hungary. He sometimes secured irregular employment as a labourer or mason, but was generally identified as a tramp or a tinker. His wanderings did not end after his family was complete, for in the eight months in 1786 between his wife's death and his own he moved from Herbolzheim to Münchweier.

The wife bore nine children, five of whom survived them to create the next generation shown in Figure 5.3. On the far left is the oldest son, Anton. He was described as a tramp, and took to wife a woman who also lacked a fixed address. Thereafter, they spent most of their lives in Ringsheim, moving to Rust only in the late 1780s. From there they proceeded to Grafenhausen before passing from the records.[23] Johann Georg Sartori had already done likewise immediately following his marriage in Grafenhausen to the daughter of a labourer with a history of wandering.

The third brother, Landolin, wed in Ringsheim and died there, but in between functioned as a tinsmith and plumber in Münchweier, Orschweier, Oberhausen, Altdorf, and Kappel. As the daughter of a tramp and bookseller, his wife was familiar with the itinerant life. Their children took after them, but pursued at least part of their reproductive careers out of wedlock. Daughter Katharina[24] gave birth to an illegitimate child in Grafenhausen in 1815 and again in 1824, having produced two others in Ringsheim in the interim. Following each of the births in Grafenhausen, a soldier appeared at the priest's house to acknowledge paternity. The couple were finally able to marry in 1825 in Altdorf, by which point the groom had taken up retailing. Katharina survived the wedding by less than two years, but one of her pre-marital children founded a line in Grafenhausen.

Her sister Magdalena was in certain respects even less fortunate. During the same years that Katharina was settling down, Magdalena bore six children in five locations, including Ringsheim, Münchweier, Grafenhausen, and an urban jail cell. Conniving to send her to her lover's hometown, local authorities stipulated that she was rich enough to wed, but the fraud was unmasked before the couple could be united. In 1826, Magdalena and her children were consigned by the Baden government to Ringsheim.[25] There, two of the daughters went on to bear illegitimate children of their own before emigrating to the United States in 1845.[26]

The next branch of the family begins with the fourth surviving son of Franz Anton. Johann Jacob Sartori was born in Grafenhausen, but left it as a child. He had wed a French woman in Alsace shortly before the revolution, but the 1790s found them travelling from Münchweier to Herbolzheim to Orschweier to Rheinhausen to Rust—not necessarily in that order, for they doubled back at least twice. Together with their children, they were finally settled in Grafenhausen.[27] Although the municipality refused to grant them citizenship, Johann Jacob scrounged work as a plumber, tinker, and gardener.

Two of his adult daughters produced illegitimate children. The youngest, Maria Magdalena, left the records after the death in infancy of the second of her children by a man from Ettenheim. Catharina, the eldest daughter of Johann Jacob, appeared in two separate OSB entries, but all of the eight children listed shared the same father, a plumber from Offenburg. He acknowledged paternity following most of the births, and all of the survivors bore his surname—as did three other children born before the family moved to Grafenhausen. The strength of this union may be gauged from the fact that the lovers and their offspring were all living together in 1839.[28]

The plumber would have welcomed more formal recognition; in 1843 he petitioned for acceptance as a citizen of Grafenhausen. The municipal council and citizens' committee turned deaf ears, hoping to expel him entirely. They derided the plumber's claim to be supporting his children, pointing out that they could be seen begging daily. Moreover, the municipality was underwriting their house tax, firewood, education, and medical care.[29] The following year brought a more permanent resolution as the municipality paid to have Catharina and her eight surviving children emigrate.[30]

The final branch of the lineage begins with Johann Sartori on the far right of Figure 5.3. In Altdorf, he wed a native of Niederhausen, after which he pursued a rootless career as a basket weaver and plumber. In the years between 1794 and 1816, the couple produced children successively in Münchweier, Ringsheim, Herbolzheim, Münchweier again, Rust, Oberhausen, Münchweier once more, and Grafenhausen. They were finally forced to settle in Orschweier,[31] where both husband and wife died after seeing two of their daughters enter nonmarital liaisons.

This repetitive recital underlines certain realities in the lives of people like the Sartoris. The descent from itinerant to petty to illegitimate occurred over and over, pushing non-marital fertility to new heights.[32] Likewise typical were the close ties within this seemingly disorganized sector of the population, for its members roamed together and roomed together. They also provided mates and godparents for one another. Family life endured even after marital bonds fell away, as the faithfulness of the Sartoris' lovers indicated.[33] In the early nineteenth century, illegitimacy and emigration marked those families as much as non-citizenship and wandering had characterized their ancestors.

These characteristics were not entirely of their own choosing. The itinerant had always dwelt on the margins of village society, but those margins became less hospitable as the population grew. Even minor jobs such as herding grew inaccessible as municipalities reserved them for their own citizens. Non-citizens and vagrants were left on the outside, limited to providing goods and services that nobody really needed. The consequence was a peripatetic life, as they wore out their welcome in place after place. Individuals and families cruised the countryside, heedless of the porous borders between the petty principalities.

Those borders solidified considerably in the nineteenth century, as did State control generally. The Baden government made every effort to fix the itinerant population in place, but imposing a permanent residence did little to better their lot. What it did do was concentrate their demographic impact, in that municipalities were now responsible for maintaining whole families rather than merely playing host to a succession of births to different couples. It was also at this point that the turn to illegitimacy took place.

The timing of these developments suggests that they had little to do with a subculture of free love. After all, during the eighteenth century when restrictions on their behaviour had been least, itinerant couples had married.[34] What changed in the early nineteenth century was not their willingness to wed but the willingness of the authorities to allow them to wed. New laws and more rigorous enforcement of customary practices hindered marriage by the poor, and over the long term perpetuated both poverty and illegitimacy.[35] These measures bore most strongly on the petty, but they also weighed on the far more numerous group of poor citizens.

This can be seen in the over-representation of Labour and Local Positions in Table 5.2—and to a lesser extent in the strong representation of the ordinary crafts. The link can be made tighter by comparing the ascending curves of illegitimacy and emigration in the first half of the nineteenth century. Both quadrupled from eighteenth-century levels, and then fluctuated around peaks from the 1820s through the 1850s. The close match in novelty, timing, and extent completes the theoretical connections between both phenomena and population growth. The suddenness and strength of those developments marked the fracturing of the Malthusian system. So many people had accumulated that they could not all be accommodated at accepted standards of living. Balancing the population would have meant raising ages at marriage to heights that were even less acceptable. One way out was emigration, in which the illegitimate played a prominent part.

So strong was the tie between illegitimacy and emigration that by the 1840s the positive relationship between them on the local level had reversed. The illegitimacy ratio of Figure 5.1 subsided somewhat, from 14 % to about 10 %, because women who left no longer gave birth locally, and their daughters no longer grew up to share their mothers' unwed condition. Illegitimacy—or rather, the social conditions and groups producing it—was exported to territories better able to accommodate it. Throughout, marginality mediated the link between emigration and illegitimacy.

The best way to appreciate the marginal character of nineteenth-century illegitimacy is to examine the social backgrounds of the unwed mothers. The second column of Table 5.2 indicates dramatically lower percentages for Order, Industry, and Menial in the occupational distributions of their parents[36] than among the lovers. These occupations temporarily supported many young men at the time they indulged in liaisons, but their partners derived from less exotic strata. Daughters from farming, affluent, substantial, commercial, and professional backgrounds contributed to illegitimacy, but not in proportion to their numbers. Rather it was poor labourers and lesser artisans—and of course the petty tradespeople—whose daughters could not wed and therefore reproduced outside of wedlock if at all.

This returns me to the theme of Malthusianism, which moulded the laws that stood in their way. Fearing that the poor would breed themselves into misery and society as a whole into revolution, bureaucrats set property qualifications for marriage.[37] In doing so, they were merely codifying practice,[38] and municipal councils exercised their renewed authority with enthusiasm. The respectable citizens who dominated local government saw the multiplication of the poor as a drain on the treasury, and were quite prepared to impose discipline and restraint on others.[39] As division of property and longer life expectancy pushed more and more holdings below the legal minimum, these regulations were enforced with increasing urgency. Marriage was delayed for large sectors of the population, in some cases past the point at which they began to have intercourse.[40]

For the growing number of couples with no hope of ever accumulating the property required for marriage, the only choices were abstinence and illicit sex. In setting a target out of reach, the laws ensured that this group would continue to grow. As long as the number of heirs exceeded the number of parents, adding together meagre inheritances simply produced smaller holdings each generation. This was accentuated among the illegitimate, for if the father took advantage of the new legal régime by failing to acknowledge paternity, the children inherited from only one side of the family.

Unwed mothers who began with tiny fortunes were unable to build up larger ones. Unskilled labour paid little, and the welfare system was far from generous. To ease the burden on the municipal purse, local councils obtained licenses for unwed mothers, entitling them to peddle inconsequential goods, but these were hardly tickets to prosperity. The situation of their children, brought up in destitution, was if anything worse. They found it difficult to attract partners, except from within the circle of misery, and were in any case unable to wed when they found them. The Sartoris were just one of the illegitimate dynasties to spring up under these conditions.

Towards the other end of the social scale, the legal changes were more benign, manifesting themselves primarily in an increase in pre-nuptial conceptions. By the second quarter of the nineteenth century, one-quarter of brides were pregnant, a figure double the eighteenth-century rate. Couples who had postponed marriage hastened to conclude it once they became aware of a pregnancy. This added impetus could overcome customary and legal obstacles provided they or their families were sufficiently well off.

Couples of limited means found it more difficult to surmount those hurdles and, like Katharina Sartori and her soldier, produced several children out of wedlock before they were able to marry. During the years when the illegitimacy ratio was at its height, such experiences were common, accounting for a further eighth of couples. They represented the fate of inhabitants whose assets fell short of the legal minimum at one point, but who subsequently amassed the difference.[41] This group felt the cutting edge of the law most keenly.

The occupational distribution of the husbands of women who had borne illegitimate children[42] reveals where the social fault line ran. The third column of Table 5.2 divides the citizenry cleanly between the predominantly rich categories, who were under-represented relative to the population as a whole, and the poor ones, who were over-represented.[43] Outside the forces of order, men married women in much the same proportions as they seduced them.[44] This is further evidence that these couples were not rejecting social norms so much as being rejected by them.

Even those who never wed remained attached to the social framework of matrimony. The history of the Sartoris brought out several instances of stable relationships amounting to marriages without the benefit of a ceremony. Some unmarried couples had even been wed, after a fashion. The sources are replete with references to marriages valid only in other jurisdictions,[45] "left-handed marriages",[46] and common-law couplings.[47]

The conflict between personal values, customary expectations, and legal norms granted a measure of tolerance to these near-marriages. This was of considerable concern to the Baden government, and in 1855 the prefect inquired whether municipal councils allowed unmarried couples to live together within their jurisdictions. Understanding what was expected of them, Grafenhausen, Kappel, and Rust replied with a chorus of no's, adding that no forms of suspicious conduct were tolerated.[48] However, in Rust the very same report later mentioned two labouring couples who cohabited none the less.[49]

The nonchalance of Rust's municipal authorities reflected the fact that neither pair constituted a burden on the taxpayers. One couple had raised three children together—a fourth died in infancy—and continued to support themselves as a family. They had been punished without result. Dealing with the other couple was regarded as less urgent, for both were old and hence incapable of producing further children. Moreover, they caused their neighbours no disturbance.

The prefect was unmoved, and ordered the pairs to separate. He too proved powerless, for the same situation was recorded in each of the next two years. Both couples were eager to wed, but could not meet the legal requirements. They tried to use the pressure from above to manipulate the local government into granting their wishes. The stalemate endured until the property qualifications were waived for them in 1857 and 1858. By that point the grooms were thirty-six and forty-seven, the brides thirty-nine and forty-six.

The abolition of marriage laws in the 1860s owed something to the persistence of ordinary citizens like these. Repression on the scale available to the government could not prevent reproduction, and often simply accentuated poverty. Poor couples did produce fewer children than they might have, but because those children were born out of wedlock they were poorer than they might have been. The next generation stood even less chance of meeting the property qualifications, and illegitimacy was perpetuated.[50] The system was creating the very proletariat it was designed to forestall. In the face of this evidence, Baden's new liberal government followed its convictions and abolished such legal restrictions on marriage.

The shift to laissez-faire sent the illegitimacy ratio plunging. To begin with, marriages between couples who had been waiting for years cut off the stream of illegitimate children they had been producing. In addition, their counterparts in the generation coming up were now able to wed before they began reproducing. The illegitimacy ratio was cut in three after the 1860s. Emigration had already mitigated its peak, but the suddenness of the fall confirms that the legal situation had sustained the second wave of illegitimacy the revolutionary wars had stimulated.

The alternative hypothesis is that unmarried men and women began using contraception during their sexual encounters.[51] I find this implausible for a number of reasons, among them the fact that the decline came rather earlier than conventional accounts allow.[52] To be sure, at the time illegitimacy fell off, some villagers were practising family limitation, but not in the numbers required to produce the plummet in births out of wedlock. Moreover, limiters were generally wealthier than the poor couples who were the predominant source of illegitimate children, earlier as well as later.

The uniform pattern of decline across villages also argues against attributing the decline in non-marital fertility to contraception. Between the 1860s and the 1880s, the illegitimacy ratio fell from 10 % to 2 % in Grafenhausen, from 7 % to 2 % in Kappel, and from 9 % to 4 % in Rust. Because the frequency of family limitation varied widely across villages, the universality of the decline indicates that it had some other source.

This imperviousness to local effects held good of illegitimacy in general. The broad shape of the curve over time was the same in all three villages, although there were some differences in the absolute illegitimacy ratio. Over the years from 1700 to 1919, births out of wedlock made up 6 %, 5 %, and 8 % of all births in Grafenhausen, Kappel, and Rust respectively. The higher figure for Rust reflected more widespread poverty, which produced higher peaks when marriage was difficult. I emphasize this point because the effects of locality on marital fertility could not be accounted for in this fashion.

Illegitimacy did not disappear with the easing of marriage laws. There remained several pools of institutions, people, and behaviours that could be counted upon to generate births out of wedlock. One of these was the régime of impartible inheritance on the other side of the county,[53] but developments there affected Grafenhausen, Kappel, and Rust only indirectly. Another was domestic service abroad. Baden women working in Alsace were subject to less scrutiny and protection than at home, and some returned to their native villages pregnant.[54] Factory work in towns was reputed a hotbed of illegitimacy, and observers anticipated that industrialization would extend such practices to the villages.[55]

These were not the only circumstances that placed women at risk, for as the nineteenth century drew to a close, prefects, journalists, and priests evinced concern over dancing, drinking, night roaming, and the like.[56] Yet the simple fact was that births out of wedlock had stabilized at a level far below their peak. Both in terms of raw numbers and in terms of significance for understanding overall fertility, illegitimacy had ceased to be important.

A review of the findings of this section shows that that had not always been the case. In the eighteenth century, births out of wedlock were rare. Malthusian controls were tested only in times of dislocation, when outside forces or the discrediting of authority altered the balance of power. Even then illegitimate births were seldom repeated. The sustained rise in population during the eighteenth century posed a more thoroughgoing challenge to the system. Both informally and formally, the response was to delay marriage.

However, human prolific power was too strong to be checked in this way. Increasing numbers of couples found themselves forced to postpone marriage, not just for a year or two, but indefinitely. Some did not accept that fate, and produced children anyway. Even if the parents eventually managed to wed, the next generation was apt to be poorer still. Within the confines of the local Malthusian régime, there was no escaping the bind. The short-term outlet was emigration, and the long-term solution was family limitation.

Age at First Marriage

From the material presented in Chapter Two and in the preceding sections, one can straightforwardly predict the history of entry into marriage. In the eighteenth century, under the European marriage pattern, brides and grooms would be fairly old. Over time, ages at marriage would rise, at first in tempo with variations in economic conditions, and later in a more rigorous way as legal restraints came into play. Elevated ages would persist until those restrictions were lifted, after which they would be free to fall.

Such a rise and fall indeed occurred. In the eighteenth century, women wed in their mid-twenties, while first-time grooms were almost two years older. That gap held in the early nineteenth century as average ages for both sexes climbed by a year or two (to twenty-seven and twenty-nine respectively). Only in the third quarter of the century did brides' ages begin to drop, a trend which accelerated in the final cohort. Grooms' ages were slower to fall, and so the gap between the sexes widened to almost three years in 1850–1874 (twenty-five vs. twenty-eight). As I have already indicated the forces behind overall trends, what follows concentrates on differences between villages. Those differences became particularly large at the end of the nineteenth century, as neo-Malthusianism permeated the villages to varying extents.

This diversity was itself a sign of neo-Malthusianism, for controlling fertility by couple rather than by community at first opened still wider scope for personal variation. In particular, awareness that fertility could be limited within marriage—and the plan to do so—permitted couples to wed young, confident

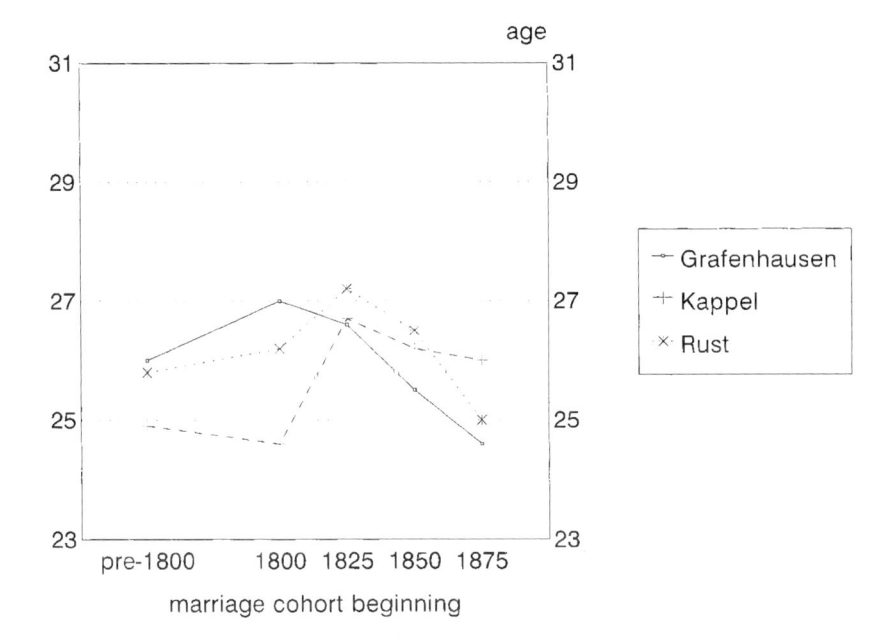

FIGURE 5.4 AVERAGE AGE OF WIFE AT FIRST MARRIAGE IN DOCUMENTED MARRIAGES IN GRAFENHAUSEN, KAPPEL, AND RUST, BY DATE OF WEDDING

that their fecundity would not be expressed throughout their life together. This new confidence lay behind the drop in ages at marriage at the end of the nineteenth century.

Figure 5.4 shows how the transition from Malthusianism to neo-Malthusianism came to each village.[57] Eighteenth-century brides were younger in Kappel than in Rust or Grafenhausen. That contrast deepened in the first quarter of the nineteenth century as ages at marriage rose in the latter two villages. By the next cohort, the Kapplers had joined their neighbours, only to be left behind once more after 1850, as ages fell, first in Grafenhausen, and then in Rust.

These trends emerged from the interaction between economic structures and fertility patterns.[58] Kappel's inhabitants included a number of very rich families, who were insulated from the pressures population growth put on the living standards of other villagers. They continued to wed young as late as the first quarter of the eighteenth century, while the less outstandingly rich in Grafenhausen and Rust joined the general movement to higher ages at marriage. The Kapplers' wealth only postponed the day of reckoning, and the next generation was obliged to delay weddings for two extra years, on average.

As marriage laws were relaxed, ages in Kappel declined slightly, but even at the end of the century the average bride was twenty-six, a year older than she had been a century earlier. In contrast, Rusters and Grafenhauseners had driven brides' ages not merely below their nineteenth-century peak but also below their original eighteenth-century level. The mass response in both villages was a function of the greater equality within their populations. In the early nineteenth century, they responded to economic threats by shifting the entire distribution of ages upwards. In the second half of the century, family limitation spread rapidly, and again large numbers responded, this time by depressing the distribution. Ages in Kappel, still largely[59] subject to natural fertility, remained fixed in a pattern reminiscent of the one Grafenhauseners had abandoned over half a century earlier.

A look at the distribution of brides' ages at two crucial points brings these tendencies out clearly.[60] At the beginning of the nineteenth century the strongest contrasts were between Grafenhausen and Kappel. Between 1800 and 1824, Kappel women wed twice as frequently under age twenty-two (39 % vs. 19 %). The Kappel rate had even increased since the eighteenth century. Rust occupied an intermediate position.

By the end of the nineteenth century, the situation had reversed. Grafenhausen now boasted twice the proportion of young brides that Kappel did (33 % vs. 17 %). Moreover, Grafenhausen also enjoyed an advantage in women wed between twenty-two and twenty-five. Rusters were concentrated (41 %) in that middle range, having recovered from the most extended postponement of marriage by any of the villagers. Even at the end of the century, Kappel brides were still strung out in the late twenties, relying for the most part on Malthusian fertility control while their counterparts deepened their neo-Malthusian dive.

The different receptions the villages afforded family limitation provide a bridge between this chapter and the next. Here I have been concerned for the most part with the workings of the old demographic régime, built around postponement of marriage and with it childbearing. This system kept fertility well below any theoretical maximum, but the moderate increase it did permit overwhelmed it when growth extended over a century. Preventing the population from outpacing the resources available to most villagers would have pushed ages at marriage to insupportable heights. Custom, even reinforced and made rigid by law, proved inadequate to this task, but it remained no less urgent for all that.

As long as marriage was tied to childbearing, and partible inheritance gave free play to youthful marriages while binding later generations to poverty, the Malthusian snare could not be eluded. Neo-Malthusianism severed this Gordian knot. Instead of the community restricting access to marriage, individual couples limited fertility within it through their own efforts. The next chapter examines those efforts directly.

Notes

1. I use this term to cover all births out of wedlock, including those subsequently legitimized.
2. For a different way of setting up the theoretical issues, see Edward Shorter, "Capitalism, Culture, and Sexuality: Some Competing Models", *Social Science Quarterly*, 53 (1972), 338–356.
3. For example, Edward Shorter, "Bastardy in South Germany: A Comment", *Journal of Interdisciplinary History*, 8 (1978), 460, and David Levine and Keith Wrightson, "The Social Context of Illegitimacy in Early Modern England", in Peter Laslett, Klara Oosterveen, and Richard Smith (ed.), *Bastardy and its Comparative History* (London, 1980), 174. A similar point is attributed to M. Mitterauer by Pier Paolo Viazzo, "Illegitimacy and the European Marriage Pattern: Comparative Evidence from the Alpine Area", in Bonfield, Smith, and Wrightson, *Gained*, 118.
4. As is customary, I use this somewhat inaccurate term to denote the percentage of children born out of wedlock. For a discussion of the shortcomings of this measure, see Edward Shorter, John Knodel, and Etienne van de Walle, "The Decline of Non-Marital Fertility in Europe, 1880–1940", *Population Studies*, 25 (1971), 379–381.
5. Typical pairings involved a lord's son and a servant in the palace (OSB *Rust* entries 452 and 453—births in 1710 and 1712) or a proprietor and one of the hired help (Pf A Kappel family register: description of entry 1563 in OSB *Kappel*—before 1898). Incest between generations perhaps belongs here as well.
6. Here are two examples. (1) OSB *Rust* entries 1375 (marriage from 1752 through 1770) and 1378 (births from 1769 to 1778). At their deaths the mother of the man's children was termed a spouse ("MARITA"), and the other woman his legal wife ("UXOR"). Pf A Rust Marriage and death register. (2) OSB *Rust* entry 570. The marriage began in 1796 but fell apart soon after, for the husband fathered children by other women in 1801 and 1809. (OSB *Rust* entries 572 and 573.) In 1810 he was living with his mother. (1810 dues listing by house in GLA 314/2248.) A land survey the next year splits the couple's holding, assigning assets to husband and wife separately. (Gem A Rust C I/8.)
7. Before 1800, only one illegitimate birth can be found for 85 % of unwed mothers. In the following fifty years, that figure fell to 60 % before climbing back to the old level by the end of the nineteenth century.
8. It is not possible to analyse the mothers' occupations, which were generally not given in the OSBs. The few women who were described pursued careers as domestic servants, factory workers, and so on. I take these designations to be typical of their age-group and so of little independent social significance. For another view, see Edward Shorter, "Illegitimacy, Sexual Revolution, and Social Change in Modern Europe", *Journal of Interdisciplinary History*, 2 (1971), 249–251; Shorter, "Emancipation", 624, or Shorter, *Making*, 117, 259–262.
9. The distributions are compared directly, without weighting for fluctuations over time.
10. Itinerant two-thirds as often and the rest even less. Categories grouped together in Table 5.2 did not differ significantly in their relative frequency among lovers, fathers, or husbands.
11. Border guards and police made only modest contributions to illegitimacy rates.
12. Edward Shorter, "«La vie intime» Beiträge zu seiner Geschichte am Beispiel des kulturellen Wandels in den bayerischen Unterschichten im 19. Jahrhundert", *Kölner Zeitschrift für Soziologie und Sozialpsychologie*, 16 (1973), 532. Christian Pfister, *Bevölkerungsgeschichte und historische Demographie 1500–1800* (Munich, 1994), 89.

13. On rape in the early modern era more generally, see Edward Shorter, "On Writing the History of Rape", *Signs*, 3 (1977), 473–475, and the references given there.
14. Entry 2390a (birth in 1703) in Albert Köbele and Hans Scheer, *Ortssippenbuch Altdorf* (Grafenhausen, 1976), entry 246 (birth in 1677) in Albert Köbele, Klaus Siefert, and Hans Scheer, *Ortssippenbuch Kippenheim* (Grafenhausen, 1979), and entry 1937 (birth in 1797) in *OSB Ringsheim*.
15. *OSB Kappel* entry 2570 ascribes the paternity of twins born in 1715 to three soldiers, while the father of an infant born in 1796 is described in *OSB Rust* entry 5071 as an Austrian military official whose name the mother did not know. Note also *OSB Grafenhausen* page 144 on soldiers treating girls roughly in 1791 and Jörg Sieger, *Kardinal in Schatten der Revolution* (Kehl, 1986), 138–139 (assault by eight soldiers in 1791).
16. In 1908 Rust's priest complained to the prefect that factories seated male and female cigar makers next to one another on the workbenches. Report on inspection tour of Rust in St A LA Lahr 3454.
17. Visitation reports of 1889 and 1913 for Rust in Ord A B4/10504.
18. Much the same reasoning applies to apprentice artisans, some of whom were found among the lovers. (No husbands were described as apprentices in the OSBs.) In this case, the occupational distribution is not distorted, since apprentices usually went on to become masters within the same occupational category.
19. The Order category surged back thanks to renewed warfare in the second decade of the twentieth century.
20. The concept began as "something like a sub-society of the illegitimacy-prone" (Peter Laslett and Klara Oosterveen, "Long-term Trends in Bastardy in England", *Population Studies*, 27 (1973), 257—compare 282–284), and was used as the title of an article by Peter Laslett in Laslett, Oosterveen, and Smith, Bastardy, 217–240.
21. Compare the Vebers briefly treated in Viazzo, "Alpine", 114–115. My account draws on information in the OSBs for Grafenhausen, Kappel, Rust, Altdorf, Friesenheim (Adolf Gänshirt, Klaus Siefert, and Erich Reinbold, *Ortssippenbuch Friesenheim* (Lahr, 1986)), Kippenheim, Münchweier (Albert Köbele, *Ortssippenbuch Münchweier* (Grafenhausen, 1977)), Niederhausen and Oberhausen (Albert Köbele and Margarete Kirner, *Ortssippenbuch Rheinhausen* (Grafenhausen, 1975)), Orschweier (Albert Köbele and Klaus Siefert, *Ortssippenbuch Mahlberg-Orschweier* (Grafenhausen, 1977)), and Ringsheim. OSB entries were checked against the registers in Pf A Grafenhausen, Pf A Kappel, and Pf A Rust, and in GLA 390/1419 through GLA 390/1423 (for Ringsheim).
22. The Figure is limited to married or reproducing adults bearing the surname Sartori. Readers may follow their peregrinations on Map 3.2. This lineage should be distinguished from more eminent families bearing the same surname who held high civil service positions throughout the region.
23. Some of their descendants remained in Ringsheim, experiencing vicissitudes much like those to be described for their cousins.
24. Not to be confused with her cousin Catharina. Incidentally, officials did confuse Magdalena and Maria Magdalena. GLA 239/1643 (correspondence from 1827 in which the latter is taken for the former).
25. GLA 239/1643.
26. At municipal expense. GLA 360/1935–11/1115.
27. GLA 239/1607 (correspondence from 1828–1829).
28. Gem A Grafenhausen B XV/809 (1839 census).
29. Protocol of 10 July 1843 in Gem A Grafenhausen C VIII 2/1.
30. Gem A Grafenhausen C VIII 2/1 (protocol of 4 March 1844). The plumber's costs were met independently, it seems.
31. GLA 239/1637 (correspondence 1826–1827).

32. The Sartoris were only one family, but in the 1830s Catharina and Maria Magdalena produced between them one-sixth of Grafenhausen's illegitimate children. Petty occupations would be even more over-represented in Table 5.2 if one calculated the distribution per child rather than per mother.
33. I emphasize this point because the Napoleonic Code (applying to Baden after 1810) forbade inquiries into paternity. Short of a court order, no legal sanctions awaited fathers who refused to declare themselves. Quite the reverse: those who acknowledged paternity were obliged to support the children.
34. Itinerant occupations were under-represented among unwed fathers in the first column of Table 5.2. Nineteenth-century officials insisted that vagrants had paid to become subjects of a territorial lord only out of desire to wed, whereupon they had moved on. See prefect's argument of 28 October 1827 in GLA 239/1651.
35. On the general situation see John Knodel, "Law, Marriage, and Illegitimacy in Nineteenth Century Germany", *Population Studies*, 20 (1967), 279–294.
36. The calculations make no allowance for variations in the number of daughters in families in different occupational categories.
37. In addition to reducing fertility, such measures were supposed to ensure support for the children who were born. (Compare Matthias Schäfle, *Vier Lustren oder zwanzig Jahre im conferenziellen Leben eines Geistlichen* (Rastatt, 1870), 128–131.) When conjoined with the laws making it easier for unwed fathers to shirk family responsibilities, these measures sometimes left children in poverty instead.
38. I referred in Chapter Two to the entry fees charged immigrants and citizens who imported a spouse. All couples, regardless of origin, had to demonstrate a minimum fortune—the level was higher for outsiders—well in excess of those fees. GLA 314/2256 (1801 regulation in Rust). For the later period see, in addition to the GLA files referred to in Chapter Two, Gem A Grafenhausen C VIII 2/1 (municipal council record book 1838 on), and GLA 239/5476 (marriage into Rust in 1845–1846).
39. Compare Edward Shorter, "Middle-Class Anxiety in the German Revolution of 1848", *Journal of Social History*, 2 (1969), 189–215.
40. It is interesting that the average age at which as yet unmarried women bore their first illegitimate child did not vary by more than one-tenth of a year from 24.2 through all the cohorts before 1875.
41. Possibly by waiting for more of their parents to die. Others simply outlasted the patience of the authorities or outlived the laws. For an example, see below.
42. My wording ignores the 5 % who arrived after the first wedding, typically to widows.
43. With the significant exception of the itinerant, who were under-represented.
44. The straightforward interpretation is that the man who married an unwed mother had usually fathered her children.
45. In the 1830's a Jewish man from Rust who had taken advantage of the laxer legal climate in Alsace found his marriage annulled by the county prefect. Both he and his wife (a non-Ruster) petitioned the authorities for years, each seeking residence rights for the other. While the paperwork mounted, the number of their children grew to six, all officially illegitimate. GLA 239/1659 (correspondence 1831–1837). Only one of the children is listed in *OSB Rust* entry 5125.
46. "[Z]ur linken Hand verheiratet" (*OSB Rust* page 95). Having spent several years in Rhinau in that condition, a Ruster declared in 1851 that he wished to solemnize the union before the law. The couple had a twelve-year-old child.
47. Some of the children born "in Concubinate" in Switzerland found their way back to these villages over the years. GLA 360/1935–11/1163 (report on 1856 inspection tour of Rust).
48. Reports on 1855 inspection tours of Grafenhausen (GLA 360/1935–11/778), Kappel (GLA 360/1935–11/821), and Rust (GLA 360/1935–11/1163).

49. Ibid. See also the reports on the 1856 and 1857 tours ibid. The relevant entries in *OSB Rust* are 3352 (illegitimacy) and 679 (marriage), and entries 1194 (illegitimacy) and 3293 (marriage).
50. "The apple falls near the tree", as Kappel's municipal council put it in 1835 (GLA 239/1613), ignoring its own rôle in the process. In that case, the two illegitimate daughters of the woman Kappel failed to exclude did go on to bear children out of wedlock themselves. *OSB Kappel* entries 1151 through 1154.
51. I pass over accounts attributing the decline to shifts in mentalités, whether Victorian prudery stifling Romantic liberation, or ultramontane discipline supplanting Enlightened laxity. (For the latter view, see Hennig, *Chronik*, 62–68, and Michael Hennig, *Geschichte des Landkapitels Lahr* (Lahr, 1893), 264–266. Compare Jonathan Sperber, *Popular Catholicism in Nineteenth-Century Germany* (Princeton, 1984), 17, 76, 92–97.) Such interpretations must displace the more basic theories that I consider in the text before obtaining a hearing.
52. Shorter, "Emancipation", 605–640. Shorter, Knodel, and van de Walle, "Non-Marital", 382, 392. The title of the latter work dates the decline from 1880. John Knodel and Steven Hochstadt, "Urban and rural illegitimacy in Imperial Germany", in Laslett, Oosterveen, and Smith, *Bastardy*, 284, 292, 297–299 is occasionally less definite about timing.
53. See reports on county Ettenheim for 1865 (in GLA 236/10289), 1866, 1872, and 1873 (in GLA 236/10290).
54. Cases are mentioned in the reports on inspection tours of Kappel in 1855, 1858, and 1860 (GLA 360/1935-11/821), and in the report on the 1867 tour of Rust (GLA 360/1935-11/1164). See also Gem A Grafenhausen B XIV/808 (general circulars on the matter from 1879 on). Episodes like these cast doubt on the assumption (in Massimo Livi-Bacci, "Social Group Forerunners of Fertility Control in Europe", in Coale and Watkins, *Europe*, 196) that towns experienced a higher share of illegitimate births than of illegitimate conceptions.
55. Report on county Ettenheim for 1873 (GLA 236/10290). See also the reports for 1874 (ibid.) and 1884–1885 (GLA 236/10463). Visitation reports for Rust in 1889 (Ord A B4/10504) and for Kappel in 1891 (Ord A B4/5632). As seen above, the fears expressed in these sources were not borne out.
56. A regular section on dances began in the 1882–1883 report on county Ettenheim (GLA 236/10293). An article in the *Breisgauer Zeitung* of 31 October 1879 denounced usury, dances, and alcoholism, and called for the return of restrictive marriage laws. The 1889 visitation report for Rust (Ord A B4/10504) described how the priest combatted night roaming ("Nachtschwärmerei"). On night roaming in Grafenhausen in 1905–1913, see Ord A B4/3742.
57. I use women's ages because they were far more important to fertility than men's.
58. On the idea that the variability of the Malthusian system was concentrated in the poor, compare Chapter Seven and Bernard Derouet, "Une démographie différentielle: clés pour un système auto-régulateur des populations rurales d'Ancien Régime", *Annales Economies Sociétés Civilisations*, 35 (1980), especially 6–8. David Levine drew Derouet's works to my attention.
59. As will be seen in subsequent chapters, the exceptions were drawn from the élite referred to in the previous paragraph.
60. The following discussion is based on the wives in documented first marriages whose dates of birth were given to the day in the OSBs. 470 such women wed in 1800–1824 and 669 in 1875–1899.

6

Natural Fertility and Family Limitation

At several points in the first five chapters, I have declared that family limitation was practised in Grafenhausen and Rust, and to lesser extent in Kappel, during the nineteenth century. The time has come to document those claims. A range of aggregate indices show significant and rising levels of family limitation from the third quarter of the nineteenth century. Applying the same battery of measures to the villages separately reveals that they participated in this movement to varying degrees. Grafenhauseners of the 1820s were the first to abandon natural fertility in large numbers, and by 1900, their descendants had left it far behind. In contrast, Kapplers as a group remained subject to natural fertility practically to the end of the century. Rust shows yet another pattern. There fecundity increased at the same time as family limitation spread, and globally these two developments offset each other. Tracing these differences among individual couples and attempting to account for the strength of local effects form the central concern of the remainder of the book.

This chapter dwells to a considerable extent on the statistical manipulation of demographic data. I shall be making a number of precise points, and mathematics lends itself to precision. I hasten to reassure readers uncomfortable with numbers that I summarize with a simple, indeed overly simple, checklist of indices of family limitation and their interpretation. Non-specialists should consider the more detailed discussion none the less, for it clarifies the theoretical implications of my research by making explicit the models and assumptions underlying it.

THE CLASSICAL THEORY OF FAMILY LIMITATION

I begin by rehearsing some features of fertility rates and then move to increasingly sophisticated interpretations of the patterns they form. In a general and admittedly biased way, this presentation recapitulates the development of the classical theory of family limitation. Although I withhold full endorsement from some common inferences from that hypothesis, in its essentials it provides an excellent model for the fertility transitions in Grafenhausen, Kappel, and Rust.

Fertility there declined through parity-dependent restriction of childbearing within marriage, as couples took deliberate action to stop reproducing while the wives were still fecund.[1] Appreciating the import of this proposition requires a deeper acquaintance with the terms that occur in it.

A fertility rate is the average number of births that take place within a given unit of time. For example, in these three villages married women between twenty and fifty years old produced children about once every three and a half years over the eighteenth and nineteenth centuries. In other words, had a woman been married right from age twenty to age fifty, and experienced the average fertility of married women at each age in between, she would have produced 8.8 children. This figure, 8.8, is the total marital fertility rate.

However, births were not evenly distributed across the thirty years, and so it is useful to consider fertility rates for more restricted ranges of ages. Demographers customarily break women's fecund years into five-year age-groups.[2] The frequency of births to women within those groups is an age-specific marital fertility rate, that is, the birth rate specific to that five-year range of wives' ages. In Grafenhausen, Kappel, and Rust, wives in their twenties produced a child in just over two years, a feat that took wives in their forties that entire decade.

Because these figures summarize the experience of villagers over two centuries, they hide as much as they reveal about historic change. I therefore break them down yet further by the wedding date. Beginning from a figure just below the two-century average, total marital fertility rates rose somewhat through marriages beginning in the first two quarters of the nineteenth century, hitting a peak at 9.2 in 1825–1849. They then fell rather farther in the next fifty years, reaching 8.55 for couples wed in 1875–1899. Age-specific rates for women in their twenties increased consistently over time, while those for women in their forties declined almost as consistently. Rates in the thirties were rather more like the overall pattern, rising tentatively and then dropping substantially.

It is natural to attempt to compare these rates and trends to those found in other populations. One standard reference group is North American Hutterites of the 1920s and 1930s, for whom reliable records report unusually high rates.[3] If one regards the organization of Hutterite communities as permitting something near the biological maximum fertility to be expressed within marriage, the extent to which a population's rates fall below the Hutterites' can be seen as a measure of how far social and cultural factors act to restrict fertility. In the Baden villages, marital fertility was about one-fifth below that experienced by the Hutterites.[4]

However, the idea of a stark contrast between biological capacity and individual control is mistaken. That marital fertility in Grafenhausen, Kappel, and Rust was less than among the Hutterites did not mean that anyone was trying to prevent births, or even that they were aware that marital fertility rates were lower than they might have been. For contemporaries, the most obvious limits on childbearing were the Malthusian restraints on entry into marriage discussed in Chapters Four and Five. It was primarily those restraints that kept women from giving birth to the nine children they were capable of producing.[5] Instead, the average wife whose marriage endured until she was at least forty-five bore about five children. Over the generations, that average increased slightly to 5.6 children. At all times completed family size[6] remained well below the total marital fertility rate.

Differences between societies in marital fertility, however measured, are not direct evidence of differences in family limitation.[7] A more promising line of inquiry into that phenomenon begins by examining the end of a woman's reproductive career. As time passed, wives ceased childbearing younger. Although average ages at last birth were effectively constant at about 40.5 before 1825, they fell steadily thereafter to three years lower.[8] It was this drop that lay behind the decline in age-specific marital fertility rates at higher ages described earlier. The rates fell, not because all women bore fewer children at those ages, but because increasing numbers bore none at all. Reflecting on phenomena like these led demographers to a more sophisticated understanding of fertility control.

This understanding grew out of the classical theory of family limitation, which in turn rests on several contentions about the transformation of fertility in the modern world.[9] According to this model, the distinctive characteristic of the transition to relatively low fertility was the spread of parity-dependent contraception.[10] For the first time, parity, meaning the number of children a wife had already borne, became an important independent determinant of her future fertility. Couples began to behave as if they desired to have no more than a certain number of children, in particular by ceasing reproduction once that family size was reached.[11] Such couples typically did nothing to control their fertility in the early years of marriage, and then switched abruptly to attempting to prevent all births.

At least two points concerning this approach deserve to be highlighted. First, it emphasizes stopping rather than spacing births.[12] The empirical evidence indicates that wider spacing was not important early in the fertility transition.[13] In historical treatments that do not extend into very recent times, it may safely be ignored, and perhaps should be ignored, in the interests of clarity.[14]

A potentially more serious cause for concern with the classical theory of family limitation lies in the fact that the link between the psychological hypotheses about target family sizes and the empirical observations, typically age-specific marital fertility rates, is merely statistical. By and large, older women have produced more children, and by and large, women who have borne many children have more surviving children.[15] The indirect nature of the connections between attitudes, ages, and extant family sizes determines the tests that can be performed.[16] I stick to the classical approach based on age rather than parity.

I summarize my presentation of this theory with a few terminological points. "Natural fertility" denotes a state in which married couples do not limit their fertility as a function of parity or age of the wife.[17] It is natural in that the slowing and ceasing of childbearing as wives age show no sign of artifice. By contrast, "family limitation" covers just such restriction of childbearing. Family limitation and natural fertility are opposites, by definition; where there is more of one, there must be less of the other.

"Fertility control" is a much wider notion, encompassing any measure to influence births. Property qualifications for marriage, breastfeeding on demand, abortion laws, selective breeding, hormone treatments, clerical celibacy, sacred prostitution, husbandly restraint, and wifely modesty are just a few of the many means of fertility control. In that sense it is clear that fertility is always controlled, even natural fertility.

Control can mean increasing fertility as well as decreasing it. Control can be a deliberate conscious choice or an unintended and even unappreciated byproduct. Control can be exercised over those reproducing as well as by them. Even if attention is limited to deliberate decreases engineered by the reproducing couple, control can appear in different patterns of births. The classical theory of family limitation singles out one pattern from this vast array, namely stopping young, and asserts that it alone is the historically relevant feature of the fertility transition. The theory thus boldly courts refutation, and earns historical credit by surviving confrontation with evidence that could go against it.

Within the classical theory then, "the fertility transition" refers to European populations' passage from natural fertility to historically low fertility by means of increasing family limitation. "A fertility transition" would be any similar decline, in another time or place perhaps.

Using these terms does not imply full endorsement of the theoretical baggage which usually accompanies them. In particular, it is not necessary to accept that all past societies were uniformly characterized by natural fertility, nor that all societies must undergo a fertility transition as part of modernization, nor that such transitions cannot be contained, halted, or reversed.[18] Likewise, I do not consider myself committed to the strong version of the theory according to which (1) target sizes are fixed from the outset of the marriage, (2) the desire to prevent further births becomes active only after the target size has been reached, and (3) that desire attains its maximum strength immediately thereafter.[19] It is enough for my purposes that reluctance to produce further children increased substantially with each birth after a certain point.[20]

There may well have been other patterns of fertility control, not involving family limitation,[21] operating in the past, and they may have continued to operate right up to the present. What the classical model contends is that such controls played insignificant rôles in the fertility transition. They did not spread or intensify.

Armed with this theory, one may analyse observed schedules of age-specific marital fertility rates in terms of two separate indices: M, which measures the underlying level of natural fertility, and m, which measures the extent of family limitation.[22] M is a scaling factor which conveys information about the absolute level of fertility abstracting from efforts to prevent or reduce further childbearing. It incorporates such social factors as customs concerning breast-feeding (which may lengthen the duration of sterility after each delivery and thus space births more widely), infant mortality (which could cut off breast-feeding), malnutrition and ill health generally (which may disrupt ovulation or promote miscarriages), frequency of intercourse (in so far as choices regarding sex[23] are independent of a desire to stop having children), and involuntary separation of spouses. M also takes in any relevant genetic differences in age at menarche or menopause, or in propensity for multiple births or spontaneous abortions.[24] In general, M rises as fecundity increases and falls as gaps between births widen.[25]

Intuitive interpretations of absolute values of M are not hard to come by. Under natural fertility, the standard schedule of fertility rates corresponds to a total marital fertility rate of 9.0.[26] Thus, an M value of 1 signifies the potential for nine children, and other values scale that number up or down. An M of 1.5 corresponds to potential for 13.5 children, an M of .5 corresponds to potential for 4.5 children, and so on.

When changes in M are coupled with attempts to halt childbearing, the effects can be more complicated. However, in such circumstances one may still imagine that a woman married from age twenty through fifty would average 9 × M births were it not for the efforts she and/or her partner are making to curtail the number of their offspring.

As it happens, in the eighteenth century the underlying level of natural fertility fell very close to 1 in the three Baden villages. Beginning in the second quarter of the nineteenth century, M rose noticeably in each marriage cohort, eventually reaching a level about one-quarter higher.[27] Thus, a twenty-year-old bride in 1875–1899 could produce over two children beyond the nine that faced her great-grandmother in similar circumstances. Delaying marriage mitigated the absolute impact of fecundity in both generations, but at equal ages later brides would still experience one-quarter more children unless they took some new action. This dilemma was general. The rise in M fits the findings of other researchers, who detect an increase in fecundity in central Europe across a wide range of measures.[28] In the absence of family limitation, this trend would have increased fertility considerably.

The other of the distinct measures in the Coale-Trussell model, m, requires more explanation. Studies of the progress of family limitation have revealed that the shape of the graph of age-specific marital fertility rates changes over time.[29] Under natural fertility, the curve keeps to a plateau only slightly below the maximum reached when the wife is in her early twenties until she reaches her late thirties. That is, the frequency with which couples produce children falls only slightly and gradually with wife's age until the mid-thirties. Thereafter, however, it rapidly declines. Yet the curve remains convex upwards even at that point. Fertility falls more sharply in each year of age than it did in the previous one.

By contrast, as family limitation intensifies, fertility rates at advanced ages of the wife are progressively depressed until the curve becomes concave upwards. Overall births at moderate ages are cut so low by the growing number of women who bear children only by accident that fertility declines less in each subsequent year. The m index measures the extent to which a given fertility schedule has deformed from convexity to concavity in accordance with this pattern.

Values of m are rather less easily interpreted than those of M. Although populations subject to natural fertility should theoretically all score 0 on the m scale, statistical fluctuations may produce other values, including negative ones. As the empirical schedules on which the standard level of natural fertility is based turn out to have m values from −.18 to +.23,[30] values within .2 of 0 cannot be regarded as definitely indicating family limitation. Values below −.2 call the applicability of the model itself into question. Coale and Trussell suggest regarding values around +.2 as signs of family limitation only when they form part of a sequence of increasing values over time.[31]

Values of m near 1, on the other hand, mean only that the fertility schedule in question diverges from natural fertility by an amount equal to the average deviation of the schedules reported in the 1960s by those United Nations members used to draw up the model. Czechoslovakia and Hungary had values as high as 2.[32] The figure for Canada in 1961 was about 1. Thus, fractions of 1 can be regarded as the extent to which villagers had duplicated the passage made by Canadian populations between 1700–1730 and 1961.[33]

The three Baden villages proceeded about halfway along that passage in the nineteenth century. On a global level there was no definite evidence of family limitation before 1825.[34] For marriages beginning 1825–1849, m registered .15, significantly above 0 for over six thousand births.[35] The possibility of incipient family limitation during those years is reinforced by the more dramatic experiences of the next two cohorts: .31 in 1850–1874 and .52 in 1875–1899.[36] By itself, introducing this much family limitation would have cut total marital fertility by one fifth. Because fecundity was rising at the same time, actual shifts in overall fertility were more modest, as seen earlier.

Throughout this discussion I have referred simply to "M" and "m", but the values reported are actually estimates.[37] In effect, I have chosen from the family of curves within the Coale-Trussell model the one curve which the observed rates best fit.[38] Values of M and m are maximum likelihood estimates.[39] The close match between observations and models[40] suggests that actual fertility was consonant with the assumptions of the theory of family limitation. Since in addition, the number of cases was comfortably high, almost twenty thousand births in sixty thousand woman-years, the behaviour of the population of Grafenhausen, Kappel, and Rust can profitably be investigated within the confines of their model.

A greater appreciation of the sharpness of that model can be obtained from an examination of the gaps between deliveries. The study of birth intervals[41]

TABLE 6.1
Average interval, in years, Between wedding and first legitimate birth, Between all confinements but the last two, and Between the second-last and last confinements in documented completed families, by date of wedding

	Wedding to first birth	Between confinements excluding the last	Final birth interval
pre-1800	1.33	2.36	3.31
1800–1824	1.17	2.37	3.41
1825–1849	1.08	2.40	3.46
1850–1874	1.09	2.20	3.66
1875–1899	1.07	2.20	3.84
Change	−.25	−.16	+.53

Notes
(1) *Source:* OSB Grafenhausen, OSB Kappel, and OSB Rust.
(2) Each marriage is counted only once, that is, the second column is the average of the averages within each family.
(3) The Table is based on 2332 cases.

acquires importance from the assertion by theorists of family limitation that attempts to space births more widely were non-existent, ineffectual, or otherwise irrelevant to the fertility transition.[42] In addition, the analysis of intervals leads naturally to further techniques for detecting family limitation.

In order to deal with these issues in a systematic way, I distinguish three sorts of intervals. A couple's childbearing years can be divided into three segments: (1) the period from the wedding until the first legitimate birth, which need not have been conceived during the marriage, (2) the period from that birth until the second-last confinement, and (3) the period between the final two confinements.[43] These intervals mark out couples starting, spacing, and stopping childbearing respectively.

The empirical results in Table 6.1 bring out clearly the virtue of drawing these distinctions, as the three sorts of intervals differed markedly in length. Right from the outset, first intervals were a year shorter than subsequent ones, and final intervals were a year longer still. The gap between wedding and first birth was only one and a third years because it did not include the period of infecundity after delivery that began every other interval.[44] The first interval was also reduced by premarital conceptions, and so shrank by a quarter-year when pregnant brides became more common.

Change came more slowly to the other two sorts of intervals. The gap between deliveries held constant for the average woman wed before 1850, and then dropped sharply to 2.2 years. This decline corresponds to the increases in completed family size and in M already noted.[45]

Final birth intervals were significantly longer even under natural fertility, for the onset of infecundity at advanced ages is gradual.[46] More significant was the steady increase in average last interval, totalling an extra half-year by the final quarter of the nineteenth century. Such widening gaps between the last two confinements often mark family limitation.

The classical theory of family limitation suggests a number of reasons couples whose families had attained a desired size might resume childbearing after an extended period. Some re-evaluate the worth of another child, perhaps in response to changes in economic fortunes, which may even have been anticipated or hoped for. Other couples, without changing their target, produce more children in the face of unexpectedly high mortality among those already born. In the simplest case, they replace a child who has just died. Such substitutions tend to come well after the previous birth, because contraception has been practised in the interim.

More sophisticated connections can also be drawn between family limitation and long late intervals. Where a couple has no definite target, but merely becomes increasingly reluctant to continue producing children as the number of their offspring mounts, the methods of contraception employed may become more efficient only gradually.[47] More interesting, contraceptive methods that are less than perfect, either because of inherent limitations or because of the inexperience of the practitioners, have much the same effect. Indeed, it has been suggested that a rough idea of the extent of reliance on coitus interruptus (withdrawal) rather than abstinence to prevent births can be derived from a comparison of final birth intervals and ages at last birth.[48]

All these lines of reasoning support the proposition that, statistically, extended gaps between the last two confinements characterize couples attempting to limit their fertility. On the other hand, as age at last birth falls, it becomes harder to lengthen the last interval. A delay of four years between ages thirty and thirty-four, for example, in general reflects considerably more effort, conscious or unconscious, than an equal gap between ages forty and forty-four, since younger women are more fecund. If fertility were controlled by absolute and irrevocable stopping at an age well below forty, the final birth interval would be reduced by about one year to match the length of the other inter-birth intervals. That final birth intervals followed a course opposite to the one pursued by other intervals at a time when fecundity was increasing and ages at last birth were falling thus provides striking confirmation of a dramatic change in the approaches nineteenth-century villagers took towards childbearing.

This impression can be rendered more rigorous by examining the separate effects of the elements of marital fertility that I distinguished earlier.[49] In general, a reduction in legitimate births may be brought about (1) by starting older—in the form of increased ages at marriage or extended waits before commencement of childbearing—or (2) by spacing wider, or (3) by stopping younger—through low ages at last birth or extended final intervals—or by some combination of the three. The classical theory of family limitation claims that only the third element, stopping, was historically important. The theory would be refuted if it turned out that fertility declined instead because of later starting or wider spacing.

Assessing all the possibilities together requires limiting attention to couples with at least two legitimate confinements.[50] This eliminates wives who wed so old that they had no time to produce children. It also rules out couples who wanted just one child and ceased reproducing once he or she arrived. Removing from consideration the most dramatic practitioners of starting and stopping in this fashion may understate their contributions, but even under these conditions, spacing had nothing to do with the fertility decline in these three villages.

Overall, the average number of births in such families fell 7 % between the 1700s and 1875–1899, but that trend resulted from the superposition of two contrary forces.[51] The average inter-confinement interval (excluding the last)[52] fell sufficiently during the nineteenth century to increase fertility by 10 %. Moreover, both age at marriage and the gap between the wedding and the first legitimate birth also fell, potentially increasing the number of confinements by a further 7 % and 1 % respectively. Thus, spacing and starting worked to increase fertility rather than decrease it. Had there been no changes in stopping, completed family size would have risen by about one-fifth. However, both the age at last birth and the final birth interval changed in ways that tended to reduce fertility by 20 % and a further 4 %. It was only because this effect was greater than the countervailing forces that fertility fell at all.

This pattern confirms a basic contention of the classical theory of family limitation. Particularly noteworthy is the contrast between the effect of final birth intervals and that of other intervals. Only the last interval is strongly linked to family limitation by the theory, and only the last interval contributed to the fertility decline.

Historically, birth rates first fell thanks to stopping younger, not spacing wider or starting older. Wider spacing between young births emerged only late in the fertility transition, when falling family sizes moved the longer final intervals right next to the start of childbearing. Likewise, it took a strong acceptance of contraception and a consequent uncoupling of marriage and reproduction before the idea of delaying the first birth caught on among married couples. Tentative hints of such developments can be seen in the decline in age at marriage among neo Malthusians,[53] but they did not come to fruition until well into the twentieth century. By that point the fertility transition was virtually complete.

Estimating the Percentage Limiting

Thus far, the measures I have described are standard tools in the kit of the historical demographer. I propose now to add a new instrument of my own devising. Like the others it is calibrated according to the classical theory of family limitation. That theory's attractiveness reflects its empirical success and precision. Yet even the sharp classical theory of family limitation makes equivocal predictions about the birth patterns of limiters. On the one hand, they might be found among families with low ages at last birth, and on the other hand they might be found where final birth intervals were extended.

Presumably it was this sort of reflection that led Knodel to muse about an index combining age at last birth and length of final birth interval.[54] This might be done in any number of intricate ways, but one straightforward procedure is to consider age at second-last confinement.[55]

As explained, couples endeavouring to follow the very same strategy could display two fertility patterns.[56] This index promises to reunite the two sorts of couples for the purposes of analysis, much as it did implicitly in the analysis of birth intervals. Whether it succeeds depends on the extent to which the classical theory of family limitation actually applies to what was taking place in Grafenhausen, Kappel, and Rust. The history of these three villages provides a variety of demographic conditions under which to test this approach.

The evolving distribution of ages at second-last confinement over the nineteenth century can be used to estimate how many villagers were taking up family limitation. For example, the percentage of wives giving birth twice after turning forty fell from 27 % in the 1700s under natural fertility to 12 % among women wed 1875–1899. Conversely, the percentage with one or no births after their twenties rose from 7 % to 25 %. From this last pair of numbers, one might suspect that at least 18 % of the population had begun to practise family limitation. Refining such observations yields an estimate of the percentage limiting within the population.[57]

This new tool for measuring family limitation delivers slightly different information from the indices previously considered. It is now possible to determine, for example, whether a long fall in average age at last birth reflects an increasing number of women who gave birth for the last time just a bit earlier than their mothers had or larger reductions among a correspondingly smaller segment of the population.[58]

Applying the new measure reveals a reassuringly familiar picture. The estimated percentages limiting fall into much the same patterns over time and across villages as uncovered previously. After recording insignificant or even mildly paradoxical levels for couples wed before 1825,[59] it rises to an arguably interesting 16 % for 1825–1849. The 30 % and then 43 % limiting in the final two cohorts are definitely respectable.

Such estimates should not be regarded as pinpoint measurements. Small groups or corrupt data easily throw off an intricate calculation such as this one. As with the m index of family limitation, it is safer to interpret a sequence of values than an isolated reading. In this case, the sustained rise in the 1800s reinforces the impact of each separate value. Still, one needs to bear in mind the distorting influence of younger marriage, which reduces age at second-last birth only slightly less than it does age at last birth. In either case, marrying young can create a false appearance of modest family limitation.

These reflections make it appropriate to present here the promised checklist of indices of fertility. Table 6.2 is arranged in the order in which I discuss findings in the next section.[60] For each measure the Table states values typical of natural fertility in these villages and notes forces that influence it independent of family limitation. Readers previously unfamiliar with these instruments may find it helpful to refer to this Table as they read on.

THE COURSE OF MARITAL FERTILITY IN GRAFENHAUSEN, KAPPEL, AND RUST

The aggregate figures presented thus far show that family limitation eventually came to dominate the behaviour of some inhabitants of all three villages. However, that does not mean that each village participated equally. In fact, the most outstanding feature of the fertility transition was its diversity. I therefore analyse the experiences of Grafenhausen, Kappel, and Rust separately, drawing attention to peculiar features of more general interest.

Grafenhausen provides a textbook illustration of the turn to family limitation, and one important for its timing. Studies of German fertility at the federal, regional, and district levels had suggested that one should not look for substantial declines in fertility until well after the unification of 1871.[61] Nevertheless, all the classic marks of family limitation were present in Grafenhausen

TABLE 6.2
Simplified checklist of measures of fertility and their interpretation

---

Wife's age at last birth
  Average under natural fertility: 40 to 41 years old
  Sensitive to age at marriage—lower if bride younger

Final birth interval
  Average under natural fertility: 3.0 to 3.5 years
  Sensitive to age at last birth—lower if last birth sooner

Completed family size
  Average under natural fertility: 5 to 6 children
  Sensitive to age at marriage—higher if bride younger

Total marital fertility rate
  Under natural fertility: M × 9 children (see below for M)
  Sensitive to birth intervals—greater if fecundity higher

M index of underlying natural fertility
  1 corresponds to the potential for 9 children;
  1.5 to the potential for 13.5 children
  Sensitive to birth intervals—greater if fecundity higher

m index of family limitation
  Under natural fertility: −.2 to +.2
  1 corresponds to the level for Canada in 1961
  Sensitive to age at marriage—slightly greater if brides younger

Percentage limiting
  Under natural fertility: −15 % to +15 %
  Sensitive to age at marriage—greater if brides younger

from the third decade of the nineteenth century. Table 6.3 displays a consistent fall in the average age at last birth that cut it five years below its original level. The extreme lengthening of the final birth interval further compressed childbearing into the early years of marriage. Because age at marriage was falling, women came to be at risk of giving birth during ages when they had always been more fecund. Completed family size therefore decreased less dramatically, though still substantially.[62]

Family limitation was so strong in Grafenhausen that it overpowered all other demographic trends. The total marital fertility rate, for instance, hesitated a bit around 8.6 in the early nineteenth century, but then plunged in subsequent cohorts to finish at 6.3 children. It was borne along by an accelerating current of family limitation. Breaking m down by decade reveals that it jumped to .4 in the 1820s, paused around that level until the 1860s, and then ballooned, passing .88 for the final quarter-century. Indeed, Grafenhauseners wed in the 1890s surpassed the Canadians of 1961. The parallel fall in age at marriage during these years (shown in Figure 5.4) conveys an impression of increasing control and confidence that the old Malthusian restraints were no longer necessary to a growing segment of the population.

They achieved these solid results in the face of increases in the underlying level of natural fertility. Indeed, the strength of family limitation can even be seen in the pattern traced by the M index. It increased 18 % between the first and third quarters of the nineteenth century, much as it did for the villages as a group. However, the rise was choked off thereafter. Just at the point where M accelerated in Rust and Kappel, Grafenhausen's M fell to 1.07. By the final cohort, family sizes had dropped so far that increasing fecundity could no longer express itself. That is, in some cases the number of children desired over an entire marriage had fallen below the number that could now be produced within a five-year span.[63] This capped age-specific marital fertility rates, and so muted the rise in M.

The experience of Kappel provides an almost complete contrast. There the curves remained resolutely convex even at advanced ages. This left the way

TABLE 6.3
Average age of wife at last birth and Final birth interval, both in years, together with the Number of legitimate children in documented completed families in Grafenhausen, by date of wedding

	Age at last birth	Final birth interval	Number of children
pre-1800	40.6	3.18	5.3
1800–1824	39.7	3.38	4.9
1825–1849	38.5	3.55	4.7
1850–1874	37.5	3.87	5.0
1875–1899	35.2	4.35	4.0

Source: OSB Grafenhausen.

clear for the rise in underlying natural fertility to buoy total marital fertility rates. They remained over nine children for the last three quarters of the century. Only[64] in the final cohort does the m index report a fully reliable sign of family limitation, and even then the score is just .28. That development had been anticipated slightly by the modest decline in age at last birth shown in Table 6.4. Final birth intervals varied but little right to 1900. Completed families grew by about one child despite the resort to high ages at marriage (depicted in Figure 5.4).

The same divergence between Grafenhausen and Kappel is evident in the percentages limiting. The estimate rises markedly in nineteenth-century Grafenhausen, where 36 % of couples practised family limitation as early as 1825–1849. Half of Grafenhauseners did so in the next cohort, and almost three-quarters of completed families beginning between 1875 and 1899 were limited. Kappel, where the estimate for the final cohort was a barely noticeable 18 %, lagged generations behind.

Combining the percentage limiting with the Coale-Trussell indices produces a new way of looking at family limitation. The percentage limiting indicates how widespread family limitation was within a population, while m measures its overall intensity. These make up two dimensions of family limitation, which may be graphed as width and depth respectively. Thus, a rectangle combining a low percentage limiting with a high m value shows that that small fraction practised family limitation deeply. Conversely, a square shows less intense family limitation per practising couple.[65] Adding a temporal perspective creates the three-dimensional shape of family limitation.

Two distinct shapes are illustrated in Figure 6.5, which compares family limitation in Grafenhausen and Kappel in a dramatic and accessible way. For each cohort I provide a background grid. Its full width represents 100 % of the population, while its depth is bordered by an m value of 1. A completely filled square therefore means that every couple was successfully practising contraception with results in terms of family limitation equivalent to those achieved by the Canadian population in 1961. The cohorts are arranged next to each

TABLE 6.4
Average age of wife at last birth and Final birth interval, both in years, together with the Number of legitimate children in documented completed families in Kappel, by date of wedding

	Age at last birth	Final birth interval	Number of children
pre-1800	40.9	3.46	5.2
1800–1824	40.0	3.46	5.1
1825–1849	40.4	3.57	5.8
1850–1874	39.5	3.65	5.7
1875–1899	38.8	3.48	6.0

Source: OSB Kappel.

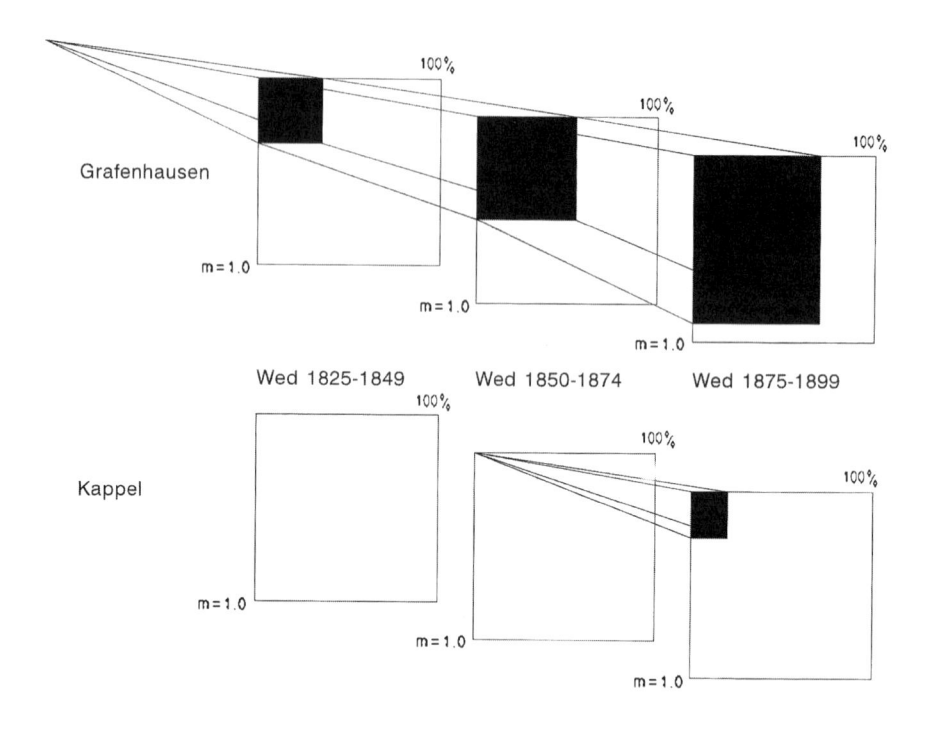

FIGURE 6.5   THE SHAPE OF FAMILY LIMITATION IN GRAFENHAUSEN AND IN KAPPEL

other, displaced slightly downwards to create perspective. This effect is heightened by joining the corners of the shapes.[66] Where family limitation is snowballing, the diagram displays the avalanche clearly.

At a glance, one can tell from Figure 6.5 that family limitation was longer in Grafenhausen, that is, extended over a greater period. It was also wider, that is, at any given point a larger percentage of Grafenhausen's population practised contraception. Finally, family limitation was deeper, that is, the relative reductions in fertility at higher ages were more extensive than in Kappel. On this scale family limitation before 1875 was no deeper than it was wide, indicating that many Grafenhauseners were limiting family size with results in keeping with their numbers. The final cohort shows a deep rectangle rather than a rough square. The limiters, by then a substantial majority of Grafenhausen's population, intensified their efforts, forestalling even more births per couple than earlier. In Kappel, few couples turned to contraception. After 1875, they made deep cuts in their own families, but their rarity limited their overall impact.

These results do not rule out the possibility that some Kapplers were limiting their fertility earlier, but in numbers too small to affect the vital statistics for the village as a whole. Even if that did happen,[67] the sharp division between Kapplers and Grafenhauseners, who lived just minutes apart, poses perplexing

TABLE 6.6
Average age of wife at last birth and Final birth interval, both in years, together with the Number of legitimate children in documented completed families in Rust, by date of wedding

	Age at last birth	Final birth interval	Number of children
pre-1800	40.2	3.30	4.6
1800–1824	41.5	3.41	5.6
1825–1849	40.0	3.29	5.2
1850–1874	39.3	3.50	5.5
1875–1899	38.7	3.70	6.8

Source: OSB Rust.

problems. Since an appeal to "Ortsgeister", the spirits peculiar to localities,[68] provides only a verbal solution, subsequent chapters classify the population of all three villages in ways that do not rely on brute differences of residence or ineffable local culture.[69] Nevertheless, few of the social or economic variables so beloved of the modern social scientist provide the same predictive power as home village.[70] "Heimat" really matters.[71]

Although Rust's fertility transition fell between Grafenhausen's and Kappel's, a closer look at the interplay of family limitation and underlying natural fertility brings out interesting differences between individuals, there and elsewhere. Table 6.6 presents evidence of family limitation in Rust, but not until about twenty-five years later than in Grafenhausen. Mother's ages at last birth fell from a particularly high value in the first quarter of the nineteenth century. Final birth intervals increased in the second half of the nineteenth century, although not on the scale seen in Grafenhausen. These trends were insufficient to reduce average completed family size.

Indeed, the number of legitimate children per couple was accelerating at the end of the century, drawn upwards by a total marital fertility rate that exceeded ten children at that point. Significant values of m were recorded just a generation later than in Grafenhausen, but even in marriages starting after 1850 family limitation did not bring smaller families in the aggregate. The great rise in M (to 1.47) and in the other measures considered by Knodel and Wilson[72] suggests that increases in fecundity more than offset the growth in family limitation.

The evidence presented thus far does not disentangle the chronological sequence. Thus, although I have written as if increasing fecundity undercut prior family limitation, it is as appropriate to imagine an increasing resort to family limitation in the face of a rise in underlying natural fertility. To assert either that each couple saw its hopes for a smaller family dashed or that each couple took up contraception just to the extent necessary to keep its family from growing beyond traditional bounds would be to commit the ecological fallacy.[73] It is more accurate to regard Rust as splitting into two villages, one successfully reducing family size and the other bearing the full weight of increasing fecundity.

The size of the first group may be gauged from the percentage limiting. It

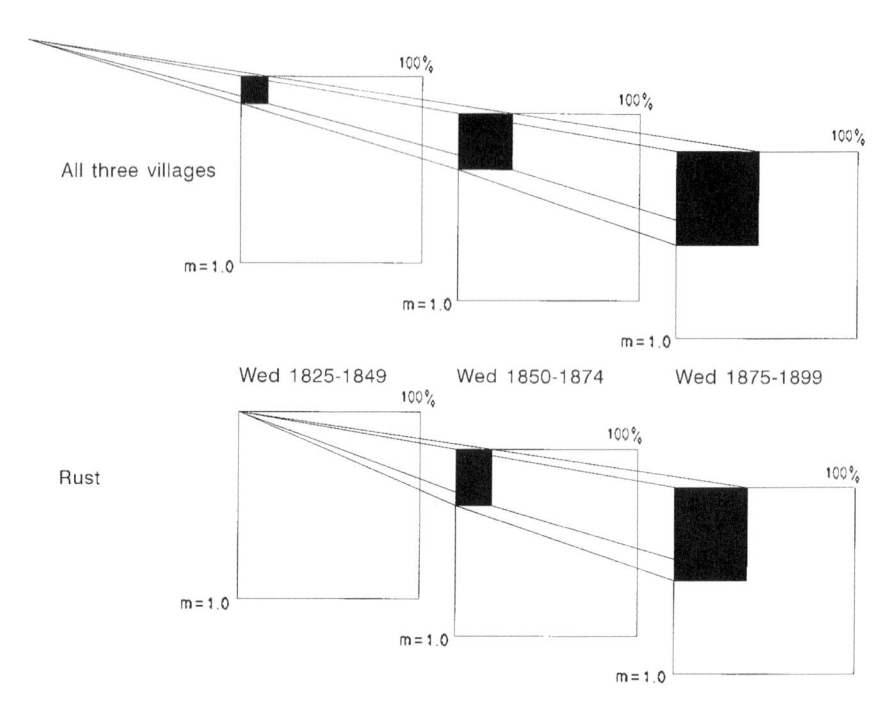

FIGURE 6.7   THE SHAPE OF FAMILY LIMITATION OVERALL AND IN RUST

reached 22 % among Rusters wed 1850–1874. In the final quarter of the nineteenth century it hit 38 %. Grafenhauseners had achieved such a level of family limitation half a century earlier, but Rusters were still a least a generation ahead of Kapplers. Three of every eight Rusters had found a way to overcome rising fecundity.

In this respect, Rust was a microcosm of the three villages combined, as Figure 6.7 brings out. Family limitation was shorter in Rust, indicating that the bulk of limiters before 1850 lived in Grafenhausen instead. Despite its later start, the extent of family limitation in Rust came to match closely the m for the villages as a whole. In each case, family limitation continued over two cohorts, becoming both wider and deeper with time. Over all three OSBs, these two dimensions were about equal. In Rust, on the other hand, the rectangles were much deeper than they were wide. Proportionately fewer couples had taken up family limitation there than in Grafenhausen, but those who had, practised it quite intensively.[74] Their strenuous efforts exempted them from the rise in family size that engulfed most of their neighbours.

A look at the distribution of family sizes confirms the suggestion of a split within Rust.[75] The percentage of couples with five to nine children shrank from 64 % to 45 % between the eighteenth century and the end of the nineteenth. Both larger and smaller families became more prominent. On the one hand the frequency of families with two to four children rose from 15 % to 26 %, reflecting increased family limitation by some. At the same time, the share of families with ten or more children grew about equally (15 % to 27 %). Because I have controlled for age at marriage, most of the differences result from diverging patterns of marital fertility. The concentrations of villagers at the upper and lower ends of the scale provide suggestive support for the hypothesis that Rust was polarizing.

The aggregate experience of increasing fecundity and increasing family limitation, in Rust and elsewhere, was in fact an amalgam of disparate experiences, experiences rendered disparate by the choices of individual couples. Villagers did not respond to population pressure in a uniform way, but rather split, with only some couples taking up family limitation. Because all inhabitants did not participate equally in the fertility transition, examining the characteristics of pioneers in family limitation promises to shed light on how that transition occurred. Trends within a group of pioneers would be especially significant where they went beyond the singular fluctuations inherent in individual family histories. Can such pioneering limiters be reliably identified?

With its deft predictions, the classical theory of family limitation offers the greatest hope of separating true limiters from spurious anomalies. Yet, as lamented previously, it is just at this point that the theory makes equivocal predictions, namely, low ages at last birth and long final birth intervals. These characteristics work against each other. Considering only the age at which wives ceased reproducing risks misclassifying partners who relied on contraceptive methods that were less than perfect or who altered their behaviour in response to unanticipated events.[76] On the other hand, exclusive reliance on the length of the period between the final two confinements overlooks couples who successfully terminated childbearing while young. The previous interval, coming at a fecund age when no attempt was made to prevent conceptions, tended to be short.[77]

Faced with this bifurcation in birth patterns at the end of a limiter's reproductive career, I move back to an earlier stage. I propose to search for practitioners of family limitation among couples whose second-last child arrived while the wife was unusually young. In doing so I hedge my bets. By allowing for one episode of contraceptive failure per family, this measure detects couples relying on methods that were less than perfect. It is also capable of spotting couples who resumed childbearing to replace a child who died unexpectedly.

I therefore single out from the completed well-documented families in each marriage cohort and village the twenty youngest wives at second-last confinement.[78] In the eighteenth century, this young group should be a near-random assortment if no couples were practising contraception. As time passed, greater prevalence of family limitation would make the young group a purer and purer collection of limiters. In so far as sub-populations practised family limitation more frequently or more intensively, the young group would come to differ from the population as a whole with respect to the relevant characteristics. Still later, after family limitation became close to universal, the young group would again become a random assortment from the total population.

Confirmation of this supposition comes from the fact that the other characteristics of the young group fell into suggestive patterns over time. Just at the time family limitation became detectable overall, the percentage of Farming occupations in the young group rose from 37 % to 62 %. At the same time, the percentage of Labour dropped from 19 % to 7 %.[79] Moreover, the extent to which their wealth exceeded that of other villagers grew. There was also a rise in the percentage of families including officeholders in municipal government. Finally, displays of religious and political independence became more typical of these groups.

Each of these claims is documented in a more rigorous way in subsequent chapters and then followed up in detail. Chapter Seven looks at the influence of occupation and status, Chapters Eight and Nine at wealth, and Chapters Ten to Twelve at politics and religion.

Notes

1. Fecundity is the capacity to bear children; "fertility" refers to actual births.
2. I ignore fertility rates under twenty because too few women were married at those ages and because there are problems interpreting adolescent sterility. See Louis Henry, *Anciennes Familles Genevoises* (Paris, 1956), 112–113, 117–118, Etienne Gautier and Louis Henry, *La population de Crulai paroisse normande* (Paris, 1958), 103–104, Coale, "Factors", 205, 209, and Ansley Coale and Roy Treadway, "A Summary of the Changing Distribution of Overall Fertility, Marital Fertility, and the Proportion Married in the Provinces of Europe", in Coale and Watkins, *Europe*, 154.
3. I allude here to the Ig index developed by Ansley Coale and used extensively by the Princeton European Fertility Project. It uses the number of married women to weight the ratios of age-specific marital fertility rates to those of the Hutterites. Coale, "Factors", 205–206. Coale, "Decline", 3–5. Coale and Treadway, "Summary", 33–35, 153–162. The Hutterites were studied in Joseph Eaton and Albert Mayer, "The Social Biology of Very High Fertility Among the Hutterites. The Demography of a Unique Population", *Human Biology*, 25 (1953), 206–264. John Knodel has devised a modified index Ig' for work with German populations. On how this measure differs from the original see John Knodel, "From Natural Fertility to Family Limitation: The Onset of Fertility Transition in a Sample of German Villages", *Demography*, 16 (1979), 497–499, 519.
4. Ibid. Because Ig' considers only births within wedlock, this reduction is over and above that brought on by late marriage and considered in Chapter Four.
5. Comparing the values of Ig' and Im (see Chapter Four) shows that entry into marriage was three times as important as behaviour within it in reducing fertility.
6. So called because the wife's childbearing years were effectively complete at that point. Fertility rates over forty-five were negligible.
7. Even within marriage, unquestioned infant feeding practices may influence Ig as much as conscious choices by couples. As a result, a wide range of values of Ig have been uncovered in societies apparently subject to natural fertility. Knodel, *Germany*, 59–61. Ansley Coale, "The Decline of Fertility in Europe since the Eighteenth Century As a Chapter in Demographic History", in Coale and Watkins, *Europe*, 8–10.

Coale and Treadway, "Summary", 36–37, 46. See also Henri Leridon, *Human Fertility* (Chicago, 1977), 118–119. Because it is such a blunt instrument, I make little use of Ig henceforth. See also the criticisms of Timothy Guinane, Barbara Okun, and James Trussell, "What Do We Know About the Timing of Fertility Transitions in Europe?", *Demography*, 31 (1994), 1–20.

8. The difference is very significant by almost any measure. Even in the half-village cohorts studied later in this book, standard deviations for ages at last birth were about two-thirds of a year.
9. A systematic statement of this theory can be found in Louis Henry, "Some Data on Natural Fertility", *Eugenics Quarterly*, 8 (1961), 81–91. For subsequent expositions of the founder's views, see Louis Henry, *Population Analysis and Models* (London, 1976), 90–104, and Louis Henry, "Concepts actuels et résultats empiriques sur la fécondité naturelle", in *International Population Conference Mexico 1977* (Liège, 1977), 5–15. Although much of the evidence on which the theory was based came from studies of Europeans and their descendants, other populations also fit the model. John Knodel, "Family Limitation and the Fertility Transition: Evidence from Age-Patterns of Fertility in Europe and Asia", *Population Studies*, 31 (1977), 219–249. John Knodel, "Natural Fertility: Age Patterns, Levels, and Trends", in Rodolfo Bulatao and Ronald Lee (ed.), *Determinants of Fertility in Developing Countries* (New York, 1983), 61–102.
10. Contraception should of course be distinguished from birth control. In particular, induced abortion is a method of birth control but not of contraception. Edward Shorter (in "Has a desire to limit fertility always existed? The question of drug abortion in traditional Europe", a paper prepared for the International Union for the Scientific Study of Population's Conference on Determinants of Fertility Trends, held in Bad Homburg in 1980, ms. 1–4, 26, and in *A History of Women's Bodies* (New York, 1982), 177–191) argues against downplaying induced abortion as a factor limiting fertility in early modern Europe. Susan Watkins, "Conclusions", in Coale and Watkins, *Europe*, 426, 435 likewise lists abortion as a means of birth control that had always been available. In contrast, Coale ("Chapter", 9, 10, 14) and Coale and Treadway ("Summary", 22, 35, 37) add abortion to contraception when describing how the fertility transition took place in Europe as a whole. John Knodel and Etienne van de Walle, ("Lessons from the Past: Policy Implications of Historical Fertility Studies", ibid., 390) assign rather less importance to induced abortion, especially in the early years of the fertility decline (and a fortiori before that point). I found no evidence of widespread or increasing resort to induced abortion in the Baden villages, and therefore presume throughout that family limitation took place through contraception.
11. The assumption is that the number of children that they could have had was greater.
12. Attempts to space that did not begin until a certain number of children had been born, or that became more intense as family size increased, are captured. Slowing down counts as partially effective stopping.
13. I show this below for three villages.
14. An exchange on this subject took place in *Annales*. John Knodel, "Espacement des naissances et planification familiale: une critique de la méthode Dupâquier-Lachiver", *Annales Economies Sociétés Civilisations*, 36 (1981), 473–488. Jacques Dupâquier and Marcel Lachiver, "Du contresens à l'illusion technique", ibid., 489–492. "Réponse de John Knodel à Jacques Dupâquier", ibid., 493–494.
15. Than mothers of low parity. On whether family limitation might be linked directly to age, rather than indirectly via parity, see Watkins, "Conclusions", 434.
16. Calculating fertility rates by parity rather than by the wife's age leads to formidable practical and theoretical obstacles, some of which are discussed in Knodel, "Onset", 502, 513–517, 520. For an example of perseverance in the face of these

obstacles see David Weir, "Fertility Transition in Rural France, 1740–1829", *Journal of Economic History*, 44 (1984), 612–614, summarizing his 1983 Ph.D. dissertation at Stanford.
17. Thus, it is the product of very general genetic and environmental conditions among human beings. Compare John Knodel and Chris Wilson, "The Secular Increase in Fecundity in German Village Populations: An Analysis of Reproductive Histories of Couples Married 1750–1899", *Population Studies*, 35 (1981), 61. See also Chris Wilson, Jim Oeppen, and Mike Pardoe, "What is Natural Fertility? The Modelling of a Concept", *Population Index*, 54 (1988), 4–5, 11–12, 14.
18. On irreversibility, see Coale, "Chapter", 21, Coale and Treadway, "Summary", 37, and more persuasively, Knodel and van de Walle, "Lessons", 408–412.
19. These assumptions have been criticized by Wally Seccombe. See "Starting to Stop: Working-Class Fertility Decline in Britain", *Past and Present*, 126 (February 1990), 151–188.
20. The possibility that a desire to limit births strengthened with advancing age without there being any target family size is left open.
21. Examples include delaying marriage and extending the breastfeeding of each child. Both clearly reduced fertility substantially, before and after the fertility transition in these villages.
22. M and m were introduced by Ansley Coale ("Age Patterns of Marriage", *Population Studies*, 25 (1971), 206-208), developed by Ansley Coale and James Trussell ("Model fertility schedules: variations in the age-structure of childbearing in human populations", *Population Index*, 40 (1974), 185–258, and "Erratum", *Population Index*, 41 (1975), 572), and refined by the same two authors ("Technical Note: Finding the Two Parameters that Specify a Model Schedule of Natural Fertility", *Population Index*, 44 (1978), 203–213). On calculating M and m, see Göran Broström and Kenneth Lockridge, "Coale and Trussell's "m" visits Sweden, or, why do we get such lousy fits?", in Kenneth Lockridge, *The Fertility Transition in Sweden* (Umea, 1984), 98–110, and Göran Broström, "Practical Aspects of the Estimation of the Parameters in Coale's Model for Marital Fertility", *Demography*, 22 (1985), 625–631.
23. Such as prohibitions against or distaste for intercourse at specific times of year or during lactation or at points during a woman's menstrual cycle or lifespan, or a generally lower sex drive.
24. As this list brings out, separating genetic and social factors is not at all straightforward. Fortunately, there is no need to disentangle the joint influence of heredity and environment in each of these areas. Indeed, that is one of the virtues of M.
25. Provided the widening is independent of the number of children already born.
26. Or 11.0, if the calculation is based on all ages from fifteen on.
27. A small part of this rise was due to the increase in premarital conceptions mentioned in Chapter Five. (A pregnant bride raises fertility rates because she contributes a birth to the numerator but less time to the denominator than wives who did not enter marriage pregnant.) Making allowances for this following a method outlined by John Knodel (adding to the age-group in which the woman wed the difference between the number of months before she gave birth and the average number of months it took non-pregnant brides to produce their first child) reduces the increase in M, but only from 24 % to 22 %. (The rise in m becomes 44 points instead of 47.)
28. Knodel and Wilson ("Fecundity", 53–84) report that brides became pregnant more swiftly, that the proportion remaining sterile fell among wives wed before age forty, that the seasonal pattern of conceptions, and presumably of intercourse, smoothed, and that births came closer together.
29. The pattern was first observed systematically in Henry, *Genevoises*, 77–78.
30. Or –.15 to +.24 on an older calculation. Coale and Trussell, "Finding", 205–206. See also Wilson, Oeppen, and Pardoe, "Modelling", 10. The confidence intervals ibid., 8 make a similar sweep of ±.2 for populations with 500–1000 births, about

half the size of a village marriage cohort in this book. Compare Broström, "Practical", 630–631. It is therefore prudent to allow a range ±.2 in a cohort divided between rich and poor or between political parties.
31. Coale and Trussell, "Finding", 205–206. John Knodel (in "Child Mortality and Reproductive Behaviour in German Village Populations in the Past: A Micro-Level Analysis of the Replacement Effect", *Population Studies*, 36 (1982), 180, and elsewhere) uses +.3 as a dividing line. The highest "natural" value, +.23, belongs to families of Genevan citizens born 1600–1649. The corresponding ellipse in Wilson, Oeppen, and Pardoe, "Modelling", 10 is also well to the right. Since subsequent cohorts definitely practised family limitation, it may have been incipient in Geneva at that point.
32. Coale and Trussell, "Model", 188–189. Government policies in China may have pushed urban m over 4. William Lavely, "Age Patterns of Chinese Marital Fertility, 1950–1981", *Demography*, 23 (1986), 419–434.
33. Data from Jacques Henripin, *La population canadienne au début du XVIIIe siècle* (Paris, 1954) give m = −.14. Compare Coale and Trussell, "Finding", 205. For data on Canadian fertility at other points, see Jacques Henripin, *Trends and Factors of Fertility in Canada* (Ottawa, 1972), 378, and Warren Kalbach and Wayne McVey, *The Demographic Bases of Canadian Society* (Toronto, 1979), 105.
34. Values of m: .05 in the pre-1800 cohort, .06 in 1800–1824.
35. That is, significant statistically, a discrepancy greater than two standard deviations. Age at marriage, bridal pregnancy, corrupt data, and feedback between m and M also distort readings of m.
36. Each value is significantly higher than the one for the previous cohort.
37. Coale and Trussell, "Finding". Broström, "Practical". Wilson, Oeppen, and Pardoe, "Modelling".
38. This eliminates the confusion that multiple estimates (one for each age-range) might produce, as in the exchange between Richard Morrow, "Family Limitation in Pre-Industrial England: A Reappraisal", *Economic History Review*, second series, 31 (1978), 423, and Anthony Wrigley, "Marital Fertility in Seventeenth-Century Colyton: A Note", ibid., 430–432.
39. Each observation from ages 20–24 to 45–49 is weighted by the number of births in that span. Weighting naturally compensates for statistical fluctuations in the rare births after age forty-five. (Compare Coale and Trussell, "Finding", 204, and Knodel, "Asia", 221.) It also dampens the influence of bridal pregnancy, because births in general are less frequent in the age-ranges where weddings are taking place.
40. Both mean square errors (Coale and Trussell, "Finding", 204) and residual sums of squares (Broström, "Practical", 629) are unobjectionable for all cohorts reported thus far.
41. For variety of expression I occasionally ignore the possibility of twins or triplets, and speak of intervals between births rather than intervals between confinements. At all times I refer to the latter.
42. Louis Henry, *On the Measurement of Human Fertility* (New York, 1972), 211–217. For a different view, see Douglas Anderton and Lee Bean, "Birth Spacing and Fertility Limitation: A Behavioral Analysis of Nineteenth Century Frontier Populations", *Demography*, 22 (1985), 169–183, and Lee Bean, Geraldine Mineau, and Douglas Anderton, *Fertility Change on the American Frontier* (Berkeley, 1990).
43. (3) has little theoretical significance in marriages that end prematurely, so I calculate these intervals only for completed families, ones that endure until the wife turns forty-five.
44. Unless there had been a birth shortly before the wedding, either out of wedlock or in a previous marriage.
45. In Chapter Seven I suggest that a reduction in breastfeeding, particularly among working women, accounts for part of this decline.

46. For empirical data, see Gerhard Döring, "The Incidence of Anovular Cycles in Women", *Journal of Reproduction and Fertility*, supplement no. 6 (1969), 77–81. For theoretical treatment of this and other features of intervals, see Henry, *Measurement*, 12–17, and Leridon, *Human*, especially 148–162.
47. For instance, they may engage in intercourse less and less frequently.
48. Knodel, "Transitions", 378–379.
49. The following analysis is based on ideas from John Knodel, "Starting, Stopping, and Spacing During the Early Stages of Fertility Transition: The Experience of German Village Populations in the Eighteenth and Nineteenth Centuries", *Demography*, 24 (1987), 143–162, which in turn acknowledges Peter McDonald, "Nuptiality and Completed Fertility: A Study of Starting, Stopping, and Spacing Behavior", World Fertility Survey *Comparative Studies*, 35 (1984), 25–27. I restore one of McDonald's distinctions and add one of my own.
50. So that first and last birth do not coincide, and so forth. Couples with just two confinements can be considered provided others with larger families are available for the calculation of gaps between births before the last.
51. 624 couples wed before 1800 averaged 6.54 confinements, with 2.25 years between pairs of births before the last. Wives' ages at marriage, first legitimate birth, second-last confinement, and last birth were 26.03, 27.24, 37.46, and 40.77 respectively. 446 couples wed 1875–1899 averaged 6.11 confinements, with pairs separated by 1.96 years. The transitional ages were 24.95, 25.97, 34.03, and 37.87.
52. Measured per pair of consecutive births and not as earlier, per woman.
53. And in slightly longer second-last intervals in Grafenhausen. On second-last intervals, see Leridon, *Human*, 112. Compare Henry, *Genevoises*, 105–107, 123–124, and Gautier and Henry, *Crulai*, 146-148.
54. Knodel, "Espacement", 486.
55. For a more detailed justification of this measure and its calculation, see Benz, Thesis.
56. Strictly, once family limitation sets in, the second-last birth does not come at the same stage of family building for all couples. For those who suffered contraceptive failure, it represents the point at which they wished to stop. For those who did not suffer contraceptive failure, that point came only with the last birth, a short interval later. Compare Henry, *Genevoises*, 102.
57. I sum over the ages of the wife (up to forty) the differences between the number of couples whose second-last birth came at that age and the number of second-last births that would have been expected then had the aptitude to stop been identical to that displayed in marriages beginning 1730–1799 in any of the three villages. For instance, under natural fertility, 4 % of women in well-documented completed families with second-last births at age thirty-three or greater actually experienced that second-last birth at thirty-three. For age thirty-four, the statistic was 6 %, for age thirty-five 9 %, and so on. If corresponding rates vary in another population, the surpluses and deficits count towards the percentage limiting there. Weir, Thesis, uses a similar calculation on ages at last birth.
58. The classical theory of family limitation suggests the latter.
59. Pre-1800 cohort: +1 %, 1800–1824: –1 %. Negative percentages are possible because random fluctuations under natural fertility are as apt to lower the number of second-last births coming at a particular age as to raise it. Among Rusters wed 1800–1824, a small population whose ages at marriage were rising, the estimate fell as low as –14 %. Since that figure must be off by at least 14 %, I regard positive values in the same range as unreliable.
60. Pride of place goes to age at last birth, a stable statistic under natural fertility with clear sensitivity to family limitation. It also comes closer to the intuitive reasoning of limiters than does the elaborate mathematics behind m and the percentage limiting.

61. Knodel, *Germany*, 55–68. Map 2.1 accompanying Coale and Treadway, "Summary" places the onset of fertility decline in this part of Baden in the 1880s.
62. The magnitude of the average decrease is more impressive in light of the increases overall and in Kappel and Rust. See below. Of course, it was lower still among just that segment of Grafenhausen's population who were practising family limitation. Similarly, their ages at last birth were even lower, their final intervals even longer, and their m even higher.
63. Another way of appreciating this phenomenon is to note that the deformation of fertility rates that began at advanced ages in the 1825–1849 cohort had by 1875–1899 worked its way back to fertility rates for wives in their twenties.
64. The m of .17 for 1800–1824 just barely differs from 0 statistically.
65. The intensity or true depth of family limitation is more precisely measured by the ratio of m to the percentage limiting. Nevertheless, for ease of presentation I stick with the format described in the body. John Knodel called my attention to its weaknesses.
66. I do not colour in the shape at all unless the m value is significantly greater than zero. Otherwise, the quadrilateral is the point in the upper left corner.
67. In later chapters I argue that it did.
68. Albert Köbele, "Die deutschen Ortssippenbücher", manuscript. Johannes Hohlfeld, "Die Dorfsippenbucher", *Familiengeschichtliche Blätter*, 42 (1944), 69.
69. Compare Barbara Anderson, "Regional and Cultural Factors in the Decline of Marital Fertility in Europe", in Coale and Watkins, *Europe*, especially 296–299, 304–311, 313.
70. Indeed, when the data are purified by the exclusion of outsiders (meaning here families who appear in more than one OSB or in which at least three of the parents and children were born elsewhere), Grafenhausen shows even stronger family limitation while Kappel displays less.
71. As the compilers of the OSBs claimed all along. On geographic differences dwarfing socio-economic variation, see Pierre Chaunu, "Réflexions sur la démographie normande", in *Sur la population française au XVIIIe et au XIXe siècles* (Paris, 1973), 115–116, which too hastily attributes all such differences to family limitation.
72. "Fecundity", 59 singles out Rust for special attention.
73. Inferring that members have characteristics of the whole.
74. As elsewhere, intensive family limitation coincided with high fecundity.
75. I compared the number of legitimate children in completed documented marriages in which the bride was under thirty. There were 200 such families before 1800 and 164 beginning 1875–1899.
76. A possible example is *OSB Grafenhausen* entry 1611. The wife wed in 1825 at age twenty-six, and gave birth at twenty-seven, twenty-nine, thirty, and not again until age forty-six.
77. *OSB Rust* entry 185 provides a possible example. The wife bore one child before marrying in 1839 at twenty-four. She produced two more children a year and a quarter apart, and stopped at age twenty-six.
78. Family histories that are well-documented by the criteria set out in Chapter One record this event more reliably. Benz, Thesis, describes the young group in more detail.
79. Calculations based on 180 families from village-cohorts with m under .2 and 120 from village-cohorts where m was greater.
80. In the nine cohorts subject to natural fertility, 58 % (of 148 young stoppers) were rich, but the rich made up 72 % (of 98) in the six cohorts where family limitation was practised. Wealth was calculated only for the mature marriages defined and described in Chapters Eight and Nine.

7

Proprietors and Notables

The previous chapter uncovered widely varying levels of marital fertility between and within Grafenhausen, Kappel, and Rust. This chapter explores the extent to which social differences, as reflected in occupation and status, shed light on this diversity. Occupation exerted strong influence on illegitimate fertility, as seen in Chapter Five. Did the peculiar marital fertility patterns apparently associated with each village actually arise from occupational trends broader than the municipality?

I begin by pointing to evidence that suggests a positive response to this question. I then examine the fertility of three broad occupational groupings: farming, labour, and artisanal pursuits. Those holding offices in municipal government, dubbed notables, receive separate attention. The results show that family limitation appeared earliest and most extensively among those engaged in farming, the affluent, and the local notability. This pattern is apparent in each village, but the differences between villages remain just as striking after occupation is taken into account. Thus, these findings point to a more finely tuned examination of the importance of landed wealth (Chapters Eight and Nine) and beyond that to a consideration of the political matrix of the municipality (Chapters Ten to Twelve).

In Chapter Six, I singled out the twenty completed families from each village and marriage cohort with the youngest wives at second-last confinement. Exaggerating slightly, one may declare that these couples were practising family limitation if any couples were.[1] Since this relationship is both hypothetical and statistical, changes in the composition of the young group over time are more significant than its makeup at any given point or in any given village.

In the case of occupations, the most notable change is the substantial increase in the frequency of Farming mentioned at the end of Chapter Six. In each village the occupational distribution within young cohorts wed after there is evidence of family limitation in the population as a whole diverged from its predecessors. Despite the wide variation in the distributions from village to village, in each case the percentage of Farming occupations increased substantially: in Grafenhausen from 45 % to 74 %, in Kappel from 41 % to 65 %, and in Rust from 27 % to 43 %.[2] This trend was especially pronounced in the earliest cohorts practising family limitation. As time passed, other occupational categories, led by the artisans, joined in. Day labourers lagged behind.[3] The consistency and strength of these results hint that occupation may have been the key to the behaviour of individual villagers and entire populations.

In particular, the differences in the occupational distributions of documented families in the three villages parallel those for family limitation. Farming occupations were most common (49 %) in Grafenhausen, while in Rust occupational designations fell most frequently (47 %) into the artisan categories. If, as was suggested in the previous paragraph, artisans took up family limitation somewhat later than landed proprietors, that circumstance would fit the lag in its spread from Grafenhausen to Rust.

Although the Farming and artisan categories were also prominent in Kappel, the most striking feature of that village's occupational distribution was the relatively high proportion of day labourers.[4] If labourers had less incentive or inclination to control their fertility than other occupational groups, Kapplers' stubborn failure to take up the contraceptive practices spreading around them would be less surprising. However, a closer look at each of the occupational categories shows that the villages' demographic histories cannot be linked quite so straightforwardly with differences in their social structure.

FERTILITY CONTROL FOR FARMING AND LABOUR

In Chapter Three, I suggested that farming and labouring were at opposite ends of the social scale, at least as far as agriculture was concerned. Their demographic experiences diverged as well, especially as family limitation began to spread. At that point, landed proprietors increasingly restricted reproduction within marriage, while day labourers remained under Malthusian controls.

Figure 7.1 contrasts the two trends clearly. Age at second-last confinement fell away among the landed proprietors from the beginning of the nineteenth century. Day labourers continued at the old level until 1875, though they experienced a significant decline thereafter. Because the landed proprietors pressed further downwards at that point, the gap between categories narrowed only slightly.[5]

Table 7.2 shows that the advantage of farming couples in the middle of the nineteenth century derived from a significantly lower age at last birth and a somewhat more extended final birth interval. They maintained much of their lead in both respects even in the final cohort. Moreover, at that point, their more intensive family limitation gave them lower completed family sizes for the first time.

That reversal of rank owed almost as much to the increase in underlying natural fertility, which hit labouring couples particularly hard. Their total marital fertility rate, already over 9, jumped by a full child between the final two cohorts. M rose an even sharper 23 % at that point to 1.42 . By contrast, landed proprietors held underlying natural fertility at the less elevated level (1.2) reached in earlier cohorts. This corresponded to a continuing fall in their total marital fertility rate.

The contrast in levels of family limitation is evident in every dimension of

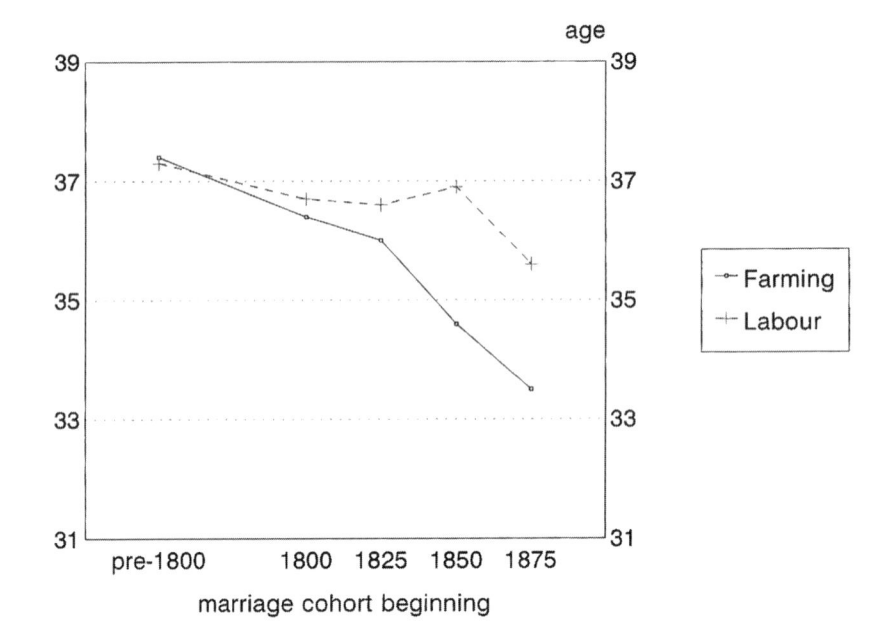

FIGURE 7.1 AVERAGE AGE OF WIFE AT SECOND-LAST CONFINEMENT IN DOCUMENTED COMPLETED FAMILIES IN FARMING AND LABOUR CATEGORIES, BY DATE OF WEDDING

TABLE 7.2
Average age of wife at last birth and Final birth interval, both in years, together with the Number of legitimate children in documented completed families engaged in Farming and Labour, by date of wedding

	Age at last birth		Final birth interval		Number of children	
	Farming	Labour	Farming	Labour	Farming	Labour
pre-1800	40.3	40.8	3.20	3.45	5.4	4.7
1800–1824	39.8	39.9	3.41	3.44	5.3	4.6
1825–1849	39.4	39.8	3.56	3.30	5.6	3.7
1850–1874	38.3	40.3	3.84	3.43	6.0	4.9
1875–1899	36.9	38.9	3.78	3.49	5.2	5.5
Change	−3.4	−1.9	+.58	+.04	−.2	+.9

Notes
(1) Source: OSB Grafenhausen, OSB Kappel, and OSB Rust.
(2) The Table is based on 1638 cases:
1106 in Farming and 533 in Labour.

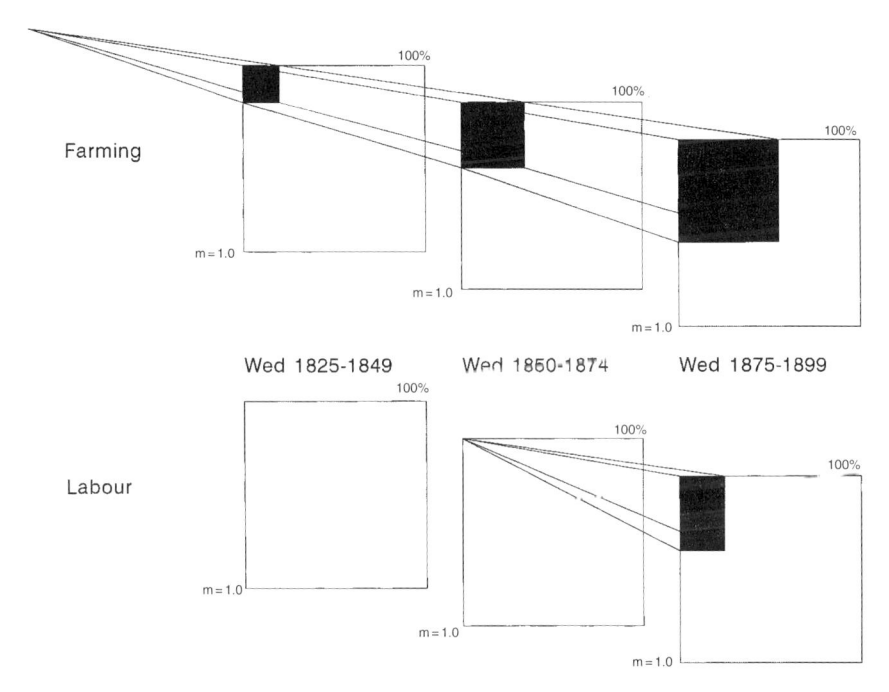

FIGURE 7.3 THE SHAPE OF FAMILY LIMITATION IN THE FARMING AND LABOUR CATEGORIES

the shapes in Figure 7.3. It was longer among landed proprietors, and at every point wider and deeper.[6] Even at the end of the nineteenth century, the greater percentage of farming couples practising contraception kept their m value ahead. However, the intensity with which the smaller proportion of day labourers joined in immediately made up most of their lag in m.

With the exception of this last development, these results fit the hypothesis that it was the threat of excessive division of landholdings that prompted villagers to resort to family limitation. That pressure weighed most heavily on landed proprietors with assets extensive enough to form independent economic units. Most labourers possessed only marginal holdings, and so lacked this incentive to control family size. The difference in economic interests could account for differences in fertility through at least 1875.

However, this reasoning overlooks the elevated ages at marriage in the labour category. Figure 7.4 shows that, on average, labourers had to wait two years longer than landed proprietors to wed in the eighteenth century. Moreover, labourers's ages at marriage increased more in hard times. Thus, the gap between categories for grooms widened to three years in the middle cohorts of the nineteenth century, when the average day labourer celebrated his thirtieth birthday before his first wedding. Population pressure weighed harder on labour,

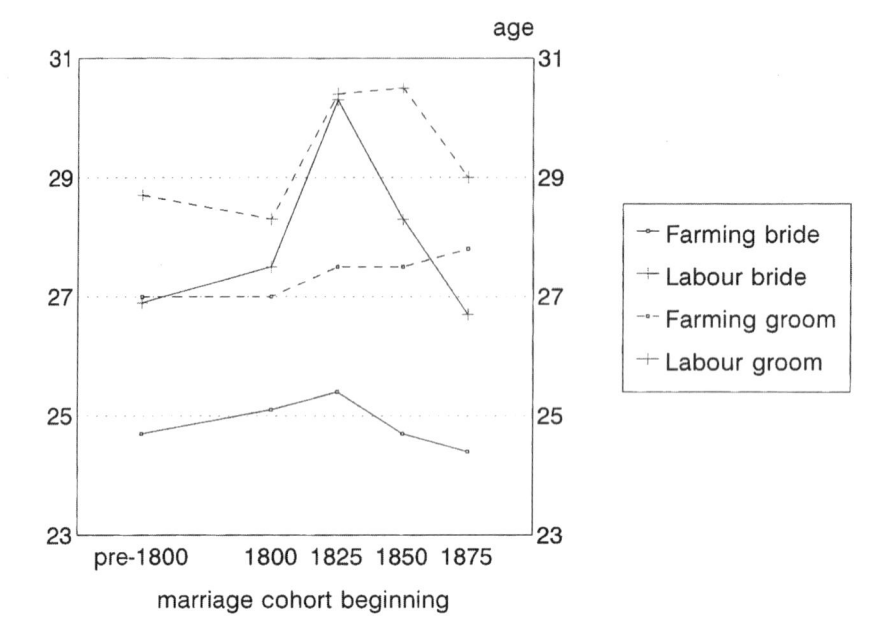

FIGURE 7.4 AVERAGE AGE AT FIRST MARRIAGE OF HUSBANDS AND WIVES IN DOCUMENTED MARRIAGES IN FARMING AND LABOUR CATEGORIES, BY DATE OF WEDDING

which was bound more tightly by customary and legal restrictions on marriage.[7] This was especially true of women, who wed five years later than their farming counterparts between 1825 and 1849. Even under the less extreme circumstances half a century later, the gap between brides was twice that between grooms.[8]

This trend reduced family size among labourers far more effectively than family limitation. For instance, Table 7.2 showed that fewer than four children were born to the average labouring marriage beginning in 1825–1849. Even at the end of the century, the effects of half a century of family limitation among landed proprietors did not match those late marriage had long bestowed on labourers. Under those conditions, many labouring couples who desired only a few offspring had no need to resort to contraception before the end of the wife's fecund years.

Thus, as long as their ages at marriage remained high, labourers had no real opportunity to demonstrate whatever affinity for family limitation they might have had. When they were able to wed younger in the final decades of the nineteenth century, they displayed levels of family limitation not far removed from farming couples'. The timing of the onset of family limitation in the latter category suggests that landed proprietors preferred contraception to accepting the longer postponement of marriage forced on humble villagers. In short, in the terms introduced in Chapters Four and Five, the difference between farming and labouring families was as much one between neo-Malthusian and Malthusian fertility control as one between family limitation and natural fertility.

Family Limitation among Artisans

Because the artisanal categories were both more diverse and smaller, I do not analyse their fertility in as much detail. Nevertheless, similar patterns can be seen, with the Affluent and Substantial categories enjoying a considerable lead in family limitation over the run-of-the-mill crafts. Families who survived the crises in fishing and weaving lagged still further behind.

Because of the importance of brides' ages for the fertility of farming and labouring couples, I begin by examining the distinct shifts between cohorts and between occupational categories in entry into marriage. Brides establishing affluent or substantial families, and fishing families in eras when they too did well, averaged twenty-four years of age, two years younger than women forming craft families. By contrast, weavers' brides in early periods, and fishers' later, were much older (twenty-seven to twenty-nine).

These results accord with the tripartite analysis implicit in the discussion of Figure 7.4, according to which delaying marriage was associated with poverty, hard times, and femaleness. At all times, the better off categories wed younger than average, while the poor endured longer periods of celibacy. Hard times intensified those patterns, lengthening the delay of marriage disproportionately for those who had always wed older. As the economy turned down, more people were pushed into poverty, and the reinforced ranks of the poor bore almost the entire weight of the extra postponement of marriage. That is, an increase in overall average ages at marriage was achieved through a more hefty jump among the poor.

The jump was both voluntary and involuntary. The more numerous poor grew more cautious about forming a family. More important, they were subject to more searching scrutiny by the wealthy, who eagerly enforced prudence on others. The rich moved more slowly to discipline themselves, but eventually came to prefer the self-discipline of contraception to the imposed rigours of postponed marriage.

Gender intensified variations across occupations and over time. Women's ages at first marriage underwent wider swings than men's. In the first half of the nineteenth century brides' ages rose by more than grooms' ages, and later they fell even further. The first movement corresponded to the tightening of Malthusian controls, the second to their easing through neo-Malthusianism. Grooms' ages bunched more closely within cohorts.

In each occupational category grooms' ages deviated less from the population average than brides'. Labouring and weaving grooms were older than the average husband, but their wives had waited even longer relative to the average for women. Conversely, innkeepers and landed proprietors were younger than average at marriage, but the youthfulness of their womenfolk was even more outstanding. In other words, a bride's age was slightly more sensitive than a groom's to his own occupational category.[9] This regularity reflected the fact that marriage was a genuine economic partnership. Occupations were not characteristics of the husband alone, but of the couple, and even of the entire family. Because daughters inherited equally with sons, a husband's occupation was often determined by the assets his bride brought to the new family.[10] Because those assets helped to determine the age at which she wed, the association between husband's occupation and wife's age makes perfect sense.[11]

Occupation continued to relate to demographic behaviour after marriage, as Figure 7.5 illustrates. The second quarter of the nineteenth century saw a dramatic fall in age at second-last confinement among affluent and substantial couples. The fall continued at a reduced rate in the next two cohorts. The decline in the Craft category was at first more gradual, as average age dropped decisively only in the final quarter of the nineteenth century. At that point, however, it practically reached the level attained by the affluent and substantial. The sharp decline for Fishing after 1825 was partly due to the extreme value obtaining in the previous cohort. For the final seventy-five years ages stagnated with the fortunes of their enterprises. Advanced ages at marriage among weavers kept their ages at second-last birth high as long as there were sufficient cases to trace them.

Table 7.6 breaks these trends down to produce a fuller picture. For the larger categories, age at last birth followed the course made familiar by Figure 7.5,

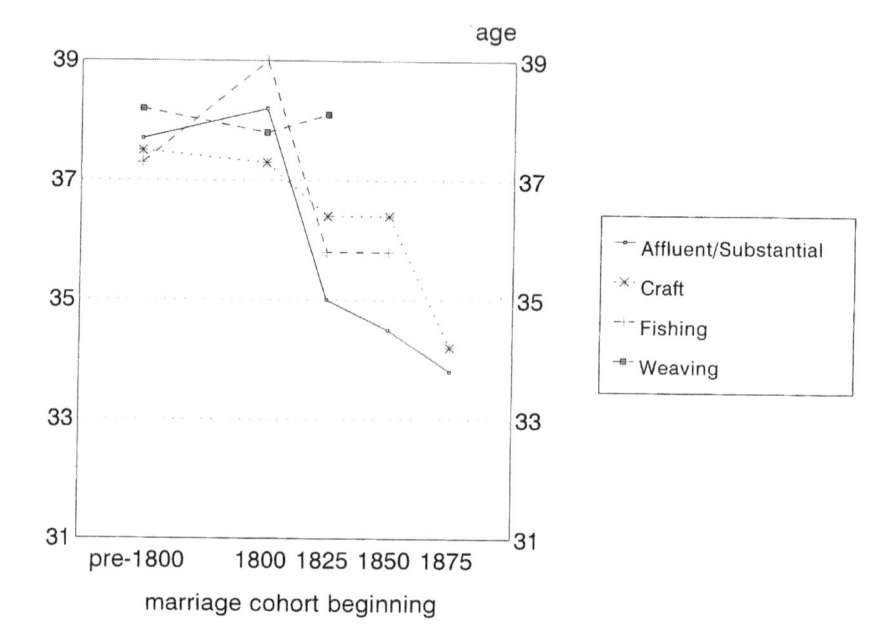

FIGURE 7.5 AVERAGE AGE OF WIFE AT SECOND-LAST CONFINEMENT IN DOCUMENTED COMPLETED FAMILIES IN ARTISANAL OCCUPATIONAL CATEGORIES, BY DATE OF WEDDING

TABLE 7.6
Average age of wife at last birth and Final birth interval, both in years, together with the Number of legitimate children in documented completed families in artisanal occupational categories, by date of wedding

Age at last birth	Affluent or Substantial	Craft	Fishing	Weaving
pre-1800	41.3	40.6	40.0	41.8
1800–1824	41.0	40.4	42.2	41.2
1825–1849	38.5	39.8	39.0	41.1
1850–1874	38.0	39.3	39.6	(36.8)
1875–1899	37.5	38.5	39.9	(38.7)
Change	–3.8	–2.1	–.1	–3.1
Final birth interval (in years)				
pre-1800	3.33	3.35	3.22	3.66
1800–1824	2.84	3.65	3.14	3.37
1825–1849	3.29	3.78	3.51	2.95
1850–1874	3.68	3.42	3.81	(2.64)
1875–1899	4.37	4.43	(4.20)	(3.73)
Change	+1.04	+1.08	+.98	1.08
Number of children				
pre-1800	6.3	5.2	5.9	5.3
1800–1824	5.3	5.2	7.9	4.6
1825–1849	5.2	5.9	5.5	5.3
1850–1874	5.2	5.5	6.2	(5.7)
1875–1899	6.6	5.7	6.0	(5.2)
Change	+.3	+.5	+.1	–.1

Notes
(1) Values in brackets are based on 10–19 cases.
(2) The Table is based on 1160 cases: 250 Substantial or Affluent, 537 in Crafts, 202 in Fishing, and 171 in Weaving.

declining consistently from the outset. Affluent and substantial couples posted larger reductions than craft couples until the final cohort. This trend was far less decisive for fishers, among whom extended final intervals were the only possible signs of family limitation. Still longer intervals characterized the first two categories at the end of the nineteenth century.

Whatever family limitation was present did not decrease the average size of completed families for any category as a whole. The affluent and substantial, who boasted the largest families in the eighteenth century, made some progress in this regard for the next seventy-five years, but their gains were wiped out in the final cohort. The other categories could not claim even this temporary success. The rise in underlying natural fertility boosted actual family sizes despite reductions in total marital fertility rates that continued to the end of the

118   CHAPTER SEVEN

Affluent or Substantial

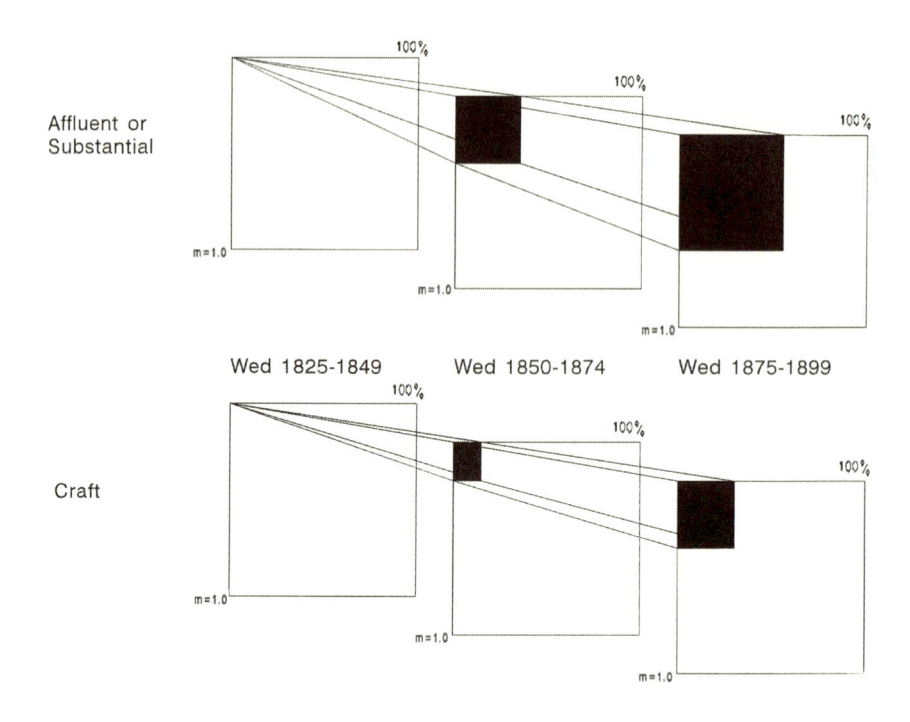

Craft

Wed 1825-1849   Wed 1850-1874   Wed 1875-1899

FIGURE 7.7 THE SHAPE OF FAMILY LIMITATION IN COMBINED AFFLUENT AND SUBSTANTIAL CATEGORIES AND IN THE CRAFT CATEGORY

century.[12] The wave of increasing fecundity that swept unresisted through most of the population swamped the minorities whose efforts at family limitation can be seen in the drops in age at last birth.

Changes in the m index of family limitation were rather more dramatic, as Figure 7.7 brings out.[13] For both categories, the third quarter of the nineteenth century saw a rise from suggestive but insignificant values. Moreover, in each case the shape deepens a bit faster than it widens. The biggest difference was that family limitation was more prevalent among the affluent and substantial in each cohort.

Indeed, the acceleration in family limitation took the affluent and substantial to values of m and the percentage limiting higher than those achieved by farming couples. Craft families, on the other hand, had two cohorts to reach the level labour attained in one. These results reaffirm the association between prosperity and family limitation.

OTHER OCCUPATIONS

The occupations still to be considered present a more variegated appearance. Because these residual categories were smaller, I do not treat their fertility in depth. Only in the case of Industry does their experience have important implications for my overall account. The spread of factory work helped to increase underlying natural fertility in the second half of the nineteenth century. A few comments suffice to place the other categories within the framework I have been developing.

The mobility of their members makes it especially hard to analyse the families classified under Menial, Order, Itinerant, and Petty. As seen in Chapter Five, they made their major contributions to fertility outside the realm of settled family life. Those who wed and left detailed traces in the records were unfamiliar with family limitation, as the average woman continued to bear children into her forties.

Much the same was true of couples engaged in commerce, at least as long as the villages contained enough families to permit serious study. Because Jewish dealers and traders dominated this category, its fertility followed theirs, holding at a high level until the emancipation of the 1860s.[14] The greater mobility of professionals and the diffuseness of their backgrounds make it even harder to pin down their fertility. Professional men wed late in their twenties, but they chose women younger than almost every other category. Perhaps because of the gap in spousal ages, they did not produce unusually large families.[15]

The demographic behaviour of holders of local positions differed only slightly from that of day labourers. Because their dual careers offered more security, both men and women wed a bit younger than their labouring colleagues. Under natural fertility, that meant larger families. In the second quarter of the nineteenth century, there were indications that some of them were adopting contraception, following the example set by the notables with whom they associated. However, that trend was not sustained. Decisive evidence of family limitation within this category comes only in the final cohort.

Because industry arrived in the villages after contraception, workers displayed the strongest family limitation of any category when date of marriage is disregarded. However, absolute levels were no different from those found among contemporary labourers. Workers differed from that category much as the holders of local positions did, in that they wed younger. Acquaintanceships struck up in the factory setting facilitated youthful marriage.[16]

An even more striking characteristic of industrial families was their large size. Despite considerable family limitation, women surviving to forty-five bore over seven children. However, these children also endured much higher mortality than most villagers. A closer look at this circumstance sheds light on the general rise in underlying natural fertility in the late nineteenth century.

Table 7.8 sets out the distribution of ages at death for children from two key occupational categories in the final cohort. Infant mortality rates were a third higher in families where the husband pursued an industrial or labouring career. In the case of the day labourers, the low percentage surviving to adulthood reflected greater mortality throughout childhood, but for workers the high death rates were limited to infancy. The total marital fertility rate and underlying natural fertility (M) were very high for both Industry and Labour. The lower part

TABLE 7.8
Mortality and fertility in documented marriages formed 1875–1899 and engaged in Industry, Labour, or neither

	Industry	Labour	Non-Industrial and non-Labouring
Children's ages at death			
Died before age 1	33 %	32 %	24 %
Died between 1 and 15	6 %	10 %	8 %
Survived to age 15	60 %	58 %	68 %
Total marital fertility rate	10.56	10.49	8.08
M	1.50	1.42	1.20
Average birth interval (excluding the last)	2.12	2.05	2.24
Number of children	7.2	5.5	5.4

Notes
(1) *Source: OSB Grafenhausen, OSB Kappel,* and *OSB Rust.*
(2) Children whose fates are not given in the OSBs are assumed to have survived to age fifteen.
(3) Birth intervals are averaged within families before being averaged across them.
(4) Because some husbands were assigned both industrial and labouring occupations, the Table is based on 724 marriages:
72 in Industry, 106 in Labour, and 546 in neither.

of the Table shows that births came more frequently to wives in these categories. The consequence was two extra children for the workers.[17]

The shorter birth intervals may mean that the higher infant mortality was not directly the product of general poverty, as the deaths of labourers' children between ages one and fifteen might be, but of curtailed breastfeeding.[18] Failing to nurse or weaning young contribute to infant deaths while also hastening, statistically, the resumption of ovulation and the arrival of the next child.[19] These practices might have been especially prevalent among the poorer inhabitants of the village, and so produced Table 7.8's occupational patterns. More generally, turning away from breastfeeding would shrink birth intervals and increase fecundity, both phenomena that have been observed for the villages as a whole. Such trends would account for the rising frequency of exceptionally large families, especially in Rust.

Rather different accounts are also conceivable. Higher mortality might have cut off breastfeeding by mothers who would otherwise have continued to nurse. That in itself would increase fecundity and lower the average birth interval. Alternatively, the arrival of several children in succession, whether permitted by the absence of breastfeeding or not, might increase infant mortality.[20] The numbers cannot decide alone between these speculations.

However, contemporary evidence on these questions supports the hypothesis of an independent decline in breastfeeding. The high infant mortality among children of factory workers was also noted by the county prefects. On six inspection tours of Rust between 1903 and 1914 they inquired into its cause.[21] Municipal councillors, nurses, the doctor, the priest, and the midwives all claimed that factory work diminished the care mothers provided their children. They called particular attention to the practice of putting infants out to be babysat while the mother returned to work in the factory. The exigencies of earning a living often ruled out the standard schedule of breastfeeding. The problem was compounded by the shortage, or maldistribution, of dairy cattle in Rust, which meant that milk had to be imported for workers' families. Even so, goats' milk was preferable to well water in a municipality that made no effort to install a modern sewage system. The absence of child care facilities and the draining effect of factory work on parents' capacity to nurture their children also came in for criticism.[22]

Thus, factory work for married women led to a decline in breastfeeding which in turn increased family size and infant mortality. These effects were strongest in poor families, who stood in greatest need of the wages wives could provide. Moreover, those households were least able to use their labour profitably outside industry. The cigar plants offered a way to fend off poverty, but only by accepting more births and more infant deaths.[23]

These trends account for some of the relations between occupation and fertility. Part of the rise in underlying natural fertility has been traced to a decline in breastfeeding, a decline which proceeded unevenly across social groups. Among industrial and labouring families, wage work for women was more common, and so they tended towards higher fecundity than women in more prosperous households. Moreover, the ease with which family limitation overcame the rise in underlying natural fertility in Grafenhausen is also clarified. Factory work penetrated each sector of the economy more slowly there, as married women—and men—made more attractive opportunities in agriculture. The insights generated by this discussion of factory work in Rust thus go well beyond that restricted topic.

Notables

Having passed in review each of the major occupational groupings, I now turn to groups based on status, or more narrowly to officers in local government. These notables differed from the mass of the population in several respects. In the eighteenth century they produced larger families than ordinary citizens. However, they were among the first to turn to family limitation, and drove their fertility down substantially in the middle years of the nineteenth century. Thereafter, their efforts slackened, and they blended back into the rest of the population.

Assessing the significance of these trends requires examining who rose to leadership within the villages. That in turn requires an understanding of the structure of municipal government. I therefore begin with a description of that structure.[24]

Within the Holy Roman Empire, each community exercised minor administrative and judicial powers. The court which heard petty cases in the first instance was made up of half a dozen men,[25] and presided over by the mayor. In theory, all power flowed downwards. Bearing, at least figuratively, a staff of office, the village mayor acted on behalf of the lordship and was responsible to it. Like the other members of the government and even holders of local positions, the court served at the pleasure of the sovereign, and offices were to be renewed each year.

In practice, members of the court enjoyed security of tenure except in the event of gross malfeasance or incompetence. In this regard their status matched that of the municipal clerk. As head of the local civil service, the clerk was in charge of the day-to-day business of the municipality. Recording commercial transactions and decisions of municipal bodies, together with keeping the village archives in good order, required literary, computational, and social skills. Experience was an asset in carrying out such tasks, and clerks tended to serve under lifetime contracts. The rights of members of the court were not as explicit, but they were sometimes enforced against the lord.[26]

Despite customs and regulations prohibiting close relatives from sitting on the court at any one time, it tended to function as a patrician oligarchy.[27] Occasionally, the lordship disrupted this arrangement by bringing in a newcomer as staffbearer rather than simply promoting a longtime councillor, but even this did not guarantee that its will was carried out. On paper, the subjects' only check on the lord's officials lay through the special representatives they elected, but disputes typically saw the local leadership and citizenry united against the outside world in all its manifestations. Citizens also exercised a certain amount of control through the election each year of one member of the court to act as treasurer. He supervised the collection of dues and taxes, and produced the municipal accounts.[28]

Under the more democratic systems of local government in nineteenth-century Baden, the central power exerted more authority than ever. Mayors, treasurers, and councillors were now chosen through direct or indirect popular elections in which each male citizen had a vote. To ensure stability, at least against pressures from below, the government insisted on long terms of office. Mayors were elected for nine years and councillors for six, while treasurers and clerks could serve as long as their work was satisfactory. The State reserved the right to appoint any candidate or unseat any office-holder. It was not shy about using those rights to secure political ends, most notably in suppressing the revolution of 1848.[29]

In general, offices continued to go to solid citizens with a stake in the community. Property holders were regarded as more responsible in maintaining order. Individuals with a high profile locally, thanks to wealth, prominence in a local guild, or wide family ties, were perennial candidates. In practice, established families contributed representatives to the municipal council each generation, except when some conflict so invigorated political life that partisanship over-rode tradition. Otherwise, status ran in families as much as occupation did.

Virtually all notable families have already been considered under one or more occupational categories, normally the better-off ones. Affluent, Professional, and Farming occupations were represented about twice as strongly among notables as among the entire population. By contrast, Crafts and Fishing were somewhat under-represented in government. That left virtually no positions for the remaining categories.

The hold of the affluent, professionals, and landed proprietors on local power reflected their generally high social standing, but there were also specific circumstances that made each of these categories more apt to lead. Considerable immovable property was required of responsible officers such as treasurers, so that the community could recoup its losses in the event of embezzlement or flight. Thus, only the wealthy were eligible for certain positions. The prominence of professionals derived additionally from their special expertise. In the 1700s, the schoolmaster, as one of the few residents who could write legibly as well as read and calculate, often doubled as court clerk. Even in the nineteenth century, the senior teacher was to fill in whenever the post of clerk fell vacant.

Other links between these categories reflected the lords' interests rather than the villagers'. It was convenient for an absentee administration to channel all its dealings with a territory through a single person. As a result, the man who was mayor often collected taxes, dues, and tithes.[30] Whether undertaken by an agent or by a tax farmer, such tasks required ready cash, and so wealthy innkeepers and peasants were favoured candidates. Conversely, financial dealings outside the village built up expertise, and brought rich and competent individuals to the attention of the lord. Since trade in tithed commodities and tax collection were among the most lucrative of early modern occupations, the ties between prosperity and local leadership were reinforced.

Their occupational distribution accounts for the unusual marriage patterns found among notables. They wed two years younger than the average villager, younger than members of any occupational group. Their headstart was at first just as large among men as among women. That testifies to the unusual youthfulness of notable grooms. In addition, male notables married slightly more often than the rest of the population.[31] These patterns reflected the attractiveness of a match with an eminent lineage, as well as the greater social and economic responsibilities that went with such status.

Notable men joined in the postponement of marriage common to all nineteenth-century villagers. Moreover, their ages were still rising at the end of the nineteenth century (to twenty-seven). The average age of first-time brides, on the other hand, fluctuated only slightly, remaining less than a year from 23.5 in all cohorts. Couples aware of family limitation did not shy away from marrying young, and those subject to natural fertility were in a position to support large families in any case.

The coincidence of economic and political leadership carried over into demographic behaviour. Comparison of the ranks of the notables and the group stopping young suggests that notables practised family limitation in greater numbers than the general population. This relationship emerged only after the eighteenth century. Before 1800, the governing élite represented about the same proportion in the young group as in the general population (10 % vs. 12 %). In the nineteenth century, by contrast, notables were encountered twice as frequently among youthful stoppers as among the populace at large (16 % vs. 7 %). Yet this relationship grew weaker at the end of the 1800s.

The graph in Figure 7.9 shows that these trends were also evident on a larger scale. The initial fall in age at second-last confinement was the earliest and steepest of any category considered thus far. The lead over the rest of the population widened for two cohorts, but then closed abruptly. This convergence reflected not merely a substantial drop in the ages at which ordinary citizens stopped childbearing, but also a regression on the part of the notability.

More complete statistics confirm these phenomena. Even in the eighteenth century, notable women ceased childbearing almost one year younger than other villagers, but that was simply a consequence of their substantially earlier start. From 1825 on, both age at last birth and final birth interval altered as family limitation caught on, and together reduced completed family size. However, in the final cohort all values swung back in the direction of natural fertility.[32]

This reversal contrasts sharply with the experience of ordinary citizens. Despite the general increase in underlying natural fertility (M), total marital fertility rates declined for almost all occupational categories. Even the day labourers

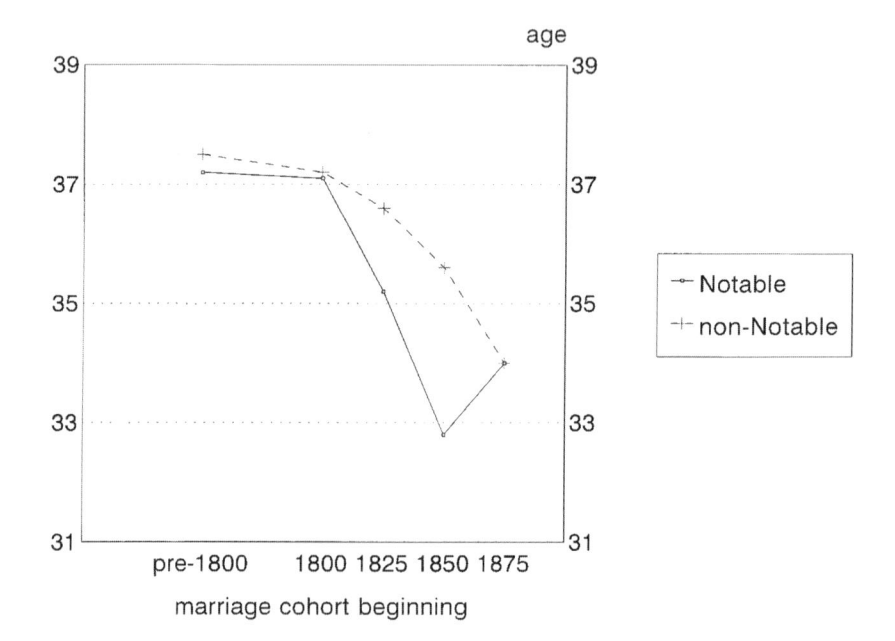

FIGURE 7.9 AVERAGE AGE OF WIFE AT SECOND-LAST CONFINEMENT IN DOCUMENTED COMPLETED FAMILIES, BY STATUS AND BY DATE OF WEDDING

and factory workers whose wives curtailed breastfeeding posted reductions in average age at last birth. Yet notable fertility jumped by more than a quarter across the board between the final two cohorts.[33] Since notable wives were least apt to supplement the family income by working in the plants, one must look to political developments to understand this shift.[34]

The shapes of family limitation in Figure 7.10 clarify both the early lead among the notability and the later regression. Notable couples were distinguished by width[35] rather than length.[36] They soon added depth. Their jump in m to .54 for the third quarter of the nineteenth century outdid every occupational category. Sharp increases took place in each of the villages, including Kappel.[37] Contraception was therefore not unknown within Kappel's élite, however resistant the rest of the population may have proven.

The slackening in family limitation among notables wed in the final quarter of the nineteenth century was a function of width rather than depth. m rose a bit more in this cohort, but all other measures showed strong trends in the other direction, as has been seen. Notables retained a slight lead as far as the shapes in Figure 7.10 are concerned, but the days during which they led their citizens towards family limitation were clearly over.

One of the striking features of the notability was that at the end of the nineteenth century family limitation was equally strong among families of municipal

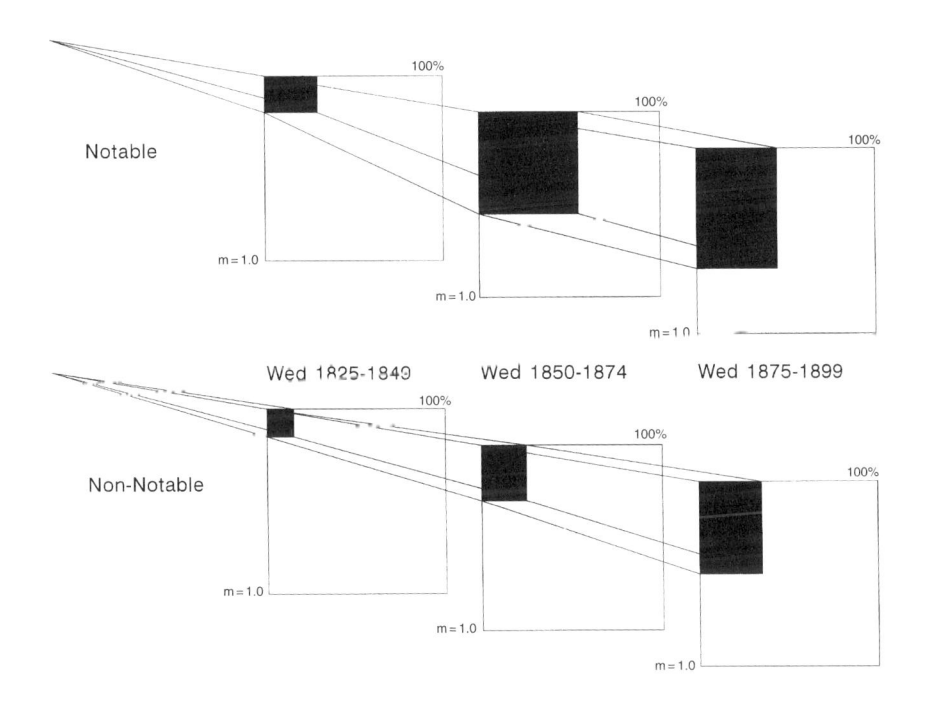

FIGURE 7.10 THE SHAPE OF FAMILY LIMITATION BY STATUS

officials in Grafenhausen, Kappel, and Rust. This similarity suggests that local élites shared common habits across the three villages. In other words, being a village leader was a far better predictor of one's fertility than which village one led. Common status over-rode the differences between villages detailed in Chapter Six.

The same cannot be said for occupation. Figure 7.11 reveals clearly that villagers with different occupations were far more alike than occupational categories from different villages were.[38] At the end of the nineteenth century, every occupational grouping in Grafenhausen had a higher m value than every one in Rust, and each of their values in turn exceeded those for all of Kappel's occupations. These differences were roughly as large as those between the entire villages. In addition, there was no strong or consistent pattern of differentiation among occupations. For example, day labourers lagged behind in Grafenhausen, but not in Kappel or Rust.

Even where membership in an occupational category seemed to outweigh the influence of home village, the results can be interpreted in a way which re-emphasizes the importance of the latter. The families classified under Petty, Itinerant, Order, and Menial did show affinities which transcended their origins. For the most part that simply meant statistical fluctuations within the

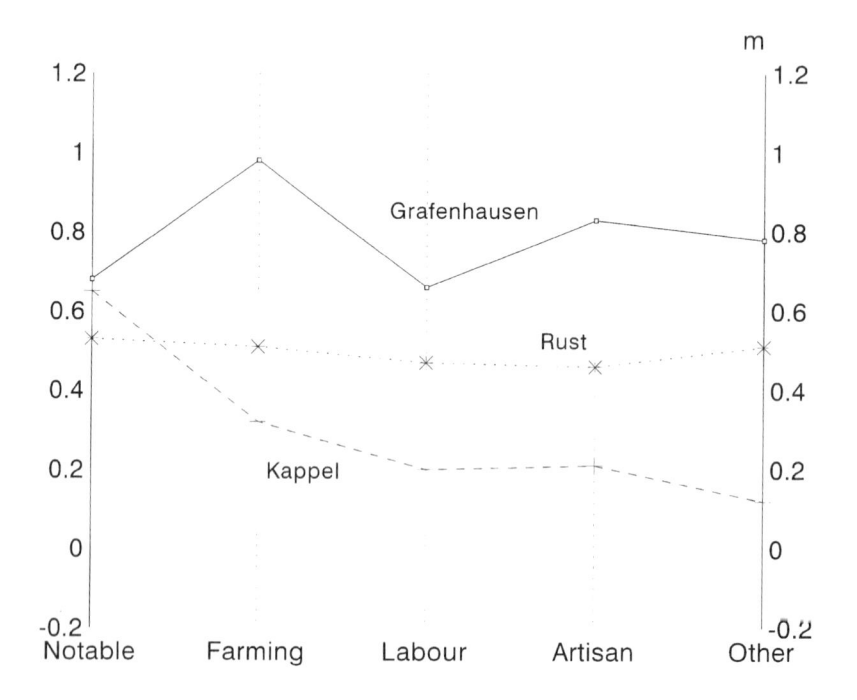

FIGURE 7.11 M INDEX OF FAMILY LIMITATION IN DOCUMENTED MARRIAGES BEGINNING 1875–1899 ACCORDING TO OCCUPATION AND STATUS, AND BY OSB

European range of natural fertility. The more numerous professionals and dealers also diverged somewhat from the surrounding population, the former by practising family limitation only in an spotty way, the latter by adopting family limitation late but at a high level. However, it was precisely these categories who, because of greater mobility or religion, had the least identification with their municipalities of residence. It was not so much that social forces broke the bonds of locality, as that those bonds were not very strong in these categories to begin with.

In any case, for most couples locality mattered more than occupation. Figure 7.11 shows that differences in occupation or occupational structure simply do not account for differences in fertility between villagers and between villages. However, it should not be thought that this chapter has shed no light on demographic behaviour. For example, the coming of cigar-manufacturing plants has been seen to have raised infant mortality and underlying natural fertility.

Moreover, significant differences were uncovered in the speed with which occupational categories took up family limitation. Although they did not maintain their early leads, landed proprietors, the affluent, and substantial artisans all displayed strong family limitation well in advance of the general population. Moreover, along with the local notability, they practised contraception more assiduously for most of the nineteenth century. One prominent characteristic these groups shared was wealth. Its relations to fertility are explored directly in the next two chapters.

Notes

1. In the eighteenth century this proposition is true simply if no couple practised family limitation. Even at the end of the nineteenth century it stands to reason that the young group includes some anomalous cases, thanks for example to extended jail terms or typographical errors in the OSBs.
2. This trend is partly compositional, for the overall percentage Farming increased with time. Nevertheless, the magnitude of the initial rise among the young group (to 90 % in Grafenhausen from 1850–1874) and the significant fall in Labour show an independent occupational effect.
3. After family limitation began, Labour made up just 5 % of the occupations of the young groups in Grafenhausen and Kappel, and 10 % in Rust. In earlier cohorts, it accounted for 28 %, 16 %, and 18 % respectively.
4. Labour made up 19 % of Kappel's occupational distribution, the highest percentage of the three. Because labourers there were often assigned another occupation as well, they actually encompassed almost a quarter of the families.
5. Standard deviations for age at second-last confinement were roughly equal to those for age at last birth. A two-year drop or gap corresponds to three standard deviations in the smaller sub-populations reported in this book.
6. There are tentative indications in the m values for the first two nineteenth-century cohorts (.24), that family limitation was not entirely absent among labourers before 1875. Because they were not sustained and because they are contradicted by other indices, including the percentage limiting (9 % in 1800–1824), that trend is not depicted in Figure 7.3.

128   CHAPTER SEVEN

7. Charles Tilly, "Demographic Origins of the European Proletariat", in David Levine (ed.), *Proletarianization and Family History* (New York, 1984), 42–43 operates on the opposite view. His second reason proletarians would wed young, that they reached maximum earning capacity sooner, may fail where that capacity was low.
8. Compare Smith, "Reflections", 83–84, 96. The gap had been just over two years before 1800, but labouring brides' ages increased three and a half years in the next two cohorts while landed brides aged by less than one year. In the next section, I explore the significance of the greater responsiveness of brides' ages to occupational differences.
9. Reflecting on similar findings, Knodel ("Transitions", 354) pronounces them "noteworthy", seemingly "inconsistent with our [Oedipal] understanding of the traditional European marriage pattern", "intriguing", and "clearly deserving of further investigation".
10. In keeping with the analysis that closes Chapter Four, it might be the amount of land one wife held that made her husband a landed proprietor rather than a day labourer, and the bakery another woman stood to inherit that made her sweetheart a baker, and so on.
11. Had this not been so, demographic adjustments to economic conditions would have been much less efficient. That brides' ages responded more strongly than grooms', especially to poverty, reflects the fact that women tended to wed younger than men. There was therefore more room for their ages at marriage to rise when they found themselves in straitened circumstances.
12. For instance, M for the affluent or substantial jumped to 1.23 among couples wed between 1875 and 1899 following two cohorts at 1.1.
13. Because of the small number of weaving and fishing families in the final cohorts, those categories are not depicted.
14. The fertility of Jews as such is covered in Chapter Eleven.
15. Some professional couples may have begun to practise family limitation in the second half of the nineteenth century, but there are too few cases to draw any definite conclusions.
16. This tendency should not be exaggerated. At twenty-six overall (twenty-five in the final cohort), brides of workers were younger than contemporaries who chose craftsmen or labourers, but farming, affluent, and substantial brides were younger still. The same intermediate placing had characterized weavers' brides in earlier centuries.
17. Labourers' families were smaller because they wed old.
18. For what they are worth, surveys relying on midwives' diaries reported that 95 % of 252 newborns in Grafenhausen, Kappel, and Rust in 1886–1887 were breastfed by their mothers. This percentage was a bit higher than the county averages reported by the health officer from 1884 through 1896–1897. GLA 236/15840 and GLA 236/15841.
19. See John Knodel and Etienne van de Walle, "Breast Feeding, Fertility and Infant Mortality: An Analysis of some Early German Data", *Population Studies*, 21 (1967), 109–131, John Knodel and Hallie Kintner, "The Impact of Breast Feeding on the Biometric Analysis of Infant Mortality", *Demography*, 14 (1977), 391–409, John Knodel, "Breast feeding and population growth", *Science*, 198 (1977), 1111–1115, or almost anything from Knodel's pen.
20. The parents' attention would be that much more divided, and communicable diseases would spread that much more quickly.
21. The following remarks are based on the reports on the 1903, 1905, 1907, 1908, 1909, and 1914 inspection tours of Rust (St A LA Lahr 3454). The references to factory workers cover the wives rather than the husbands on whom Table 7.8 was based. Three-quarters of the families of those male workers came from Rust.

22. The need for child care for workers' families had been mentioned as early as 1889 (visitation report in Ord A B4/10504).
23. These speculations bear on larger controversies concerning the significance of wage labour. Some (such as Shorter, *Making*, 248, 259–264) have argued that by removing traditional restraints, including poverty, and exposing people to a value system stressing self-gratification, capitalism promoted a new style of family, held together by bonds of love between mother and child. The experience of Rust's workers does not sit well in that framework. It may be that the early factory system did not allow quite as much scope for self-fulfilment as this theory postulates, or that the new world proved just as confining in certain respects as the old. (For a version of this interpretation, see Louise Tilly, Joan Scott, and Miriam Cohen, "Women's Work and European Fertility Patterns", *Journal of Interdisciplinary History*, 6 (1976), 470–473.) However, it is also possible that it was precisely a new economic and social individualism that led to relative neglect of children. Concern for individual interests, narrowly defined, might as easily prompt rejection of family responsibilities as affirmation of the nuclear nest. Shorter (*Making*, 269 and following) has in fact postulated just such a trend for later periods.
24. Compare the more general account in Jerome Blum, "The Internal Structure and Polity of the European Village Community from the Fifteenth to the Nineteenth Century", *Journal of Modern History*, 43 (1971), 556–562.
25. Women did not serve on government bodies or run municipal affairs during the periods with which I am concerned.
26. See Chapter Ten for the example of Michel Ott.
27. Compare Sabean, *Property*, 38, 48, 69.
28. The position customarily rotated, but when villagers found a champion they sometimes stuck with him. Rusters in 1789–1791 refused to replace their treasurer, heedless of the lord's ostentatious solicitude for their long-term interests. GLA 229/90539.
29. See Chapters Ten to Twelve for this and other examples.
30. BvB A U. 910 (agreement between lord and mayor in Rust in 1770).
31. One quarter of notable marriages involved a groom who had already been wed, while the corresponding figure for the population at large was just 18 %.
32. Between 1850–1874 and 1875–1899, average age at last birth rose from 36.5 to 37.5, final birth interval fell from 4.51 to 3.75 years, and the number of legitimate children rose from 4.9 to 6.9. In all, there were 303 documented completed families of notables.
33. Their total marital fertility rate rose from 7.12 to 8.92 children, while M rose from 1.05 to 1.38.
34. Compare the speculations of Jacques Houdaille, "La Population de Remmesweiler en Sarre aux XVIIIe et XIXe siècles", *Population*, 20 (1970), 1187–1188. In the three Baden villages, a major part of the trend was compositional, as groups with less affinity for family limitation took over municipal office. The break was especially sharp in Kappel, where the liberal élite was ousted wholesale as the Centre party rose to power. At the same time, the emergence of new sources of income may have reduced the incentive for the wealthy to control the size of their families. In Rust for example, the change coincided with a general deceleration in family limitation among the rich. Detailed discussion of these matters is postponed until the relations between fertility, wealth, and politics have been more fully explored in Chapters Nine and Eleven.
35. That family limitation was so much wider than it was deep suggests that the estimate of the percentage limiting was misleadingly buoyed by low ages at marriage.
36. Indeed, their m value for 1825–1849 (.19), although greater than that registered by the ordinary citizens (.15, significant by virtue of their greater numbers), was not quite significant statistically. I show it none the less to make the point about width.

37. In the nineteenth century, notable m there fell below .6 only for the 1850–1874 cohort, which saw the religious and political ferment described in Chapter Eleven. (The small numbers involved expand the confidence ellipses.)
38. Because my purpose here is heuristic, Figure 7.11 includes some quite small populations.

8

Fragmentation and Accumulation

This Chapter develops the methodological tools needed to investigate relations between economics and fertility. I present a theory linking greater wealth and stronger family limitation, and refine it to permit testing. I then analyse the economic structures of the villages, emphasizing differentiation within their populations as well as contrasts between municipalities. An extended comparison of Grafenhausen and Kappel reinforces this analysis and sets the stage for Chapter Nine.

Conclusions reached in earlier chapters point to the significance of landed wealth for the fertility transitions in Grafenhausen, Kappel, and Rust. Grafenhausen, where family limitation was adopted early and massively, was distinguished by a higher ratio of cultivated land to population. The percentage of its inhabitants described as landed proprietors was even more out of line. Furthermore, over all three villages the farming category practised family limitation earlier and more intensively than most other occupational groups in the middle years of the nineteenth century. The strong leads opened up by notables and by the small affluent and substantial categories constituted exceptions that proved the rule. Those very groups tended to possess extensive assets of all kinds, including real estate. An association between landed wealth and family limitation would render intelligible these less fundamental correlations.

THE REFINED MORCELLEMENT HYPOTHESIS

In interpreting these results as they emerged, I have alluded to theories attributing deliberate restriction of fertility to fear of excessive fragmentation of the family holding. Since this chapter and the next test such views from several angles, I present an explicit account of this morcellement[1] hypothesis before proceeding further. Briefly, it has been an academic commonplace since at least the time of Frédéric Le Play[2] that partible inheritance established a close association in the minds of rural householders between family size and the fortunes of future generations, and that one natural response to this observation was to restrict the former in the interests of the latter.

The mathematics of the situation are clear enough. Whenever the quantity of land to be inherited is constant, and the number of inheriting offspring exceeds the number of parents from whom they might inherit, average holdings fall. If sustained, even a slight surplus of heirs over parents sharply reduces assets. Limiting reproduction counteracts this tendency. That much is generally recognized. More important here are a number of assumptions and auxiliary hypotheses which usually remain implicit in discussions of this model.

The idea that the current population should take thought for the living conditions of its descendants is seldom felt to need justification, and indeed will not receive much examination here.[3] However, before such dispositions can affect behaviour in the manner hypothesized, at least two related attitudes must be present. First, the well-being of the next generation must be seen as something that can be balanced against other desiderata.[4] Such utilitarian calculation may be innate in humans, or in the ways in which they describe their behaviour, but in so far as it is not, the rural environment fostered the required states of mind in any case. Determining the appropriate amounts of seed, labour, or fertilizer to devote to one or another parcel of land, experimenting with new crops, buying and selling at rural markets, all favoured the emergence of a canny temperament accustomed to weighing alternatives in a hardheaded fashion.

It is particularly noteworthy that agriculture required balancing interests over time. Sacrifices in the form of increased effort or postponement of consumption were made good only in the future.[5] Moreover, investments of time and money did not guarantee the desired payoff, although the relationship was reliable enough statistically to entice all peasants to a greater or lesser extent. As this last observation brings out, there were considerable variations in the confidence with which villagers took risks and in the sorts of risks they took. The agrarian histories of individuals and communities predisposed them to participate in this Benthamite world to different degrees.

A brief digression may make the point more concrete. Consider Grafenhausen's venture into tobacco marketing described in Chapter Three. Its late nineteenth-century inhabitants could look back on several generations of forebears who had grasped eagerly at innovations and prospered as a result. Their confidence and solidarity enabled them to strive together to make the market work for them through their cooperatives. Readers will recall how they resisted the blandishments of urban merchants, holding products back from sale until a preset higher price was offered, and eventually processed part of the crop themselves, thereby earning returns well above their neighbours'. When one considers the psychology involved, one is not surprised to find that the same discipline and deferred gratification characterized villagers' sexual behaviour.

Yet at least some measure of surprise is called for. Applying this sort of calculation in the bedroom requires a further conviction, namely that contraception is both feasible and appropriate. The latter position, at least, cannot be presumed to be universal. It is true that common sense, reinforced if necessary by country life, from the breeding of livestock to the sowing of seed in furrows, would have encouraged villagers to recognize the efficacy of abstinence and withdrawal in preventing conceptions,[6] were they to have considered the question seriously.

But that is just the point. Practical and ideological controls on sex and childbearing functioned precisely by contrast with the unfettered expression of impulse within marriage.[7] Active awareness of power to limit marital fertility went hand in hand with regarding it as a legitimate option, a goal to be preferred and vigorously prosecuted.

A model which presents family limitation as a response to economic interests should include some account of the origins of this mentality. In short, appeals to general theory are not sufficient to bypass the subject of popular attitudes and consciousness. The scope which economics allows to individual decision-making and cultural norms does add another dimension to the picture of village life, but giving a full history requires broadening that dimension still further. Establishing this claim of course involves seeing just how far economics alone can take the demographic historian. I now return to that task.

In examining the experience of these three villages for links between wealth and fertility, one should note a few natural refinements to the model sketched above. First, assessments of wealth apply most appropriately to an entire lifetime. To be rich is not to possess much for an instant, but to store up treasure over the long term. Conversely, to be poor means more than to lack assets at a particular moment. That little property was assigned to individuals in childhood, adolescence, and old age does not make all of them poor; rather it means those are inappropriate times to measure wealth. Because of this, and because this book focuses on marital fertility, I limit attention in what follows to the holdings of married men.[8] Even the experiences of that group were not limited to the progressive division and fragmentation of holdings. On the contrary, accumulation and consolidation were much more typical of their adult lives.

Adding a temporal dimension to economic careers brings out another shortcoming of standard accounts of morcellement. One alternative response to population pressure that threatened to divide holdings to an extent deemed unacceptable by their owners would be to reduce the period of time any single individual enjoyed maximum control over property. This might take the form of postponing marriage or disconnecting entry into marriage from accession to a livelihood.[9] The same result could be brought about by earlier retirement. Either method would permit more people to be supported from the same amount of land in the style to which they had become accustomed—albeit for a shorter time.

Other options which this sort of model generally neglects also merit attention. As more people come to occupy an area of cultivated land, the ratio of land to mouths can be maintained either by incorporating more land into the community or, where additional land is more distant, by sending part of the population there. Without migrating, a greater part of the population might take up handicrafts or invest more time in such by-occupations. The political and economic relations that determine the part of agricultural production assigned to the actual tillers of the soil might be challenged and altered. Such moves need not involve any great dislocation of agricultural practices. Moreover, qualitative changes, such as intensive cultivation and even industrialization, could also break the bottleneck which conventional theories of morcellement take for granted.

The failure of such theories to consider these possibilities makes it harder to apply them to concrete situations. On the one hand, presenting such courses of action as options would mean highlighting individual and social choices. As I have argued above, this would undercut the model's reliance on narrow economics, and with it much of its attractiveness. In addition, demonstrating that approaches other than family limitation were not viable in a particular case would complicate the account considerably.[10] This is especially true of Grafenhausen, Kappel, and Rust, where Chapters Two through Five showed the villagers using all these techniques and more to cope with population growth. Overly simple theories are ill-equipped to disentangle the complex web of challenge, choice, and response.[11]

For instance, it is by no means clear where morcellement theory would have one look for innovation within a differentiated peasantry. It might be maintained that the hypothesis does at least rule out family limitation among the absolutely landless. It would be more accurate to state that the theory makes no claims about such groups, since landlessness might equally distinguish rich families, in towns for example, who simply did not invest in real estate. Be that as it may, the issue is moot, for virtually no couple in Grafenhausen, Kappel, or Rust was literally landless.[12]

As far as family limitation by landed peasants is concerned, explanations in terms of fear of fragmenting holdings are, if anything, too versatile. For instance, the richest proprietors had the most to lose, in both material and psychological terms, from division of their assets. However, they also possessed the resources to support large families, and even splitting those resources many times would still leave them well above any literal margin of subsistence. Smallholders whose plots could not maintain families of the customary size might equally be argued to have no interest in family limitation and to have the strongest interest. On the one hand, they might have lost hope of climbing back to self-sufficiency. On the other hand, only by consolidating the family fortunes could their descendants regain the independence of their ancestors. Moreover, as even these sketches of reasoning indicate, personal and group evaluations of what was customary, adequate, or desirable could vary.

What this means is that an explanation for the inception of family limitation can be offered within the model regardless of which groups were involved. A theory with so many successful predictions can claim no credit for any of them. It therefore behooves me to tighten up the argument somewhat. In what follows, I attempt to establish a refined morcellement hypothesis to the effect that the rich took the lead in practising family limitation. Especially when concentrating on its spread, I emphasize the rôle played by the moderately rich, rather than the very rich.

In testing such a theory, one must be wary of at least two factors that could produce artefactual results seeming to support it. The first takes the reasoning of the morcellement hypothesis a step further. If the hypothesis is correct, then children of marriages whose fertility was reduced for any reason became richer. If that pattern of behaviour were continued by those offspring, they too would produce fewer children without necessarily being prompted to do so by their wealth. This would set up a misleading association between rich families and small families.

Second, it should be remembered that family limitation might appeal more to the rich for reasons only indirectly related to economics. As outlined in Chapter Four, the Malthusian repertoire of late entry into marriage and continence outside it sufficed to keep fertility far below any hypothetical biological maximum. Chapter Seven showed this was especially true of the rural poor, who typically postponed marriage until their late twenties. In contrast, youths with enough assets to support a new household went on to produce considerably more children. In the event of a general shift in preference towards smaller families, it was primarily this latter group who needed to submit to new controls. Put another way, the point is that to reach any particular low target number of children, rich couples had to do something new and extraordinary, while poor ones might carry on as they always had.

The preceding argument holds independent of inheritance systems or reflections upon them, and so provides a new reason to look to the rich, albeit this time the very rich, to take the lead in limiting family size. However, it can readily be adapted to fit morcellement theory. Couples who wed old produced few children, and even fewer survived to claim a share of the inheritance. Such families, by and large poor ones, had less fear of dividing the holding too far. The reverse was true of the rich. With these possibilities in mind, one can see that only a very special set of findings could confirm the refined morcellement hypothesis over its rivals, friendly and unfriendly.

I trust that I have not so far reduced the credibility of this sort of theory as to convince readers that testing it is nugatory. Fully undoing its tenacious appeal requires more extensive efforts than I can muster here, and in any case I do mean to end by bolstering it after a fashion. The value of that exercise can be gauged by noting that despite its popularity, there is little empirical evidence for this model, in Germany at least.[13]

The most methodologically sound study deals directly with the region in which the three villages are located. Hermann Schubnell compares the sizes of the families of established peasants and near-landless workers in the Rhine plain and the Black Forest using data from the 1933 census.[14] He carefully takes into account the far more intensive agriculture of the first area, differences in age at marriage, changes over time, and a number of other complicating factors.

Schubnell's results for the Rhine plain show that the larger the holding, the smaller the proprietor's family. In the Black Forest, where impartible inheritance was the rule, the pattern was reversed. On the plain, the decline in family size across cohorts wed from 1880 to 1923 was least pronounced for the best-endowed families, but this was because they were considerably smaller to begin with.

Schubnell sees a pattern in which the very rich were the first to practise family limitation, followed by the merely rich.[15] Although the predominantly urban families of cigar makers whom he also studies were the smallest of all, that reflected advanced ages at marriage rather than greater family limitation.[16] Despite the considerable local variations within his data,[17] Schubnell's findings are striking, and justify more detailed examination of the region and of the years before 1880.

So far in this section I have linked economics and demography by reviewing selected results from earlier chapters, introducing a refined theory of morcellement, and surveying some salient literature. I turn now to specific reasons for tying prosperity to family limitation in these villages. In particular, I look at the percentages of rich couples among those chosen in Chapter Six for youth at second-last birth. Couples with above average holdings were encountered only slightly more often among the young families in the natural fertility cohorts than they were in those cohorts as a whole.[18] However, in each village the rich dominate the young groups following the turn to contraception. This relationship is strongest in the first cohorts to practise family limitation and recedes in Grafenhausen and Rust at the end of the nineteenth century.[19]

These results dictate pursuing this inquiry further. Couples apt to be practising family limitation were indeed wealthier than other villagers. They were also better off in a relative sense than their counterparts in earlier generations who were less prone to family limitation. These relationships were neither strong nor enduring, and so care will be required in investigating them.

The Land Market

I begin my examination of economic structure by recalling Figure 4.3, the graph of the average landholding career. Although typically low in endowments at marriage, couples could look forward to decades of increasing wealth and an extended plateau near their maximum. For perhaps half a century, the average couple experienced accumulation, with fragmentation reserved for old age.

Naturally, all careers did not match Figure 4.3 exactly.[20] Some villagers never possessed even the fractional holdings typical of young men, while others exceeded the average by considerably more than the 38 % that marked the highpoint of aggregate experience. The shape of the curve, however, is the same for rich and poor.[21] Regardless of absolute levels of wealth, villagers built up their holdings in the first decades of their marriages and nurtured them to a height in their mature years, before relinquishing them in old age.

These patterns of accumulation and divestment were the result of purchase and inheritance. In most of what follows, I stress the latter, but the former should not be neglected entirely. For instance, just over half the documented claims to land in Grafenhausen in 1727 were based on purchases.[22] Clearly, there was a thriving land market at all times.[23]

Opportunities to acquire control over land arose in a number of ways. Individuals migrating between villages to marry or to establish a new business often disposed of their local assets before leaving. Families prompted by straitened circumstances, political peril, or wanderlust to seek their fortunes abroad did likewise. Indeed, both local and central governments limited mobility until assured that the fees migrants were assessed would be covered, along with back taxes and debts.[24] The goods of emigrants were commonly auctioned off, either beforehand to raise the funds necessary to travel or afterwards in confiscation for illegal emigration.

Individual parcels might also be sold to meet small debts. Wealth could be dissipated in other ways as well. In 1901 the county prefect claimed one alcoholic was literally converting his assets from solid to liquid.[25] However, the more usual course was first to take out a mortgage on pieces of property or use them to secure a loan.[26] Such a move might simply presage a sale, as there were natural limits to the number of times one could pawn one's holdings in this fashion.[27]

As has become clear, the availability of money was crucial to property transactions in the rural economy. With coin hard to come by, credit became almost as valuable as land. This increased the economic leverage of those whose everyday businesses and salaries blessed them with cash.

Affluent individuals took advantage of their good fortune in a whole range of ways. On the one hand, they built up their own holdings, with the result that innkeepers and people of substance often possessed the most extensive tracts of land. Strangers to the area, including doctors, clerics, teachers, and officials, preferred to invest in their hometowns or to acquire scattered pieces of property throughout the region.[28]

The cash they had on hand also allowed them to stake other villagers to purchases, and this may have been an even more important basis for their social prominence. By standing surety, offering loans, or taking on mortgages, they made it possible for landhungry but cashpoor households to acquire more land. If the labour of those households had previously been underemployed, both parties could benefit from such transactions. However, the abundance of labour and the scarcity of cash promoted relations of dependence. For the most part, the needy looked to better-established family members or to long-time patrons for assistance, and this mitigated or at least regularized that dependence.

Auction records in Grafenhausen give a more concrete idea of the dynamics of land transfers. Documents concerning the disposition of the assets of would-be emigrants have been preserved in a number of cases. Two come from the year 1844,[29] and so the bidders may be compared with the landowners in an 1843 tithe register.[30] Auctions were held in two sessions a week apart. In the interim, information circulated concerning the pieces of property at stake, including their assessed values and the current high bids. This protected the seller's interests by keeping prices in line. Purchases were to be paid off in four equal annual instalments at five percent interest. Each purchaser had to be backed by a guarantor, who ensured payment.

Some forty-two sales were finalized in the two auctions. The parcels went to thirty-nine different bidders, but only twenty-seven villagers stood surety. More than a quarter of the buyers were unmarried men and women who were staked by their fathers. According to the register the previous year, the remaining purchasers already possessed almost one-quarter more assets than the average married man. Quite a few were backed by a brother or brother-in-law, whom they might in turn stand behind in a later bid.[31] Sibling guarantors were generally not as well off. This suggests that to compete, some extended families treated the auction as a joint venture. The other guarantors were even richer than the purchasers, as their holdings were assessed at more than one-and-a-half times the average.

To some extent the rôles of the affluent grew directly out of their social positions. Auctions were typically held in inns, for example, and it was natural to turn to the proprietor for support when the bidding got heavy. The greater involvement of the rich in public life also brought them opportunities. The municipal officials who presided over the auction, including the not necessarily wealthy clerk who recorded the proceedings, appeared repeatedly as guarantors. Clearly, to succeed bidders required access to the resources of family or patrons.

The small scale of the local auction illuminates relations within the citizenry. The results show the importance of cash even in that egalitarian setting. When villagers sought funds on a broader scale, they were often forced to look outside the community. Table 8.1's examination of mortgaging in Rust, where it was most widespread, brings home once again the significance of money.

Because many villagers did not own outright the land they tilled, Table 8.1 provides a solid picture of the sources of rural credit. The existence of a mortgage did not always signify that a commercial transaction had taken place. On the one hand, the many outside institutions represented in Table 8.1, notably pension and scholarship funds, dealt with the village as investors only. On the other hand, the far more numerous plots devoted to the maintenance of the church or the poor were generally acquired through donation rather than purchase. Nevertheless, over time those holdings were valued primarily for the surpluses they generated for the beneficiaries.

Indebtedness could be a sign of investment by the debtor as well as the creditor.[32] Mortgagors included large families who sought access to as much land as possible to maximize the average return on their labour, agents who were rapidly paying off the mortgages on the businesses they ran, and entrepreneurs with connections beyond the village which they used to bring in cash to finance their other projects. Such families might already be well off or they might be making progress towards that state. In addition, mortgages held within a family,

Fragmentation and Accumulation

TABLE 8.1
Distributions of Holders of mortgages and Mortgages held in Rust in 1827, by the character, location, and occupation of the mortgagee

	Mortgagees	Mortgages
Local institutions	5 %	17 %
Institutions outside Rust	24 %	25 %
Local persons		
Farming	3 %	8 %
Other occupations	4 %	2 %
No occupation	8 %	3 %
Persons outside Rust		
Aristocrat	10 %	14 %
Professional	6 %	5 %
Government official	6 %	7 %
Commercial	6 %	6 %
Other occupations	7 %	5 %
No occupation	22 %	10 %
Absolute total	142	443

Notes
(1) *Source*: Gem A Rust C IV/46 through Gem A Rust C IV/50.
(2) All mortgagor-mortgagee relationships are weighted equally, i.e. no allowance is made for the number, size, or value of parcels.
(3) "Other occupations" locally are: innkeeper, trader, tailor, and mason. "Other occupations" outside Rust are: peasant, innkeeper, postmaster, saddler, shoemaker, tailor, hosier, brazier, and tanner.
(4) Those with "no occupation" locally include the unmarried, heirs, children, and relatives. Outsiders whose occupations were not specified include adults from places without OSBs.
(5) Professional occupations are: doctor, teacher, minister, rabbi, and dean. Government officials are: prefect, auditor, and counsel to the grand duke. Here, "Commercial" occupations are: merchant, trader, and furrier.

possibly as part of an inheritance settlement, said little in themselves about the relative economic standing of the parties. Thus, the significance of the debt to a mortgagor varied considerably.

The interests of the other party to the transaction were generally clearer, as a second look at Table 8.1 brings out. Although a smattering of mortgagees were relatives and even young heiresses, such individuals generally entered into only a single transaction each. By contrast, a handful of local magnates held mortgages on numerous parcels worked by other villagers. Note the almost perfect counterpoise within the category of local persons. Those with no occupation predominated among such mortgagees, while landed proprietors held the bulk of these mortgages. These adult male mortgagees were indeed the village élite, for they possessed in their own right five times as much land as the average. This reinforces the impression of a concentration of wealth with important social and economic consequences.

So far, the results are broadly in keeping with those turned up in Grafenhausen's auction records, once allowance is made for the greater equality there. The non-Rusters appearing in the lower half of the Table add another dimension to the analysis. Here too the distribution is quite uneven. Many outsiders whose occupations could not be determined held but one mortgage. Quite possibly they represented distant branches of the family, and so occupied a position parallel to the local heirs'. In contrast, those whose occupations were specified in the register typically held several mortgages each. They rise above the local mortgagees in both wealth and social standing.

Most had enjoyed some connection with Rust at one point or another. Merchants trading over long distances and urban businesspeople who drew raw materials from this region easily developed contacts with needy villagers. Salaried professionals and government officials stationed in the vicinity became acquainted with economic opportunities and had the resources to take advantage of them. Aristocrats such as the Böcklins and Berstetts had holdings of their own in Rust, and family or institutional ties brought in still others. In all these cases, creditors tended to be both geographically and emotionally distant. In consequence, their relations with villagers were primarily economic.

The prominence of these outside investors indicates that few residents were in a position to buy land on a large scale. Most entered the land market only through their families or on behalf of relatives. A small group did enjoy considerable success by converting its rare cash assets into real estate. Yet affluent and substantial villagers were unable to meet the demand for credit, and outside capital was drawn in along all the networks that linked the community to the wider world. The relations so engendered drew off the surplus produced by local labour, and thereby perpetuated the situation. These patterns were not substantially altered until the rise of rural credit unions at the end of the period under study.

Both the theoretical account of the importance of cash and these two sources indicate that it took money to make money. Yet the growth in villagers' assets with age was so strong that it could not have been financed by simply reinvesting the profits earned from the small plots with which they began. The foundations of their fortunes must therefore be sought elsewhere. As it turns out, inheritance provides the key to understanding Figure 4.3.

The Lifetime Career of Landholding

Together with the patterns of purchase just described, inheritance customs accounted for the rapidity with which property changed hands. Without even considering the impact of leasing and other devices for transferring the use of land but not title to it, one can see that the landholding system was quite flexible.[33] In consequence, fluctuations in ownership took place easily. This point merits emphasis, as early modern rural society is often described as static. Actually, the landscape could become a dizzying kaleidoscope as parcels whirled first this way and then that.

A single example illustrates the possibilities. In 1727, as the Grafenhausen land survey was being renewed by establishing the occupants of all parcels and the bases of their rights over them, a dispute broke out over a half-acre.[34] One claimant had married first in Grafenhausen, but had been living with his second wife in Kappel for over twenty years. He had retained almost as much property in Grafenhausen as he had acquired in Kappel, making him one of the richest peasants in either village. He based his argument on an entry in a 1683 register which is no longer extant, but which presumably assigned the plot to one of his parents.

However, it turned out that the parcel had been sold at least once within Grafenhausen, and then to the mayor of neighbouring Orschweier, at whose death in 1707 it passed to his married daughter. Her husband in turn exchanged it for some vineland in Altdorf—which borders Orschweier but not Grafenhausen. (See Map 3.2.) That transaction brought the land into the hands of a day labourer whose incomplete family history can be traced in Kippenheim (a town again one tier away from Grafenhausen) and Grafenhausen. At his death in Grafenhausen in 1724, it came to his widow, who was ultimately credited with it in the 1727 survey. Presumably she held it until her death in 1742, also in Grafenhausen. Not all of the three thousand parcels in the survey enjoyed such an active career, but the countryside was clearly a much livelier place than it is sometimes made to appear.

The marriage strategies engendered by partible inheritance had direct consequences for the relationship between wealth and fertility. Each villager was acquainted with the division of assets among heirs and saw how large families broke up the holdings painstakingly amassed over a lifetime. Those who married down could halt their fall only by working harder or by restricting the number of their offspring so that each would have a larger share of the smaller inheritance. Thus, the basics of morcellement theory were familiar to villagers.

Considering the analogy of a rural marriage market brings out other channels along which a desire to limit family size could arise and spread. As noted in Chapter Four, when individuals desire to find spouses for themselves and their children who are as rich as possible, there is a tendency towards intermarriage between similarly situated families. Having fewer siblings improves the chances of poorer villagers in such a competition. Moreover, if some families begin to employ that strategy, their rivals feel pressure to follow suit. Where wealth is distributed evenly, the pool of potential partners—and hence the range of couples to whom family limitation appeals—is correspondingly wide. Under the right circumstances, there is general recognition that the chances of one's children in making a match are a function of one's own fertility. These reflections add theoretical weight to the refined morcellement hypothesis.

With these points behind me, I am in a position to return to the landholding patterns of Figure 4.3. Underlying the graph by age (or by years married) is the similar curve representing parental mortality. Because villagers wed before their natural parents and those of their spouses had all died, they spent their first years of marriage in control of far fewer assets than eventually came their way. Only as the older generation died off, one at a time, did a couple's holding expand to its full extent. It stabilized at that level for a number of years, and declined only with the death or serious physical incapacity of a partner.

These relationships were so tight as to be taken for granted by village common sense. Figure 4.3 shows a gradual increase as the aggregate experience, but for individuals the death of each parent signified a substantial accretion of resources. Over a lifetime, entitlement moved upwards in four great leaps. When the fortunes of individuals or couples were assessed by themselves or by the rest of the community, these underlying potentials loomed large.[35] As will be seen, I endeavour to have them determine the placement of couples in my analysis as well.

The longitudinal pattern of Figure 4.3 has significant implications for the interpretation of the cross-section one encounters in a single source of economic information. Consider for a moment the couples assigned fewer assets than average in a survey or tax roll. For some of them this was a straightforward measure of their lifetime prospects, for they would never rise to even mediocre levels of wealth. A few, on the other hand, were retired, possibly enjoying a modest income from investments made at a time when they had disposed of considerably greater resources. Even more could look forward to inheriting large holdings once their surviving parents relinquished them.[36] The apparently poor were thus a heterogeneous group.

This phenomenon was accentuated by demographic factors that make it particularly important for my analysis. Recently formed marriages are always numerous, for they have had less chance to dissolve through the death of either spouse. They therefore predominate among the poor at any given point. Because their poverty is deceptive in many cases, these newlyweds distort any examination of economic standing. This compositional effect becomes especially serious when the introduction and spread of family limitation are being investigated. The new patterns of behaviour grew more popular as time passed, and so were more prevalent at each stage among younger couples. Thus, apparent poverty and affinity for family limitation were confounded in an entirely artefactual way.

My resolution of this problem grows out of a reconsideration of the trends revealed in Figure 4.3. In the early stages of a villager's landholding career, differences between rich and poor families mattered less, for most assets were still controlled by the previous generation. Old age likewise functioned as a great leveller. Only in the intervening period did differences in wealth show through clearly. Therefore, the way to obtain accurate measures of long-term wealth is to restrict attention to couples whose property was recorded during that intervening period.

It seems logical that the chance of detecting villagers whose assets rose above the average was greatest in the age-groups whose wealth as a whole was at least average.[37] From the graph, this means looking at the holdings credited to men who had wed for the first time fifteen to forty-five years before the date of the source. Those poorer than average at that time tended to be poor throughout their lives. By the same token, those who were ever richer than average were apt to be so at that stage in their careers. Making due allowance for the vagaries of individual cases, one may conclude that restricting attention to "mature" marriages, meaning those in which the husband had been married between fifteen and forty-five years, permits the clearest demarcation of rich and poor possible with the data.[38]

The fact that property typically did not change hands at the marriage of the children, but rather later, at the death or retirement at advanced age of the parents, plays a significant part in the analysis of landholding undertaken below. This fact also has important consequences for the structure of arguments linking wealth and fertility, for it shows that the influence of the former was only prospective. Couples with surviving parents by and large did not receive their full inheritances until their childbearing years were practically complete. In particular, villagers destined to be rich achieved that destiny only when they were well into middle age. Until that point, they were not that much wealthier than other villagers, on average. In so far as their demographic behaviour differed from their neighbours', they were not responding directly to existing economic circumstances.

Now, the link between inheritance and wealth was so strong as to be obvious to all. Thus, apparently poor villagers who were to become rich were well aware of that fact and could act accordingly.[39] Still, even where a villager's reactions to the prospects of wealth were customary or unconsidered, economic forces acted only indirectly. Moreover, this book focuses precisely on a switch from customary patterns of behaviour to conscious consideration and planning of fertility. Against such a background it is salutary once again to stress psychology rather than raw economics.

For the moment, I remain concerned with economic realities. Until one's parents or one's spouse's parents died—or one's father or father-in-law turned seventy or more—one could not count on acquiring substantial property. This lag means that an investigation of the significance of landholdings cannot rely on evidence concerning the assets of most villagers while they were under age forty. Looking instead at the older generation, one can see that the best time to ascertain a man's fortune extended into his sixties, provided he survived that long. Paradoxically, then, assessing the impact of wealth on fertility requires measuring wealth at a point when fertility was zero. In what follows, I do just that, first for several selected points in the history of Grafenhausen and Kappel, and then in more detail for each of the villages in turn.

Grafenhausen and Kappel Compared

The contrasts between the population histories of Grafenhausen and Kappel make it particularly appropriate to examine more closely the economic structures of these adjacent villages. For centuries their inhabitants laboured side by side, sharing the fortunes and misfortunes of weather and soil, war and politics. That their responses to these apparently uniform circumstances diverged so far reflected in part the different social organizations with which they confronted them. Originally, Grafenhauseners of all stripes tended to possess more land than Kapplers, and land of slightly better quality at that. Moreover, these assets were distributed far more equally in Grafenhausen than in Kappel. This equality endured even as holdings shrank over the eighteenth and nineteenth centuries.

Claims like those made in the preceding paragraph are difficult to establish. Sources of economic information are rarely reliable, systematic, or consistent enough to permit an assessment of the global characteristics of the distribution of wealth or of trends over time in one location, let alone two. Fortunately, Grafenhausen and Kappel shared administrative history as well as geography.[40] At several points, the authorities ordered land surveys for both villages in accordance with a common methodology. Three such surveys, from 1727–1728, 1842–1846, and 1877 have survived.[41] In all three cases, the proprietors of each parcel of farmland within the municipal boundaries were noted, and so it is possible to analyse the data in parallel fashion.

The average holding of a Grafenhausener was initially more extensive than that of a Kappler (4.73 hectares vs. 3.61). Over 150 years, holdings in both villages shrank, but the decline was sharper and more sustained in Grafenhausen. By 1877 the average holding there was just 1.78 hectares, as against 2.11 hectares in Kappel. The figures for mature marriages show that these differences were not produced by variations in age at marriage or life expectancy, but rather represented genuine features of the economic structures of the villages.[42]

The greater value of land in Grafenhausen to some extent counterbalanced the more rapid fragmentation of holdings there. Comparing the 1842 and 1846 registers shows that although the average couple possessed only 5 % more land than its counterpart in Kappel, its land tax assessment was 19 % higher. The surplus was in part a measure of the more extensive improvements that had been made in Grafenhausen. Right at this time, in the course of negotiating the amount required to redeem the tithe, Church authorities insisted that their rights in Grafenhausen covered some of the best land in all of Baden.[43] Even in 1877, many parcels of land in Kappel were part marsh. For this comparison, however, I simply take land as land. Regardless of its quality, increasingly less was available to the average couple.

In part these results are a function of the number of married men among whom the land was divided. As the number of husbands in Grafenhausen climbed further above that in Kappel, their average holding tumbled. Developments in Rust, which boasted a larger population throughout, are consistent with this reasoning. From an already low 2.74 hectares in 1759, average holdings in Rust fell to 2.07 ha. in 1827, and were hovering around 1.55 ha. in the 1870s and 1880s.[44] On an aggregate basis, both Grafenhauseners and Kapplers were considerably better off.

However, the distribution of landholdings within the population is a more important characteristic of an agrarian community than their average size. In this case, the trends confirm the fragmentation of property, but at the same time bring out a significant contrast between the two villages. In both communities, the percentage of large holdings diminished. This decline was most marked in Grafenhausen, so that its considerable advantage in the frequency of holdings over five hectares in 1727 was reversed 150 years later. In 1877 the percentage of such great enterprises in Kappel was still three-quarters what it had been in 1728 (17 % as opposed to the original 23 %). Over the same period it was cut by a factor of five in Grafenhausen (to 9 % from 43 %).

Underlying this transition were more enduring features of the distribution. Grafenhausen's initial clustering at the highest level did not come at the expense of the middle category (one to five hectares), which was almost as large as in Kappel.[45] Instead, Grafenhausen was the home of fewer landpoor families. Only 21 % held less than one hectare, as against 34 % in Kappel. Thus, the greater prosperity was shared widely within Grafenhausen's population. This commonality of condition persisted over the centuries, as the fragmentation of holdings increased the middle category more than the lowest one. In 1877, 61 % of holdings in Grafenhausen fell between one and five hectares. At all times, then, landed property was distributed more uniformly in Grafenhausen than in Kappel.[46]

A 1902 inquiry into grain marketing[47] suggests that modest differences between the villages persisted into the twentieth century. It classified villagers in accordance with ideas stirred up by early social discussions of the agrarian question. The instructions limited the focus to grains destined to be made into bread, and thus ignored the cash crops so prominent in this area of intensive agriculture. To the extent that traditional accounts of the transformation of natural economies into commodity economies are inadequate, the approach loses force. The results are nevertheless of some interest.

They indicate that turn-of-the-century Grafenhausen was the home of a few more non-agricultural families (9 % vs. 6 %). These are described as officials, teachers, and pensioners, as well as smallholders and workers growing only fodder crops and vegetables. Thus, they were not necessarily poor. Poor families who had to purchase grain to supplement their own production were encountered equally frequently (15 %) in the two villages. At the other end of the scale, slightly more Grafenhauseners (51 % vs. 45 %) produced surplus grain which they brought to market or sold to bakers, millers, and brokers. Like the study of landholdings, the survey of grain marketing finds that economic differences between the villages were diminishing at the very time that demographic contrasts were approaching their peak.

Other measures continued to show greater prosperity in Grafenhausen, and even suggested that its lead over Kappel was growing. When the old land tax assessments based on 1828–1847 prices were replaced at the turn of the century using 1895–1899 prices, Grafenhausen's overall tax bill increased 39 %.[48] The rise in Kappel was just 33 %, despite the extensive irrigation projects that had been undertaken there.

Taxable income per head is far from satisfactory as a measure of the living standards of rustics who did not depend solely on traceable earnings. Nevertheless, trends in that variable provide insight into the pace of agricultural improvement. In 1885, taxable income per head was 11 % lower in Grafenhausen than in Kappel, but by 1909 the relationship was reversed. In the intervening years, the figure for Kappel grew by an impressive 65 %, but in Grafenhausen it more than doubled. These increases largely reflected the earnings to be made from livestock and crops such as tobacco. If one were to judge from these figures alone, one would be forced to conclude that Grafenhausen's qualitative advantage endured until at least the end of the period under study.

For my purposes, the longstanding disparities are more important. The trends uncovered thus far can be interpreted fairly straightforwardly in terms of the agrarian histories of the two villages presented in Chapters Two and Three. Moreover, that interpretation fits rather well into the refined morcellement hypothesis. Together, the two promise to illuminate the fertility of both sets of villagers. The strengths and weaknesses of this account are instructive.

The eighteenth century brought an end to an era of devastation and periodic depopulation on the Rhine frontier. At first at least, the abundance of land attracted settlers. Grafenhausen's acquisition of the lands of Reichenweier (see Map 2.2) helped to lift holdings there well above the regional average. Much of Kappel's land, on the other hand, was marsh or other terrain unsuitable for cultivation by the techniques of the time. It provided a reserve for later expansion.

This geographic safety valve proved a mixed blessing. As time passed, population growth and partible inheritance combined to cut holdings again and again. Grafenhauseners responded by intensifying their exploitation of the land, introducing new crops and crop rotations, while the municipal government developed the infrastructure to maximize returns for the citizenry. Such changes were slower and less far-reaching in Kappel, because the natural constituency for improvements was smaller. No innovation could have made the petty holdings of the numerous labourers viable, while the great landholders were slower to feel the economic pinch. In any case, the day of reckoning was postponed by mere quantitative expansion, as the lands west of the Elz were reclaimed.[49] (Again, see Map 2.2.)

Against this background, differential fertility becomes intelligible. With no opportunity to extend their holdings, large numbers of Grafenhauseners were pressed towards living standards for themselves and their children that they considered unacceptable. Alive to qualitative changes that might relieve the pressure, they endeavoured to acquire the same control over themselves that they were exercising over the natural world. In Kappel, less urgency was felt, and less imagination and confidence were brought to bear. The extension of Kappel's farmland roughly kept pace with population increases—less emigration—in the mid-nineteenth century. The continuing high proportion of the smallest holdings suggests that the rich benefitted most from this expansion. In any case, there were fewer families of the less rich but still solid variety so prevalent in Grafenhausen. All these circumstances dulled the cutting edge of change in Kappel.

This sort of reasoning was not foreign to villagers then or later. Albert Köbele, himself a Grafenhausener, portrays Kappel's socio-economic history in many of the same terms. I do not endorse all his speculations, but the sketch is worth quoting at length.

> But only after the correction of the Rhine could the territory to the west be increased, parcel by parcel, through reclamation. Because fishing declined more and more at this time, Kappel became a purely peasant village. In the second half of the last century, this development reached its high point. The largest part of the landholdings was at that time in the hands of a relatively small number of richer peasants. The division of property, which through the practice of partible inheritance, still dominant here to-day, always hindered the formation of larger holdings, was not so extensive at that point. The social differences between the various strata within the village population appeared more clearly then; the contrast between peasant and fisher may have been sharper than one can imagine to-day.[50] In consequence, the poor and usually also childrich families were forced from earliest youth to eke out a bare existence as domestic servants, as farmhands and maids.[51]

Although here large families are linked to poverty, on the previous page he writes more broadly of

> the noteworthy treasuring of children which always distinguished Kappel above all surrounding localities.[52]

In short, when Grafenhauseners looked at Kappel, they saw social polarization and big families.

Because the villages varied so widely in family limitation and in the distribution of landholdings, it makes sense to analyse relations between rich and poor within a single village. There are also practical reasons for adopting the village as the unit of study. Relatively few sources of economic information permit direct comparisons between villages in the same year. The diversity of the data, even for a single village, calls for a more refined technique. In what follows, I divide mature marriages into rich and poor along a line drawn at the average value for each measure of wealth.[53] A couple's position is therefore assessed by an ongoing comparison against its peers. Such an evaluation reflects more closely the economic, social, and psychological realities of contemporaries.

Since this extensive digression on economic matters has at times taken me rather far from the themes introduced in the opening sections of this chapter, I summarize the findings to be applied in the substantive discussion in Chapter Nine. The basic point is that there was considerable differentiation within the peasantry at all times. Purchase and inheritance acted to maintain that inequality as well as to set bounds to it. On the one hand, the economic system benefitted those who already controlled substantial resources. On the other hand, few families fell all the way into pauperism.

Economic inequality presents a complex face in other respects as well. Both the absolute level of wealth and its distribution within the population varied from village to village. There were, however, strong universal trends growing out of shared customs of inheritance. As the generations passed, morcellement proceeded apace. Even in lineages that maintained their ranks in the social hierarchy, the raw resources available to successive couples dwindled steadily.

The lives of individuals were dominated less by the menace of long-term impoverishment than by the lifetime advance of landownership. The road to complete control of one's inheritance was a long one. Not until their fifth, sixth, and seventh decades did couples enjoy full economic independence. Even then, the vagaries of mortality, personality, weather, floods, and a thousand other natural shocks affected the fortunes of each villager differently.

Economic structure emerged from the overlaying of all these forces. Analysing it therefore proceeds by stripping them away one at a time. Statistical methods smooth out the anomalies of individual experience. Restricting attention to mature marriages abstracts from the process of inheritance to give a reliable summary of landholding careers. Comparing assets to those held on average controls at the same time for the increasing division of property and for the increasing productivity of land. Finally, the interplay of economics, social organization, and psychology that produced patterns specific to each village must be studied in that context.

Notes

1. From the French for cutting into small pieces, as the multiplication of heirs ate away the holding.
2. Frédéric Le Play, *On Family, Work, and Social Change* (Chicago, 1982), 278 (original 1855).
3. My data do not add much of substance to the inchoate debates between partisans of sociobiology, feminism, behaviourism, and the rest, over the origins and significance of such parental instincts. For my purposes it does not matter whether the actual concern was for the family business, or for the family name, or merely for one's own position in a society which officially valued those things. I shall accept without further argument that villagers preferred, ceteris paribus, a world in which their children were richer, or more respected, or happier.
4. Compare "fertility must be within the calculus of conscious choice", the first of Ansley Coale's three prerequisites for a major fall in marital fertility. "The Demographic Transition Reconsidered", in *International Population Conference Liège 1973* (Liège, 1973), 65.
5. This might have eased the move to consideration for the fate of one's enterprise and one's family.
6. Compare Greer, *Destiny*, 138, which does not continue as I do.
7. Later, the same attitude that everything is permitted within marriage nurtured contraception.
8. This approach is defended in Benz, Thesis, appendix D.
9. In so far as they had been connected to begin with.
10. Compare Rudolf Andorka, "Un exemple de faible fécondité légitime dans une région de la Hongrie L'Ormànsàg à la fin du XVIIIe et au début du XIXe siècle: contrôle des naissances ou faux-semblants?", *Annales de Démographie Historique*, 1972, 38. He is less guarded elsewhere ("Birth control in the eighteenth and nineteenth centuries in some Hungarian villages", *Local Population Studies*, 22 (1979), 41–42, and "La

prévention des naissances en Hongrie dans la région 'Ormansag' depuis la fin du XVIIIe siècle", *Population*, 16 (1971), 74–75) about endorsing morcellement theories (and many others). Ironically, a similar eagerness to backdate family limitation leads David Gaunt ("Family Planning and the Preindustrial Society: Some Swedish Evidence", in Kurt Agren (ed.), *Aristocrats, Farmers, Proletarians* (Uppsala, 1973)) to an overhasty rejection of interpretations invoking morcellement.

11. Compare Kingsley Davis, "The Theory of Change and Response in Modern Demographic History", *Population Index*, 29 (1963), 345–366.
12. Appendix D of Benz, Thesis documents this in detail.
13. In his review of the German fertility transition, Knodel (*Germany*, 125–130, 232–239) notes only a few studies bearing directly on the issues involved, and those tend to run against the hypothesis. Census material from 1939 revealed that those with larger tracts of land generally had *larger* families and were slower to reduce the number of their offspring. Among Breslau householders in 1905, family size fell as rents increased, but house owners had more children than the groups paying high rents. (R. Manschke, "Beruf und Kinderzahl", *Schmollers Jahrbuch*, 40 (1916), 1876–1881. Manschke was arguing for the importance of wealth on grounds other than the morcellement hypothesis.) Other studies deal only with aggregates, or use proxies in place of wealth.
14. Hermann Schubnell, *Der Kinderreichtum bei Bauern und Arbeitern* (Freiburg, 1941), 111–120 in particular.
15. All those he considers peasants possessed more land than the average inhabitant of Grafenhausen, Kappel, or Rust.
16. Average family size in both groups was cut in half over the period. (The later marriages were not yet complete in 1933. This truncation affects all groups, not necessarily equally.)
17. Schubnell's samples of peasants and workers enjoyed practically identical fertility in each of the three villages under study here. Grafenhausen: peasants—3.4 children/marriage, workers—3.3; Kappel: peasants—4.9, workers—5.2; Rust: peasants—6.0, workers—5.5. Calculated from ibid., 187, 191.
18. Rich couples were just one-tenth more frequent among the young than among all marriages meeting the criteria for selection in Grafenhausen and Rust under natural fertility, and two-tenths more frequent in Kappel. The somewhat higher value in Kappel is compatible with some couples there limiting family size out of economic considerations even before there is evidence of family limitation on a global scale. I take up this speculation in Chapter Nine.
19. For the family limitation cohorts as a whole the relative frequency was 1.3 in Grafenhausen and Rust, and 1.6 in Kappel.
20. For instance, many men were still unmarried in their early twenties, while others died well before becoming senior citizens.
21. It also applies, within a year or two, to all three villages and all marriage cohorts.
22. The calculation covers 1184 parcels (of 2989 in Gem A Grafenhausen C VII/1) whose provenance is specified. It overstates the proportion of purchases because inherited holdings were less open to question. In addition, the unsettled conditions of the previous half-century (described in Chapter Two) had promoted the alienation of property.
23. That market appears to have been dominated by kinship, along the lines documented for Neckarhausen by Sabean, *Property*, 368–369, 391, 412–413.
24. See the paperwork surrounding the moves of two Grafenhauseners to Rust in 1813, when both villages were under the same administration, in Gem A Grafenhausen B XIV/798.
25. St A LA Lahr 2130 (report on inspection tour of Grafenhausen).
26. For the reasons explained in Chapter Two, selling the land and working as a wage labourer, even at market rates, made less sense.

27. In 1827, 10 % of Rust's married male landowners had mortgages on every piece of their property. (Calculations based on Gem A Rust C IV/46 through Gem A Rust C IV/50.)
28. Because these assets are difficult to trace, the true wealth of these groups is greatly understated when attention is restricted to local holdings, as in most of this chapter. However, when information is available on income, the wealth of professionals and the representatives of the State shows through clearly. Benz, Thesis, appendix D shows that in late nineteenth-century Kappel investment income was negative for all occupational categories but Professions and Order.
29. Gem A Grafenhausen B XIV/799 and Gem A Grafenhausen B XIV/800.
30. Gem A Grafenhausen C I/10.
31. On patterns of alliance between brothers and brothers-in-law under partible inheritance, see the Württemberg example in Sabean, "bees", 171–186.
32. In "Die Lage der bäuerlichen Bevölkerung im Grossherzogthum Baden", in *Bäuerliche Zustände in Deutschland* (Leipzig, 1883), 286–289, Adolf Buchenberger, later Baden's minister of finance, repeatedly makes this point in arguing that in most areas rural indebtedness did not constitute a crisis.
33. Bernard Derouet ("Famille, ménage paysan et mobilité de la terre et des personnes en Thimerais au XVIIIe siècle", *Etudes rurales*, 86 (April 1982), 47–48, 54–55, and "différentielle", 3, 22–33) also associates partible inheritance and flexibility.
34. Gem A Grafenhausen C VII/1 (folio 211). The account there is supplemented by information from entries in the Grafenhausen, Kippenheim, and Mahlberg-Orschweier OSBs.
35. In assessing ability to pay fines, nineteenth-century officials customarily inquired not only how much the convicted possessed, but also how much they had to hope for in future inheritances. Gem A Grafenhausen C VIII 2/1 (individual cases 1839–1843). Compare a marriage-minded economist inquiring after lifetime earning potentials or permanent income streams.
36. In practice, they might even be working that land already.
37. My approach aims to make one qualitative distinction within the population, between rich and poor. Finer gradations, say separating out those with holdings over double the average, would require looking at still more limited age-ranges. More generally, it is not possible to employ regression analysis on these economic data. That one family held two and a half times the average at a time when another held one and a half times the average says nothing about which was richer over the long term, let alone by how much. Nor does learning that these figures represented the maxima observed for these two families help, unless they were both observed every year that their marriages endured. My data are that detailed only in Kappel from 1872 to 1902, where the prevalence of natural fertility makes sophisticated statistical manipulation less valuable.
38. Limiting consideration to mature marriages uncovers differences in fertility between economic categories that remain hidden in the mixed statistics for all marriages. See Benz, Thesis, appendix D. Using more than one source refines the accuracy of this method. All marriages observed fifteen to forty-five years after the husband first wed are classified as rich or poor using the maximum value of their wealth. Anomalous values between, say ten and twenty years married or forty and fifty years married, then do not matter provided some other observation is available in which the true wealth of a couple shows through. This further purifies the economic categories. To preserve comparability, I do not classify as either rich or poor any marriage which was never observed in a mature state.
39. Anticipating one's inheritance ran risks. A parent who lived to a ripe old age without incapacity—or an impulse to share—might deprive a child of property for much or even all of his or her life. In practice, the statistical regularities of mortality among

a couple's four parents and the emotional and economic ties between the living generally ensured that a family enjoyed some semblance of the standard of living it had anticipated.
40. This practical consideration accounts for the near-exclusion of Rust from the remarks that follow.
41. Gem A Grafenhausen C VII/1 (99 cases from 1727 of which 47 were mature), Gem A Kappel C VII/2 ii (95 cases from 1728 of which 35 were mature); Gem A Grafenhausen C I/10 (245 cases from 1842 of which 109 were mature), Gem A Kappel Tithe register (215 cases from 1846 of which 110 were mature); Gem A Grafenhausen C VII/3 (299 cases from 1877 of which 148 were mature), Gem A Kappel C VII/3 (226 cases from 1877 of which 119 were mature).
42. From an initial advantage in 1727–1728 of 6.42 hectares over 5.21 hectares, Grafenhauseners in mature marriages fell to rough equality with Kapplers in the 1840s, and then to a deficit of 2.27 hectares as against 2.81 in 1877. These numbers provide a more realistic idea of the sizes of individual farming operations. If anything, they are still too low, for they make no allowance for leasing.
43. Ord A B4/3753 (letter of 22 March 1845). The tithe-payers refused to concede this and the Church acquiesced. Ibid. (letters of 26 April and 2 May 1845).
44. Gem A Rust C I/6 (1759 renewal of tax rolls). Gem A Rust C IV/46 through Gem A Rust C IV/50 (1827 land register). Gem A Rust B XIII/311 (bundles of property slips from 1872–1883).
45. 36 % of Grafenhausen's mature marriages, 43 % of Kappel's. Relative to all marriages, this category was larger in Grafenhausen.
46. An 1873 agricultural census that took account of leasing reported that 71 % of agricultural households in Grafenhausen controlled over 1.8 ha., but the figure for Kappel was only 57 %. (In Rust it was a mere 48 %. *Beiträge zur Statistik der inneren Verwaltung des Grossherzogthums Baden*, 37 (1878), 94–95.) On the other hand, no striking contrast emerged when the larger holdings were compared. The census's findings were thus more in keeping with the older distribution than with the patterns in the 1877 surveys. Because of the contrasting methodologies involved, not much will be made of these differences here. Evaluations of the 1873 census can be found in Buchenberger, "Lage", 243–245, and in Hecht, *Landwirtschaft*, 35–37.
47. Gem A Grafenhausen B XV/811 covering 356 families and Gem A Kappel B XV/713 covering 290 families. The term "family" ("Familie") in the original corresponds to "household" ("Haushalt") as used in the German censuses of the period. (Hecht, *Landwirtschaft*, 66.) Hecht, who instigated the research, provides an extensive discussion of the results by county (ibid., 60–86), on which parts of the following are based.
48. This and later figures are derived from Hassinger, *Tabakbau*, 31–36, 51, 55, 57.
49. Compare the logic of the frontier advanced by Rudolf Andorka and Sandor Balazs-Kovacs, "The Social Demography of Hungarian Villages in the Eighteenth and Nineteenth Centuries (With Special Attention to Sarpilis, 1792–1804)", *Journal of Family History*, 11 (1986), 169–192.
50. This association of fishing with poverty is incorrect. See Chapter Three.
51. OSB *Kappel* page 66.
52. OSB *Kappel* page 65.
53. The interaction between the quantity of economic information available for each village and the distribution of wealth within it puts this value close to the median. I therefore stick with this intuitive approach.

9

Rich and Poor

This chapter studies relations between wealth and fertility in Grafenhausen, Kappel, and Rust, applying the concepts and methods developed in Chapter Eight. It treats the villages sequentially, focusing on the years surrounding the inception of family limitation. In each case, better-off villagers were the innovators. Moreover, rich couples employed contraception assiduously. Yet this relationship was short-lived. In Grafenhausen and Rust, it was already waning at the end of the nineteenth century. That fact, together with some of the obstacles to the spread of family limitation beyond the village élite, especially in Kappel, suggests that wealth was only part of the story. Both the strengths and weaknesses of this association argue for the importance of psychological factors, such as the religious and political attitudes to be taken up in the following three chapters.

Grafenhausen

Like other topics, the direct analysis of links between wealth and fertility begins with Grafenhausen. I do this partly out of deference to alphabetical order, but also because that village constituted an especially suitable setting for such an investigation. Family limitation spread early and widely among its inhabitants, and so the concomitants of the new patterns of behaviour can be observed over an extended period. Moreover, as Chapter Eight showed, those inhabitants included a substantial number of solid peasants, who are precisely the group the refined morcellement hypothesis singles out as apt to limit fertility within marriage. As it happens, the results do reveal differences between economic categories compatible with the theory.

Table 9.1 summarizes the experience of the first three cohorts.[1] The figures for all marriages show differences in the predicted direction for average ages at last birth[2] and completed family size. Rich Grafenhauseners wed from 1825 to 1849 ceased childbearing younger than their grandparents had, and produced smaller families. Poor couples showed only a weak tendency in the same direction. However, there was no similar contrast in final birth intervals at any point. Moreover, the shrunken families of the rich still averaged as many children as those of the poor.

TABLE 9.1
Comparison, for rich and poor couples, of Average age of wife at last birth and Final birth interval, both in years, together with the Number of legitimate children in mature documented completed families in Grafenhausen, by marriage cohort and age of bride

	Age at last birth		Final birth interval		Number of children	
	Rich	Poor	Rich	Poor	Rich	Poor
All brides						
pre-1800	40.4	39.7	3.44	3.09	6.5	5.4
1800–1824	39.4	39.6	3.33	3.12	5.7	4.5
1825–1849	37.7	39.3	3.58	3.60	4.8	4.6
Change	−2.7	−.4	+.14	+.50	−1.7	−.9
Bride under 25						
1825–1849	36.2	38.1	3.41	3.71	6.1	6.4
Change	−2.9	−1.1	−.24	+.42	−1.8	−1.5
Bride 25–29						
1825–1849	38.3	(39.6)	4.17	(3.58)	4.6	(5.7)
Change	−3.7	−.0	+.80	+.61	−3.0	−.0

Notes
(1) The sources of economic information are listed in connection with Figure 4.3 and described in Benz, Thesis.
(2) A rich couple is one whose holding at its zenith exceeded the average holding at that time. All others are poor couples.
(3) Values based on 10–19 cases are shown in brackets.
(4) The Table is based on 390 marriages, 209 rich and 181 poor.

To these considerations must be added the fact that both measures in which a difference appears are sensitive to age at marriage. The more uniform distribution of wealth in Grafenhausen meant that differences in ages at marriage were less extreme than elsewhere, but gaps as wide as three years did open up between the averages for rich and poor.[3] This gap artificially deflated measures of family limitation for the poor.[4] Even changes between cohorts are not entirely reliable, for they are confounded with increasing delay of weddings and declining proportions of remarriages in the first half of the nineteenth century. Therefore, I break down the results by the age of the bride.[5]

The figures for the young brides are rather mixed. As in the overall population, ages at last birth dropped quite a bit more among rich couples. On the other hand, part of this difference is undercut by the finding that the length of final birth intervals increased among the poor, while it fell among the rich. Finally, there is not much to choose between the trends in family size. In both categories it fell by more than the increase in age at marriage would have led one to expect. Overall, the clearest lesson is the wisdom of making the division by bride's age to begin with, for ages at last birth are consistently lower and the number of children consistently higher for these couples.

The women who wed between twenty-five and thirty are considerably more interesting. There is no trend in any of the variables for the poor families, but rich ones move sharply in the predicted directions. In each case the changes are greater than for the young brides.[6] Within this group, some rich couples had begun to compress their period of childbearing at a time when poorer villagers showed no such tendency.

Unfortunately, it is not possible to trace developments after 1850 in the same manner. Perhaps because the municipality had no need to collect annual levies from its citizens, no tax records of the type analysed below for Kappel and Rust have been preserved in Grafenhausen.[7] I must therefore turn to two less useful documents, the 1894 animal census and the voters' list for the 1905 municipal election.[8]

Table 9.2 uses the same format as Table 9.1 to summarize the information in these sources. Its clearest feature is that both rich and poor, however defined, participated in the fertility transition. In fact, between 1877 and 1905,[9] the overall figures for both categories shifted strongly in the direction of family limitation for all measures. Women from all ranges of wealth stopped having children earlier, and did so at lower parities. Sharp rises in last birth interval, indicating an unsuccessful or temporary resort to contraception by some couples, appeared from time to time in each category.

Within the limitations imposed by the nature of the sources, the differences between rich and poor were broadly consistent with the refined morcellement hypothesis. For example, the figures for 1877 roughly parallel those for the 1825–1849 marriage cohort, as they should, but usually at a slightly less advanced level. This retreat among both rich and poor confirms Chapter Six's surmise that there was a general pause before family limitation resumed its progress later in the century.[10]

The small overall advantage of the rich was concentrated in the group wed at twenty-five to twenty-nine. This fits the pattern of Table 9.1. Moreover, the slight hint there, in the figures for final birth intervals, that the poor who wed young might also be taking up family limitation, is borne out here. In 1905 they led rich brides under twenty-five in age at last birth and completed family size. Each figure represents the largest reduction since 1877 for any group.

The denseness of Table 9.2, the vagaries of the sources, and the convolutions of the preceding reasoning may have left readers with a sense that the account of events in Grafenhausen is becoming obscure. Figure 9.3 should restore some clarity. By reuniting those who ended childbearing while still young with those who extended their final birth intervals, age at second-last confinement simplifies the picture considerably. In addition, it is slightly less sensitive than the measures considered thus far to variations in age at marriage. Although the switch after the 1825–1849 cohort from summaries of lifetime wealth to cross-sectional measures complicates the picture, the overall trend is clear.

TABLE 9.2
Comparison, across economic categories, of Average age of wife at last birth and Final birth interval, both in years, together with the Number of legitimate children in mature documented completed families in Grafenhausen, by year of source and by age of bride

	Age at last birth		Final birth interval		Number of children	
	Rich	Poor	Rich	Poor	Rich	Poor
All brides						
1877	38.2	39.9	3.76	3.53	5.8	5.5
1894	36.4	36.9	4.03	4.08	5.2	4.9
1905	36.1	37.2	4.35	4.11	4.9	4.5
Change	−2.1	−2.8	+.59	+.58	−.9	−.9
Bride under 25						
1905	35.8	34.9	4.49	3.71	5.6	4.9
Change	−1.6	−4.6	+.87	−.42	−1.3	−2.3
Bride 25–29						
1905	36.3	39.6	4.14	4.82	3.8	5.0
Change	−1.6	−.7	−.01	+1.45	−.7	−1.5

Notes
(1) The sources of economic information, here the 1877 land survey, the 1894 animal census, and the 1905 voters' list, are described in Benz, Thesis.
(2) Mature marriages are those in which the husband first wed
   (a) in 1832 through 1861 (in 1877), or
   (b) in 1854 through 1883 (in 1894), or
   (c) in 1860 through 1889 (in 1905).
(3) Poor couples are those
   (a) with below average holdings (in 1877), or
   (b) with no horse (in 1894), or
   (c) in the least taxed class (in 1905).
   All others are rich couples.
(4) The Table is based on 441 marriages, 235 rich at some point and 206 poor at some point.

From the steeper slope of the solid graph, one can see that family limitation at first proceeded more rapidly among rich couples. Indeed, the flatness of the dashed graph suggests that natural fertility was dominant among poor couples until the middle of the nineteenth century. However, the next few decades saw ages plummet for both categories. Since overall m continued to shoot upwards in the 1890s as family limitation spread to three-quarters and more of couples, both curves would continue to fall if the graphs were extended to the right. If the rich did show the rest the way at first, there was no difference in the rapidity with which family limitation spread through Grafenhausen thereafter.

Figure 9.3 fits nicely the reasoning advanced in Chapter Eight. The moderately rich were among the first to feel an impulse to control fertility within marriage. If it was indeed fear of further division of the family holding that

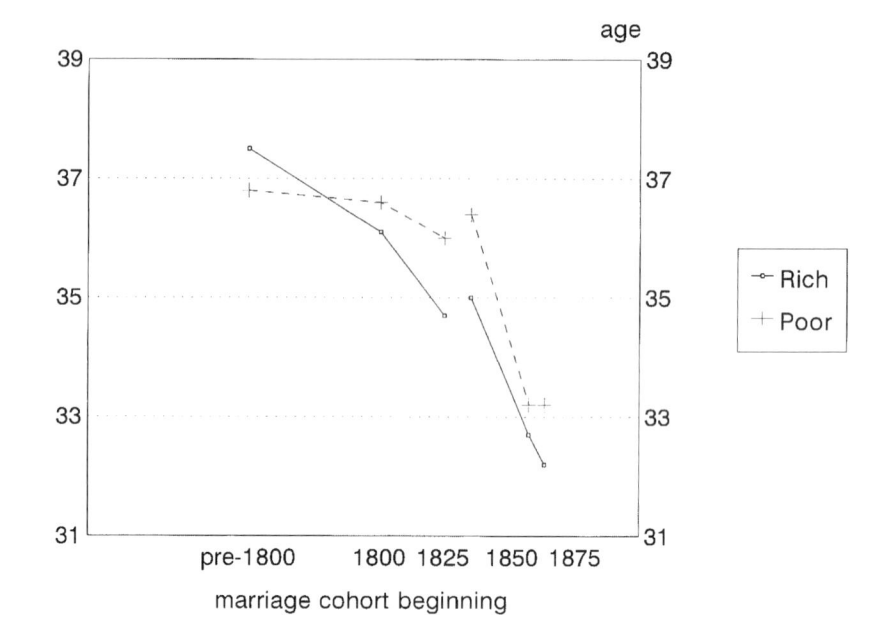

FIGURE 9.3 AVERAGE AGE OF WIFE AT SECOND-LAST CONFINEMENT FOR RICH AND POOR COUPLES IN MATURE DOCUMENTED COMPLETED FAMILIES IN GRAFENHAUSEN, BY DATE OF WEDDING

motivated them, that concern roused sympathetic echoes throughout Grafenhausen, where ideas congenial to the solid peasantry found a wide audience. The fairly egalitarian economic structure promoted the diffusion of innovations. What differences in wealth there were proved no barrier to the spread of family limitation.

All the measures presented thus far confound the intensity of family limitation and its extent. Matching the data to the Coale-Trussell model fertility schedules begins to disentangle these tendencies in a way that strengthens the case I have been making. As these indices are based on all documented couples, not just completed families as the earlier ones were, they provide a broader picture.[11]

In the case of total marital fertility rates, that picture is the clearest of any so far. Although beginning at a higher level (9.42 vs. 8.83), the figures for rich couples fell steadily. An upward trend can be discerned among poor couples for much of the nineteenth century. After a sharp peak at 10 children for the mature marriages in the 1877 survey, the rate among the poor dropped rapidly, and only the continuing fall among the rich kept them a bit ahead (7.01 vs. 7.39) as the century drew to a close. Except perhaps at their zenith, the high rates among the poor were primarily statistical abstractions. Since most of them wed old, fertility rates in the younger age-groups seldom had concrete conse-

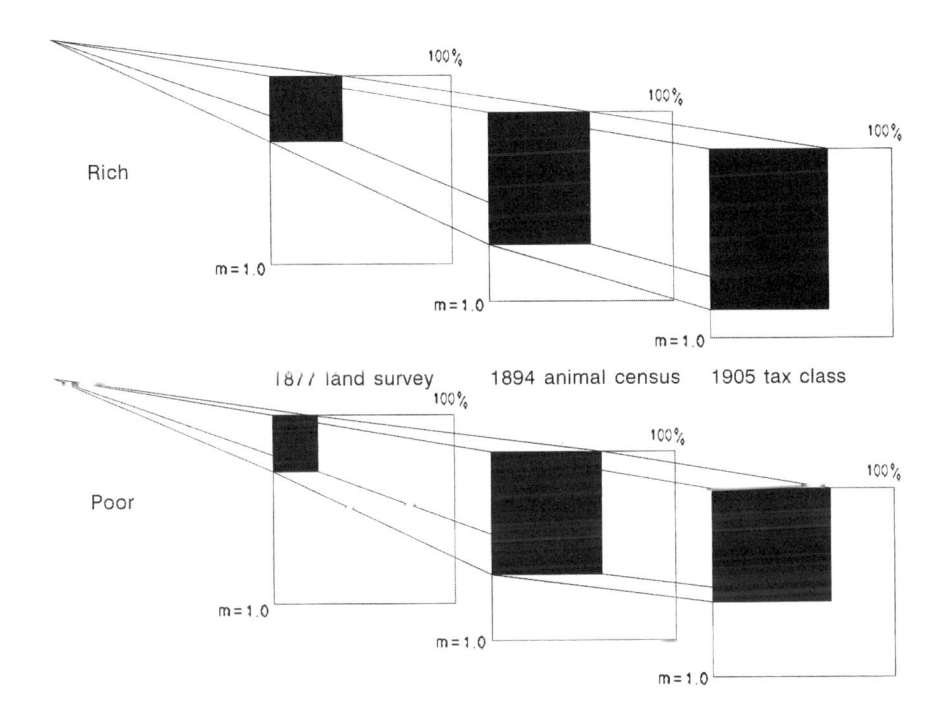

FIGURE 9.4 THE SHAPE OF FAMILY LIMITATION AMONG RICH AND POOR IN GRAFENHAUSEN

quences. The overall pattern of increase and decline does, however, bespeak a more vibrant demographic environment than that conjured up by Figure 9.3.

These developments corresponded closely to trends in the M index of underlying natural fertility, which also hit a peak for the poor in 1877 before returning to more modest levels. I argued in Chapter Six that Grafenhauseners' extensive family limitation masked the strong increase in fecundity evident in Rust and Kappel. M values confirm that interpretation. Following a rise between the second and third cohorts, the rich held to a narrow band (1.07 to 1.16) for the rest of the nineteenth century. Because family limitation caught on more slowly among the poor, they suffered a further sharp increase (to 1.27) before bringing underlying natural fertility back within bounds (1.12 for 1905).

A deeper understanding of the ways in which different economic categories participated in the spread of family limitation can be gathered by comparing its shapes among rich and poor. In the cohorts before 1825, neither the m index nor the percentage limiting rose above insignificance. The change to the third cohort was dramatic as both rich and poor couples took up family limitation to a considerable extent.[12] Its slightly greater strength among the rich reflected a higher proportion practising contraception (41 % vs. 29 %). Wealthy Grafenhauseners did not enjoy any lead in time or in the intensity of family limitation, but more of them did display an affinity for it. At first at least, their control of fertility within marriage was wider, rather than deeper or longer.

The more episodic data from later in the century depicted in Figure 9.4 reveal a slightly different pattern.[13] For the mature unions included in the 1877 land survey, m values were just below those in the overlapping marriage cohort. They rose rapidly thereafter, and more continuously among the rich.[14] At the same time, differences between economic categories in the percentage practising family limitation effectively disappeared. That suggests that the more permanent pattern saw deeper, but not wider family limitation among the solid landed proprietors.

Overall, then, the refined morcellement hypothesis has passed through the ordeal of testing without sustaining fatal damage. The first generation to take up family limitation included disproportionate numbers of villagers with holdings greater than the average. Even after roughly equal percentages of other groups joined in, these innovators practised contraception more intensively. There are hints in the data that this was particularly true of rich couples who wed old and poor couples who wed young. In so far as ages at marriage were influenced by economic considerations, these two groups tended to be quite similar. Especially in Grafenhausen, both were found near the dividing line between rich and poor, close to where this version of morcellement theory locates the greatest incentive to limit family size.

However, because this sort of peasant was prevalent in Grafenhausen, and because, perhaps coincidentally, family limitation was strongest there, the theory has faced easy going thus far. I now turn to Kappel to see whether appeals to fear of morcellement can account for failure to control fertility within marriage as well as for success.

Kappel

As might be expected, relations between wealth and fertility were rather different in Kappel. The overall patterns of Chapter Six rule out any strong, widespread, or consistent family limitation there. All the same, there have been hints at several points that it was not entirely absent. Municipal officers, for instance, reduced fertility within marriage right from the opening of the nineteenth century. This small group of notables overlapped to a considerable extent the élite of great proprietors who concentrated much of Kappel's land in their hands. This coincidence fits morcellement theory rather well. In this section, I explore how far the resistance to family limitation by large sectors of Kappel's population can also be accommodated within this framework.

Table 9.5 presents data on completed families, broken down by economic category.[15] The overall figures show a modest but sustained decline in age at last birth among the rich. There was no trend in the age at which the poor ceased childbearing, nor in the gap between their penultimate and final births. This last variable did increase for the rich, but the entire increase came in the first cohort of the nineteenth century following an unusually low value before 1800. These tendencies towards lower fertility did not reduce the average

TABLE 9.5
Comparison, for rich and poor couples, of Average age of wife at last birth and Final birth interval, both in years, together with the Number of legitimate children in mature documented completed families in Kappel, by date of wedding and age of bride

	Age at last birth		Final birth interval		Number of children	
	Rich	Poor	Rich	Poor	Rich	Poor
All brides						
pre-1800	40.5	40.8	3.11	3.85	5.7	5.3
1800–1824	39.0	40.7	4.07	3.45	5.0	4.7
1825–1849	39.3	41.3	3.73	3.37	6.7	5.4
1850–1874	39.2	39.8	3.80	3.55	6.2	5.2
1875–1899	37.9	40.3	3.56	3.89	6.0	6.3
Change	–2.5	–.5	+.44	+.04	+.3	+1.0
Bride under 25						
1875–1899	35.3	39.8	3.84	4.43	6.0	7.8
Change	–4.6	–.5	+.64	+.19	–1.8	+.7
Bride 25 to 29						
1875–1899	40.4	40.3	3.22	3.35	6.9	6.7
Change	–.1	–1.8	+.31	–1.23	+.7	+1.2

Notes
(1) The sources of economic information are described in Benz, Thesis. In addition to those cited in connection with Figure 4.3, they include an 1812 building assessment (Gem A Kappel B IV/193) and tax assessments on voters' lists for 1880 and 1883 (Gem A Kappel B IV/135).
(2) A rich couple is one whose holding at its zenith exceeded the average holding at that time. All others are poor couples.
(3) The Table is based on 604 marriages, 299 rich and 305 poor.

number of children rich women bore, although maintaining family sizes at a time when they were driven up among the poor represented an achievement of sorts.[16]

However, these overall trends hide as much as they reveal. The concentration of wealth in Kappel meant that differences in age at marriage across economic categories were also extreme. They peaked in the 1825–1849 cohort, when the average rich woman wed five full years ahead of her poor counterpart. Breaking the results down by age of bride is therefore imperative.

The lower part of Table 9.5 reveals that the advantage of the rich in family limitation was exclusive to couples where the bride wed before turning twenty-five. At the end of the nineteenth century, a four-year gap in age at last birth separated them from both subgroups of the poor and even from rich couples who were slower to wed. This phenomenon was so strong that, despite being married four years longer, rich young brides produced almost one child fewer than older brides, regardless of their wealth.

160 CHAPTER NINE

The pattern of change in the final birth intervals of young brides was less striking, but still consonant with the overall trend. For the rich the gap between the final two confinements grew over the nineteenth century. Figures among the poor fluctuated until after 1875, when their jump muddied the picture somewhat. Among the rich there is no downward trend in completed family size before 1875, but a dramatic decline distinguishes the final cohort from the poor and from earlier generations of the rich. In fact, rich women who wed under twenty-five were the only ones to produce fewer children at the end of the nineteenth century than had their predecessors a century earlier. Significant family limitation was thus found in Kappel only among the rich who wed young.

Trends for brides aged twenty-five to twenty-nine should not be judged solely on the changes to 1875–1899. Had the Table ended a quarter-century earlier, there would have been reason to locate incipient family limitation among the rich who wed old. Up to 1875, age at last birth fell to thirty-nine and completed family size to five children, while final birth intervals rose above four years. The poor showed, if anything, a tendency in the other direction. The changes to the final cohort among the poor were equally unremarkable, but the rich slipped back to natural fertility across the board. Thus, any spread of family limitation to this group proved abortive.

Because they make no distinction by age at marriage, Figure 9.6's graphs of

FIGURE 9.6 AVERAGE AGE OF WIFE AT SECOND-LAST CONFINEMENT FOR RICH AND POOR COUPLES IN MATURE DOCUMENTED COMPLETED FAMILIES IN KAPPEL, BY DATE OF WEDDING

ages at second-last confinement are rather simpler. The countervailing tendencies within the rich made overall trends less dramatic. At no point can one see the steep declines typical of both categories in Grafenhausen. Instead, the modest advantage of the rich over the poor, which emerged as early as the first quarter of the nineteenth century, was maintained. At the end of the century, it was even increasing, as each category moved away from the other.

Less refined measures reveal less striking differences between economic categories. The rich experienced higher total marital fertility rates than the poor at first (8.80 vs. 8.31), but this relationship reversed itself over the years. The shift primarily reflected a rise among the poor to almost 10 children, as rates among the rich fluctuated, finishing at 8.56. Even at the end of the nineteenth century, neither category had begun the descent couples in Grafenhausen had entered on half a century earlier. Underlying natural fertility (M) increased consistently. The rich advanced steadily from .96 to 1.19 between the eighteenth century and the 1875–1899 marriage cohort. After a nadir at .87 in 1800–1824, the poor likewise closed at 1.19.[17]

From the results thus far it seems that the shape of family limitation in Kappel varied considerably, and in some respects unexpectedly, from that in Grafenhausen. The final pattern there, as seen in Figure 9.4, was extended in time, wide within and across economic categories, and deeper among the rich. In Kappel, it was by all indications longer for the rich, yet thin and shallow.

Figure 9.7 confirms all three characteristics. There was a clear contrast between rich and poor in the percentage of couples practising family limitation in each cohort wed after 1800. However, even among the rich, no consistent trend towards higher values emerged. When this is combined with m's directionless tumble along the border of significance,[18] the result is a twisted shape. A small minority limited the size of its families over an extended period without its neighbours, rich or poor, being tempted to join in.

Thus, the overall lines of development are clear. Throughout the nineteenth century, a few rich couples compressed their childbearing into the early and middle years of their marriages. Their poor counterparts displayed no tendency to follow this lead. Indeed, at the end of the century, even a segment of the rich reverted to natural fertility. At the same time, the richest of the rich redoubled their efforts. Those efforts were deep enough to lift the village as a whole out of the zone of insignificance for the first time.

If taken at face value, these findings pose some difficulty for conventional American theories of fertility transition, according to which the spread of family limitation is a unique and irresistible phenomenon. Be that as it may, the refined morcellement hypothesis can digest them without much embarrassment. To put it simply: the unequal distribution of wealth in Kappel cut down the number of couples to whom family limitation might appeal.

The contrast with Grafenhausen is instructive. There, the couples I have dubbed poor possessed on average one-third as much as the rich. In Kappel, a more typical ratio was one-fifth. The rich were richer and the poor were

162   CHAPTER NINE

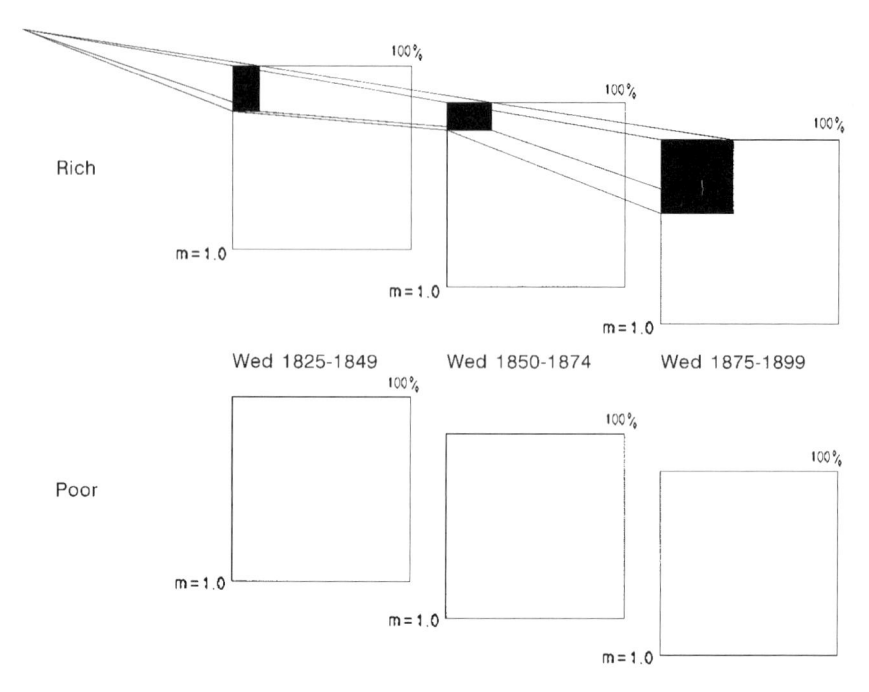

FIGURE 9.7   THE SHAPE OF FAMILY LIMITATION AMONG RICH AND POOR
IN KAPPEL

poorer.[19] The more exalted social and economic position of Kappel's rich families depended on maintaining their outsized holdings. Population growth threatened that position earlier than in Grafenhausen, and so a few Kapplers turned to family limitation right at the beginning of the nineteenth century.

Their example was not followed, as few other residents felt the same pressure. The poor had nothing to preserve, while those who wed old produced fewer children in any case. In the course of the nineteenth century, reclamation of land postponed any crisis among families who relied on their holdings for a living. Those who could not maintain themselves from their own land resorted first to emigration and later to the cigar plants to ease their circumstances. By all appearances, these approaches were preferred to contraception. Thus, occasional moves in that direction by the rich who wed old or the poor who wed young were not sustained.

The social isolation of Kappel's élite also helps to account for the failure of contraceptive practices to spread. In Chapter Eight, I indicated how a rural marriage market might diffuse family limitation throughout a community. A couple who produced fewer children would see them wed up, and pressure rivals to follow suit lest they be leap-frogged. Developments in Grafenhausen could easily be interpreted along these lines. In Kappel, on the other hand, the gulf separating rich and poor, and the frequency with which the rich looked outside the village for mates, kept the same mechanisms from coming into operation. Even if this interpretation is far too simple to represent the whole story, it does illustrate how a whole range of social contacts between rich and poor were curtailed. In Kappel it was more difficult for new ideas and practices to trickle down to the mass of the population. Here again, morcellement theory provides a plausible summary of the leading features of Kapplers' fertility.

However, the account does not mesh perfectly with the one I offered for Grafenhausen. There I emphasized the rôle of solid peasants, such as the rich who wed old or the medium taxpayer, in sustaining and strengthening the turn to family limitation. In Kappel, on the other hand, only some of the rich joined in. It is true that these individuals were quite well off, even by Grafenhausen's standards, but wealth alone is clearly insufficient to explain the distribution of attitudes towards family limitation in either village.

The previous two pages indicate how economic history and social structure can go some distance towards bridging the gap. For example, the greater wealth of Kappel's élite and the slower pace of agrarian reform there gave an early impetus to family limitation. In a like manner, the eventual expansion of farmland and the social isolation of the prosperous proprietors accounted for the steady state of the first three nineteenth-century cohorts. However, the sudden concentration after 1875, as some groups abandoned their incipient family traditions while others pursued them all the more avidly, lies wholly outside morcellement theory. Rather than concoct an ad hoc economic explanation here, I leave discussion of these issues until the conclusion of this chapter, and ultimately to Chapter Eleven.

Rust

Because Rust is the last municipality to be considered, evaluating the pattern of events there also completes the assessment of the refined morcellement hypothesis. That assessment requires rather more information about the economic structure of this village than I have made available thus far. The outline of Rust's agrarian history in Chapter Three supported the popular image of a poor community inhabited by some of the most downtrodden peasants in the region. In almost all respects, the average wealth of a Ruster fell below that of a Grafenhausener or a Kappler. Demographic measures, including age at marriage, the emigration rate, and the illegitimacy ratio, corroborated that poverty. Rust's intermediate position in family limitation therefore seems to make it inhospitable ground for morcellement theory. Still, in the absence of the sort of detail that Chapter Eight's comparison of Grafenhausen and Kappel provided for each of those villages, it is best to proceed cautiously.

Making a plausible link between low levels of wealth and moderate levels of family limitation requires uncovering some economic measure according to which Rust stood between Grafenhausen and Kappel. I have rehearsed at various points the reasons my data cannot establish a substantive finding of this kind. Discrepancies in the timing of sources and in the types of wealth they cover make tight comparisons across villages virtually impossible. It is nevertheless interesting from a technical point of view to examine the distribution of mature marriages with respect to each of the local averages. The results may shed more light on the methods I have been employing than on economic reality, but that does not make them any less relevant to interpreting the demographic results.

As it happens, the data from Rust[20] occupy an intermediate position at both extremes of wealth. The proportion of mature marriages whose holdings peaked at less than half the village average is lowest in Grafenhausen (17 %). As expected, Kappel features a considerably higher percentage of such very poor families. Rust slips in just below Kappel (27 % vs. 29 %). The same order emerges at the other end of the scale.[21]

One way of appreciating these figures is to consider what they imply about the makeup of the economic categories in each village. In Grafenhausen, two-thirds of the poor possessed at least half as much as the average villager.[22] In Kappel, and to a lesser extent in Rust, the poor category was more heavily weighted towards the very poor. At the other end of the scale, two-thirds of Grafenhausen's rich had less than double the village average. In Rust the corresponding figure was three-fifths, but in Kappel it fell to one-half. In broad terms, the economic contrasts within the data were sharpest in Kappel, somewhat duller in Rust, and least in Grafenhausen.

This pattern is in keeping with Chapter Seven's study of occupational distributions. As the largest of the three villages, Rust boasted the most varied social structure. The proliferation of non-agricultural activities bespoke the relative poverty of many of its inhabitants, who could not make a living from the land alone.[23] Although a few residents' holdings rivalled the ones to be found in Grafenhausen and Kappel, the average was at all times below the neighbouring villages'. Numerous by-employments to some extent alleviated poverty, and produced clustering around that average. The social equality obtaining within this group was accentuated by the contrast with the extensive holdings of the Böcklins. In short, though poorer even than Kapplers, Rusters displayed some of the egalitarian spirit of the considerably wealthier Grafenhauseners.

In using this economic information to interpret fertility, one should bear in mind a couple of peculiarities of Rust's demographic experience. The village featured the highest average ages at marriage, so much so that brides in their thirties were not uncommon. This phenomenon reached its peak in the middle of the nineteenth century. At about the same time, Rust began to experience a striking increase in underlying natural fertility, with the global result that actual fertility did not fall even as family limitation spread. All these developments complicated relations between wealth and fertility.

To reduce those complexities, I begin this time with the graphs of age at second-last confinement. Figure 9.8 reveals a deceptively simple pattern. Among

FIGURE 9.8 AVERAGE AGE OF WIFE AT SECOND-LAST CONFINEMENT FOR RICH AND POOR COUPLES IN MATURE DOCUMENTED COMPLETED FAMILIES IN RUST, BY DATE OF WEDDING

the rich, ages at second-last birth started to decline in the second quarter of the nineteenth century, and the next cohort opened up a wide lead over the poor. Ages in the latter category were basically constant until 1875–1899, when they declined precipitously. Because family limitation receded among the rich at that point, neither category had an edge as the century drew to a close. In brief, the rich showed an earlier affinity for family limitation, but once the poor joined in at all, no economic distinction persisted.

Having, I hope, established this pattern in readers' minds, I now turn to the more detailed, but also more dispersed, results of Table 9.9. Average age at last birth for the rich dropped for two cohorts from a peak between 1800 and 1824, but rebounded at the end of the century. The decline among the poor came entirely in that last cohort.

There was little to distinguish either economic category according to the other measures. Final intervals changed little. The increase among the rich, again choked off after 1875, brought them only to the level attained by the poor all along. Where ages at last birth are falling rapidly, as in Grafenhausen, maintaining the length of this interval is an achievement, but there is no question of that here.[24]

The decline in completed family size among the poor in the second quarter of the nineteenth century reflected the sharp increase in age at marriage for

TABLE 9.9
Comparison, for rich and poor couples, of Average age of wife at last birth and Final birth interval, both in years, together with the Number of legitimate children in mature documented completed families in Rust, by date of wedding and age of bride

	Age at last birth		Final birth interval		Number of children	
	Rich	Poor	Rich	Poor	Rich	Poor
All brides						
pre-1800	39.6	39.9	3.24	3.62	6.9	5.1
1800–1824	41.2	41.1	3.34	3.37	5.9	5.5
1825–1849	39.7	39.9	3.42	3.13	6.1	4.6
1850–1874	38.1	40.8	3.67	3.43	6.2	5.5
1875–1899	38.5	38.7	3.55	3.63	7.3	6.3
Change	−1.1	−1.2	+.30	+.02	+.5	+1.2
Bride under 25						
1875–1899	38.7	38.6	3.82	4.30	8.2	7.9
Change	−.4	+.7	+.63	+.90	+.4	+1.2
Bride 25 to 29						
1875–1899	38.0	38.4	3.06	3.13	6.2	5.8
Change	−1.4	−3.0	+.31	−.91	+.6	−.1

Notes
(1) The sources of economic information are described in Benz, Thesis. In addition to those cited in connection with Figure 4.3, they include an 1811 land survey (Gem A Rust C I/8) and an 1855 building assessment (Gem A Rust A U. 32).
(2) A rich couple is one whose holding at its zenith exceeded the average holding at that time. All others are poor couples.
(3) The Table is based on 729 marriages, 361 rich and 368 poor.

couples who found it difficult to wed. The trend reversed in the 1860s when marriage became easier once more. The reversal among the rich hit even harder, as the weakening in family limitation in the last cohort brought them an extra child each on average.

These nondescript findings become considerably more interesting once age at marriage is factored out. The lower part of Table 9.9 inverts Table 9.5 for Kappel. There, only the rich who wed young could claim in 1900 to have made any progress out of natural fertility. Although there was a parallel tendency in Rust prior to 1875, in the final cohort every other group showed declines in age at last birth, while many young rich brides abandoned family limitation.

Trends in the other two variables were less strikingly different for young brides. Final birth intervals rose among the rich, but the poor displayed a greater increase from, moreover, a higher base. Both categories suffered an increase in completed family size. Taken as a whole, the results for young brides do not support a strong association between wealth and family limitation.

Poverty pushed many brides over the ceiling I imposed at age thirty. The few women wed between twenty-five and thirty posted clear reductions in age at last birth for rich and poor alike. The short final birth intervals may reflect the greater ease of conception at those lower ages. In any case, they render all the more impressive the increases registered by the young brides. Little change took place in the number of children, and what did favoured the poor.

Before attempting to reconcile these disparate findings, I add more raw material. On some measures, differences between economic categories were more modest. Total marital fertility rates fell gently below 9 for the first three nineteenth-century cohorts among the rich, but then jumped to almost 10. The poor experienced much of that increase earlier, hitting 10 in 1825–1849 and holding to that level even as family limitation began to spread amongst them.

No such ambiguity emerged in underlying levels of natural fertility as the M index traced a strong and consistent upward course for both categories. M advanced almost 50 % among both rich and poor between the 1700s and 1875–1899.[25] On the other hand, Figure 9.10 shows that the m index of family limitation echoed Figure 9.8's graphs of age at second-last birth. After three cohorts characterized by natural fertility for both economic categories, m values for the 1850–1874 cohort showed a significant level of family limitation, especially among the rich. The rate of increase slowed for that category in the next twenty-five years, allowing the poor to keep pace.[26]

A similar pattern shows up in the estimates of the percentage of the population practising family limitation.[27] Few, if any, poor couples compressed their childbearing years before 1875, but a number of rich couples did do so from at least 1850. Because they made few converts, birth control became deeper than it was wide, producing the final rectangle shown in Figure 9.10. At the same time, family limitation caught on among a third of the poor. With respect to width, there was no strong difference in the two categories' affinities for contraception by the turn of the century. Relations between economic categories were thus much more like Grafenhausen's than like Kappel's.

It follows that much the same evaluation of the refined morcellement hypothesis as I offered for Grafenhausen can be given in Rust. However, it is hard to account for the timing of developments within this framework. Since holdings in Rust had always been smaller, the incentive to control family size should have been higher earlier. This reasoning is confirmed by the fact that the preventive Malthusian check of late marriage operated most stringently in Rust, and kept down the number of offspring born to the poor. When that proved insufficient, heavy emigration ensued from the 1830s on.

The options of those left behind were limited. Rust had little room to expand, and even in the late nineteenth century did not match Kappel in upgrading land on the Rhine side. With its generally poorer citizenry, the municipality was in no position to take on the fiscal burdens required to finance extensive

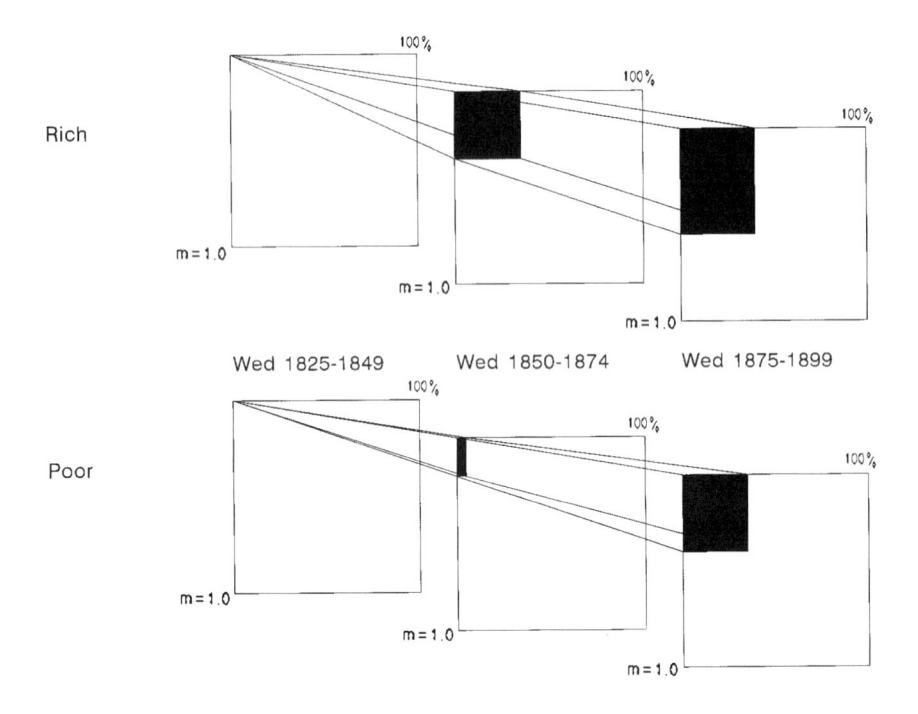

FIGURE 9.10 THE SHAPE OF FAMILY LIMITATION AMONG RICH AND POOR IN RUST

agricultural improvements. If anything, these circumstances make it all the more surprising that family limitation was not resorted to before the mid-nineteenth century.

The hypothesis fares rather better in dealing with the economic patterns that emerged at that point. Family limitation did appear first among the rich and was almost exclusive to them for a couple of decades. In a regional perspective, one sees them following the example set by the rich in Grafenhausen and perhaps elsewhere. From this point of view, their rôle was analogous to that of the middling Grafenhauseners whose economic circumstances they shared. In that respect at least, the refined morcellement hypothesis is borne out.

To some extent, the spread of family limitation to poor couples wed after 1875 can be seen as a simple extension of that process. As in Grafenhausen, the dense ordering of villagers by wealth, and the climate of common interests it fostered, transmitted new practices down the economic scale. Few of these families possessed so little property that reducing the number of heirs held no advantages. The other qualities necessary to prompt a shift to family limitation were no less common than among the rich, and soon roughly equal proportions of rich and poor couples had taken it up. Since the latter betrayed a lingering attachment to late marriage, they did not need to practise family limitation as intensively, and so the rich retained a small lead in that respect.

If that were all there were to the story, the refined morcellement hypothesis could claim a victory. However, as in Kappel, a few features of the villagers' demographic experience do not sit comfortably within the model. I have already indicated that the onset of family limitation does not seem to have been a response to local landholding trends. A more general objection is that the data do not show a reduction in actual family sizes. At least in the aggregate, family limitation did not forestall the division of holdings. At most it headed off even more rapid fragmentation as underlying natural fertility soared. The steady state that resulted poses a dilemma for any account of the attraction of family limitation in Rust.

Even with the aid of findings from earlier chapters, the refined morcellement hypothesis provides only a partial solution. At the end of Chapter Six, I pointed out that the deceptive overall balance was actually the product of two strong opposing tendencies. Those who practised contraception did cut family size considerably, while those who did not produced more children than ever. The late nineteenth-century proliferation of cigar-manufacturing plants offering paid employment to adolescents and women made large families more attractive. Table 7.8 suggested that it may also have made them more likely, as married women cut short the nursing of their infants in order to return to work.

It would fit morcellement theory very nicely if the citizenry had divided between those with land and those whose primary resource was labour. The former would restrict fertility in order to maintain a viable family enterprise, while the latter maximized the number of their newly valuable offspring in order to create one. There is some evidence of such a trend in cohorts wed before 1875, but it disappears entirely in the final quarter of the century.

Linked to this problem is the plateau in family limitation among the rich. The parallel with Kappel, where family limitation also failed to make progress after establishing itself among a segment of the rich, is interesting, but does not render either development more intelligible. Likewise, the similar level of absolute wealth enjoyed by the rich who wed young in Rust and the rich who wed old in Kappel by itself provides no understanding of why family limitation weakened among both groups in the final cohort. Appealing to the new opportunities created by factory work is of little assistance here, for they applied more strongly to the poor than to the rich. Interpreting differential fertility within either category requires looking beyond economics.

The Refined Morcellement Hypothesis Evaluated

Where does this leave the refined morcellement hypothesis? My overall appraisal distinguishes four elements within the theory. They involve, on the one hand, the timing of the onset of family limitation and the groups who took the lead then, and on the other, the timing of its spread and the groups who became involved only at that point. In each area, the refined morcellement hypothesis, abetted by appropriate auxiliary data, sheds some light on the course of events. Both its successes and its failures point to the importance of popular attitudes, and thus lead naturally into the themes of Chapters Ten to Twelve.

I begin with the initial turn to family limitation. As I have just indicated in discussing Rust, I do not see that the finer points of timing can be captured within the hypothesis. The account would be just as plausible, or implausible, if family limitation had been detected a cohort earlier or a cohort later in all the villages. Still, a wider discrepancy would occasion some legitimate surprise. Not until the artificial depopulation of the seventeenth century had been made good and the benefits of the transformation of the three-field system had dissipated did villagers need to resort to other means to preserve their livelihoods. Once that point had been reached, starting afresh in the New World appealed least to those who still had something to hang on to in the old one. The rough coincidence of emigration by one part of the population while another adopted family limitation therefore makes sense within the model.

However, the order in which this development came to the villages is not so easily accommodated. The few in Kappel who perhaps practised family limitation right at the beginning of the nineteenth century may have been richer than the many Grafenhauseners who joined in in the following generation, and both were definitely better off than the families in Rust who took it up later still. However, this very pattern runs against the hypothesis, for morcellement pushed each of these groups below any particular economic threshold in the reverse order. Rusters should have been first to counteract the fragmentation of holdings, for it had proceeded furthest amongst them. Clearly they were not.

This point has important theoretical consequences, as it shows that resort to contraception was not a mechanical adaptation to gradual change. If family limitation had been part of a traditional repertoire of demographic behaviour, merely in abeyance during the eighteenth century because of a particularly favourable constellation of economic circumstances, it would have re-emerged incrementally and automatically precisely where it was most needed. That that did not occur strengthens the case for regarding family limitation as a radical departure from longstanding demographic patterns. As such, it is linked, however tentatively, with other novel ideas that struck popular consciousness in the nineteenth century.

Despite the fact that its timing is a bit awry, the hypothesis does pick out the economic categories in which to look for innovators. In the eighteenth century, no measure of family limitation shows a significant difference between rich and poor once age at marriage is taken into account. Just as the hypothesis would have it, the emergence of economic differences coincided with the emergence of family limitation itself. In Rust the practice was found among the rich a full cohort ahead of the poor, and in Kappel the lead was even larger. Even if one discounts the figures before 1875 there as too shaky, the results for the last cohort are clear enough. In Grafenhausen, some measures show family limitation among the rich before it appears among the poor, and in those where no distinction in timing was present, such as m, the representation of the rich was larger and stronger. In each case, then, peasants with something substantial to lose through the division of holdings dominated the first cohort to practise family limitation.

In introducing morcellement theory, I pointed out that this pattern could also come about for a variety of other reasons, some of them purely technical. Indeed, I noted early in Chapter Eight that it would take a most unusual combination of results to confirm the refined morcellement hypothesis alone. As it turns out, just such a combination has emerged. To begin with, the suggestion that family limitation was a cause rather than an effect of the greater wealth observed among its practitioners has been rendered implausible. They possessed significant assets even before they turned to it. For example, from Chapter Eight it is clear that Grafenhauseners were rich well before they took up family limitation. Indeed, its adoption coincided with a decline in their holdings relative to Kapplers, a decline which family limitation, at least in its early stages, failed to halt.

The more important objection that younger marriage meant that only the rich needed to control fertility within marriage has also been undercut. Not all the poor wed at advanced ages, nor did all the rich begin bearing children in their early twenties.[28] In Kappel before 1875 and in Grafenhausen and Rust throughout the century, rich women wed between twenty-five and thirty cut the number of their children by at least as much as those wed young.[29] The contrasts between economic categories in other respects were generally also greatest for brides of twenty-five to twenty-nine. Economics, and not simply demography, had something to do with the attraction of family limitation right from the start.

The refined morcellement hypothesis fares even better with respect to the spread of the new demographic régime. In Grafenhausen and Rust, respectable citizens from all walks of life rapidly joined the innovators, and soon equal numbers of rich and poor were limiting family size. It is noteworthy that family limitation did not saturate the rich category before spreading downwards. Only theories that locate an affinity for family limitation somewhere around the economic average can accommodate such a pattern.

Kappel's experience proves the rule, as its expansion towards the Rhine had precisely the consequences predicted by morcellement theory. By making more farmland available, especially to the rich, that expansion took away the incentive to reduce family size. More generally, like emigration and even the coming of the factory, it permitted important aspects of village life to continue without qualitative change. In the face of these developments, the minority practising family limitation made few converts, for the intermediate elements were especially weak in Kappel. Their absence hindered transmission of new behaviours, demographic or otherwise. It is not necessary to endorse speculations about a marriage market to see that sharper economic contrasts minimized common interests, and perhaps more important, the perception of common interests.

In all three cases then, the key rôle the refined morcellement hypothesis assigns to solid peasants in spreading family limitation is borne out. Where they were present, it appeared. Where they were threatened, it spread fast. Where they were numerous, it spread widely. Where they were strong, it became accepted.

I have felt free in the foregoing summary to draw on certain social and psychological factors linked to the distribution of landholdings. After all, I have been arguing from the outset that economics alone cannot supply a full understanding of demographic history. Even within the perspective of morcellement theory, it is possible to ask whether the attitudes of those who took up family limitation were only indirectly the product of economic realities. How far, that is, did the behaviour of Grafenhauseners whose holdings had been cut below those of the average Kappler still reflect the proud independence of their ancestors? How far did poor Rusters' willingness to follow the lead of their rich counterparts grow out of a feeling of village solidarity built up through years of confrontation with the lord? How far did the economic gulf in Kappel make the mores of the rich something that the poor could not share?

The shortcomings of the refined morcellement hypothesis render such questions all the more acute. After all, differences in economic structure were not that large. A family moving with its property from any village to any other would not have found itself out of place. In each municipality there were a certain number of the solid citizens I have labelled the natural constituency of family limitation. They may have made up a smaller proportion of the population in Kappel than elsewhere, but even there their representation was not negligible. The modest economic differences can bear the explanatory weight I have placed on them only because of my buttressing claims about what they meant for the social and psychological life of the communities. To make such views plausible, I have to show that attitudes in other spheres also varied considerably from village to village.

The study of popular psychology holds out hope of filling in gaps in the preceding account. For all the aggregate differences between economic categories, one can find pairs of villagers in virtually identical straits who chose to deal with them in contrary ways. Pressure to maintain the size of landholdings provided only part of the attraction to family limitation. The factors required to turn attraction into practice, to make contraception accepted, had to come from somewhere else. The triumph of these new attitudes was not uniform, as the pauses and even regressions for different economic categories in each village have revealed. Examining other local conflicts promises to uncover important insights into this contest for villagers' hearts and minds, and bodies. In Chapters Ten, Eleven, and Twelve, I look to political and religious life in Grafenhausen, Kappel and Rust to round out the economic account I have given in the past two chapters and to deepen understanding of their histories.

Notes

1. Couples wed after 1850 require a different treatment. See below.
2. In populations of this size, standard deviations are roughly two-thirds of a year.
3. Because age at marriage indirectly attested to wealth, adding it to the mix refines my analysis.
4. Within a given marriage cohort, decisions to stop childbearing were taken later in the century for brides who wed young. For instance, a rich woman wed at twenty in 1850 turned thirty-five in 1865, while a poor woman who had waited till thirty to wed reached thirty-five in 1855. Because family limitation spread with each passing year, grouping by marriage cohort (or mature marriage) bestows an artificial advantage on couples belonging to later birth cohorts, in this case rich couples.
5. No figures are provided for brides over thirty, who were too few to permit reliable calculations. In any case, couples wed that late had less need to control fertility within marriage.
6. To some extent the contrast is exaggerated by the extreme values attained by the pre-1800 cohort, but even evaluating the changes against the levels of their poor counterparts leaves a measurable difference.
7. In April 1881 Grafenhausen proposed to dispense with its cadastre entirely, but the prefect ordered that it be drawn up even though it would not be used. Gem A Grafenhausen B IV/248. Apparently no copy has survived.
8. Gem A Grafenhausen B VII/525 and Gem A Grafenhausen B IV/172, respectively. In 1894 the rich are those with at least one horse, the poor are horseless. In 1905 the rich are those in the highest- and medium-taxed groups; the poor are the lowest-taxed. The intricacies of working with these sources are covered in Benz, Thesis, appendix D. One complication is that the poor of 1894 or of 1905 include couples who were better off at other times. Unfortunately, they cannot be recognized, as there is only one observation with each type of source. To compensate, in what follows I also present figures based on the 1877 land survey (Gem A Grafenhausen C VII/3), separating rich from poor as in Table 9.1. Because this information is more directly comparable to the measures of landed wealth used for earlier cohorts, it isolates the distortion produced by using snapshots of the distribution of wealth.
9. Note that these dates refer to mature marriages, formed about thirty years earlier.
10. It may also be an artefact of an isolated measure of wealth.
11. The calculations are based on a total of 21162 woman-years, 11779 rich and 9383 poor.
12. Rich wed before 1800 m = .03, 1800–1824 m = –.01, 1825–1849 m = .40. Poor wed before 1800 m = .19, 1800–1824 m = .13, 1825–1849 m = .31.
13. Note that I use the three sources of economic information here rather than the marriage cohorts employed in other diagrams.
14. It is noteworthy that the gap between categories was widest in 1905 when the rich one incorporated the poorest medium taxpayers, who fell into the poor category at other times.
15. Kappel's tax records are more complete than Grafenhausen's, and so a uniform account can be given of all cohorts.
16. The pure minority of limiters boasted genuine reductions, of course.
17. Because of the abundance of economic data for Kappel, most of the estimates are based on comfortable numbers of woman-years (totalling 7921 for the rich and 7410 for the poor).
18. The .15 score for 1850–1874 is depicted despite the fact that it did not differ significantly from 0. Strictly, the shape could wink to a point for that cohort.

174 CHAPTER NINE

19. Relative to the local average.
20. In addition to the measures noted in connection with Figure 4.3, they include the extent of land in an 1811 land survey (Gem A Rust C I/8) and an 1855 building assessment (Gem A Rust A U. 32).
21. The percentage of couples with more than four times the average is over twice as great in Kappel as in Grafenhausen (7 % vs. 3 %), while Rust occupies a position dead between the two. These results cannot be pushed too far, which is why I have not dignified them with a Table. The frequency of very rich couples detected is highly sensitive to the number of observations available, as momentary peaks easily escape detection. From that point of view, the percentages of very rich couples match all too well the range of information from each village. However, the same reasoning makes Kappel's, and to a lesser extent Rust's, heavier weighting in the lowest category all the more impressive, as couples who ever managed to rise even halfway to the average had a much greater chance of being detected there. If the results at the top of the range of wealth are artefactual, those at the lower end are all the more genuine.
22. Their characteristics and thinking were therefore close to those of the solid proprietors on the other side of the average.
23. Especially because much of it belonged to lords.
24. One might speculate that final intervals were at least bucking the trend towards higher fecundity, but it is hard to predict how that development would affect these intervals. It might for instance extend them, by drawing out the period of intermittent infecundity many women experienced as their reproductive spans drew to a close.
25. The rich from 1.03 to 1.48, the poor from .96 to 1.43.
26. Overall, 18806 woman-years were considered, 9823 for the rich and 8983 for the poor.
27. It registered impossible values in 1800–1824 for both categories (rich –20 % and poor –11 %).
28. Too few older brides were involved in remarriages for step-children to be a factor. For example, just 19 % of rich brides wed at twenty-five to twenty-nine chose a widower. (Among the poor, the corresponding figure was 14 %.)
29. Despite the fact that the latter group made their decisions about contraception later in the century.

10

Subjects and Citizens

Chapters Two through Five linked local occurrences such as population decline, tobacco cultivation, and illegitimate births to the broader military and political history of this border region. In contrast, the past few chapters have concentrated on small-scale features of rural life. Even the notables of Chapter Seven were studied in relation to the communities they governed, rather than in relation to the wider world. In the next three chapters, general and local themes come together as I explore political life in Grafenhausen, Kappel, and Rust.

Politics can relate to fertility in ways both banal and exciting. On the one hand, political structures facilitate the transmission of information, including information about contraception. Conversely, political organization is often parasitic on social networks, exploiting whatever structure already exists within a population to mobilize its members. Whatever contacts between villagers permitted family limitation to spread could likewise become nodes for political movements. In either case, political divisions come to correspond with demographic ones, but the links are purely coincidental.

The more exciting possibility is that political affiliation might be tied to demographic behaviour in substantive ways as well. In the two previous chapters I emphasized the novelty of the psychology involved in the turn to family limitation. If those new ideas were part of a broader ideology, then popular attitudes might provide the key to the fertility transition. This would hold if an outside movement brought villagers new attitudes towards fertility or if affinity for contraception attracted villagers to particular worldviews—or repelled villagers from them.

Because the vast majority of inhabitants of the three villages were Catholics, and because the natalist position of the Roman Catholic Church has become a subject of public controversy in the twentieth century,[1] it is tempting to place eighteenth- and nineteenth-century villagers in the same debate. Interpretations along these lines are taken up in Chapters Eleven and Twelve as I deal with the religiously charged politics of late nineteenth-century Baden. However, I do not endorse those views. This chapter, covering political life through 1850, bypasses those arguments, and allows me to set up issues and themes in my own way.

A third sort of interpretation falls between the coincidental and the substantive.

The particular content of political or religious stances taken by villagers might be less relevant than what patterns of engagement reveal about their approaches to the world. In previous chapters, I have dwelt on the psychology of the solid peasants, who were alert to economic opportunities and who responded creatively to population pressure. These attitudes have natural analogues in the political realm.

Aggressive pursuit of interests, hard bargaining, and manipulation of others while preserving their own flexibility promoted villagers' control over their lives. Economic independence made it possible to undertake political activities that reinforced that independence. Furthermore, a record of success in economics, politics, or family life fostered initiative and dynamism in confronting challenges of all kinds. Thus, if these speculations are correct, there should be links between prosperity, family limitation, and political independence.[2]

Because of the striking differences in fertility between villages, I am especially interested in local variations in political life. Here the institution of the municipality provides the key.[3] By focusing the attention of the inhabitants and at the same time isolating them from conflicts elsewhere, the organization of local government set the political agenda. The municipality became the arena for small-scale rivalries, where kinship and personal animosity dominated.[4] In addition, it constituted the prize in those disputes, bestowing power, prestige, and patronage on the victors. Finally, it provided an enduring base from which villagers wore down opponents outside the community.

In the eighteenth century, Rust and Grafenhausen distinguished themselves in this regard, as their citizens pursued autonomy by challenging external centres of political and economic power. These struggles both reflected and reinforced local solidarity. As it happens, these episodes also form a backdrop against which later patterns of engagement and apathy can be understood. In particular, local traditions of resistance and self-assertion merged into the general currents of nineteenth-century radicalism that culminated in the revolution of 1848.

Unfortunately, only rarely has direct evidence of the stances taken by individual villagers survived. As a result, links with fertility remain tentative. Nevertheless, a study of political factions in Grafenhausen in the 1820s brings to light what may be the first villagers to practise family limitation. Similarly, the divisions between the élite in Kappel and the mass of the population can be traced in political sources. Finally, examining leading figures in the upheavals of 1848–1850 brings out an association between radical politics and strong family limitation.

I re-emphasize that this link need not exist on the level of ideology. If the revolution directly represented anything demographic, it was an attempt to resolve the population problem politically, without altering fertility.[5] Rather, what I associate with family limitation is striving for control and willingness to undertake qualitative change.[6] Those characteristics were found more frequently among Grafenhauseners, more generally among solid proprietors, and more actively among revolutionary leaders. Their confident attempts to manipulate the environment, institutions, and even themselves were all of a piece.

Although my main line of argument traces the vicissitudes of this Promethean approach to the world, a few related themes arise repeatedly. The first concerns the status of women. In previous chapters I have several times noted the social and economic prominence of women in this area. It should come as little surprise then to find them intervening in the political process on behalf of the causes that also engaged their menfolk. Occasionally, they even entered the lists in their own right. The possible relevance of this activism to family formation and fertility cannot be tested in any sharp way, but it does illuminate another aspect of ordinary life.

A second theme that recurs, at least in episodes where villagers held their own, is their ability to exploit splits in the forces confronting them from outside the municipality. Finding their way through the administrative mazes set above them required a certain legal sophistication. Still more important was political judgement, which enabled them to play lord against overlord, ecclesiastical authority against secular power, government patronage against popular pressure. As in other spheres of life, success here fed on itself, building ambition as well as the confidence to ride out setbacks.

Political action rested ultimately on organization. The structure of village life constituted the framework around which factions solidified and entered the public arena to contest power. Within the community, gathering places such as the smithy or the priest's house, and above all inns, became the homes of identifiable tendencies.

Inns stood at the confluence of economic, political, and social networks, and so innkeepers appear prominently throughout the next three chapters. As part of the agrarian economy, they experienced growing population pressure and responded early with strong family limitation. As eminent figures on the local scene they took office in municipal government. At the same time their horizons extended farther than ordinary citizens'. As agents for outside firms, they brought new products and ideas into the community. In a era before mass-circulation periodicals, they were the centres of news and the main subscribers to the journals that did reach the villages. By bringing people together in an atmosphere where the exchange of opinions was encouraged, inns became the settings within which reflection and debate took place. Moreover, they were among the few buildings able to accommodate mass meetings. These features put innkeepers at the nodal point of the connections I am drawing.

To understand the turn to family limitation, one must regard the inhabitants of Grafenhausen, Kappel, and Rust as agents. Each of the characteristics I have been discussing, from the drive to control their fates, through the active rôles taken by women, to the persistence and solidarity with which villagers pursued their bargaining with the external world, bears out the value of that approach.

The Ruster Rebellion[7]

As it happens, the first event to be considered highlights all these themes. In 1747 tensions between the municipality of Rust and its lord came to a head in a confrontation that lasted for four years. At this time the Böcklin family resided in Strasbourg and left administration of the village in the hands of the municipal council. Although originally appointed by the lord, its members had acquired considerable independent authority with the citizenry at large. In particular, the municipality had become accustomed to effective self-government and saw its relation to the lordship as one of negotiation rather than outright subordination.

This arrangement was threatened by the determination of Franz Jacob Christian Böcklin von Böcklinsau, the heir to the Böcklin territories, to take a more active rôle in their governance, especially where lordly revenues were concerned. His insistence on having written copies of the municipal accounts delivered to him personally put the villagers on guard, none more so than the treasurer, Philipp Werner, and the mayor, Michel Ott. In the disputes to come, the lordship alleged that they had exploited their free hand in the collection of dues to line their own pockets. Whatever the merits of these claims,[8] citizens came to see the lords' innovations as far greater threats.

This point is illustrated neatly by the issue that provoked the rebellion: the assessment of the fee for allowing each villager's pigs to forage in the lordly—and municipal—forests. This levy had been collected in a manner harmful to both subject and lord, the Böcklins claimed. For example, in 1741 it had been set at five shillings per pig, but only half the sum generated by the estimated 150 swine had been remitted to Strasbourg. However, when the lord proceeded to set the fee for 1747 at seven-and-a-half shillings per pig, all of which would flow to himself, it became clear that the elimination of corruption would not ease the burden on the ordinary proprietor.

The manner in which this decision was taken also aroused protest. Normally, the woods were surveyed annually by the lordly forester, accompanied by members of the municipal council. Their estimate of the total value of the acorns and so forth available, which was then divided over the porcine population, varied from year to year. To the Böcklins this was evidence that the level of the due was at the lord's discretion; to the municipality it connoted bargaining.[9] In any case, the entire process was bypassed in 1747 when the lord sent a foreign forester to make the assessment and council members boycotted that survey.

When the herders attempted to apportion the new fee as the swine were led out to the forest, the villagers present overbore them by force. Suspended from office for instigating this revolt, Werner and Ott insisted that they had counselled obedience in the face of challenges by the populace to act like real leaders. Ordinary citizens were vague about what had happened, maintaining that everyone had taken part, but that they could not pinpoint anybody by name, especially under oath. These interrogations themselves were forcibly brought to a close by a crowd of villagers who broke into the room where they were being conducted.[10]

In a climate of widespread disrespect for the authority and even the person of the lord, Böcklin called in imperial troops.[11] The intervention of these twenty-six hussars was important less for the sullen acquiescence they enforced within the village than for the mounting costs to support them. In accordance with established practice, the goods of the ringleaders of the uprising were declared forfeit. Werner's attempts to divert the contents of the municipal storehouse to the soldiers' upkeep were blocked, and a guard placed on it. At the same time, preparations were made to market the cattle and horses of the deposed officials.

In response, the male population of the village went on strike. Some fled to neighbouring municipalities, including Grafenhausen and Kappel, while most remained hidden in their homes. New labourers recruited from the surrounding area to thresh the confiscated grain and to drive off the livestock were met on the way to work with threats from the men of Rust. Those strikebreakers who persisted were subjected to verbal and physical abuse from the women. The same fate met the hussars, who made no progress confronted by angry women of all ages, wielding wooden knives and hurling stones.[12]

In the time bought by their physical resistance, the villagers belatedly entered the legal arena. The municipality responded to the Böcklins' accusations of mutiny with a counter-suit alleging oppression. Individual petitions for redress were filed by the notables, who had been definitively replaced in February 1748.[13] The Rusters enlisted in their cause the archbishop of Strasbourg, from whom the Böcklins held Rust in fief. However, aside from granting sanctuary to refugees, the archiepiscopate was blocked from intervening in the legal process before imperial courts.[14] Nevertheless, it was able to use its stated concern about the Böcklins running down the capital assets entrusted to them, namely the village and its inhabitants, to get the hussars withdrawn. Both sides settled in for a campaign of attrition.

After a sequence of decisions, investigations, commissions, and reports, lord and subjects came to an agreement in August 1751.[15] Each side dropped its suits and promised to observe the customs governing their relationship, many of which were set out explicitly in the settlement. For example, foresters were to be elected by the citizenry and then invested by the lord, who was to draw up regulations which they would swear to uphold. The contested forage fee was fixed at six shillings. Each side was to bear its own costs, but the municipality committed itself to pay 1500 fl. to the lord.[16] In view of this token of obedience, the Böcklins revoked all fines imposed in the course of the dispute.

This left outstanding only Ott's personal fate. Böcklin had resisted attempts to reinstate him, but his prestige among the villagers endured undiminished. Eventually a compromise was reached, under which Ott was entitled to use the term "mayor" for the rest of his life, leaving his replacement to be content as a mere "staffbearer".[17] With the title, Ott retained his exemption from taxation, and lived out his days the richest man in the village.[18] Over the long haul, Michel Ott has outlasted Franz Jacob Christian Böcklin von Böcklinsau.[19]

THE REICHENWEIER TITHE[20]

The municipality as a whole had not fared so well in the struggle. For a more successful engagement with feudal reaction, one may look to the experience of Grafenhausen. Like Kappel, it was not exposed to the direct control of a secular lord.[21] The administration of the prince-bishops did not possess outposts in the villages themselves, relying instead on the county office in nearby Ettenheim. In the eighteenth century at least, the villagers' resentment was directed less against their titular overlord than against the monastery of Ettenheimmünster, which held the rights to most tithes from Grafenhausen's fields.[22]

Like other municipalities in the area, Grafenhausen had striven in the 1740s and afterwards to free new crops including the potato from the tithe, but those attempts had ended in failure. The continuing transformation of the agricultural system in subsequent years provided the occasion for renewed disputes over how to divide the increasing production. Around 1770, the municipality launched a series of cases designed to minimize its obligations through strict adherence to the letter of the mediaeval agreements in which they were set out. When their arguments were dismissed by lower courts reluctant to overturn longstanding practices, the citizenry pursued appeals through all the twists and turns of the Holy Roman Empire's legal machinery. Where there was leeway for judicial interpretation, the municipality could count on the age-old enmity between the archiepiscopate and the monastery, as well as on the increasingly Enlightened tone of the higher reaches of the lay imperial bureaucracy.

For example, in a case stretching from 1771 to 1776, Grafenhausen won a ruling that the monastery was to measure and collect the grain tithe in the village, thereby sparing its citizens the expense of transport.[23] Verdicts were not always so favourable. Renewal of the claims to exemption from tithes which had been rejected in the 1740s foundered on Grafenhauseners' inability to produce new evidence, despite the numerous delays they won to keep the cases alive.[24]

Procrastination is a common tactic of the more powerful party in judicial proceedings, but in cases like these, postponement could favour the tithe-payers. Because of its effective control of the local scene, the municipality was able to impose its will pending a legal decision. Overcoming that advantage required outside intervention, as in 1798 when the monastery sent in troops to collect tithed straw and present a bill for 780 fl.

In the end Grafenhausen's legal manoeuvres paid off in a manner which more than made up for that setback. In discussing Map 2.2, I explained that Grafenhausen had acquired the abandoned territory of Reichenweier. Much of that land was converted to meadow as the population grew in the course of the eighteenth century. In 1772 the municipality went to court to free this area of tithes to outsiders. Twenty-seven years later, the case was finally settled when the imperial supreme court in Vienna ruled in Grafenhausen's favour and awarded it costs. In the statement of settlement drawn up in October 1799, the municipality waived its claims of over 2000 fl. in expenses in return for 1100 fl. and the forgiving of the 1798 debt.[25] In addition, of course, it retained the tithes (69 fl. per year) withheld over the previous two decades.

The sums involved in these cases constituted a serious burden on litigants who fared less well than Grafenhauseners. In 1800 this was forcibly brought home to seven deputies representing Rusters who had long refused to pay tithes to the monastery Ettenheimmünster from newly cleared land.[26] They lost the substantive issue, despite a recognition that military measures taken against them a dozen years earlier had been illegal. That left them liable for 4000 fl. and the interest that had accumulated on it since the original judgement in 1793. The courts and the lordship[27] had insisted that the deputies were personally liable, as they were the defendants of record.

Fortunately for the seven, they were able to turn to the rest of the village for support. In December 1800, an assembly of 114 citizens unanimously supported having the community take on the debts of its deputies, including the expenses they had incurred.[28] Solidarity meant sharing adversity as well as good fortune. Such sharing respectively strained or strengthened communal bonds in future struggles.

The significance of these episodes went well beyond the immediate economic transfers. The descent of troops, striking confrontations, and the arrest of prominent citizens were often the biggest news to hit the communities in years. These events were recounted in word and song, rapidly acquiring legendary qualities. Heroes like Ott were celebrated, villains like the lord mistrusted, comic or tragic anecdotes involving one's ancestors treasured. Young Grafenhauseners, for instance, learned how their forebears had resisted the monastery for decades, pursuing appeal after appeal before winning vindication. The morals were then applied in their own lives.

I pause to sketch, in deliberately overdrawn stereotypes, the consequences for popular psychology in each village. Grafenhauseners brought with them into the nineteenth century a material surplus and a confidence that the system could be made to work for them. They were painstaking in enumerating their claims, aggressive in asserting them, and stubborn in pursuing them. Rusters could also look back on a tradition of collective action, but their approach to the world was tempered by the recognition that victory had proven elusive. Kappel, in contrast to both its neighbours, was relatively quiet. Whatever resistance to economic or political domination did exist there apparently never went so far as to provoke military retaliation against Kappel alone.

Incorporation into Baden after 1803 brought new challenges to what villagers perceived as their individual and collective rights. Moreover, the tumults of the nineteenth century were often characterized by divisions within the populations of the three communities. Even so, the patterns implicit in the events of the eighteenth century endured.

Kapplers, for instance, seldom took conspicuous individual stands. Instead most of them kept to the line of least resistance. In practice, the initiative—and the responsibility—were left in the hands of the local élite. This state of affairs reflected the economic power the wealthy few exercised over much of the citizenry. By and large, Kapplers entered politics only under the wing of a protector, and did not abandon that patron until they had found another.

Rusters were considerably more active, but circumstances repeatedly conspired to undercut their efforts. The typical Ruster lacked the material resources traditionally available to a Grafenhausener, and with them the strength to win through in a protracted struggle. This meant that the authorities could maintain rather tighter control in Rust, so that even determined villagers met with setback after setback. These experiences added an air of desperation to their strivings.

Grafenhauseners generally insisted that the world heed their will, and took for granted that it would eventually do so. They were economically and psychologically capable of taking independent positions, often to the discomfiture of those governing them. When their wishes were frustrated, Grafenhauseners persevered, standing up to authority and regrouping their forces, strong in the assurance that they would triumph in the end. This attitude was clearest in legal matters, where unfavourable judgements were treated merely as occasions to appeal.

The parallels between the villagers' demographic characteristics and these stereotypes are intriguing. The pages that follow document and refine them as I trace the evolution of the local matrices that emerged from the eighteenth century. Both outside forces and local personalities were constrained by psychological realities even as they worked to transform or manipulate them. The dynamics of these processes can be observed particularly clearly in times of controversy.

The Restless Minds of Grafenhausen[29]

In the late 1810s a number of Grafenhauseners became increasingly dissatisfied with what they saw as the corruption and cronyism of their municipal government. Each had or soon acquired personal grudges against the treasurer, Ignaz Mutschler, who dominated the day-to-day administration of the village, only nominally under the control of its ineffectual mayor, Anton Herzog. The malcontents frequented the Crown inn and won a following among its clientèle of "restless minds".[30] Hoping to take advantage of the prevailing fear of revolutionary conspiracies, their opponents, who preferred the semi-official Ox inn next to the village hall, hastened to label them a cabal or club.

Spreading accusations of malfeasance against Mutschler—and Herzog, who had preceded him as treasurer—brought demands from individual citizens to see the municipal account-books. However, the treasurer, and to a lesser extent the mayor, found support in Ettenheim, now the seat of the Baden county administration. In 1819, the county prefect, Christian Donsbach, refused to dismiss Herzog despite evidence of misconduct and incompetence. When six citizens formally denounced Mutschler in 1821, Donsbach prevented them from gaining access to the accounts. In May 1822, the resulting case went against them, and the six were sentenced to fourteen days each for slander. They launched an appeal and renewed the request to open the books.

Donsbach brought the situation to flashpoint on the night of 24 June 1822 by sending a band of officials, including local Ettenheim police, to Grafenhausen to take the slanderers into custody. The expedition went astray and entered the house of the trader Damas Rauch, who until then had had nothing to do with the case. Fleeing the intruders, the Rauchs sounded the alarm, and the outsiders found themselves confronted by a crowd of aroused citizens. Those playing leading rôles included three of the slanderers and four of their wives, as well as seven other men and women. The Ettenheimers retired empty-handed.

Donsbach seized upon this turn of events to declare Grafenhausen in a state of riot and called in troops to suppress the apprehended insurrection. As in Rust three-quarters of a century earlier, this move ran up the costs that would ultimately have to be borne by the rioters. In the wake of the troops came an investigation by an outside prefect, who rapidly reached conclusions favourable to Mutschler and Donsbach. In August 1822, Rauch was sentenced to six months imprisonment, and the other men to four-, three- or one-month terms. The six women got one, two, or three weeks. All were to apologize publicly to mayor Herzog.

Appeals were again launched, and Grafenhauseners set to work inundating the government and the courts with petitions. The slightest altercation, from the destruction of flowers around the schoolhouse to the appropriation of proceeds from a timber auction in the municipal forest, produced a renewed shower of memoranda from both sides. When the flow of incidents flagged, dismissals of lawyers and mutual accusations of intimidation in the gathering of signatures for earlier petitions filled the gap.

The torrent of paper prompted higher officials to investigate. Concerned as much over the expenditure of public money and the evident division within the community as over who might be in the right, the regional authority deposed Herzog in January 1823 and ordered a mayoral election. It further ruled that only the impartial were to be accepted as candidates, thereby frustrating Donsbach's plan to install Mutschler. The voters' choice fell on Georg Sattler, who had played no active rôle in the disorders thus far, but proved to support the key contentions of the slanderers and rioters.

This added credibility drew further attention to the issues underlying the two cases. January 1824 saw a surprise audit of Mutschler's management of municipal and parish finances, which uncovered numerous irregularities. His supporters maintained that he had not proceeded any differently from his predecessors, but Mutschler's conduct fell far short of the efficiency and integrity the auditors demanded. They recommended dismissing him, along with the rest of the municipal council, to make way for new elections.

Because voting was public, this provided the occasion for an open test of strength. Over 60 % of the 170–180 citizens[31] who turned out on 5 February 1824 favoured candidates identified with the dissidents. Their nominee for treasurer emerged victorious, while Rauch and one of the original slanderers headed the list of councillors. The winners announced their intention to name as municipal clerk the instigator of the denunciation. Together with his wife, that man had taken part in the riot as well. Donsbach refused to swear in those who had been convicted, and cast doubt on the suitability and impartiality of the rest. In the end, the results were obscured by a fresh flurry of petitions, and a new election was set for March 11.

Free pending the outcome of their appeals and with their credibility increasing with each new revelation, the dissidents demanded a ducal commission to review the two cases. Rauch took the lead, pressing their cause within legal forums and without. Indeed, he and others now extended their agitation to Kappel and other municipalities, arousing in the authorities fear of revolutionary unrest.[32]

The aftermath of the first election had complicated the strategy of the dissidents. Confident of their popular support, they nevertheless had to choose candidates whom Donsbach could not impeach. That ruled out those currently under sentence, but no agreement was reached on how much further compromise was advisable. On election day, pride of place went to the relatively moderate mayor Sattler, who voted for a like-minded clerk and proposed a slate of councillors leaning only partly to the dissidents. Seeking to protect his own position, he cleverly selected for treasurer a supporter of Mutschler who had finished second in the mayoral race. However, the next dozen citizens to approach the voting register were not to be swayed and declared their support for the slate chosen by the hardline malcontents. Although a few others came forward to strengthen Sattler's hand and the partisans of Mutschler remained numerous, at the end of the balloting 50 % of the votes had again fallen on candidates who stood little chance of confirmation. The old order in the municipal government commanded the support of about one-quarter of the electorate, while the rest were scattered somewhere in between.

I have dwelt at such length on this election because a copy of the poll-book has survived, and so the views of individual citizens may be compared with their fertility.[33] In Table 10.1, I distinguish three broad factions: the numerous restless minds, the previous incumbents grouped around the ousted Mutschler, and the remainder, who split their votes as Sattler did or cast ballots along other lines altogether. In each faction, the average date of marriage was 1810, well before family limitation became either strong or widespread in Grafenhausen.

That makes it all the more interesting to note that there are distinct, though weak, indications that Mutschler's supporters (second column) were not uniformly subject to natural fertility. Their wives ceased childbearing almost three years ahead of their main opponents'. To some extent, this was offset by shorter final birth intervals, but even so their families were smaller than the other two factions'.[34]

TABLE 10.1
Fertility of documented marriages of Voters in the 11 March 1824 municipal election in Grafenhausen, by political faction

	Restless minds	Old order	Intermediate
For completed families			
Wife's age at last birth	40.3	37.5	40.7
Final birth interval (in years)	3.66	2.83	3.30
Number of legitimate children	5.0	4.9	6.6
Total marital fertility rate	8.92	7.60	9.97
M	1.05	.95	1.08
m	.11	.23	−.06
Percentage limiting	8 %	14 %	−6 %

Notes
(1) *Source*: Gem A Grafenhausen B IV/129 and OSB *Grafenhausen*.
(2) The assignment to factions is described in Benz, Thesis.
(3) The table is based on 217 marriages: 105 involving restless minds, 53 involving partisans of the old order, and 59 involving intermediate voters.

Similar advantages appear in the lower part of the Table, but there they are more attenuated. Total marital fertility rates were least among the partisans of the old order, partly because they displayed a lower level of underlying natural fertility (M). The m index, which is not apt to increase before a definite turn to family limitation sets in, approached significance only for Mutschler's followers. The more volatile estimate of the percentage limiting was likewise highest for those couples. Taking one consideration with another, one suspects a few members of Mutschler's faction adopted new patterns of fertility.

At first blush, these results are not surprising. It was the prominent citizens who had controlled the previous municipal government who identified with Mutschler. In addition, pleas to restore order won a sympathetic hearing among those who stood to lose in material terms from revolutionary upheaval. From those points of view, Table 10.1 fits the patterns of Chapters Seven and Nine in which notable and rich villagers led the turn to family limitation.

In fact, however, both factions recruited equally from rich and poor.[35] At this early date, political cleavages matched demographic distinctions better than economic ones. At the very least, the data fit the view that shared political affiliation eased the spread of family limitation. In so far as politics coincided with kinship ties and social connections within the divided community, that link is plausible.[36]

The resolute adherence to natural fertility by the intermediate couples, who were the best off economically, is particularly striking.[37] They were wealthy enough to resist falling into line behind either side, and perhaps so wealthy that they had no need to restrict family size. Alternatively, their views and the ranges of contacts that they permitted or inhibited did not compass family limitation.

Whatever insights these election results may stimulate a century and a half later, they were treated with little respect at the time. Donsbach persuaded the chief returning officer to recommend that the outcome be disregarded in so far as it reflected a spirit of factionalism. The first-place finishers in the balloting for treasurer and clerk were ruled out as too poor and incompetent respectively. The democratic principle was then honoured by elevating to those offices the candidates who had come second, that is Mutschler's choices. The candidates for councillor were dealt with similarly; two victors were disqualified as partisan, and their opponents named in their place. In the end, only one of the six positions was filled by a candidate supported by the restless minds. By August, mayor Sattler too had been replaced by his rival.

The long-delayed legal verdict also proved unfavourable. Having lost their last appeals in May 1824, the accused sought clemency, pointing out that their original claims had been vindicated. This carried some weight, and in August 1824 the sentences of the slanderers were waived. However, the hard fact remained that the rioters had openly challenged those set over them. Moreover, they could scarcely be described as repentant. Accordingly, the sentences were cut in half and the requirement to apologize to ex-mayor Herzog was dropped, but the defendants were still held responsible for the costs incurred by the military and legal manoeuvres.

Further appeals in their own names and by the female members of their families proved unavailing. Those still at large surrendered one by one to do their time. When Rauch relied too long on a promised delay to set his affairs in order, he was carted off to prison in chains. Although his wife had proven unable to shield him from arrest, conviction, and imprisonment, she did manage to deflect some of the financial burden by pointing out that much of Rauch's property was held in her name, and thus not liable to confiscation.[38]

It should not be supposed that this marked the end of the conflict. The dissidents possessed a base in the citizens' committee, whose membership the prefect did not control so tightly. Moreover, Donsbach's conduct led to his transfer in 1825. With time, the force of numbers overcame the government's willingness to set aside election results. By the late 1830s, restless minds were again found in municipal offices. In 1840 a visiting dean remarked on the persistence of factionalism.[39] Vestiges of the split remained as late as 1855, when a prefect newly assigned to Ettenheim discovered on touring Grafenhausen that his rôle in investigating and condemning the rioters thirty years earlier had not been forgotten.[40] By then, that uprising had been overshadowed by the revolutions of 1848–1849. As will become clear shortly, the allegiances forged in the disputes of the 1820s played no small part in that larger upheaval.

THE REVOLUTION OF 1848

This is not the place to recount the political history of Baden in the first half of the nineteenth century, but a few pieces of background information will put the events of 1848–1849 in these three villages into context.[41] Baden's 1818 constitution established a bicameral parliament with a wide franchise for elections to the lower house.[42] Lively debates there drew widespread public interest, as progressive deputies[43] attacked the restrictions on liberty and national self-determination identified with the Metternichean system. The proximity of France and Switzerland, as well as the growing range of contacts with the United States of America, made the population of the grand duchy aware of alternative political forms. The indefatigable Adam von Itzstein time and again rallied the increasingly variegated opposition, holding within its ranks disgruntled office-seekers, moderate reformers, free traders, civil libertarians, radical republicans, and social democrats.[44] Even the system of indirect elections, under which voters in each locality chose electors who in turn chose the deputies, was harnessed to the task of organization.[45] Both government and opposition campaigned hard.[46]

These struggles were matched on the local level, as the experience of Nepomuk Winkler, bookbinder and proprietor of the Angel inn in Grafenhausen, makes clear. Although his father was an outsider, his mother was the daughter of the keeper of the Crown inn, headquarters of the restless minds. Having learnt the bookbinding trade on tramp as far afield as Slovenia,[47] Winkler married into Grafenhausen in 1831. The connections of his womenfolk elevated him to the municipal council from 1838 to 1842.[48]

As a bookbinder, Winkler constantly confronted censorship. Each time a work was banned, he had to certify that he had seen and acknowledged the order.[49] He made his attitude towards such measures clear in 1843 when he taunted an official in the next county by presenting him with such a publication and offering to supply multiple copies of the next edition.[50] In January 1846 Winkler again found himself in trouble with the authorities, this time for showing off an anti-government cartoon in four taverns in Ettenheim.[51] In April 1847 the prefect finally nailed him when an early-morning search of the Angel inn turned up quantities of subversive literature, including songbooks and political pamphlets Winkler realized were illegal.[52]

The pursuit of Winkler grew out of the government's conviction that he was the "captain" of radicalism throughout the region.[53] Indeed, members of parliament grew familiar with Winkler's handwriting on a host of mass petitions in the 1840s. When public declarations of support for the parliamentary opposition embarrassed the government in 1844, the county office reported to the Interior Ministry that they were mainly the work of an unholy trio ("Kleeblatt") consisting of Winkler and two town-dwellers of private means. The prefect assigned the leading rôle to Winkler, who travelled several times a week to neighbouring towns and villages to stir up resistance. "If this Winkler did not exist, the *radical demonstrations* would cease immediately", the harassed official assured his superiors.[54]

Regardless of who led whom, Winkler's travels did allow him to concert with like-minded individuals. In Kippenheim in 1846 he joined in a petition for German unification begun by the other two-thirds of the trio.[55] His nationalism took a Rousseauite turn, as the document went on to declare that the national will could be expressed only where civil rights were guaranteed and free elections safeguarded popular sovereignty. Signing with Winkler were Rauch and three other Grafenhauseners, as well as a lone Kappler, Karl Richter, of whom more in due course.

In fact, a closer look at Kappel reveals that some of Winkler's ideas enjoyed considerable support. In the flush of revolutionary enthusiasm in the spring of 1848, 136 men called for radical reforms.[56] In an address to the lower house of parliament, they petitioned for: (1) reduction of dues through taxes on income and capital, (2) reduction of the standing army, (3) election of army officers by the troops, (4) jury trials on the English model, (5) reduction of pensions through abolition of mandatory retirement, (6) abolition of hunting rights, (7) ministerial responsibility and an end to Crown agents' immunity from prosecution, (8) unconditional freedom of the press, (9) abolition of bridge tolls with these costs and those of tithe redemption to be borne by the State, (10) fixed government salaries for priests, with surplus funds going to educational services, (11) a German parliament in place of the confederation, and (12) a requirement that the military swear an oath to the constitution.[57]

Table 10.2 summarizes the fertility of the petitioners' families, with special attention to the one-fifth who were notables. The overall results are well within the range of natural fertility. As in Kappel as a whole at this time, the average woman in a completed family gave birth to her sixth and final child at age forty following a modest final interval. Only elevated ages at marriage pre-

TABLE 10.2
Fertility of documented marriages of All husbands and Notable husbands Signing 2 March 1848 petition in Kappel

	All	Notables only
For completed families		
Wife's age at last birth	39.9	37.9
Final birth interval (in years)	3.50	4.27
Number of legitimate children	5.9	5.7
Total marital fertility rate	8.68	(7.04)
M	1.00	.99
m	.07	.44
Percentage limiting	5 %	48 %

Notes
(1) *Source:* GLA 236/7894 and *OSB Kappel*.
(2) Total marital fertility rates in parentheses are based on 500–999 woman-years.
(3) The Table is based on 130 marriages, in 30 of which the husband was a notable.

vented high marital fertility rates from translating into even larger completed families. The m index of family limitation and the percentage limiting were both so low as to be insignificant.

The second column indicates that notable couples diverged from this pattern. Their lower ages at last birth and their long final intervals kept their families relatively small, despite the fact that the brides were three years younger than average.[58] Underlying natural fertility was effectively identical. The m index of family limitation was six times higher among the notables.[59] The large difference in the percentage limiting confirms the gap.

As I argued in Chapters Seven and Nine, a segment of Kappel's élite did practise family limitation for much of the nineteenth century, but its behaviour was swamped by the natural fertility of the bulk of the population. Here then, social barriers prevented the spread of contraception even among those espousing similar political views.

Detailed information is not available on how attitudes in these localities changed as the revolution progressed. Nevertheless, a few episodes give a feeling for overall trends. The most recent elections in February-March 1846 had featured "intrigues" in Grafenhausen and Kappel, which may be taken as an indication of radical agitation.[60] These proved more successful in Kappel than in Grafenhausen. In the first location, Karl Richter headed the slate of electors, while in the latter, the choice fell on moderates including the priest and dean, Franz Sales Steiger, and the mayor. Rust also returned an establishment slate.[61] In the electoral college as a whole, government and opposition candidates won exactly equal votes; the radical took the seat on a drawing of lots.

By the April-May 1848 balloting for the constituent assembly in Frankfurt, opinion had apparently shifted to the left. Grafenhausen's electors included Winkler and Rauch, the radical Kappel slate was again returned, and affluent militants displaced the municipal officials Rusters had chosen two years earlier. The sentiments of these electors may be gauged from the fact that at their first assembly in May, two-thirds voted for Lorenz Brentano, who was to head the provisional republican government a year later.[62] When he declined, having already been chosen for another seat, they turned in even larger numbers to Ettenheim's representative in the Baden lower house.[63] That man, a Kappler by birth,[64] sat on the far left in Frankfurt.

Even at this point, events were moving too slowly for some. Hardly was Winkler's jail sentence quashed by the revolutionary amnesty for political crimes than he pushed beyond the new legal boundaries. In April 1848 he joined an abortive uprising.[65] After its failure, he went underground as a fugitive, skipping both electoral colleges. When Grafenhauseners were offered an opportunity to replace him, they simply stayed away from the polls.[66] The attitude of the hardliners was further manifested in September 1848, during the second move to establish a German social republic.[67] Grafenhausen contributed a contingent to the saboteurs who ripped up the railway tracks between Orschweier and Ringsheim to hinder the passage of troops sent to subdue the insurgents.[68] In the end, their efforts went for naught, but even under martial law the county remained unstable.[69]

The population polarized as the deliberations and negotiations at Frankfurt seemed to make no concrete progress. Dissatisfied with the Baden government's failure to follow through on the few measures that had been passed, for example by abolishing the aristocratic upper house of parliament, radical deputies indicated their lack of confidence by resigning their seats in the lower house. Among them was the member from Ettenheim.[70] The government called a by-election, in which the electoral college chosen in the relative calm of 1846 was to reassemble to select a new deputy. Karl Richter had fled to America in the aftermath of the September attack on the railroad,[71] but Kapplers dutifully chose a replacement for him.

The electors met in March 1849 and again in April, but each time were unable to proceed to a vote as the number willing to participate did not constitute a quorum. Both before and during the assemblies, just over half the electors, including all three from Kappel, declared that they too had no confidence in the current Baden parliament, and demanded the convening of a constituent assembly for Baden. The four Rusters and the three Grafenhauseners chosen in 1846 stood fast on the side of constituted order.[72]

In May 1849, a third revolutionary upsurge swept that order away, and proclaimed a republic. Much of Baden's army and civil service went over to the new régime. Elections to a constituent assembly were held, but the outcome in these three villages has not been preserved.[73] In practice, power passed into the hands of Nepomuk Winkler, functioning temporarily as revolutionary civil commissar in place of the county prefect.

Full details of his activities are not available, but he was much concerned to build up the citizens' militia.[74] He organized the raising of troops and arranged for arming and provisioning them. He threatened disobedient municipalities with military occupation.[75] The atmosphere was tense as the revolutionaries braced for outside intervention. Facing opposition from Grafenhausen itself, Winkler deposed the mayor and replaced the municipal clerk.[76] At one point, Winkler had Steiger arrested, but the priest was released by Brentano within a week.[77] On returning to his parish, Steiger committed his mistrust of Grafenhausen's republican schoolteachers to paper, but only in Latin.[78] To some at least, revolutionary terror lay close at hand.[79]

The character of the Baden republic is moot, for it was crushed within two months by Prussian troops. Municipal officials were ousted and politically reliable citizens put in their place. A good many villagers were arrested temporarily, but most were released without having been charged. In determining whom to punish, the government relied on informers, among them the keeper of the Crown inn in Kappel.[80]

Prosecutions for treason and resistance to legitimate authority, occasionally coupled with manslaughter, violence, and extortion, were initiated against eight Grafenhauseners, four Rusters, and four Kapplers. The activities of the Kapplers were not that consequential, for their cases were among the seven to be dropped. The list of the convicted was headed by Winkler with a fifteen-year sentence, and Rauch, who drew ten years.[81] Winkler lived out his days in Paris,[82] but Rauch was captured and died in prison.

Not every revolutionary was dealt with harshly. Complicity with the republican cause had been so widespread that it was impracticable to punish all those involved,[83] and generous amnesties were granted. Attempts by the government to recover costs also tended to end in negotiation, as many revolutionaries lacked the property to cover their fines.[84] Winkler's deserted wife divided the family assets and took over the Angel inn herself. The government closed it down, citing her loss of citizenship through her husband's conviction and the revolutionary tendencies of the Angel's clientèle. She appealed the decision, lost, and appealed again, highlighting the issue's significance for the status of Baden's wives. In 1852, she finally won the right to reopen the inn.[85]

The restored government took advantage of the presence of the occupying troops to renew parliament in January 1850. Campaigns were quiet, and turnout was fairly light. By and large, the voters made safe choices, although in each of Grafenhausen, Kappel, and Rust, one elector of a left-wing stripe was chosen.[86] In February, the electors unanimously endorsed the government official recommended to them by the chief returning officer.[87]

The same meekness characterized that month's voting for the house of the abortive new German confederation in Erfurt. Only a few citizens bothered to take part, and their choice generally fell on the municipal leaders recently imposed upon them. Those electors proved quite reliable, at least in public, voting virtually unanimously for the candidate put forward by the government.[88]

In the absence of detailed information from Grafenhausen, Kappel, and Rust, it is difficult to gauge popular responses to these developments. The petition from Kappel and the behaviour of citizens throughout the region indicate that radical democratic ideas, if not the methods of the republican insurgents, commanded a great deal of popular sympathy.[89] Looking at the revolution as a whole, one can see that it found its most active supporters, as well as its most obdurate opponents, in Grafenhausen. Rusters were less prominent before the uprising, but like many radical Grafenhausener maintained their commitment to the bitter end. Kappel featured plenty of radicals on paper in the springtime of peoples, but they were nowhere to be found the following summer when the day of glory arrived.

The implications of this state of affairs for population history are less clear. Because records of the first stage of voting have not survived, one can study only the electors who emerged from it. Within that élite, Radicalism was associated with family limitation, but Moderation was not.[90] Table 10.3 shows the Radicals further from natural fertility in every respect.

Last births came just a bit younger to Radical women, but they followed much longer intervals and fewer pregnancies.[91] Total marital fertility rates were considerably higher among the Moderates, despite the fact that their underlying level of natural fertility (M) was identical to the Radicals'. The entire difference

TABLE 10.3
Fertility of documented marriages of Radical and Moderate electors in Ettenheim and Kenzingen ridings from 1846 to 1850

	Radical	Moderate
For completed families		
Wife's age at last birth	38.8	39.4
Final birth interval (in years)	4.62	3.50
Number of legitimate children	4.8	6.5
Total marital fertility rate	7.40	8.73
M	1.03	1.03
m	.44	.10
Percentage limiting	58 %	26 %

Notes
(1) The sources and the definitions of the two tendencies are outlined in the text.
(2) The Table is based on 122 marriages: 57 involving Radicals and 65 involving Moderates.

derived from family limitation, for the Radicals' m is elevated while the Moderates' remains insignificant. The percentage of Moderates practising family limitation is higher than the m value would have led one to anticipate, possibly because the estimate is inflated by the low ages of their brides. In any case, it does not reach half the figure for the Radicals. All these measures, then, indicate that Radicals were prone to innovate within the family as well as within the State.

One must be wary of extrapolating from so few leaders to the mass of followers. The youthfulness of their brides suggests that electors of both tendencies were considerably better off than the voters who chose them. Table 10.4 bears this out. The radicals' occupational distribution was skewed, with one-quarter falling in the Affluent category, typically innkeeping. Such occupations were only half as common, although still heavily over-represented, in the Moderate camp. Artisanal, and to a lesser extent Farming occupations, made up the shortfall. Humble activities were rare on both sides.

From the pattern in Kappel (Table 10.2), one may speculate that although leaders of the revolution were adopting family limitation, their followers were less apt to do so. Given Chapter Nine's links between wealth and fertility, the notorious concern of Moderates for property rights might make family limitation more popular among counter-revolutionaries.[92] Such a division would fit the pattern obtaining in Grafenhausen in 1824. Testing these assumptions requires a body of evidence on the political behaviour of ordinary citizens. In its absence, they have to stand as merely plausible.

The 1850s and 1860s were a period of transition in Baden's political life. The suppression of the revolution had dampened popular enthusiasm for political involvement.[93] Prudence dictated withdrawal from the public arena, where conspicuous commitment brought only repression. Until new forces had organ-

TABLE 10.4
Distributions of occupations of Radical and Moderate electors in Ettenheim and Kenzingen ridings from 1846 to 1850

	Radical	Moderate
Affluent	26 %	13 %
Craft, Fishing, Weaving	9 %	20 %
Farming	34 %	40 %
Profession, Substantial, Commerce	29 %	26 %
Local Position, Labour	1 %	1 %
Absolute total	48	50

Notes
(1) The sources and the definitions of the two tendencies are outlined in the text.
(2) In the one case where an elector was not assigned an occupation in the OSBs, he was classified by the designation used on the list of electors.

ized themselves on the local level, the mass of the population remained ensconced in private affairs. Politics was left to the politicians. The result was a transformed agenda, dominated by relations between Church and State and the broader problems of governance of the new German empire.

Notes

1. J. Stengers ("Les pratiques anticonceptionnelles dans le mariage au XIXe et au XXe siècles: problèmes humains et attitudes réligieuses", *Revue belge de philologie et d'histoire*, 49 (1971), 1119–1174) traces the Church's aggressive public denunciation of contraception to Belgium in 1909. Beginning in 1920, Baden's visitation forms asked whether marrying couples were warned against "abuse of marriage". Priests' answers tended to be perfunctory. Ord A B4/3747, Ord A B4/5632, and Ord A B4/10504. The earliest expression I have found of clerical concern in this area comes from Herbolzheim in 1915 (Ord A B4/4632), a century after family limitation began there. Knodel, *fourteen*.
2. Independence sometimes dictated apathy rather than engagement. Where villagers had nothing to gain from either side in a dispute, independence took the form of resisting being drawn into it.
3. On the significance of the municipality more generally, see Jerome Blum, "The European Village as Community: Origins and Functions", *Agricultural History*, 45 (1971), 159–166.
4. Compare Robert Netting, *Balancing on an Alp* (Cambridge, 1981), 186–201, which downplays the broader political possibilities of villagers.
5. To meet the agricultural crises of the late 1840s by taking land from lords, churches, and states, and redistributing it. The failure of this attempt was the signal for the massive emigration of the 1850s, which the government encouraged.

6. Alternatively, French ideas, from republicanism to contraception, may have seeped into Baden in a common solution. In May 1849 the revolutionary Nepomuk Winkler, to be discussed below, declared that he was in personal touch with "the most prominent democrats of Alsace". GLA 264/7 (grounds for sentence 18 June 1850).
7. Both the title and parts of the following account draw on Benedikt Schwarz's contribution to *Das Badener Land* for 13 and 20 December 1903, reprinted in *OSB Rust* pages 76–83. Köbele, compiling the OSB, renamed it a "Revolution".
8. The cross-examination of Ott, detailing numerous accusations of misconduct together with his by and large convincing replies, is preserved in GLA 229/90576.
9. GLA 229/90580 (interrogation of Ott 27 October 1747).
10. The notary's record of the testimony and the disruption ibid.
11. See also BvB A U. 875 (24 November 1747 declaration by Neckar and Black Forest imperial knighthood).
12. Eventually, the troops managed to escort the goods out of the village while the women were attending a church service.
13. BvB A U. 876 (13 February 1748).
14. GLA 229/90580 (especially letter to Ettenheim office 5 March 1749 and response 29 March 1749 on the legal situation).
15. BvB A U. 887 (28 August 1751). On the atmosphere, consider the 1750 cases of sub-tenants, including Werner, threatening tenants-in-chief in BvB A U. 882.
16. Ordinarily, the Böcklins made about 2000 fl. a year from Rust. BvB A DEPOSITA 356 (accounts for 1763).
17. "Stabhalter", as distinct from "Schultheiss". GLA 229/90575.
18. His successor was second-richest. Gem A Rust C I/6 (tax rolls 1759–1765). In 1753, Ott and Werner loaned the lord money in return for the right to purchase the lands of bankrupts at half-price. (BvB A U. 894.)
19. The roadside cross Ott and his wife set up can still be seen (picture and description in *OSB Rust* pages 122–123) and elsewhere in Rust a street bears his name (ibid., between pages 140 and 141). The grounds of what was the Böcklins' palace are now the site of the community's lucrative Europa-Park.
20. For details of the court case that gives this section its title, I rely on Gem A Grafenhausen B IV/199 and GLA 353/1908–105/191.
21. Proverbially, it is good to live under the (bishop's) crook.
22. Ord A Konstanz Generalia Ha 582a (1762 visitation report).
23. *OSB Grafenhausen* pages 196–205.
24. GLA 229/33749 (delays 1781–1784).
25. GLA 27a/30 U. 646 (31 October 1799).
26. Because this case is less well attested, I present only a few highlights from GLA 126/37.
27. At that time embroiled in a separate dispute with the citizens over its attempts to force them to choose a new treasurer. (GLA 229/90539.) The deputies had been declared unacceptable candidates (letter of 10 June 1790).
28. Their unanimity raises suspicions of coercion.
29. The following discussion draws heavily on collections of documents in the municipal and provincial archives (Gem A Grafenhausen B IV/129 and GLA 229/33739, respectively). Only the latter were used by Karl Person, "Der Aufruhr in Grafenhausen im Jahre 1822", *Herbolzheimer Zeitung* (October–December 1937, copy in Herbolzheim town archive). All but the final instalment (4 December 1937) has survived in *OSB Grafenhausen* pages 238–251.
30. The epithet "unruhige Köpfe" was used twice to describe followers of the dissidents in a 20 December 1823 demand that the mayor be removed from office (Gem A Grafenhausen B IV/129). See also *OSB Grafenhausen* page 88 (quoting the prefect).

A factum prepared by the Böcklins in 1748 had characterized rebellious Rusters in the same terms (OSB Rust page 80).
31. The turnout was about 90 %. 192 male citizens had taken the oath of allegiance on 4 January 1819. GLA 236/1758. There were just over two hundred adult male taxpayers on the rolls for 1819. Gem A Grafenhausen C IX/1.
32. Gem A Grafenhausen B V/370 (complaints by mayors of Wittenweier, Mahlberg, Kappel, Kippenheim, Altdorf, and Ringsheim, in late February and early March 1824).
33. I treat a husband's vote as a family characteristic, like his occupation or mature landholding. Since the means of contraception available to a village couple—abstinence and withdrawal—involved cooperation or even initiative by the husband, there is little reason to fear that discrepancies between the political views of husbands and their disenfranchised wives obscure relations between fertility and politics.
34. These differences hold up when the factions are broken down by age at marriage, and a clear gap in family size becomes evident. (Details not shown.)
35. The percentage rich, in the sense of Chapter Nine, was 48 % among Mutschler's opponents and 53 % among his supporters. By contrast, 75 % of intermediate voters were rich.
36. In addition to their predilection for the Ox, prominent supporters of the old order shared an interest in Grafenhausen's band, which they founded in 1825.
37. Especially because the wives wed for the first time about one year younger than those in the other two factions.
38. Attempts to collect from the dissidents and to have their toe Mutschler make good various shortfalls were still in progress in 1829. Gem A Grafenhausen B IV/129.
39. Ord A B3/500 (visitation report).
40. GLA 360/1935–11/778.
41. For more detailed presentations of Baden's political life at this time, see Manfred Hörner, *Die Wahlen zur badischen zweiten Kammer im Vormärz (1819–1847)* (Göttingen, 1987), Norbert Deuchert, *Vom Hambacher Fest zur badischen Revolution* (Stuttgart, 1983), and Lothar Gall, *Der Liberalismus als regierende Partei* (Wiesbaden, 1968), 1–57.
42. Hörner (*Vormärz*, 131) calculates the franchise to have been the most extensive in a European monarchy. Benz, Thesis, appendix E describes the electoral system.
43. Such as Karl Theodor Welcker, who represented Ettenheim riding from 1831 to 1839. (For variety and precision, I use "riding" to mean an electoral district.) Hans Person, "Parlamentarisches aus 150 Jahren Abgeordnete aus dem Kreis Lahr", Geroldseckerland, 7 (1964–1965), 20–29 lists the region's other deputies.
44. Helmut Kramer, *Fraktionsverbindungen in den deutschen Volksvertretungen 1819–1849* (Berlin, 1968), 40–71.
45. For example, Welcker worked out his position and tactics on freedom of the press, taxation, and the customs union in consultation with his electors. Ettenheim town archive B XIII/969. The more general aspects of Welcker's career are covered in Heinz Müller-Dietz, *Das Leben des Rechtslehrers und Politikers Karl Theodor Welcker* (Freiburg, 1968).
46. The government regained Ettenheim at the end of Welcker's term in 1839 (on the campaign, see Hörner, *Vormärz*, 446), but lost it once more in the extraordinary general election of 1842. The victor that year was Karl Zittel, once the fourth child in entry 1968 of Albert Köbele, Hans Scheer, and Emil Ell, *Ortssippenbuch Schmieheim* (Grafenhausen, 1979). On his political career, see Alexander Mohr, "Karl Zittel (1802–1871), Pfarrer und liberal Politiker in der II. Ständekammer und im Paulskirchen-Parlament", in Gerhard Schwinge (ed.), *Protestantismus und Politik*

(Karlsruhe, 1996), 132–140. For Zittel's own account of political life in the 1840s, see "Die politischen Partheiungen in Baden", *Jahrbücher der Gegenwart*, 1847, 347–378 and "Der badische Landtag", *Jahrbücher der Gegenwart*, 1848, 62–64.
47. Interrogation of 20 April 1847 in GLA 264/5. At that point Winkler was concerned to deny links to France, the homeland of revolution.
48. Indeed, he was twice chosen mayor, but vetoed both times by the government. GLA 264/6 (interrogation 14 May 1847).
49. Gem A Grafenhausen C VIII/1 (1843–1848 instructions from Ettenheim to Grafenhausen). See also the similar order in Gem A Grafenhausen B XI/675.
50. GLA 233/16779 (documents surrounding appeals of Winkler's convictions for mockery of the civil service).
51. GLA 264/4. The investigation was dropped when it was discovered that the ostensible butt of the cartoon proudly displayed his own copy.
52. GLA 264/5. A previous search had turned up nothing. Winkler appealed his arrest and later his sentence to six months in jail. GLA 264/6.
53. "Hauptmann". Submission from brigadier of gendarmerie 12 May 1847 in GLA 264/6.
54. Report of 25 March 1844 in GLA 236/8159.
55. GLA 233/30013 (petition of 29 January 1846).
56. There were just over two hundred married male landowners in Kappel around this time. Gem A Kappel Tithe register for 1846.
57. GLA 236/7894 (petition of 2 March 1848). To endorse such positions publicly was of course far less egregious in 1848 than it had been earlier.
58. That difference in age at marriage did not account for the results in Table 10.2, for they show up just as strongly when only young brides are considered. (Details not shown.)
59. It was significantly greater than 0, and outside the confidence ellipse for the petitioners as a whole.
60. GLA 313/4365 (report from prefect 16 March 1846 on "Umtriebe").
61. List of electors for subsequent by-election in GLA 236/4307.
62. GLA 236/4250 (protocol of 16 May 1848 electoral college).
63. GLA 236/4249 (protocol of 3 June 1848 electoral college).
64. Brother to Karl Richter in *OSB Kappel* entry 1839.
65. Led by Friedrich Hecker.
66. GLA 236/4250 (letters of 11 and 15 May 1848 from chief returning officer). GLA 236/4249 (letter of 30 May 1848).
67. Associated with Gustav Struve.
68. Map 1.1 shows the rail line. Gem A Grafenhausen B XVII/836 assessed costs against Grafenhausen, Kappel, and Ettenheim. GLA 236/8510 names as participants six Ettenheimers, three Mahlbergers, and two Grafenhauseners, as well as one each from Rust and three other locations. A 3 October 1848 report, reprinted in Thomas Dees, "Ettenheim in den Revolutionsjahren 1848 und 1849", *Die Ortenau*, 62 (1982), 157, informed the national government in Frankfurt that twenty participants were in custody, including Rauch, while forty had fled, Winkler and a Grafenhausen schoolteacher leading the pack.
69. Ettenheim town archive B IX/791 (prefect's correspondence with the mayors of Kappel and Ettenheim).
70. GLA 231/1616 (letter of 1 March 1849).
71. Gem A Kappel C IX/12 (introduction to municipal accounts for 1848). Six other Kapplers turned themselves in. Dees, "Revolutionsjahren", 157.
72. GLA 236/4307 (protocols of 6 March and 4 April 1849 electoral colleges). GLA 236/4301 (declaration of 26 March 1849 from boycotting electors and response of 6 April 1849 from the chief returning officer).

73. On the election campaign and the assembly's debates see Sonja-Maria Bauer, *Die verfassungsgebende Versammlung in der badischen Revolution von 1849* (Düsseldorf, 1991).
74. Ettenheim town archive B IX/784.
75. GLA 264/7. Kippenheimweiler was in fact occupied.
76. GLA 240/1680.
77. GLA 264/7.
78. Pf A Grafenhausen announcement book 25 June to 4 July 1849. He employed the same discretion in recording their arrest by the restored government on 25 July 1849.
79. This aspect of the situation is emphasized from a christian democratic perspective in Johannes Ferdinand, "Die revolutionäre Bewegung 1848–1849 in Ettenheim", *Die Ortenau*, 30 (N.F. 2, 1950), 46–59, and from a national socialist one in Erich Blankenhorn, "Badens Wehr in den Jahren 1848/49", *Mein Heimatland*, 27 (1940), 188–206.
80. Gem A Kappel B VI/345.
81. GLA 237/16844 and GLA 237/16845. They were followed by a Ruster prominent in the militia (nine years reduced to six on appeal—GLA 240/1431), a Grafenhausen schoolteacher who acted as scribe for Winkler (three years reduced to two on appeal—GLA 240/1680), and a Grafenhausener who fought briefly with the revolutionary army (two-year sentence upheld—GLA 240/1434).
82. He maintained loose contact with Grafenhausen until his reported death in 1864. GLA 353/1905–105/4.
83. Confronted with the news that his part in the uprising rendered his property liable for all costs arising from the revolution, an exasperated innkeeper burst out "Didn't the entire country take part then?". Emil Ell, "War Kippenheims Kronenwirt ein Revoluzzer?", *Altvater*, 36 (May 1978), 42.
84. GLA 237/3183 through GLA 237/3185 (concerning a schoolteacher in Grafenhausen) and GLA 237/3838 through GLA 237/3846 (concerning Rauch).
85. GLA 236/7389 and *OSB Grafenhausen* pages 190–191.
86. GLA 236/4305 (list of electors and report of 24 January 1850 from the prefect). This was as far as villagers could go in demonstrating their sentiments, for when Grafenhauseners chose their Radical elector as mayor, he was not allowed to take office. GLA 360/1935–11/778 (report on 1855 inspection tour of Grafenhausen). On the election at the time, see GLA 236/3109.
87. GLA 236/4306 (report of 24 February 1850 from chief returning officer).
88. GLA 236/4220 (reports of 17 March 1850 from chief returning officer).
89. The assertion in Walter Rinderle and Bernard Norling, *The Nazi Impact on a German Village* (Lexington, Kentucky, 1993), 15, that peasants in this area were largely ignorant and apathetic may rest on anecdotal lore or on a special case.
90. Members of electoral colleges chosen from 1846–1850 in the future provincial riding of Ettenheim-Kenzingen are classified as follows. Those who refused to take part in Baden by-elections in 1849 are Radicals, those willing to vote are Moderates. GLA 236/4307 and GLA 236/4301. The Radical side is supplemented by electors for the Frankfurt assembly, the Moderates' by electors chosen at the height of reaction in 1850. GLA 236/4250, GLA 236/4247, and GLA 236/4305. Gem A Grafenhausen C IX/1 and Gem A Kappel C IX/12 (notes in municipal accounts for 1850). Herbolzheim town archive B XIII 1/3. The two tendencies overlap.
91. Radicals wed in 1835, Moderates in 1828, on average. This was less because Radicals were younger, although that was true, than because they remarried more frequently. Wives' average ages at first marriage were equal, but in completed families, Radical brides were a year and a half older than Moderate ones. Attempting to control for the later date of Radical marriages by restricting attention to couples wed from 1825 on actually accentuates the differences in fertility. For instance, the gap in final birth intervals rises to over a year and a half.

92. That is, one might postulate the following ordering in strength of family limitation: Radical leaders, Moderate leaders, Moderate followers, Radical followers.
93. This does not mean that the revolution disappeared without a trace. A century later, an octogenarian in Grafenhausen recalled the words to songs that had brought his father a stay in jail. Gem A Grafenhausen B XIII/760 and *OSB Grafenhausen* pages 189–190.

11

Anticlericals and Ultramontanes

I now extend my examination of politics into the second half of the nineteenth century, during which Baden's public life was dominated by religious controversies. This chapter links religion and fertility in Grafenhausen, Kappel, and Rust, and explores their impact on federal election campaigns. I begin by outlining several strong theories identifying ultramontanism with tradition, and anticlericalism with modernization. I do not endorse those views, but I bow to their popularity by allowing them to structure my presentation. My own interpretations, along the lines introduced in Chapter Ten, emerge as a residue, rather than as a position argued for directly.

Models of Secularization

Theories associating religion and fertility take a variety of forms, but most agree in tying orthodox Catholic religiosity to resistance to modernization, including family limitation under that vague catch-all.[1] The nature of the link is often left equally unclear, shrouded in cultural norms and aggregate correlations.[2] One specific way to make the connection is to argue that rejecting the Church symbolized rejecting a whole constellation of attitudes that had prevented resort to contraception. Alternatively, anti-religious ideologies may have included promotion of family limitation among their tenets. In either case the causal chain runs from the new attitudes to the new behaviour.

Theodore Zeldin has proposed an interesting reversal of this argument.[3] He suggests that family limitation led to anticlericalism among Catholics. The institution of confession stands at the heart of his reasoning.[4] Responding to priests' detailed questioning of their wives concerning sexual practices, or to the mere possibility of such questioning, husbands practising coitus interruptus are alleged to have turned against the Church as a whole.

Zeldin's hypothesis can be refined to take account of more varied behaviour by priests and parishioners. One might speculate, for example, that clerics who were less ultramontane or simply older were more inclined to pursue a Liguorian line[5] in the confessional, avoiding controversial topics unless a penitent brought them up, making generous allowances where the description of behaviour was ambiguous or incomplete, and prescribing token penances.[6] Such priests would retain the loyalty of voters, while doctrinaire ones would alienate them.

In a region like this one, where clericalism had to fight its way to political victory, contrary to the theory's implicit assumptions, one could build on this idea to suggest that it was villagers who forced priests to modify their behaviour, rather than vice versa. By this account, to keep the confidence of their parishioners, priests had to tolerate what the Church regarded as errant sexual practices.[7] On either version of Zeldin's theory, just as on either of the more standard accounts, anticlericalism in the voting booth went with anticlericalism in the bedchamber. I henceforth refer to such views as Secularization theories.

As I indicated earlier, this model determines the topics I take up in this chapter and the next one. Because work on Secularization has focused on the statistics generated by electoral politics, I present all the available results from contests in which ultramontanism was an issue. This gives these interpretations a full and fair test.

Let me indicate briefly what a positive outcome to this test would look like. Table 11.1 summarizes results of the 1903 federal election and the 1905 provincial election in several municipalities in the region.[8] It also includes the percentage of the population in each location who were Roman Catholics, on the assumption that that religion was especially relevant to politics on the one hand and family limitation on the other.

TABLE 11.1
Outcome of the 1903 German federal election and the 1905 Baden provincial election in selected polls in Ettenheim-Emmendingen-Lahr riding

	Percentage Roman Catholic	Federal election			Provincial election		
		On voters' list	NL	Z	On voters' list	NL	Z
Entire provincial riding	84 %	6188	20 %	57 %	6089	29 %	42 %
Schuttertal	99 %	193	1 %	87 %	183	1 %	71 %
Schmieheim	4 %	207	81 %	1 %	210	89 %	0 %
Rust	95 %	374	8 %	75 %	371	16 %	56 %
Kappel	99 %	279	8 %	74 %	294	22 %	55 %
Grafenhausen	99 %	363	9 %	64 %	369	38 %	20 %

Notes
(1) *Source*: GLA 236/15106 (official tabulation of results), supplemented by Roth and Thorbecke, *Landstände*, 194.
(2) NL is the percentage of the eligible voters who actually cast ballots for the National Liberal candidate.
   Z is the percentage of the eligible voters who actually cast ballots for the Centre candidate.
(3) The religious breakdown comes from the 1901 census of the entire population.

In this area the elections were essentially straight contests between the National Liberal party and the Centre.[9] The two parties differed sharply on religious issues, with the Centre championing the privileges of the Roman Catholic Church that anticlerical National Liberal governments had attacked. It is plausible then that a major factor in voters' choices might be Secularization.[10] The one-sided outcomes in Schuttertal and Schmieheim add strength to that assumption. In Schuttertal, an overwhelmingly Catholic poll, the Catholic Centre party won almost unanimous support. In Schmieheim, where Protestants and Jews dominated the voters' list, the Centre was virtually shut out.

The results in Grafenhausen, Kappel, and Rust were not as monolithic, perhaps because the larger size of these villages permitted more variegated politics.[11] Nevertheless, in the federal election, all three delivered very comfortable majorities to the Centre. On the federal scene, then, there is no reason to suspect differential Secularization at this point when variations in fertility were extreme. Political Catholicism also carried Kappel and Rust in the provincial election, although the turnout and the Centre's margin were reduced in both polls. However, provincially Grafenhausen proves as outstanding politically as it was demographically, delivering a surprise victory to the National Liberals by a two-to-one margin. If Grafenhausen deviated consistently in that fashion, especially at the time contraception was spreading there, theories of Secularization could claim exemplary confirmation.

Before one can determine the significance of these or any other elections, one must investigate their context.[12] I begin by sketching the course of relations between the Roman Catholic Church and the Baden State in the first half of the nineteenth century. I then briefly trace the steps by which the government brought to life the resistance that crystallized as the Centre. At first at least, these developments proceeded without much popular involvement on either side. There was generally no difference between villagers' responses, and a fortiori those responses shed little light on fertility. By the last third of the century, however, questions with religious overtones did agitate the mass of the population.

Indeed, it proves easier to link religion and politics than to tie either to demography in a conclusive fashion. For instance, both Jews and Old Catholics opted virtually unanimously for the form of liberalism that dominated Baden's political life at this time. As it happens, their fertility also diverged from that of the surrounding population. However, the differences were not always in the direction predicted by Secularization theory, and in any case reflected special social circumstances as much as religious attitudes.

Analyses of voting behaviour at the end of the century bring to light suggestive, if intricate, patterns. The Centre dominated federal politics in these villages, for reasons only partly related to religion. On the other hand, within that general framework, Grafenhausen, and to a lesser extent Rust, sometimes displayed an unusual affinity for National Liberalism. Moreover, those supporting that party on key occasions practised family limitation more assiduously than followers of the Centre. Kappel's experience proves the rule, as the minority of dissidents from the political hegemony of the Roman Catholic Church there also exhibited independent patterns of fertility.

Even so, readers anticipating a clear-cut, unilinear process of dechristianization will search the history of these villages in vain. In Baden, family limitation predated the new era of liberal dominance, and in any case was never exclusive to its proponents. Moreover, many of the most strident liberals were subject to natural fertility. Practitioners of family limitation were distinguished less by unwavering commitment to the National Liberal party than by greater flexibility.[13] That is, their political loyalties were more complicated than their neighbours'. In this respect, they again display the independence and solidity that characterized their economic and family lives.[14]

Before documenting these claims concretely, I pause to indicate in a general way what is wrong with Secularization theory. The basic problem is that it grows out of political experiences like the ones I am about to describe.[15] It is therefore one-sided. Demographic historians no less than others can benefit from pondering the proposition that the present is the product of the whole past.[16]

In particular, the Centre should not automatically be regarded as a traditional force.[17] Non-Catholics find it easy to suppose that Centre supporters, under the thumbs of their priests, resisted political enlightenment, personal freedom, and fertility control.[18] Urbanites likewise incline to see the countryside, hidebound by custom, giving ground only slowly in the face of the relentless progress of civilization.[19] Such interpretations have little to recommend them to the less dogmatic.

Only prejudice would make them more appealing initially than an alternative account according to which a falling away from the Church led reckless citizens to experiment with radicalism, liberalism, socialism, and even national socialism,[20] before the full scope of their error became clear, and they returned to the fold. At least that tale correctly notes that anticlericalism dominated the scene first, and that the Centre came on to supplant it. One is not required to endorse either of these manichean visions. I prefer to see in the histories of Grafenhausen, Kappel, and Rust, human attempts to make less dramatic choices on a range of issues.

In that context, interpretive fairness requires one to extend historical empathy to moderate ultramontanes, social Catholics, Baden particularists, and superstitious fanatics as much as to radical republicans, laissez-faire liberals, German nationalists, and blind anticlericals. Only an appreciation of the individual variations and interactions which made up villagers' lives can permit the historian to plumb the well-springs of their behaviour. That task requires specific research into the intricacies of politics, to which I now turn.[21]

Church and State

The political incorporation of this region into Baden severed its religious affiliation with the Strasbourg diocese. In the end, leadership of the two-thirds of

Badeners who were Catholics passed to Ignaz Wessenberg, functioning as interim bishop of Konstanz.[22] The chapters on the right bank of the Rhine were overseen by his colleague, Vitus Burg, priest in Kappel from 1809 to 1827 and subsequently bishop of Mainz. Both were partial to Josephism.[23] They discouraged "superstitious" customs, such as processions, recitation of the rosary, pilgrimages, orders, Sabbath observance, and periodic abstinence. Simplicity, a general humanitarianism, and a German liturgy were championed in their place. Above all, the Church was not to act independently of the State.[24]

This Enlightened religion dominated the field until the 1840s and left its imprint on priests educated under a curriculum approved by the government. Events took a rather different turn after the ultramontane Hermann von Vicari became archbishop of Freiburg.[25] His insistence on the liberties of the Church was not met with sympathy on the government side, and he eventually resolved to act unilaterally.[26] In November 1853, the Church began to make appointments and process decisions without the concurrence of the State.

Both sides proceeded to test the strength of their hierarchies. The archbishop distributed a pastoral letter defending his position, which priests were to read to their congregations. Subsequently, priests were instructed to preach on four successive Sundays on the issues at stake. On the other side, county prefects had municipal councils and citizens' committees write to their priests, urging them not to foment discord within the community and to restrict themselves to their proper sphere. Notables in Grafenhausen, Kappel, and Rust duly complied, the Rusters even going beyond their mandate by threatening to resign from parish committees and boards of foundations.[27]

Nevertheless, all three priests proceeded as directed by Vicari. Indeed, in the rural chapter of Lahr, the sole admitted exception was the dean, Steiger.[28] His fifteen-year stint in Grafenhausen (1835–1849) had coincided with the appearance of significant levels of family limitation there. Steiger had moved on by this point, but the fact that he sided with the State rather than the Church conveys something of the attitudes he had promoted in his old parish.[29]

Although these developments might be relevant to previous events in Grafenhausen, in 1854 the struggle between Church and State was sharpest in Kappel. As the dispute was approaching its height, Peter Anton Schleyer was invested as priest there. He went unrecognized by the State, which blocked his salary. On instructions, he then refused to carry out the civil service duties handled by priests, and managed to evade attempts to have them carried out at his expense.

The confrontation at the other end of the hierarchy also reached a crisis. When Vicari ordered parish treasurers to disregard commands from government officials regarding parish funds, the eighty-one-year-old archbishop was arrested. In response, Schleyer banned music and song from church services and locked out the organist. The village church bells fell silent. Despite the prefect's attempts to intercept their mail, the priests read a second pastoral letter from their pulpits in June 1854. The deadlock was broken only with the release of the archbishop.[30]

Tempers cooled somewhat thereafter. Even the agitation that blocked ratification of the new concordat negotiated between the grand duchy and the Vatican at the end of the decade died away when its object was achieved.[31] The Church had demonstrated that it commanded the loyalty of the clergy, but it was condemned to passive resistance as long as the laity remained unorganized.

This remained true in the 1860s when the government passed into the hands of moderate liberals, under the similarly minded grand duke Friedrich.[32] In earlier chapters, I have had occasion to mention their laissez-faire programme in connection with the abolition of guilds, the lifting of legal restrictions on marriage by the poor, and the extension of full civil equality to Jews. They regarded the Church too as an unfree institution whose oppressed individual members were to be liberated by the State. Over a period of years, liberals passed laws replacing religious oversight of education with school boards (1862, 1864, 1868), forcing priests to pass a State exam before taking office (1867),[33] requiring civil marriage (1869), closing schools run by religious corporations (1870), and confiscating the assets of religious foundations and transferring them to welfare agencies. Although these moves aroused the indignation of some Catholics, their response was not yet concerted enough to prevent the new régime from proceeding at its own pace. Like its head, the Church was limited to the grim declaration that it could not and ought not reconcile itself to, nor agree with, progress, liberalism, and civilization as lately introduced.[34]

These phenomena can be seen at work in the voting for district electors in Grafenhausen in September 1865. These contests were regarded as a test of support for the government's recent measures in the field of education. A year earlier, the archbishop had urged Catholics to boycott elections to the boards set up to supervise the new school system. Turnouts had been low: 13 % in Kappel, 18 % in Rust (Catholics only), and 25 % in Grafenhausen.[35] Because the archbishop called on Catholics in general and priests in particular to participate in the district elections, the stage was set for a sharper struggle.

In Grafenhausen the battle proved rather one-sided, as a slate made up of six members of the municipal council received about 70 % of the vote. Reports in the pro-government press trumpeted a complete victory for progress, led by young men, over a priest and his benighted followers, who had employed all means to prevent it.[36] The documents of the returning officers reveal a rather different picture.[37] To be sure, the priest did cast his ballot for losing candidates, but he was virtually alone in two of his choices. Nor was the priest the only voter in doubt about how best to register a protest. It is a measure of the disorganization of the clerical party at this time that opposition votes were split among eight serious candidates. Furthermore, family limitation was found among the leaders on both sides, and to a lesser extent among their followers.

Table 11.2 bears this out. It compares the family histories of backers of the straight winning ticket and supporters of the also-rans. Wives in the first faction gave birth for the last time an insignificant half-year younger than the rest of the population. Their completed families were larger, and there was little

TABLE 11.2
Fertility of documented marriages of Voters in the 4 September 1865 district election in Grafenhausen, by political faction

	Backed government	Backed opposition
For completed families		
Wife's age at last birth	38.3	38.8
Final birth interval (in years)	3.75	3.69
Number of legitimate children	5.5	4.7
Total marital fertility rate	8.37	8.76
M	1.13	1.15
m	.38	.36
Percentage limiting	40 %	34 %

Notes
(1) *Source*: Gem A Grafenhausen B XIII/768 and *OSB Grafenhausen*.
(2) The assignment to factions is described in Benz, Thesis, appendix E.
(3) The Table is based on 214 marriages: 164 involving supporters of the government and 50 involving opponents.

difference in final birth intervals. All these results reflect nothing more than younger marriage on the winning side.[38] The m index of family limitation and the percentage limiting likewise reveal no striking distinction between tendencies.

Thus, at this time, political and religious differences had no bearing on fertility, and vice versa. Since both family limitation and the polarization of politics along religious lines were only beginning, both bore little relation to voters' motivations. It is plausible to regard the losers, some of whom had held municipal office in earlier years, as citizens dissatisfied with the village government for personal reasons. They practised a certain measure of family limitation as notables, while ultramontanism was merely a convenient vehicle to express personal disaffection. In Grafenhausen in 1865, political cleavages did not mark different approaches to family life.[39]

In the foregoing pages, I have several times implicitly slipped from discussing all inhabitants of the villages to considering Catholics only. Neglect of the handful of Protestants in Grafenhausen, Kappel, and Rust, many of whom were only temporarily resident, is not particularly serious, as they were too few to permit separate demographic analysis. Rust's Jews were more numerous, and so one may compare their fertility to that of the rest of the population. It turns out that they remained subject to natural fertility even at a time when their political allegiances were distinct from their neighbours'. Finally, the Old Catholics in Kappel provide an especially acute test of links between religion, politics, and fertility. Restriction of reproduction within marriage was common in the generation that rejected Rome, but their children's political situation over-rode this attachment to family limitation. Because these patterns bear directly on the Secularization thesis, I pause to examine these two minorities before redirecting my attention to the Roman Catholic majority.

THE JEWISH COMMUNITY IN RUST

For the most part, Rust's Jews were politically inactive. They were denied the vote in the first half of the nineteenth century, and displayed none of the ingenuity of their co-religionists elsewhere, who attempted to circumvent the restrictions on their franchise.[40] When other Jewish communities in the region petitioned for equality in 1845–1846, Rusters remained silent.[41] When equality finally came, they celebrated, proudly asserting their full citizenship and voting in disproportionate numbers in the 1860s. For instance, 62 % turned out in the 1864 school board election the Catholics shunned.[42] However, Rust's Jews valued freedom of movement over suffrage, as heavy emigration set in almost immediately. Moreover, they did not display their gratitude as openly as the region's other Jews, who lined up with the government publicly.[43] The overall impression is of a community somewhat removed from the questions that agitated their Christian neighbours.

One reason Rust's Jews could lie low was the absence of virulent anti-Semitism at this time. The upheavals of 1848 did not include riots directed against them, as they did in other parts of Baden.[44] Their emancipation was received with calm in the village itself.[45] No Kappler objected to the prospect of Jews immigrating, even when a special opportunity was provided.[46] Later in the century, official anti-Semitic candidates received no votes in Rust.[47] A certain mutual diffidence in politics, then, may have preserved peace for Rust's Jews.

Their fertility was equally unremarkable.[48] Average age at last birth was forty-two, following a short final interval of 3.24 years. Women entered marriage at twenty-seven on average, and their mates were consistently older still, so that the male advantage was greater than among Christians. Marrying old kept completed family size (6.2 children) around the level for Catholic citizens despite the Jews' higher total marital fertility rate. That higher rate runs counter to any expectation of reduced fertility through absence of husbands on business trips, or observance of religious prohibitions.[49] Taken as a whole, the results clearly bespeak natural fertility.

Relaxing the limitation to documented families by taking advantage of other information on the Jewish community did not substantially alter this verdict. Only in marriages beginning after emancipation, at a time when most Jews were already leaving Rust, is there evidence of strong family limitation. This fits the findings of studies of the Jewish communities in nearby Altdorf and Nonnenweier.[50] The coincidence suggests that it would be profitable to study the fertility of this region's Jews as a unit, for co-religionists in different villages seemingly had more in common with one another than with the Christians who were their immediate neighbours.

In Rust, for instance, they lagged two decades behind the first Catholics to adopt family limitation.[51] Their religion contributed to a different political orientation but it did not predispose them to contraception. The same applied to their unusual occupational distribution. 82 % of occupations in documented marriages were classified as Commercial, and a further 16 % were Affluent or Substantial, but there is no sign of the very early family limitation that marked Catholic villagers in these categories. For the Jewish community, both economics and religion impeded the entry of innovations.[52]

Old Catholicism in Kappel

The proclamation of papal infallibility as dogma in the course of the First Vatican Council in 1870 provoked a split in the Catholic Church. Those who dissented from this decision called themselves "Old Catholics", insisting that they held fast to the true popular religion of their ancestors. With the encouragement of the government, the movement enjoyed a meteoric career in Baden. As it happens, the sole recognized Old Catholic congregation between Freiburg and Offenburg was found in Kappel.

Its history sheds surprising light on the themes considered in this chapter.[53] Old Catholics were distinguished by wealth, status, and politics, as well as by religion. The first two characteristics predisposed them towards family limitation. However, politics exerted an independent effect that eventually over-rode this predisposition. Within this group, it was politics that determined religion, and ultimately it was politics that determined fertility.

I therefore treat Old Catholicism as a social and political phenomenon rather than a strictly theological one. Its roots in Kappel lay in several developments already described. The sudden shift from the liberalism of Burg and Baptist Uebelin, who succeeded him as Kappel's priest from 1827 to 1853, to the ultramontanism of Schleyer brought the struggle between State and Church home to the parish. The easygoing Uebelin had lent his name as president to a literary society that functioned as a cover for revelry after curfew by the local élite.[54] By contrast, Schleyer on one occasion denounced the conduct of those citizens in such strong terms that they walked out of the church and subsequently attended services in Rust if at all. Embroiled in disputes with the central government and under attack from the municipal council, Schleyer was eventually forced to withdraw from Kappel.[55] Thereafter the parish was served by several vicars and priests, none of whom lasted long enough to make a positive impression.

The church assets in Kappel, accumulated through bequests from well-off peasants, constituted a perennial source of tension in the landhungry community. The idea of secularizing them, or drawing off some of the income to defray municipal expenditures and thereby cut taxes, had a particular attraction.[56] This desire was only strengthened by the behaviour of one elderly priest who took a leave of absence in 1867 but continued to live from the emolument until 1874.[57]

Still, to move from a state of endemic discontent to an open break with the Church hierarchy required energetic leadership of a kind rare in Kappel. It was provided by the forty-eighter Karl Richter, who returned from his self-imposed American exile and resumed his rise to political prominence. In short order, he became a councillor, and then in 1862 mayor. He initiated the extensive drainage and irrigation projects described in Chapter Three.[58] In 1865, Richter was elected to the Baden legislature,[59] where he associated himself with the ruling liberals. He wholeheartedly endorsed the government's anticlerical policies and worked on the local level to win support for them.

Richter enjoyed a measure of success in making Kappel a national liberal strongpoint. Under his leadership, Kapplers contributed disproportionate amounts to collections for a monument to Wessenberg and for the German cause in Schleswig-Holstein.[60] Richter intervened decisively in the 1865 district elections, speaking the day before the vote to counter the archbishop's pastoral letter and the leaflets the priest distributed. After hearing the mayor's analysis of how the clerical party aimed at its own power rather than the good of the citizenry or the promotion of religion, the voters delivered a pro-government majority.[61] In a like manner, Richter was able to turn the government's surprise defeat in the 1868 vote for the customs parliament into a National Liberal majority in the 1871 federal election. The local scene was firmly under control as Richter won re-election as mayor in 1870. As late as the November 1873 municipal elections, the liberals were in command, taking 57 % of the vote and all three council seats at stake.[62]

Carried away by this string of victories, Richter intensified the anticlerical campaign. The early 1870s saw a flood of pamphlets,[63] newspaper articles,[64] and speeches aimed at persuading Kapplers to reject Jesuitical innovations and papal domination.[65] When the citizen's union developed into a Catholic Men's Association[66] under an interim cleric, a Liberal Union emerged to combat it. The parish fell vacant in 1874, and the time seemed ripe for an open move to win it for Old Catholicism. The mayor, a majority of the municipal council, the Baden government, and the semi-official gazettes stood ready to back the cause.

Social events were arranged to rally mass support. A celebration was held to commemorate a visit by Wessenberg to Burg. A judge, son of a former teacher in Kappel, made a speech at Christmas 1874 attacking the clergy and mariolatry. Kapplers watched as an Old Catholic professor from Freiburg presided over a burial in Grafenhausen in place of the priest. An Old Catholic priest from Heidelberg spoke at yet another rally in Kappel. These activities culminated in January 1875 with the formal establishment of an Old Catholic community and the submission to the government of a request for recognition of its claims to church property and rights.

The Roman Catholics countered with sermons, a visit from the dean,[67] and the naming of a full priest to the parish in the person of Felix Koch. Koch's arrival in March 1875 was celebrated with a procession from the railway station through Grafenhausen, where he had served as interim priest some years

TABLE 11.3
Distributions of husband's occupations in Kappel, by religion 1875–1890

	Old Catholic	Roman Catholic
Affluent, Substantial, Commerce	18 %	9 %
Labour	10 %	20 %
Farming	34 %	38 %
Craft	24 %	17 %
Fishing, Weaving	7 %	12 %
Local Position	4 %	1 %
Industry, Profession, Petty	4 %	3 %
Absolute total	67	166

Source: Pf A Kappel Family register, Ord A B8 Altkatholiken 12 (January 1875 declaration), and OSB *Kappel*.

earlier.[68] Following his investiture, Koch set to work to win back waverers while preserving the Roman Catholic ranks intact. All these efforts were not without effect. When the dust settled, the Roman Catholics could count about two hundred signatures on their submissions to Church and State authorities, the Old Catholics only seventy-six.

Table 11.3's distributions of occupations within the two confessions reveal that the split followed social lines.[69] In general, the élite rejected the Church, while the masses remained true to it. For instance, a disproportionate share of affluent, substantial, and commercial villagers became Old Catholics. At the other end of the scale, day labourers were twice as strongly represented among the Roman Catholics as among the Old Catholics. Although there was little difference in the percentage of Farming occupations, similar distinctions can be seen within the artisan categories. Old Catholics pursued the more lucrative trades, such as smithing, while Roman Catholicism dominated among weavers, tailors, masons, and fishers.

The heavy preponderance of Old Catholics among holders of local positions, who were generally poor, may seem to run counter to my analysis. However, because such positions depended on patronage, that pattern actually bears out the image of Old Catholics as the in-party. Municipal employees were vulnerable to pressure from notables, and therefore tended to follow their anticlerical lead. In addition, these positions were offered to the undecided as inducements to break with Rome. When the minority status of Old Catholicism in Kappel became clear, Richter rewarded the loyalty of his followers with five-year contracts to run beyond his term as mayor.

Richter and the civic workers were not the only ones casting edgy glances at the numbers of signatures. As measures of the strength of the two tendencies, they were cited prominently in the popular press.[70] Elections, whether federal, provincial, or municipal, provided renewed tests of strength, as every aspect of village life polarized.

Recognizing that his situation had become impossible, Richter took a vacation and then resigned in 1876 to devote himself full-time to his business interests in Freiburg. The prefect named another Old Catholic in his place, but he could not survive the next election. In May 1876, 96 % of the eligible voters turned out to choose a Roman Catholic mayor by a margin of 176 to 58.[71] Six months later, three Roman Catholics swept the council elections by 166–167 to 62–65.[72] The January 1877 federal election saw the Catholic Centre defeat the National Liberals by 173 to 74, a result confirmed a year and a half later by a 165 to 76 score.[73] Clearly, the schism had mobilized virtually the entire population and then frozen it in place.

The numbers themselves seemed clear enough. Nevertheless, each side attacked the other's credibility, arguing, for example, that the presence of unmarried men in the opposition's ranks meant that its strength was over-stated.[74] This mode of argument provoked a boomlet of weddings in 1875–1876. Thirteen couples were wed in 1875 and eighteen in 1876, compared to an average of 8.7 over the previous decade. No such rise occurred elsewhere.[75] I emphasize this straightforward demographic response to the new political and religious conditions because I shall have occasion below to attribute subtler changes to the same source.

Whatever the significance of the headcount to contemporary polemicists and later demographers, at the time the Old Catholics' numbers were considerable enough for the government to recognize their congregation as a legitimate successor to the pre-Vatican Church, side by side with the Roman Catholics. Under laws passed expressly for the purpose, this entitled the Old Catholics to use of parish buildings and property. The prefect prescribed the hours each congregation was to have access to the church and arranged for the division of paraphernalia. The Roman Catholics refused to use an altar desecrated by excommunicated priests, and resorted first to Grafenhausen and then to the construction of a new emergency church of their own.

The same policy of sharp separation was followed in other spheres.[76] Old Catholics were removed from the administration of religious foundations and from service as organists.[77] As indicated earlier, Roman Catholics systematically replaced Old Catholics in municipal government, the last Old Catholic councillors being defeated when their terms expired in 1879. The new council moved to purge the civil service, recruiting only Roman Catholics as field guards, messengers, and patrollers. At the same time, a marital and business boycott of Old Catholic families was put into effect.[78]

This state of affairs endured some fifteen years. The Old Catholics were hampered from the start by their status as a minority and by their inability to match the services provided by the Roman Catholic Church. Pastors came and went with great rapidity, and sometimes with scandal.[79] For much of the period, the congregation enjoyed a minister only once a fortnight, with the schoolteacher filling in in the other weeks. Because many Old Catholic men had been distinguished by indifference to begin with, the community's religious life did not thrive. Some women were perhaps more devout, but that predisposed them to sympathy with Roman Catholicism.[80] Several quietly and informally drifted back, having their children receive sacraments from Koch. It was clear that the movement had no future.

Only following Koch's death in 1889 did the two sides find it possible to put aside accumulated personal grievances. First under a vicar and then under the new priest, dean Michael Hennig, arrangements were made for a general reunion. In 1890, a handful of Old Catholic holdouts were granted use of the emergency church,[81] and the Roman Catholics returned in triumph to the building they had left fifteen years earlier.

The Old Catholics gave up the ghost for a variety of reasons. Their enterprises had suffered economically as Roman Catholics took their business elsewhere. Innkeepers in particular saw their customers melt away, and had to draw down their capital reserves to continue functioning. The diminished pool of marriage partners, even when supplemented by the occasional Protestant or distant outsider,[82] also provided an incentive to rejoin the Catholic mainstream. Theological purity seemed increasingly irrelevant as Pius IX and Richter receded into memory. Likewise, the rise of the Centre party throughout the countryside made steadfast adherence to political principle appear pointless. Indeed, it was even counterproductive, for it denied Old Catholic families what they saw as their rightful places in village government. Neither winning converts nor natural increase could bring them to power in the foreseeable future.

On the surface, life in Kappel returned to the status quo before 1875, with a few twists. Hennig, like Richter, served as deputy to the Baden legislature, albeit for a neighbouring district, and acted to bring a broader perspective to local issues.[83] The schism, reinforced by Hennig's hegemony as priest through 1915, determined political alignments in Kappel right down to the present.[84]

Here I am concerned, not with the legacy of Old Catholicism to the twentieth century, but with the demographic patterns it generated in the nineteenth. Table 11.4 compares the fertility of the families described by Hennig as Old Catholics to that of the families maintaining their allegiance to the pope and the conforming bishops. Each confession is subdivided by the wives' dates of birth. Although this procedure shrinks the numbers involved in each calculation and with them the confidence to be placed in the results, it lays bare sharp differences between the generation of Old Catholics who reproduced before the open break with Rome and the one that bore its children while the dispute was at its height. The former led the rest of the village in adopting family limitation, but the latter reverted to natural fertility.

If one looks first at the families of women born from 1815 to 1839, one detects a sizable gap in ages at last birth.[85] The intervals before that birth were a bit longer for Old Catholics, and their completed families were smaller. Despite greater underlying natural fertility (M), their total marital fertility rates were also lower. The m index of family limitation and the percentage limiting bolster the view that Kappel's Roman Catholics were subject to natural fertility.

TABLE 11.4
Fertility of documented marriages of Old Catholics and Roman Catholics in Kappel, by wife's date of birth

	Wife born 1815–1839		Wife born 1840–1864	
	Old Catholic	Roman Catholic	Old Catholic	Roman Catholic
For completed families				
Wife's age at last birth	(37.4)	40.8	40.3	39.0
Final birth interval (in years)	(3.81)	3.67	3.34	3.96
Number of legitimate children	5.0	6.3	6.9	6.1
Total marital fertility rate	(8.46)	9.45	(9.50)	8.77
M	1.30	1.00	1.05	1.13
m	.61	–.08	–.01	.24
Percentage limiting	44 %	–13 %	8 %	22 %

Notes
(1) *Source*: Pf A Kappel Family register, Ord A B8 Altkatholiken 12 (January 1875 declaration), and OSB *Kappel*.
(2) Results based on 10–19 completed families are shown in brackets.
(3) Total marital fertility rates based on fewer than 1000 woman-years are shown in brackets.
(4) The Table is based on 216 marriages: 60 involving Old Catholic husbands and 156 involving Roman Catholics.

Although the number of cases is small, the contrast with the Old Catholics is striking on both measures. In this birth cohort, Old Catholicism typified the small minority of limiters who diverged so far from the bulk of Kappel's population.

Considering the fertility of the wives born during the following twenty-five years provides further insight into Kapplers' slow progress out of natural fertility. Entry into marriage again differed little between confessions. However, the combined effects of easier laws and the pressure to wed early so as to increase the ranks of one's faction reduced brides' ages at first marriage by two years in both camps (to twenty-five).

In this generation, it is Roman Catholics who display stronger affinity for family limitation, albeit at less than half the level of the older Old Catholics. Their last births came younger, final intervals were longer, and completed families were smaller than among their predecessors. Among the Old Catholics, these measures jumped to values as extreme as among the first generation of Roman Catholics.[86] A similar pattern holds with respect to total marital fertility rate, m,[87] and the percentage limiting. Now it is the Old Catholics whose high natural fertility masks incipient family limitation among some Roman Catholics.

One might read Table 11.4 to support Zeldin's hypothesis. After all, the schism grew out of resentment of clerical criticism. Kappel's élite much preferred the liberal priests who had overseen the beginning of family limitation among them. Disdain for the confessional was particularly strong within this group.[88] Moreover, the first two columns show that a majority of practitioners of family limitation eventually went over to Old Catholicism. The appearance of family limitation in the final column of the Table could be accounted for by the variation on Zeldin's ideas sketched at the beginning of this chapter. Here, the argument would run that in order to maintain their loyalty in the struggle against Old Catholicism, Koch had to allow the few Roman Catholic members of Kappel's élite to practise family limitation. However, on that basis there is no accounting for the Old Catholics' continuing antipathy towards him.[89]

I interpret Table 11.4 not only as strongly supporting the idea of linking politics, religion, and fertility, but also as indicating that the links were far from straightforward. In the years before the schism, Old Catholics were distinguished from their neighbours, not merely by less attachment to ultramontanism and by greater wealth, but also by greater family limitation. The same social factors that left them politically isolated account for the failure of family limitation to spread to the rest of the population.[90]

The shift in the behaviour of the younger generation argues against attributing to Old Catholicism per se an affinity for contraception. Engaged in ideological and economic warfare, and constantly reminded of their status as a minority, the Old Catholics resorted to the vengeance of the cradle. Earlier, I noted that in the years of the split unmarried individuals hastened to wed. Table 11.4 shows that the same drive carried over into their married lives, as couples strove to be fruitful and multiply the strength of their party. The result was that liberalism was tied to fertility in both generations, but its significance for family limitation altered radically between them.

Just as Secularization theory predicts, the strength of religious attitudes in Kappel did correspond to the extent of family limitation, at one point at least. If similar differences could be uncovered between villages,[91] showing much weaker piety in Grafenhausen for example, the hypothesis could claim a signal victory. However, standard measures of religiosity reveal only a small difference in the predicted direction. For example, in the decade before World War One, church attendance on a Sunday in Lent averaged 59 % of the population in Grafenhausen, 66 % in Kappel, and 69 % in Rust. Consumption of hosts, per Catholic, also varied little, though Rust lagged behind Kappel and Grafenhausen until 1911.[92]

For Grafenhausen, these figures are only slightly below those recorded by Steiger in the 1840s, when family limitation was far less extensive.[93] For Kappel, they represent a return to the level of the 1850s following a long trough from the late 1860s through the years of the schism.[94] With the obvious exception of that period, there is no sign of a drastic falling off in religious observance anywhere. I therefore resume my account of political developments, testing Secularization theory on its chosen ground.

FEDERAL ELECTIONS 1868–1912

The information presented thus far provides an introduction to the religious dimension of federal election campaigns. However, the national question and economic issues also played important rôles in political life in Grafenhausen, Kappel, and Rust. Because these themes and the relationships among them emerged clearly as early as 1868, I cover that year's critical election to the customs parliament in some detail. In key respects, including the victory of ultramontanism, that vote set the mould for the next half-century. I therefore deal more cursorily with subsequent federal elections, singling out for attention only a few striking deviations from the overall trend. These deviations involved experimentation with new ideas in Grafenhausen and susceptibility to persuasion in Rust. In the years leading up to the First World War, Rust settled into the pattern of Centre hegemony that had long characterized Kappel, while Grafenhausen displayed a marked degree of independence.

After the war of 1866, the Baden government advocated a union between the south German states and the newly created North German Confederation, excluding the Habsburg monarchy. It seized upon the February 1868 election to the parliament of the customs union to demonstrate popular sentiment and thereby build diplomatic momentum for such a little German solution.[95] Prominent figures on the government side were put forward as candidates, and proclaimed their intention, if elected, to promote unification by extending the jurisdiction of the customs parliament. By supporting men with government experience, the voters were to show their desire for an equally national and liberal state.

In the riding including the three villages, the candidate was Friedrich Kiefer, a leading member of parliament who was later to head Baden's National Liberal party for seventeen years.[96] A prominent lay Protestant, he had distinguished himself by his resolute anticlericalism. He made only a few speeches during the campaign, coming no nearer the villages than the county seat. A sympathetic press carried his message into the countryside, as did urban merchants and manufacturers who worked on their customers and suppliers.

The government hierarchy determined the structure of political organization on the local level. This naturally discouraged input from below. Thus, Richter and the mayor of Grafenhausen were among the sponsors of a rally in Lahr early in the campaign, but it was a foregone conclusion that that meeting would nominate Kiefer.[97] Later, Kiefer's organizing committee publicly coopted prominent local citizens whom it presumed would be reliable, without even consulting them.[98] In each of Grafenhausen, Kappel, and Rust, the choice fell on the mayor and the municipal clerk, with other office-holders and proprietors of inns rounding out four- or five-man committees.[99] Assisted by the civil service and police, they were counted upon to deliver a solid vote.

The Baden opposition had originally toyed with boycotting the election altogether as a protest. However, the opportunity afforded by the first[100] direct and secret vote by the whole of Baden's adult male population could not be passed up. Shortly before voting day, ballots,[101] posters, and leaflets for alternative candidates were mailed to priests in the area.[102] Door-to-door canvassing followed, generally by the sexton, but some energetic clerics worked their parishioners in person.[103] Such tactics were particularly effective the day of the vote in ensuring that well-disposed but lackadaisical citizens got to the polls.

Kiefer's antagonist was one of the handful of opposition deputies[104] in the Baden parliament. He had risen to prominence by negotiating the never-ratified concordat of 1859, a fact of which the liberals were quick to remind voters. The opposition responded in kind, pointing to Kiefer's attacks on the Roman Catholic Church.

For the most part, the struggle was between overall visions rather than personalities. The opposition derided a national liberal little Germany as merely a Greater Prussia, in which only the government and its sycophants would enjoy freedom. They pointed out that the exclusion of Austria would create an artificial Protestant majority. Moreover, the European balance of power was such that even this partial unification could be achieved only through war against France. Preparation for war meant longer terms of military service, higher taxes, perhaps on tobacco, and the prospect of seeing this border region turned into a battleground once more.

Thus, religious sentiment was far from the only reason to back the opposition. Liberalism was associated with anticlericalism, but also with Prussia, militarism, élitism, heavier taxation, and amoral diplomacy. In resisting that array of forces, ultramontanism could look for support from Baden patriots, democrats left over from 1848, and all concerned to set limits to the domestic and external power of the State.

The election results revealed that the two opposing worldviews were about equally popular in Baden as a whole. This seat and the polls in the three villages fell to the clerical opposition, with Rust delivering the highest majority and Kappel the least. Richter's liberals blamed their loss on agitation by idle youth and ambitious malcontents, who had led the poor astray, working on the men through their wives.[105] Like the government itself, they resolved never to be taken by surprise again.[106]

In the aftermath of the election, a new political culture congealed in Baden. From 1818 to 1850, rhetoric had opposed the parliament to the government, the people to the bureaucracy, freedom to exceptional laws, democracy to oligarchy, national self-determination to foreign domination, and revolution to order. Elements of that system endured, but the relations among the concepts were restructured.

Now the government and the bureaucracy were in the hands of the liberal party, and the clergy that had bolstered order in 1848 was attacking them in the name of the ostensibly oppressed masses. Ultramontanes sought to strengthen democratic rights, while anticlericals met their onslaught by suspending liberties. The grand duke championed national unification, yet it came under a Prussian élite. New issues had emerged, with appeals that cut across the old lines and eventually obliterated them.

One facet of this complex transition became apparent when the opposition that had built up in defence of the Church took institutional form as the Catholic People's Party, striving to give equal weight to both aspects of its name.[107] Its first concerted action was a petition campaign against the government. Convinced that its popular support could not be translated into seats under the prevailing system of indirect voting, the Catholic People's Party called for the dissolution of Baden's parliament and new elections on the model that had proven so successful in 1868. In this it was joined by the Democrats. That party had little presence in this area, but the Catholic People's Party did submit petitions from Grafenhausen and Rust.[108]

In the face of this assault, liberal legislators patched up their minor differences with the cabinet and created a formal party. In a counter-petition, these National Liberals urged the government to stick to its programme and make only modest electoral reforms so as to limit the power of an as yet unenlightened populace. Among the original signatories of this Offenburg address of May 1869 were one of the Böcklins and Karl Richter.[109] In the end the tens of thousands of signatures on the petitions approached the number of voters in an election. Despite the fact that the stated supporters of thoroughgoing reform outnumbered those hewing to the status quo, the National Liberals got their way.[110]

The achievement of a major part of the Baden government's programme with the establishment of the little German empire following the Franco-Prussian War brought politicians into closer touch with their counterparts elsewhere. In particular, the National Liberals allied with the Prussian party of the same name, while the Catholic People's Party became the Baden wing of the Centre.[111] These identifications strengthened in the early 1870s as Otto von Bismarck's governments pursued an anticlerical policy modelled on the one initiated by Baden.

In the riding containing Grafenhausen, Kappel, and Rust, elections pitted these two tendencies head to head. Redistricting for the first election to the federal parliament turned the seat over to Kiefer. In achieving this and subsequent victories, the National Liberals relied on overwhelming majorities among urban Protestants to outweigh the Centre's more widespread but generally less decisive margins in the Catholic countryside.[112] Recognizing the political possibilities, the Centre adopted the style of agrarian protest, attacking the economic and political privileges of the towns. Renewed struggles over the place of the Church, the rights of parliament, the military budget, and colonial policy honed the antagonisms of 1868. Gradually, the Centre tightened its hold in its strongpoints, including Grafenhausen, Kappel, and Rust, to the point where the riding became a safe Centre seat.[113] All these tendencies sit uncomfortably within models of Secularization.

There are two notable exceptions to these generalizations. Each shows that appeals based on the old radical tradition or new economic interests could break up the religious polarization. In keeping with my argument, these episodes highlight flexibility in Rust and independence in Grafenhausen. Even when voters swung away from the Centre, they did not do so in the manner hypothesized by Secularization theory.

The first of these breaks occurred in the 1880s as the National Liberals' hold on the constituency was weakening. In 1881, the incumbent resigned,[114] and the party sought out Ferdinand Sander, son of a noted parliamentary radical of the 1830s and 1840s. As head of the Lotzbeck firm in Lahr, Sander had a high profile with the region's tobacco growers. Although a Protestant, he was not known as an anticlerical. In an unusually active campaign[115] he focused on economics.

The tenor of Sander's campaign can be gauged from the content of a speech he gave at the village hall in Rust.[116] The rally was opened by the Böcklin lord, who endorsed Sander as the candidate most familiar with the riding.[117] Sander then spoke, restricting himself to substantive and technical issues, but covering them in a way that appealed to the audience's interests. He opposed social legislation, like State contributions for accident insurance, that benefitted only industrial and not agricultural workers. He borrowed a leaf from the Centre's book[118] by supporting tax reform to lighten the burden on landed proprietors and shoreline municipalities. He likewise urged lower court costs to make justice accessible to all. Reform of military punishments, a two-year term of duty, and tighter control of military spending were also championed. The key issue was the proposed tobacco monopoly, which Sander attacked in the strongest terms, painting a dire picture of the future awaiting manufacturers, dealers, and growers.

In appearances elsewhere, Sander met critics with calm and humour.[119] Those qualities proved enough to give him a slight lead after the first round of balloting, and the endorsement of the tiny Democratic party put him over the top in the runoff. In both rounds Sander captured the poll in Rust by better than one hundred votes. Given the slimness of his margin in the riding as a whole,[120] appearing in person had clearly paid off.

In parliament, Sander lived up to his reputation for tolerance, eventually leaving the National Liberal caucus to sit as an independent Moderate Liberal. Because he declared he would vote against anticlerical May Laws, the Centre resolved not to oppose his re-election in 1884. Indeed, National Liberals seem to have had doubts about Sander, requiring that he supply proof of his national and liberal sentiments before they renominated him.[121] Sander romped home with 97 % of the vote, as Rust again distinguished itself by its support for him.

In 1887, Sander's decision not to stand for re-election was privately lamented by leading National Liberals on the grounds that he could once again have commanded the votes of a great number of moderate ultramontanes.[122] As it turned out, Sander's presence was not required, for intense pressure on the civil service and an orchestrated war scare mobilized a rather different constituency to produce the highest National Liberal vote ever. However, the party's performance in the cartel government over the next three years alienated virtually every other political force. Isolated, the National Liberals failed to take a single seat in Baden in 1890. The party's fortunes rebounded elsewhere, but this seat remained securely with the Centre thereafter. Even an attempted comeback by Sander in 1893 fell short.

As it happens, the 1893 election saw the second of the exceptional events I referred to earlier. For the first time, a third party managed to win more than 3 % of the vote in one of the villages. The Social Democrats claimed a full fifth of Grafenhausen's voters, pushing the National Liberals into third place. To a certain extent, this was simply a response to the first systematic attempt by the self-styled party of the proletariat to reach rural voters. Gendarmerie reports trace the course of socialist agitation.[123] To begin with, rallies in nearby Ringsheim and Altdorf drew curious Grafenhauseners. Later, the Star inn in Grafenhausen became a socialist centre, drawing a crowd of sixty to seventy to learn the principles of social democracy.

Speakers attacked both the National Liberals and the Centre, insisting that only Social Democrats consistently resisted militarism, defended civil liberties, and promoted popular living standards. Church-State conflicts were to be ended by making religion a private matter. Capitalist exploitation and the proletarianization of middling elements were roundly denounced. At the same time, the revisionist streak in Baden Social Democracy came through as the solution was declared to lie in making the great capitalists pay higher taxes, while banning women and children from factories.

The Social Democrats did not follow up the 1893 breakthrough,[124] but it is noteworthy that it came in prosperous Grafenirhausen rather than in impoverished Rust. Then and later, a few of Rust's labourers and workers did display an intermittent and tentative attraction to socialism, but Social Democratic voters were at least as numerous in Grafenhausen. Kappel lagged far behind in this regard.[125] The absolute numbers involved are not large, but the episode does illustrate several of my themes: the importance of local centres for organization, the ubiquity and persistence of elements of Baden's radical tradition, and the willingness of Grafenhauseners to experiment politically, especially in protest.

Figure 11.5 depicts the overall response in the villages to federal politics. Except for the years of Sander's victories, the Centre enjoyed a healthy majority in nearly every election in all three localities. The variations in the size of that majority were broadly similar. Indeed, when this half-century is taken as a unit, there is little to choose between the villages. Over eighteen elections, the Centre's average share of the eligible voters was 56 % in Grafenhausen, 57 % in Kappel, and 56 % in Rust, while the National Liberals drew 20 %, 24 %, and 30 %, respectively. The close match leaves slim pickings for Secularization theory.

1877 and 1898 break Figure 11.5 naturally into three broad periods. The first decade saw the sorting out of the parties' positions as loyalties firmed. The quick and successful foundation of the little German empire won support for the

Anticlericals and Ultramontanes 219

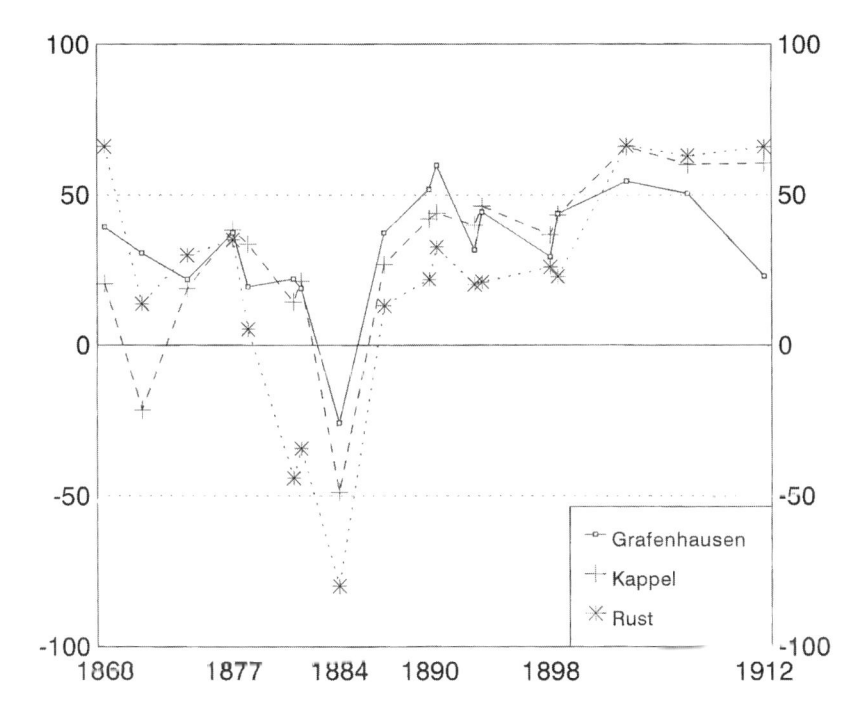

FIGURE 11.5 DIFFERENCE BETWEEN CENTRE AND NATIONAL LIBERAL VOTE AS A PERCENTAGE OF THE NUMBER OF ELIGIBLE VOTERS IN GRAFENHAUSEN, KAPPEL, AND RUST IN FEDERAL ELECTIONS FROM 1868 TO 1912

National Liberals, but except in Richter's Kappel, it was not enough to bring them victory. By 1877 the Centre had the upper hand everywhere, and its grip was equally strong in all three villages.

The graph of the years from 1877 to 1898 is dominated by the trough created by Sander's candidacies, but some longer-term features are also noteworthy. Throughout these years, Rust displayed the least loyalty to the Centre, as one might expect from the village with the greatest non-Catholic presence. The Protestant lords occasionally exerted influence on behalf of the National Liberals, and Jews were harder to persuade of the urgency of supporting the Church against the government that had emancipated them.[126] The consistent margins in Kappel, 1884 excepted, grew out of the religious stalemate there. When the Old Catholics gave up in 1890, the National Liberal vote tailed off.[127] Only thereafter did Kappel deliver a higher Centre majority than Grafenhausen, as Social Democrats and abstainers drew votes from both major parties in the latter locality.

In the third period, from 1898 to 1912, these relationships reversed. The dissolution of Old Catholicism in Kappel left the Centre unopposed. The only limit on the party's majority was the size of the turnout. In Rust, the Jewish community was shrinking fast, and the lord's passing enthusiasm for the National

Liberal cause had waned. After 1898, the Centre's margin there more than tripled, launching it to a level higher even than in one-party Kappel. Just as striking is the shrinkage of the Centre's majority in Grafenhausen, especially after the standard of the liberal bloc came to be borne by Democrats. By the final election, Grafenhausen was clearly diverging from the other two villages.[128]

Throughout all three periods, Centre organization was built around the priests. In Kappel in 1907, for example, Hennig convened a committee of sixteen agitators, staged a rally, had leaflets distributed, and organized door-to-door canvassing. During the vote, scrutineers kept track of Centre supporters who had not yet shown up and arranged to have them escorted to the polls.[129] Where priests were unwilling or unable to take such energetic action, the Centre cause flagged. Conversely, the National Liberal party often depended on the sympathy of notables for its local organization, and when they went over to the Centre, that party enjoyed a clear field.[130]

In so far as elections became votes of confidence in the priests, their results are especially relevant to Secularization theory. Unfortunately, the secret ballot makes it impossible to identify individual loyalties. Only on the rare occasions when the outcome was lop-sided does the sealed vote become transparent. Then, the list of participants provides an almost pure sample of the victorious tendency. This, the best evidence that can be gathered under such conditions, turns out to count against Secularization.

In the first round of balloting in Grafenhausen in 1898, for example, 86 % of the 129 voting chose the Centre. The fertility of the 116 documented marriages those voters began before 1900 was practically the same as that in the corresponding 210 families whose husbands refrained from exercising their franchises.[131] Those who sat out the Centre's victory gave birth for the final time .3 years earlier and produced .2 fewer children. But they lagged the mostly Centre voters by small margins in m and in final birth interval. None of these differences was significant, nor did they add up to a pattern compatible with Secularization. In 1898, the fertility of Centre voters in Grafenhausen was indistinguishable from that of the population at large. Nor is there any sign in 1898 that limiters were more difficult for priests to mobilize.[132] Those who joined the contest only for the second round of voting two weeks later displayed no more or less family limitation than residents who voted on both occasions or on neither.[133]

It is not easy to extend this approach to cover all villages and all elections in a reliable way. Taking account of all the surviving voters' lists[134] reveals a marked global association between family limitation and independence from the Centre. The key word here is "global". The results do not establish that anticlericals limited their families, but rather that geographic and chronological trends in politics and fertility coincided.

I chose to compare families of voters who cast ballots in contests in which the Centre did unusually well with those of voters whose participation coincided with a heavier non-Centre vote.[135] The two groups diverge sharply on the measures linked to family limitation. Wives of men resistant to the Centre's appeals gave birth for the last time at 36.5, two-and-a-half years younger, following slightly longer intervals, thereby producing smaller families.[136] Total marital fertility rates varied by almost two children. Both underlying natural fertility (M) and family limitation (m) were implicated in this difference, with the latter exerting a stronger influence. The percentage limiting was twice as high among families leaning to the Centre's opponents. Overall, family limitation was broader and deeper in that part of the population.[137]

It would be a mistake to presume with Secularization theory that political differences explain villagers' fertility in any direct way. The two tendencies distinguished by my measure do not recruit equally from the three communities, as one could predict from the graphs in Figure 11.5. The voters inclined away from the Centre include three-quarters of the Grafenhauseners, but only one-third of Rusters, and no Kapplers at all. This corresponds to the relative strength of family limitation in the three villages, and so the Centre polls are left with a concentration of voters subject to natural fertility.[138] Had voters' lists been available from the 1878–1893 period instead, this relationship could easily have reversed. With that point in mind, one can see in the fertility rates the influence of locality as much as political conviction.

Another way to make this point is to note that just 62 % of marriages are linked to the Centre, yet its candidates took 80 % of the vote. Conversely, the National Liberals were never shut out, and so some National Liberal voters, notably the Old Catholic holdouts in Kappel, are here attributed to the Centre. More generally, the fact that a man tended to vote on occasions when the National Liberal party did well does not guarantee that he cast his ballot for its candidate. It might be, for instance, that campaigns in which the National Liberals participated energetically mobilized supporters on both sides who otherwise remained at home or in the fields. For all these reasons, the two classes of voters cannot be identified with the two parties themselves.

However, these considerations are compatible with the more modest contention that what is being observed are local patterns, manifested in both demography and politics. A strong National Liberal presence and greater swings in party loyalties were not abstract sums of isolated decisions by individuals, but social actions which marked the life of the community as a whole. For example, in Kappel casting a National Liberal vote at this time was typically a last gesture of defiance against the hegemony of the Church. In Rust, where ideologies were more fluid, it had been easier to appear a good Catholic and yet vote liberal. In both Kappel and Rust, widespread poverty constrained political independence, but the more equal distribution of property in Rust fostered a mutual dependence which manifested itself in massive shifts in popular vote. In Grafenhausen, where innovation and experiment thrived within networks of solidarity that embraced the whole community, electoral politics was merely one more means by which the will of the independent proprietor could be brought to bear on the world.

Earlier chapters have linked such attitudes to the three villages' population histories on the one hand and to their economic structures on the other. However, these approaches were neither mechanical outgrowths of economic conditions nor consistent forces in their own right. Rather, local tendencies were formed, maintained, and modified by human desires and actions. In the next chapter, I examine provincial election campaigns in Grafenhausen, Kappel, and Rust to lay bare key features of the complex field out of which the political lives of these villages emerged.

Notes

1. See, for example, Massimo Livi-Bacci, *A Century of Portuguese Fertility* (Princeton, 1971), 129–131, Emmanuel Le Roy Ladurie, "From Waterloo to Colyton", in *The Territory of the Historian* (Hassocks, 1979), 226–227, Emmanuel Le Roy Ladurie, "Demography and the 'Sinful Secrets': The Case of Languedoc in the Late Eighteenth and Early Nineteenth Centuries", ibid., 251–253, 334, Jean-Pierre Bardet, "Les incertitudes de l'explication", in Jacques Dupâquier and others, *Histoire de la population française* (Paris, 1988), vol. 3, 372–376, Massimo Livi-Bacci, *A History of Italian Fertility During the Last Two Centuries* (Princeton, 1977), 214–215, Ron Lesthaeghe, *The Decline of Belgian Fertility 1800–1970* (Princeton, 1977), 228–231, Lockridge, *Sweden*, 62–73, Lesthaeghe, "Control", 535–543, and Ron Lesthaeghe and Chris Wilson, "Modes of Production, Secularization, and the Pace of the Fertility Decline in Western Europe, 1870–1930", in Coale and Watkins, *Europe*, 261–292.
2. For instance, regional patterns in votes on schooling in Belgium (1958), induced abortion in Switzerland (1977), and divorce in Italy (1974) correlate highly with the regional patterns of fertility decline half a century and even a century earlier. Ibid., 292.
3. Theodore Zeldin, "The Conflict of Moralities: Confession, Sin and Pleasure", in Theodore Zeldin (ed.), *Conflicts in French Society* (London, 1970), 13–50.
4. For related assumptions about confession, see Thomas Tentler, "The Summa for Confessors as an Instrument of Social Control", in Charles Trinkaus and Heiko Oberman (ed.), *The Pursuit of Holiness in Late Medieval and Renaissance Religion* (Leiden, 1974), 112–113, 125, and the less scholarly Charles Chiniquy, *The Priest, The Woman and the Confessional* (Chick Publications, no place, no date—original 1880).
5. After Alphonsus Liguori 1696–1787, declared a saint in 1839 and a doctor of the Church in 1871.
6. The history of Catholic theory on dealing with birth control is covered in John Noonan jr., *Contraception* (Cambridge, 1965). On coitus interruptus in particular, see Stengers, "pratiques", 403–481.
7. Compare ibid., 455–460.
8. This very comparison struck the eyes of contemporaries. See Hennig, *Chronik*, 209–211, and Adolf Roth and Paul Thorbecke, *Die badischen Landstände* (Karlsruhe, 1907), 194 in particular. The Baden Centre leader, Theodor Wacker, had popularized such analyses.
9. The Social Democrats received only 2 % support. Their candidate, Wilhelm Engler, made similar token runs in several constituencies. His faithfulness was rewarded with the ministry of labour in the 1920s. Engler tells his own story in *Freiburg, Baden und das Reich* (Stuttgart, 1991), especially 20–22.

10. Knodel, *fourteen*, 506–507 uses higher percentages voting Centre in the provincial election of 1925 as an index of "greater traditionalism and less secularization" in these villages.
11. I rate the capacity of villages to sustain multiple parties higher than Netting, *Alp*, 186–201, and Fred Sepainter, *Die Reichstagswahlen im Grossherzogtum Baden* (Frankfurt, 1983), 245–254.
12. Compare Charles Tilly on Lesthaeghe and Wilson, in "Review Symposium", 327.
13. For instance, many of the Grafenhauseners found backing the Centre on the federal level in this chapter will be encountered in Chapter Twelve supporting the National Liberals provincially, as Table 11.1 leads one to suspect.
14. This interpretation is limited to Catholic villagers, for the Centre exercised almost no moral suasion over Protestants and Jews. Because non-Catholics' support for the National Liberals was a given, I make no connection between their political views and their fertility. In particular, I do not treat Protestantism as more modern or as stimulating a more Weberian attitude towards the world.
15. For instance, it was Baden statistics that inspired the Weber thesis (although they do not in fact support it when analysed in depth. See Kurt Samuelsson, *Religion and Economic Action* (Stockholm, 1961), 137–147.) For an attempt to apply a version of the Weber thesis to southwestern Germany, see Günter Golde, *Catholics and Protestants Agricultural Modernization in Two German Villages* (New York, 1975). On Weberian demography, see André Bourgière, "De Malthus à Max Weber: le mariage tardif et l'esprit de l'entreprise", *Annales Economies Sociétés Civilisations*, 27 (1972), 1128–1138, Alfred Perrenoud, "Malthusianisme et protestantisme: «un modèle démographique weberien»", *Annales Economies Sociétés Civilisations*, 29 (1974), 975–988, and for that matter, Schubnell, *Kinderreichtum*, 92–111.
16. Butterfield, *Whig*, 22.
17. For an appreciation, and one explanation, of how the federal Centre party resists easy classification, see Margaret Anderson, *Windthorst A Political Biography* (Oxford, 1981).
18. Anderson goes so far as to repeat that "anti-Catholicism is the anti-Semitism of intellectuals". Ibid., vii, 192.
19. In the literal sense. Livi-Bacci's view of towns as the sources of dynamism, progress, and intelligence ("Forerunners", 198) echoes the polemics of the time. For two examples of many, see *Breisgauer Zeitung* 22 February 1868 and the circular to ambassadors 26 February 1868 in GLA 233/33851. For responses, see *Karlsruher Zeitung* 26 September 1871 (reporting a complaint that instead of bringing progress, the new railroad brought clerical propaganda) and, hurling back the insult, *Badischer Beobachter* 28 September 1873 and 4 August 1878 (the latter in GLA 236/14858).
20. Compare Edward Hales, *Pio Nono* (New York, 1954), 331.
21. Readers may find that the mass of detail to come obstructs the soaring visions with which they began. They are reminded that flightworthiness in this sense is the mark of an empirically adequate theory. In less lofty terms: if the real reasons villagers voted as they did are trivial by comparison with the great issues raised by Secularization theory, then so much the worse for Secularization theory.
22. Ord A Konstanz Strassburg 1. Parts of the following discussion draw on Hennig, *Luhr*, 256–278, and on Hennig, *Chronik*, 13.
23. The Enlightened anticlerical Habsburg emperor Joseph II had ruled territories just south of these villages from 1765 to 1790, the final ten years alone.
24. These themes recur, for example, in Burg's 1808 remarks in Ord A Konstanz Kirchenvisitationen 31 and Ord A Konstanz Kirchenvisitationen 44.
25. In 1827 that city had replaced Konstanz as the seat of Baden Catholicism.
26. On the negotiations, see the government circular of 14 November 1853 in Gem A Grafenhausen B VI/393.

27. GLA 353/1908–105/34 (letters from Kappel 9 January, from Rust 10 January, and from Grafenhausen 11 January 1854). Ord A B2–29/101.
28. Steiger appeared as a Moderate elector in Chapter Ten. Right from the outset, he had been uneasy about the reception the sermons would receive. In one of his two new parishes, the dean omitted a passage from the pastoral letter that struck him as too harsh an attack on the authorities. For this, and for presenting another priest with literature supporting the government's position, he was removed from office. In the end he repented of his actions. Ibid. Ord A B2–29/59 (report of 9 May 1854 from Steiger himself). Ord A B3/502 (elections of deans for Lahr).
29. Steiger's enemies claimed morality in Grafenhausen had suffered during his tenure. They had revolutionary politics in mind. GLA 240/1680 (schoolteacher under arrest in 1849). GLA 233/22646 (government choosing replacement in 1850).
30. GLA 353/1908–105/35.
31. *Breisgauer Zeitung* 3 March 1868 claimed Kapplers "almost unanimously" petitioned against the Convention, but the document itself (25 February 1860 in GLA 231/1440) came rather from thirty-three members of the citizens' committee (to be sure, almost all of that group). On the other side, half the citizens of Grafenhausen signed an address welcoming the concordat according to GLA 48/5271. The mayors of Grafenhausen and Kappel, but not Rust apparently, dutifully welcomed the victory of anticlericalism. GLA 48/5272 (thanks to grand duke 9 September 1860).
32. This period is covered in detail in Josef Becker, *Liberaler Staat und Kirche in der Ära von Reichsgründung und Kulturkampf* (Mainz, 1973). In upcoming sections I draw freely on Julius Dorneich, "Der Kirchenkampf in Baden (1860–1876) und die Katholische Gegenbewegung", *Freiburger Diözesan-Archiv*, 94 (1974), 547–588 and on Julius Dorneich, "Die Entstehung der badischen 'Katholischen Volkspartei' zwischen 1865 und 1869 im Tagebuch von Baurat Dr. Karl Bader", *Freiburger Diözesan-Archiv*, 84 (1964), 272–399.
33. The ultimate significance of this measure is detailed in Chapter Twelve.
34. The wording follows Henry Manning's translation of the eightieth item of Pius IX's Syllabus of Errors, in Ernst Helmreich (ed.), *A free church in a free state? The Catholic Church, Italy, Germany, France 1864–1914* (Boston, 1964), 5.
35. Officials attributed voters' absence from the polls to apathy and lack of publicity, rather than conviction. GLA 236/10289 (report on county Ettenheim for 1864). The somewhat greater defiance of the archbishop in Grafenhausen is none the less noteworthy.
36. *Breisgauer Zeitung* 10 September 1865.
37. Gem A Grafenhausen B XIII/768. See Benz, Thesis, appendix E for my attempt to crack the secret ballot.
38. By about one year over those supporting losers and two years over the abstainers. Differences between factions are inconsistent and insignificant when the figures are broken down by age at marriage. (Details not shown.)
39. Or relevant social distinctions of any kind, it seems. It is also possible that the returning officers went astray as they decoded the ostensibly secret ballots. Differences between factions were larger and consistent with Secularization for the first few dozen voters, where there is less suspicion of error.
40. GLA 236/4280 (Nonnenweier in 1843). GLA 313/4365 (Breisach in 1846). See also Hörner, *Vormärz*, 146–147, 151–152.
41. GLA 236/6053 (petitions from Altdorf, Kippenheim, and Schmieheim). Half the Rusters had participated in the mass petition drive of 1835. GLA 231/1424.
42. See above, in the text and in footnote 35.
43. Resisting the 1869 storm against the ministry, Jews joined in National Liberal petitions from Ettenheim, Kippenheim, Orschweier, and Schmieheim. GLA 233/32618. Nothing was heard from Rust's Jews. However, it may be presumed that they voted for the government whenever they voted at all.

44. Michael Riff, "The Anti-Jewish Aspect of the Revolutionary Unrest of 1848 in Baden and its Impact on Emancipation", *Leo Baeck Institute Yearbook*, 21 (1976), 27–40. Incidentally, it was Michael Riff who drew my attention to the records of provincial elections used in Chapter Twelve.
45. GLA 360/1935–11/1163 (report on 1862 inspection tour of Rust).
46. Gem A Kappel B VI/331 (1862 circulation of anti-Jewish petition). Parliament did receive objections from Christians in Nonnenweier (1860) and Schmieheim (1862), as well as more distant locations with Jewish communities. GLA 231/1425.
47. GLA 236/14913 (1893 federal election results—first round).
48. The vagaries of registration and migration limit consideration to 68 documented families, most formed from 1825 to 1874. They may thus most profitably be compared with the third and fourth cohorts for the entire village in Table 6.6 and Figure 6.7. In practice that comparison is unnecessary
49. An extremely low negative m (-.20) raises suspicions about the accuracy of the data, but it definitely does not provide evidence of family limitation. The ages of women wed in the first half of the century were often based on estimates made at death, which might well have been inflated. Over-estimated ages would account for the coincidence of a high total marital fertility rate (10.09) and a modest underlying level of natural fertility (M = 1.00). However, even women for whom exact birth dates were available show no recognizable signs of family limitation. Although they wed in 1864 on average, their last births came after age forty and m was still just .15.
50. Goldstein, "Aspects", 151–152. Goldstein, "Characteristics", 127–134, 141. On the other hand, the argument is compatible with early family limitation where Jews were numerous and active
51. Livi-Bacci ("Forerunners", 189–195) intimates that no population of European Jews has ever been found with a later fertility transition than the surrounding community. If that were true, then Rust would be the first one.
52. Just as they hastened the spread of innovations once they did enter.
53. Throughout this discussion, I draw freely on Ord A B8 Altkatholiken 12, on Hennig, *Chronik*, 13–18, 73–91, 99–113, on the relevant sections of the prefects' reports on county Ettenheim for the years 1875 through 1889–1892 (in GLA 236/10291, GLA 236/10292, GLA 236/10293, GLA 236/10434, GLA 236/10463, GLA 236/10229, and GLA 236/10490), and on the reports of inspection tours of Kappel from 1875 to 1892 (GLA 360/1935–11/822 and St A LA Lahr 2290). The statistics were calculated without consulting GLA 360/1935–11/829 and GLA 360/1935–11/830.
54. Members included affluent and substantial citizens, as well as outsiders, including the doctor and the border supervisor. St A LA Lahr 2326 (1844 correspondence over curfew-breaking).
55. GLA 360/1935–11/821 (report on 1860 inspection tour of Kappel). *Breisgauer Zeitung* 3 March 1868. GLA 240/2274 details the court cases 1854–1858 in which Schleyer was eventually convicted of endangering public peace through alleging political motives for his removal from the University of Freiburg.
56. See point (10) of the 1848 petition discussed in Chapter Ten. Kappel's parish income is detailed in Ord A Finanzkammer 12043. (For Grafenhausen and Rust, see Ord A Finanzkammer 7822 and Ord A Finanzkammer 24308, respectively.) On attempts to tax it in 1858, see GLA 360/1935–11/825.
57. That a portion also went to top up the remuneration of poorly furnished priests elsewhere (GLA 233/22750) hardly won more favour.
58. Gem A Kappel B IV/132 (award to Richter of a medal for promoting agricultural development).
59. GLA 236/4323.
60. Ettenheim town archive B XIII/969. Gem A Kappel B V/317 (contributors to Wessenberg monument in 1862).
61. *Breisgauer Zeitung* 7 September 1865.

62. GLA 236/10290 (report on county Ettenheim for 1873).
63. Examples preserved in Gem A Kappel B VI/333.
64. Such as the 3 December 1873 one in *Breisgauer Zeitung*.
65. Jesuits played a rôle in liberal demonology matched only by that of Freemasons for ultramontanes. The order was banned from Baden throughout this period.
66. Hans-Jürgen Kremer (ed.), *Mit Gott für Wahrheit, Freiheit, und Recht* (Stuttgart, 1983), 292 assigns 96 members to the Association in 1874. *Badischer Beobachter* 22 January and 24 March 1875 report numbers as high as 164, swelled by the controversies I am about to discuss.
67. Editor of the (Lahrer) *Anzeiger für Stadt und Land* and a member of the Baden parliament.
68. *Anzeiger für Stadt und Land* 11 March 1875 in Ord A B8 Altkatholiken 12.
69. The incomplete Roman Catholic figures are presented merely for comparative purposes.
70. Ibid. *Badische Landeszeitung* 19 January 1875. *Badischer Beobachter* 22 January 1875. *Breisgauer Zeitung* 2 June 1875.
71. GLA 236/10291 (report on county Ettenheim for 1876).
72. St A LA Lahr 2295. Virtually everyone who supported one of the winners supported all of them, and the losing side likewise voted in a bloc.
73. GLA 236/14862 and GLA 236/14863.
74. Gem A Kappel B IV/133 (letter of 16 March 1875 from Richter). Ord A B8 Altkatholiken 12 (letters of February-March 1875 from Koch). *Badische Landeszeitung* 29 January 1875 and 2 April 1875. *Breisgauer Zeitung* and *Badische Landeszeitung* 21 March 1875. *Badischer Beobachter* 24 March 1875.
75. In Grafenhausen and Rust combined, there were 15 % fewer weddings per year in 1875–1876 than over the previous decade.
76. When one midwife refused to take Old Catholic newborns to the church now off-limits to Roman Catholics, she was replaced. GLA 236/15840 (county health officer's report for 1875).
77. Gem A Kappel B VI/333. Gem A Kappel B IV/133 (correspondence between Koch and Richter).
78. Kapplers' behaviour refutes Netting's confidence (*Alp*, 201) that village politics never prevents opponents from becoming bedfellows—unless one regards this opposition as religious in a way that is distinct from politics.
79. *Anzeiger für Stadt und Land* 31 July 1877 (see also 19 June 1877) counted five the first two and a half years, plus three guest preachers.
80. This sentiment was not universal among women. Hennig (*Chronik*, 80) reports that the wife of a liberal councillor stiffened the resolve of her husband and Richter to persevere with their schemes at a time when they were toying with giving up.
81. Ord A Finanzkammer Altkatholiken 14. GLA 360/1935–11/829. They preferred to abandon services entirely.
82. Old Catholics from Kappel were twice as likely (11 % vs. 5 %) to wed someone from outside the county as Roman Catholics were.
83. Hennig sometimes affected a populist touch on the podium, reminding Catholics considering electing an anticlerical to represent Rust in the federal parliament that "not even the biggest calves choose their own butcher". *Anzeiger für Stadt und Land* 9 January 1877.
84. For over a century, the Centre (or its successor, the Christian Democratic Union) has carried Kappel in every single election.
85. Old Catholics wed later in the century, but at the same point in their lives. Limiting attention to brides under twenty-five cuts the gap, but only to two years.
86. Note that the Old Catholics were working against the trend in age at marriage.
87. The higher value is significantly greater than zero, as in the earlier cohort, although for the other religion.

88. One elderly Old Catholic insisted that Uebelin had declared that confession would eventually be done away with. (Hennig, *Chronik*, 14–15, 61.) Individual confession was abolished for adult Old Catholics.
89. As seen here, building too much flexibility into Secularization theory blunts its analysis of events. One is left with the uninformative assertion that as family limitation increased, the result was either clericalism or anticlericalism.
90. Moreover, once the schism had taken place, they were in no position to persuade others to innovate in any respect.
91. Compare the speculations of Manfred Welti, "Abendmahl, Zollpolitik und Sozialistengesetz in der Pfalz. Eine statistisch-quantifizierende Untersuchung zur Verbreitung von liberal-aufklärerischem Gedankengut im 19. Jahrhundert", *Geschichte und Gesellschaft*, 3 (1977), 384–405.
92. Calculations based on statistical notes for visitations in Ord A D4/3742, Ord A B4/5632, and Ord A B4/10504, supplemented by Hennig, *Chronik*, 273–286.
93. Then, an average of 63 % of the population confessed at Easter in preparation for receiving communion. Pf A Grafenhausen Announcement books 1839–1847 and 1848–1855.
94. Hennig, *Chronik*, 61–62.
95. Information on the form of the parties' campaigns comes from the January-March 1868 *Breisgauer Zeitung* and *Badischer Beobachter*, as well as from the general works mentioned in earlier footnotes. See also George Windell, *The Catholics and German Unity 1866–1871* (Minneapolis, 1954), especially 128–131. Much commentary goes back to (Carl Bader,) "Die badischen Wahlen zum Zollparlament", *Historisch-politische Blätter für das katholische Deutschland*, 61 (1868), 760–793.
96. Hermann Kalkoff (ed.), *Nationalliberale Parlamentarier 1867–1917 des Reichstags und der Einzellandtage* (Berlin, 1917), 356–360, 369. Hans-Peter Becht, *Badische Parlamentarier 1867–1874* (Düsseldorf, 1995) also provides photographs of Kiefer, his opponent Franz Rosshirt, and their colleagues.
97. *Breisgauer Zeitung* 25 and 29 January 1868.
98. This practice backfired when two of those so chosen repudiated Kiefer. *Badischer Beobachter* 18 February 1868. *Breisgauer Zeitung* 18 February 1868.
99. *Breisgauer Zeitung* 14 February 1868.
100. Or the second, if one counts the June 1849 snap election to the revolutionary constituent assembly.
101. Voters dropped envelopes containing sheets identifying their choice into the ballot box. To promote anonymity and avoid challenges, parties printed and distributed standard ballots. This system applied to all the secret ballot votes discussed in this book.
102. GLA 236/10633. The following paragraphs include material from the leaflets.
103. Where the Church had no presence, the opposition was shut out. The lone opposition ballot in Protestant Wittenweier was traced to a border guard who had received it from the Kappel cleric. St A LA Lahr Generalia XXVII/4/1.
104. Once called the Quadrilateral, by analogy with the fortress bulwark of Habsburg power in Lombardy-Venetia.
105. *Breisgauer Zeitung* 3 March 1868.
106. GLA 233/33851 (circular to ambassadors 26 February 1868).
107. Julius Dorneich, "Die Führungsschicht der Katholischen Volkspartei in Baden 1869 nach ihrer Sozialstruktur", *Zeitschrift für die Geschichte des Oberrheins*, 124 (N.F. 85, 1976), 363–368. The Centre's motto (which supplied the title of Kremer, *Mit*) tacked "with God" in front of the old radical slogan "for truth, freedom, and justice".
108. GLA 60/1284 (listed). GLA 233/31538 (petition of 24 May 1869 from 135 Grafenhauseners). GLA 233/31539 (petition of 13 May 1869 from 112 Rusters).
109. Printed copy in GLA 233/32611. In aid of the cause, Richter opened a rally in

Ettenheim at which Kiefer spoke and a county National Liberal association was founded. (Gendarmerie report of 26 July 1869 in GLA 315/45.) I found no reports of such activity in the three villages themselves.
110. I explore the implications of this victory in dealing with indirect provincial elections in Chapter Twelve.
111. It finally took over the name officially in 1888. On the process see Kremer, *Mit*, 24, 31, 77. The successive programmes of the federal National Liberal and Centre parties are set out in Fritz Specht and Paul Schwave, *Die Reichstags-Wahlen von 1867 bis 1907* (Berlin, 1908), 355–368 and 385–394, respectively. Sepainter, *Reichstagswahlen* covers numerous aspects of federal politics.
112. The classic study of Catholics' federal votes is Johannes Schauff, *Das Wahlverhalten der Deutschen Katholiken im Kaiserreich und in der Weimarer Republik* (Mainz, 1975—original 1928). The monolithic rejection of the Centre by non-Catholics, urban or rural, merits emphasis. In nearby Schmieheim, where virtually all the inhabitants were Protestant or Jewish, the Centre averaged just half a percent of the vote from 1868 to 1912. Indeed, it did not receive one single vote of the 2003 cast before 1890.
113. Elsewhere, the rise of socialism cut into National Liberal centres, but paradoxically that gave the party a new lease on life. When the Centre became the strongest party in Baden, the pragmatic calculations that had dictated the alliance of all oppositional currents against the National Liberals were reversed. Both provincially and federally, the National Liberals, Progressives, and Democrats formed a bloc, later joined informally by the Social Democrats. In this riding these later shifts were of little importance. Even when the bloc ran Democratic candidates in 1907 and 1912, Konstantin Fehrenbach, later a Weimar chancellor, won comfortably for the Centre. Fehrenbach is the first child in entry 354 in Albert Köbele and Hans Scheer, *Ortssippenbuch Dundenheim* (Grafenhausen, 1977).
114. Sepainter, *Reichstagswahlen*, 369 erroneously lists him running for re-election.
115. Sander's predecessor had refrained from speaking on the grounds that he was "no orator". *Anzeiger für Stadt und Land* 4 January 1877.
116. Reported virtually verbatim in *Breisgauer Zeitung* 11–12 October 1881.
117. The Centre's standard-bearer hailed from the Palatinate.
118. On the Centre's difficulty finding objectionable points in Sander's platform, see the reports on his speeches in *Badischer Beobachter* 20 and 22 October 1881.
119. In debate, one priest conceded that he agreed with Sander on all but two points, at which the candidate interjected "those two points are that you are black [clerical] and I [am] liberal". *Breisgauer Zeitung* 9 November 1881.
120. After the first round, Sander led by 400 votes out of almost fifteen thousand. In the runoff, which attracted three thousand more voters, the Centre finished 639 votes back. GLA 236/14864. On the runoff, see *Oberrheinischer Kurier* 5 November 1881 and Breisgauer Zeitung 4 November 1881.
121. According to Sepainter, *Reichstagswahlen*, 123, 188, 214–215.
122. "[G]emässigter Ultramontanen". GLA 360/1924–56/1 (letter of 19 January 1887 from rural commissariat). Such a phrase would not have passed their lips publicly (nor those of a Secularization theorist, for that matter).
123. GLA 315/94 (reports on rallies 30 October 1892 and 25 November 1894). A covering letter of 12 June 1893 from the Interior Ministry (GLA 236/17125) mentions a further report on a rally in Grafenhausen seven days earlier. See also GLA 236/10490 (report on county Ettenheim for 1889–1892) and GLA 236/10491 (report on county Ettenheim for 1894–1895). The story is told from the party's point of view in Hellmut Hesselbarth, *Revolutionäre Sozialdemokraten, Opportunisten und die Bauern am Vorabend des Imperialismus* (Berlin, 1968) and, critically,

Anticlericals and Ultramontanes 229

in William Maehl, "German Social Democratic Agrarian Policy, 1890–1895, Reconsidered", *Central European History*, 13 (1980), 121–157.
124. Despite a 6 June 1898 rally that attracted about 120 mostly Centre supporters to the Star. (Gendarmerie report in GLA 236/14924.)
125. Although Hennig declared his full agreement with the Social Democrats' 1893 stand against the military budget at a rally for that party, he went on at his own rally to use opposition to the proposition as a reason to vote for the Centre. GLA 236/14901 (4 July 1893 report by prefect).
126. From 1868 to 1893 that government included the first Jewish cabinet minister in Germany. Bertold Spuler, *Regenten und Regierungen der Welt* (Würzburg, 1962), pt. 2, vol. 3, 65–71.
127. This interpretation was also Hennig's (*Chronik*, 127–128, 163–164).
128. It was also diverging from villages with Catholic populations generally. See Carl Zangerl, "Courting the Catholic Vote: The Center Party in Baden, 1903–1913", *Central European History*, 10 (1977), 220–240. This political twist came well after its fertility diverged.
129. Hennig, *Chronik*, 218–219.
130. National Liberalism survived among Roman Catholics only where social networks were so ramified as to facilitate organizing independent of the State.
131. Gem A Grafenhausen B XIII/743 and *OSB Grafenhausen*.
132. Contrast Table 12.1 upcoming.
133. However, the 140 Kapplers who voted 84 % for the Centre in the first round showed stronger family limitation than Kapplers who abstained. Gem A Kappel B XIII/658 and *OSB Kappel*. Kappel's voters stopped childbearing a year and a half earlier than non-voters, although they were even further behind Grafenhauseners of both stripes. The difference is not great, and in any case counts against Secularization theories. It does fit the pattern in the final two columns of Table 11.4, as the Roman Catholics overtook the faltering Old Catholics in family limitation.
134. From 1898 to 1912 in Gem A Grafenhausen B XIII/743, Gem A Kappel B XIII/658, and Gem A Rust B XIII/294. Election results from 1868 to 1912 are given by poll in Benz, Thesis, appendix E.
135. For each voter, I compare the outcome in elections in which he chose to participate to the outcome in all elections in which he was eligible to participate. In the first group of 334 documented marriages and 6146 woman-years, average Centre support was 7 % lower than the standard. It was 4 % higher in the second group of 547 documented marriages and 9565 woman-years. The distinctions between voters are rough, but even so are finer-grained than the regional aggregates often studied by Secularization theorists. I look forward to undertaking a more thorough and wider-ranging analysis in the future.
136. For both tendencies, the average marriage began in 1880 and first-time brides were about twenty-five. Husbands' political participation had the greatest impact on age at last birth and completed family size among women who wed young. The differences between older brides were more modest, but consistent across all three variables.
137. m: .65 vs. .38; percentage limiting: 56 % vs. 28 %.
138. The results within each village offer no more comfort to Secularization theory. In Rust, voters leaning towards the Centre displayed greater family limitation. (This effect was clearest among couples wed before 1875.) In Grafenhausen, family limitation was stronger away from the Centre, but largely because its majorities shrank over time. Voters leaning its way had wed seventeen years earlier on average, at a time when family limitation was less extensive.

12

Localities and Parties

To this point my evaluation of hypotheses of Secularization has yielded a generally negative verdict. First, it is hard to see any of nineteenth-century Germany's political parties as uniformly more modern than the others. Even on clerical issues, the Centre stood no further from prejudices of the twentieth century than its opponents did. Second, ultramontanism rose to hegemony at the same time as family limitation did. The fiercest resistance to clericalism came in Kappel, where the least family limitation was manifest. Conversely, for a considerable period the Centre's hold federally was strongest in Grafenhausen, where family limitation was most widespread. Third, personal, occupational, economic, and kin ties linked religious or political attitudes to fertility as much as ideological conviction did. Sometimes, as in Kappel before the schism or in Grafenhausen in the years just before the First World War, those forces brought liberal politics and family limitation into association; at other times, as later in Kappel, or among Rust's Jews, the effect was the reverse. The values highlighted by models of Secularization faced heavy going in this environment.

Baden politics promises more hospitable terrain for Secularization theory. The provincial National Liberals remained a force locally for much longer than their federal counterparts. Moreover, the party's fortunes varied directly with the strength of family limitation. Kappel fell under the Centre's sway early, while Rust resisted longer, and Grafenhausen never fully succumbed. The existence of liberal Catholics like these villagers was crucial to wider politics, as Baden's National Liberals relied on them to supplement their base vote among the one-third of the population who were not Catholics.

Nor was that reliance misplaced, for the enduring ultramontane-liberal polarization left the National Liberals in power for over half a century. Their control over press and public service was at risk in each election, but those resources also helped to perpetuate their position as the natural governing party. Because the Centre lacked these advantages, it was forced to rely on popular organization. The government responded by clinging to the system of indirect elections, which magnified the advantages of office and reduced mass participation.

As it happens, these characteristics enhance the significance of provincial elections for a study of this kind. Because the Baden legislature retained jurisdiction over religious policy, that issue continued to mark provincial politics more strongly than it did the federal scene.¹ In addition, the fielding of slates of noted supporters in each locality made it easy to trace the personal networks around which parties were built. In such a setting, the influence of mayor and priest, patrons and clients, rallies and organizations, emerged particularly clearly. Moreover, local races and infighting over the selection of candidates gave electors ample opportunity to manifest independence or subservience to Church or State. Finally, the fact that Ettenheim-Kenzingen, the riding in which the three villages were located, swung back and forth between National Liberals and Centre in the 1870s and 1880s made politics more open and more lively.

Studying leading figures on that lively scene reveals patterns compatible with Secularization. Stronger family limitation was found among National Liberal electors, and this effect was independent of religion. However, economics clouds the picture. Because notables were at first under the sway of the prefect, the Centre had to mobilize less exalted strata, among whom family limitation was less extensive, to defend the Church. At a later point, as party politics supplanted brokerage politics, local élites realized which way the wind was blowing and hastened to affiliate with the Centre.

Far more important than any of these trends was the lingering impact of locality. Family limitation remained associated with political independence on that level right into the twentieth century. These patterns fit rather better into the themes I have been emphasizing since Chapter Ten than into the straitjacket of Secularization theory. Demonstrating this contention again requires detailed analysis of how people voted and how politics was conducted.

Notable Politics 1871–1901[2]

I pick up the story in 1871, at a point where the Centre[3] was not yet organized throughout the riding, at least not on a level where it could compete effectively in indirect elections. Polls the size of Grafenhausen, Kappel, or Rust were now assigned half a dozen or more electors, but all that meant was that mere councillors joined the mayors, clerks, and treasurers who had dominated earlier electoral colleges. In Grafenhausen and Rust, the winning slate simply was the municipal council, assigned by the voters to represent the village in yet another capacity. In Kappel, mayor Richter headed a slate including only one non-notable, a brewer and innkeeper who subsequently followed him into Old Catholicism. None of these candidates faced serious opposition. Their victories were duly recorded as National Liberal triumphs.[4]

The actual campaign began only at this point. Under the guidance of the county prefect, electors gathered formally and informally to discuss potential candidates. Ettenheim county made up most of the new riding. (See Map 3.2.) A majority of electors from its municipalities quickly agreed to renominate Richter, thereby ensuring his victory.[5] However, those from localities that had been added to the riding felt a residual loyalty to their own previous representative, also a National Liberal. Despite his urgings to unite behind Richter,[6] they cast their votes for him as a gesture of gratitude. This pushed the Catholic

People's candidate, Carl Edelmann, into third place, for he could count on the support of only those few electors who had been committed to oppose the government right from the start. For instance, although the mayor of Grafenhausen was one of the few municipal leaders to refuse to join the National Liberal party, and thereby earned the prefect's ire,[7] he nevertheless cast his vote for Richter.

The Centre's claims that religion was in danger counted for less in 1871 than the immediate pressure the prefect could bring to bear. In subsequent elections, that balance of forces was altered through the actions of the government on the one hand and the Centre's increasing organizational strength on the other. Construing their 1871 victories as mandates to press on with the anticlerical campaign, the National Liberals banned orders (1872) and shut down the institutions in which they taught. Thoroughly religious schools disappeared in 1876 with the introduction of compulsory mixed schools. This period also saw legislation recognizing Old Catholicism (1874), with the consequences described for Kappel. Other laws forbade priests to make spiritual threats or promises to influence voters or to use the pulpit for political purposes (1874).

The most striking measure was the tightening of the 1867 law referred to in Chapter Eleven. Henceforth, no one could exercise ecclesiastical functions without having passed a special State exam. The full force of the law was applied retroactively against the 1874 seminary class, who were repeatedly jailed for saying mass, teaching catechism, and the like.[8] One such priest appeared very briefly in Grafenhausen where his actions were monitored.[9] He and his classmates, along with their successors, were arrested, prosecuted, fined, jailed, and eventually forced into exile until a compromise was reached in 1880.[10] The most important effects of this dispute on these villages were delayed until Andreas Jerger, a veteran of the persecution of 1874, was assigned to Rust as priest from 1886 to 1917.

These measures were in place or rumoured during the 1873 election campaign.[11] Demonstrating that it had learnt its lesson in 1871, the Catholic People's Party entered the contest right at the outset in all three villages. In Kappel, the vicar attempted to use the newly founded Catholic Men's Association as a springboard to defeat Richter, but the slate the cleric headed succumbed to one consisting of the mayor and reliable liberal members of the council.[12] In Grafenhausen, too, the vicar took the lead, but his aggressiveness proved counterproductive, alienating voters accustomed to a low-key approach from their elderly priest.[13] A slate of up-and-coming National Liberals, most of whom had not yet achieved municipal office, emerged victorious.

The campaign in Rust was more complicated and produced more significant results. Ten days before the election, a Freiburg lawyer and an outside priest held a Catholic People's Party rally in the Eagle inn.[14] Fifty people, including eight from Kappel, heard them stress religious issues, from the Old Catholic threat to the prohibition on teaching by nuns, and call for tax reform to benefit landed proprietors. They urged citizens to choose independent-minded electors who could not be swayed from loyalty to religion and fatherland by earthly considerations.

As it happened, this rally was held on Grand Duke Friedrich's birthday, September 9. Because the celebration of that occasion was a key element in National Liberal campaigns, the coincidence afforded an opportunity to compare the two parties' styles. Rust's newly founded fire brigade, of which Friedrich was the patron, marched through the streets the night before to musical accompaniment.[15] That morning saw special services in both church and synagogue. The afternoon featured a dinner at the Ox inn during which the mayor toasted the grand duke and his policies, and sharply attacked the Centre. At the very time the clerical outsiders were speaking, an allegedly larger crowd was enjoying a banquet at the Lion inn. When voting day came, Rusters stuck to precedent by selecting the mayor and seven councillors as electors. The effects of the campaign on their views were not yet clear.

The loyalties of Rust's electors soon became an item of wider concern. Although shut out in many rural polls, the Catholic People's Party had made significant inroads in the towns of the riding, and its committed supporters were almost numerous enough to ensure victory. Just four days before the electoral college was to assemble, Edelmann was once more put forward and accepted by the Catholic People's electors.[16] He campaigned personally, but the party's main effort went into attacking Richter.

Those attacks hit home. Although National Liberal electors had earlier endorsed Richter, it became clear as the electoral college gathered that the Rusters would not vote for him.[17] Unable to settle their differences in last-minute caucuses, the National Liberals, excluding the Rusters, but including the Grafenhauseners and Kapplers, simply boycotted the electoral college, thereby denying it quorum. Seventy-two[18] electors appeared, while only fifty-six stayed away, indicating a clear victory for the Catholic People's Party had the vote been held that day.

The National Liberal press attacked Rust's electors as turncoats who had deserted the colours under which they had been chosen.[19] This betrayal was attributed to their fear of the chaplain and their wives. Their masculine pride stung, the Rusters replied in print, insisting that their position had been consistent all along: they were liberal, but they would not vote for Richter.[20] Hoping to win the eight Rusters and other independents back for the second round of balloting, at which quorum requirements would be waived,[21] the other National Liberals switched their allegiance to a merchant from Herbolzheim.[22] Richter endorsed the new candidate.

The party networks again swung into operation. For the National Liberals, notaries worked on local guardians, townspeople travelled the countryside lobbying, and the prefect raised the spectre of neglect or abolition of county institutions if the seat fell to the opposition.[23] The Catholic People's Party attempted to shield its supporters from outside contacts, and portrayed the new candidate as just as anticlerical as Richter.[24] In the end, these defensive tactics proved just enough. Sixty-four of 128 ballots were cast for Edelmann in proper form, and one incomplete ballot was acknowledged by the elector and supplemented to give the Catholic People's Party the narrowest of victories.

The intense political activity of autumn 1873 was only part of the process by which the party divisions in Baden came to be reproduced on the local level. Even municipal politics became tinged anticlerical red or clerical black,[25] as ideology competed for voters' attention against family ties, business interests, and simple competence. I have already given examples of such developments in Kappel, admittedly an extreme case. A look at local leadership in Rust and Grafenhausen brings out some of the mechanisms by which the government exercised control, and sheds light on the resources parties could bring to bear in election campaigns.

This period in Rust's history illustrates why notables were reluctant to cross the prefect in political matters. Three times between 1865 and 1879, prefects forced mayors out of office.[26] The 1874 election following one such dismissal pitted the Catholic Men's Association against liberals loyal to the government.[27] A National Liberal led after the first round, but the second-place finisher withdrew in favour of the Centre man who had come third. This enabled him to take 55 % of the vote in the runoff, in which 96 % of those eligible participated.

The prefect was not unduly concerned at first, for the victor was not decisively partisan, and he counted on the clerk and three National Liberal councillors to keep the new mayor in line. After all, in 1871 and 1873, he had eventually been persuaded to side with the government as an elector. However, the mayor fell instead under the influence of an enthusiastic vicar, and the prefect resolved to move against him.[28] The opportunity arose in 1879, and the county council, consisting of reliable National Liberals appointed by the prefect, duly dismissed Rust's mayor. This achieved the desired effect, as the voters turned to the National Liberal who had fallen short four years earlier.[29]

Events in Grafenhausen ran parallel, but the National Liberals there needed rather less help from the prefect. The mayor had maintained his leanings towards the Centre despite bowing to the prefect's wishes at election time. He ran again in 1876, finishing second behind a National Liberal in the first round, but uniting the votes of all other candidates behind him in the runoff. However, the prefect had him deposed a year later.

A new National Liberal champion emerged in the person of Leopold Sattler, who had entered politics in 1873 as an elector. He won a clear majority over three other candidates in the first round of balloting. Participation in these votes was a bit less than in Kappel and Rust, running from 82 % to 91 %. Sattler's capable leadership smoothed over the rifts within the community, and he went on to a virtually unanimous re-election in 1883.[30]

The National Liberals also maintained a strong presence on Grafenhausen's municipal council during this period. Contests were hard-fought, and interest ran high. For instance, in 1873 the third seat at stake fell to the candidate supported by the National Liberals by one vote in a 94 % turnout. Seven years later, a like margin determined the outcome.[31] On a practical level, these results highlighted the rôle of the returning officers who determined which ballots were rejected as spoiled. In broader perspective, these races kept the party vigorous on the municipal scene even as its fortunes waned on other levels.

This background makes the 1877 provincial campaigns easy to understand. In Grafenhausen, Sattler led the National Liberals to a sweep. In Kappel, the Roman Catholics rolled over the Old Catholics by the usual margin. In Rust, the victorious slate was again dominated by councillors, five of whom had served in the two previous electoral colleges. However, the vicar headed the ticket. This time Rust's electors were devout delegates rather than uncommitted representatives.

The Catholic People's Party was less successful elsewhere in the riding, despite a confirmation tour by the administrator of the bishopric that doubled as electoral agitation.[32] Edelmann continued to campaign against Richter, his foe four years earlier. In the end, the National Liberals claimed a slight margin among committed electors, but a few undecided held the balance. In a meeting at the county seat, the prefect persuaded some National Liberals to nominate a lawyer from Freiburg.[33] A few days before the electoral college assembled, Sattler welcomed a larger gathering of his party's electors to the village hall in Grafenhausen. The anticlerical principal of the county high school presided, urging solidarity and promising victory, before introducing the candidate to his supporters.[34] The National Liberals did win when the undecided electors split,[35] making Ettenheim-Kenzingen the only seat to change hands that year.

In 1879, at the height of campaigns elsewhere, the deputy so painstakingly parachuted into the riding resigned to devote himself to his legal practice. A period of confusion ensued, as electors scrambled to balance local interests against government pressure, and civic pride against party solidarity. The Catholic People's Party toyed with running the independent mayor of Ettenheim, but eventually settled on an outsider from Karlsruhe.[36] The National Liberal electors split between supporters of an Ettenheim merchant and the director of the judicial circuit including Kenzingen. The latter drew the most votes at an early caucus, but the prefect and the press were unable to swing the rest of the electors, including those from Grafenhausen, behind such a bureaucrat.[37] They eventually compromised on the merchant from Herbolzheim who had carried the party's standard in 1873 after Richter had been forced to stand aside.

The circuit director remained on the ballot for the electoral college, but dropped off after coming third in the first round.[38] His supporters then combined with the other National Liberals and independents to hold the seat for the government.

Three features of this contest stand out. The first was the tenacity of the radical tradition of preferring a civilian candidate to a government official.[39] Second, as in other elections, Herbolzheim benefitted from the stalemate between the candidates from the two larger towns. (See Maps 1.1 and 3.2.) Finally, it was clear that a convinced anticlerical of Kiefer's stripe stood no chance.[40]

Because the 1879 by-election had been limited to the electoral college chosen in 1877, the Catholic People's Party's first real chance to reverse that year's verdict came in 1881.[41] The provincial campaign overlapped the early stages of the hard-fought federal election, and the Centre used the same literature in both races.[42] For their part, the provincial National Liberals relied on the calendar to carry their campaign. As usual, the commemoration of the battle of Sedan[43] on September 4 and the grand duke's birthday five days later were celebrated in a manner calculated to emphasize their national and liberal character. This year the party also benefitted from the silver anniversary of Friedrich's accession, as well as the wedding of a princess. The liberal press rounded out its coverage with accounts of the ducal couple's honeymoon in Sweden and the emperor's visit to Baden.[44]

This sort of appeal proved insufficient in a rural constituency in the throes of the Great Depression. Low prices, flooding, poor harvests, competition from Alsatian cigar factories, and the first collection of a tobacco tax focused attention on economic issues.[45] The Centre took advantage of this discontent, slipping three Freiburg agitators to a rally at the Crown inn in Grafenhausen. Their championing of freedom of conscience and their insistence that current tax rates were more than sufficient to maintain services brought accusations of hypocrisy and irresponsibility from the National Liberals.[46] These rebuttals did not convince Grafenhauseners, who elected a Catholic People's slate for the first time.

The day of the rally in Grafenhausen saw a march by war veterans in Kappel. The National Liberals had presumed that the nationalism of veterans' associations would provide their party with a mass base, but in this constituency they were disappointed time and again. Such organizations did boast considerable memberships, but as involuntary cross-sections of the population, they reflected rather than led public opinion.[47] In 1881, for example, the religious schism once more determined Kapplers' votes, and the Catholic People's Party swept the field.

The campaign in Rust also featured a special event. The men's choral society celebrated its twentieth anniversary by dedicating its flag on the Sedan holiday. Despite inclement weather, large numbers took part in a church service and parade, followed by singing, dancing, drinking, and dining over a two-day period.[48] In this atmosphere, the new mayor led the National Liberal slate to victory on Sander's federal coattails. In accordance with National Liberal practice elsewhere, that slate included a Jew.

Rumours about candidates had flown before the voting. Judging the incumbent's chances of re-election to be slim, the National Liberals touted a lawyer from Konstanz who had been born in the district. When he declined, they were left with no choice but to fall back on the incumbent and hope to make up the lost ground. The opposition's first choice, the mayor of Ettenheim, also declined, and it turned to an outsider.[49] The Catholic People's Party had carried enough polls that its victory was not in doubt in any case. Following a postponement so that voting would not coincide with Yom Kippur,[50] its candidate was duly elected.

The defeat in Ettenheim-Kenzingen was just part of an overall setback for the National Liberals in 1881, but some remained convinced that with the right candidate the seat could be regained. In 1885, they floated the name of Stefan Leipf even before the local votes. As county surveyor, Leipf was familiar to virtually every landholder in the riding and was quite popular for a government agent.[51]

Still, local personalities mattered as much as the candidate. In Grafenhausen, the municipal council put itself forward as a block, and emerged victorious. In practice, that meant six National Liberal votes, including mayor Sattler's, against one for the Catholic People's Party. There was no question of a split in Kappel's electors, all staunch Roman Catholics. The situation in Rust mirrored that in Grafenhausen. The National Liberals no longer had the upper hand in municipal politics there, but the clerk, a perennial National Liberal elector, was selected along with seven noted partisans of the Centre.[52]

The most interesting campaign took place in the central town of Ettenheim, where Democrats and independents took advantage of lacklustre approaches by the major parties with a last-minute agitation that carried them to victory. This complicated the deliberations of the electors as civic pride and radicalism cut across shared anticlericalism. A large majority of the liberal electors stood by Leipf, but the divisions raised the Catholic People's Party's hopes of retaining the seat.[53] By the time the electoral college met, the democrats had fastened on a local candidate from an old radical centre, and supported him on the first ballot. That gave the Catholic People's incumbent a one-vote lead, but his total stagnated in the runoff as both opposing factions united behind Leipf. Ettenheim-Kenzingen changed hands once more.

This was the National Liberals' final victory, although that fact was far from clear in 1885. Understanding their eclipse requires pausing once more to focus on key local figures and events. Few of these involve Kappel, for the political framework there remained locked in place by the schism. Municipal offices were firmly in the hands of the minority of the élite who had remained true to the Church. After the general reunion in 1890, a few former Old Catholics worked their way back into government, but these were precisely the most sincere prodigals.[54]

Rust's political life was considerably more turbulent. In 1885 the voters chose as mayor a native of the village who had left it for a police career in Freiburg. On taking office, he had the mayor's salary doubled, and proceeded to administer the municipality in a highly arbitrary fashion, intimidating councillors and citizens alike. Because the mayor made no secret of his free-thinking views, his actions discredited National Liberalism. When he left in 1889 to pursue a civil service career and his successor died after serving only a year, the party was in disarray.[55]

In a straight showdown for the mayor's office, the Centre candidate decisively defeated the National Liberal clerk. A switch to indirect mayoral elections thereafter brought a measure of stability. The mayor was re-elected in 1896 and though he resigned two years later, his successor went on to hold office for a quarter-century.[56] That man was on occasion better disposed towards the government, but the real determinant of Rust's position in broader politics was the priest Jerger. He was extremely energetic, founding organizations for workers, youths, women, gymnasts, and the like, all with a Catholic tinge.[57] Jerger's sufferings at the hands of the State had persuaded him of the importance of mobilizing the people to forestall the government, and he impressed this lesson on his parishioners.[58]

In Grafenhausen, too, the priest was a leading political figure, but his relation to the laity was somewhat different. The parish's tradition of elderly priests was maintained in 1884, when Matthias Schäfle was assigned to Grafenhausen at age sixty-seven. His age, cultivation, and reasonableness impressed the county prefect, who anticipated a clear field for the National Liberals under Schäfle's pastoral care.[59] The prefect was shocked in subsequent years as the old man gave speeches, had the sexton distribute Centre ballots, and generally campaigned so actively that he made the enemies' list drawn up by the government.[60]

It was widely supposed at the time that the Church hierarchy made an effort to match the temperament and capacities of a priest with the characteristics of the parish.[61] If so, the pairing of Schäfle with Grafenhausen was an inspiration. He combined ardent partisanship with a measured approach, thereby giving the Centre the face it had to present to appeal to Grafenhauseners. Like them, he was adventuresome and paradoxical, startling fellow clerics in 1850 with the declaration that he was a socialist.[62] He brought a learned touch to the issues of the day, almost always leaving an impression of balance.[63]

Schäfle's presence alone was not enough to bring the Centre to power in Grafenhausen, for its inhabitants were not easily swayed. For instance, as mentioned above, Sattler was able to lead the National Liberals to victory provincially the year after the priest arrived. However, the mayor fell ill soon after, and died in 1888. His successor was Ludwig Häfele, who remained at the helm of the municipality for almost twenty-nine years.[64]

The prefect found Häfele to share many of Sattler's qualities, describing him as energetic, intelligent, rich, and mistrustful of all taxation. Despite his active promotion of cooperatives, the mayor held himself aloof from the Peasants Union.[65] That organization had close ties to the Centre, and set itself up in opposition to the official—and hence National Liberal—Agricultural Union.[66] Because it charged lower membership fees and focused on immediate benefits rather than education, the Peasants Union made headway in these villages. In 1908 it outnumbered the Agricultural Union by 209 to 47 in Grafenhausen, by 186 to 30 in Kappel, and by about 142 to 40 in Rust.[67] These margins were of the same magnitude as the Centre's electoral victories. However, the Peasants Union lost influence in Grafenhausen when it came out against the project to upgrade the Rittmatten. (See Map 2.2.) It also opposed construction of the railway spurline through Grafenhausen to Kappel, but Häfele and Schäfle pushed that project through.

Despite this behaviour, in the prefect's eyes Häfele had one major failing:

Localities and Parties 239

his politics. In a confidential conversation shortly before the 1889 provincial election, the mayor refused to enter the lists against the Centre.[68] He did not lead that party, but he did underwrite Schäfle's management of its cause. The result was that the priest topped the slate of Grafenhausen's electors, on which he was joined by several obscure citizens, all of them committed to the Centre. The outcomes in the other two villages were less unusual. All five electors from Kappel were Roman Catholics and followers of the Centre. Rust's electors were split much as in 1885, with Jerger delivering six votes to the Centre, including his own, while the prefect counted on the mayor and the municipal clerk to stand by the government.[69]

The results elsewhere confirmed that the Centre's targetting of Ettenheim-Kenzingen as a vulnerable seat had paid off.[70] The National Liberals had devoted most of their efforts to searching for a candidate rather than voters. Leipf had been transferred, but they remained convinced that the right figure from within the district could hold it. In the end their choice fell on a cigar manufacturer from Herbolzheim, but he failed to deliver either of the polls in his hometown.[71]

The Centre had nominated a lawyer from Freiburg before the original vote, but switched to Friedrich Hug, trustee of a foundation in Konstanz, who had sat in the legislature previously. The National Liberals criticized both choices, recalling how the Centre had used traditional radical rhetoric to decry their fondness for bureaucrats and jurists from outside the riding.[72] The Centre electors were not to be moved, and gave their party its biggest majority to that point.

This defeat, like similar losses in other ridings, did not distress the National Liberals unduly, and they confidently predicted that they would be back.[73] Those sentiments did not motivate much action in 1893. A professor from outside the district announced his intention to run, but was repudiated by the party, which went into the local elections without a candidate to face Hug.[74] Only in Rust did the National Liberals present a slate, and it went down to defeat by a solid margin. The prefect retained some hope of swaying the mayor, but Jerger and the other six electors were solidly in the Centre's column.[75]

In Grafenhausen and Kappel, the Centre had the field to itself. In a show of strength, five to six hundred inhabitants of the two villages made a joint daylong pilgrimage to a shrine in Alsace to mark Pope Leo XIII's fiftieth year as a bishop.[76] With the electoral outcome clear, turnouts were low. Surprisingly, the prefect counted on one National Liberal vote from Kappel. The end of the schism had widened the scope for personal rivalry, and one councillor was positioning himself for a run at the mayor.[77] There is no way to tell whether he stuck by this plan when the National Liberals proved unable to muster a candidate, and called on supporters in the electoral college to submit blank ballots. At that point, a few potential National Liberal votes went over to the Centre, and Hug won with a slightly larger total than in 1889.

In Grafenhausen, the Centre slate consisted of Schäfle, the head of the local chapter of the Peasants Union, and five others who had also been chosen in 1889. Facing no opposition this time, they received somewhat fewer votes. Comparing these two contests reveals an association between clericalism and resistance to family limitation. Table 12.1 classifies those eligible to vote by their apparent inclination towards the Centre. The first column comprises floating voters, who did not exercise their franchise in 1893, although they had done so in 1889 when a National Liberal slate made a challenge. The Centre's most committed supporters, who turned out even when there was no opposition in 1893, make up the second column.[78]

The floating voters wed four years later in the century, but at more advanced ages. The latter point—but not the former—renders their wives' low ages at last birth more impressive. Final birth intervals were much longer than in families whose husbands supported the Centre on both occasions, and completed families were smaller.[79] Both the index of family limitation (m) and the percentage limiting were considerably higher where voters were less enthusiastic about the Centre.[80] The levels observed are so high that they may have cut into underlying natural fertility.

Despite the smaller number of cases, Table 12.1 links anticlericalism and contraception more reliably than the 1898–1912 federal election results of Chapter Eleven did. Moreover, it does so for a period when the Centre's dominance over Grafenhausen was considerably stronger. Family limitation was found among all stripes of Grafenhauser by this time, but was least pronounced among committed followers of the Centre. The first column cannot be so easily identified with one party, for fewer than half the floating voters

TABLE 12.1
Fertility of documented marriages of Voters in provincial elections of 1889 and 1893 in Grafenhausen, by voting record

	Floating voters	Committed to Centre
For completed families		
Wife's age at last birth	36.0	37.7
Final birth interval (in years)	4.44	3.60
Number of legitimate children	4.1	5.5
Total marital fertility rate	6.48	7.85
M	1.02	1.11
m	.68	.48
Percentage limiting	63 %	38 %

Notes
(1) *Source*: Gem A Grafenhausen B XIII/757 and OSB *Grafenhausen*.
(2) The Table is based on 153 marriages: 89 involving floating voters and 64 involving committed Centre supporters.

actually chose the National Liberals in 1889. The rest were simply choosy about when they entered the political arena. In 1893 they had nowhere to go, but other opportunities to express their views lay ahead.

In the legislature, Hug won the sympathy of National Liberals by pursuing a course intermittently at odds with his party's,[81] and his position in the constituency seemed secure. But in 1897 Hug switched seats, opening supposedly safe Ettenheim-Kenzingen for Emil Armbruster, a county court judge and previously unsuccessful Centre candidate.[82] This cavalier treatment annoyed the party's supporters, who had not been consulted before Armbruster was imposed upon them. The Peasants Union threatened to run its own independent candidate, but nothing formal came of such talk in 1897.[83]

Instead, the National Liberals took advantage of this opening to test their cherished notion that a suitable candidate could swing the seat their way once more. In doing so they set up an archetypal struggle between two of the great forces invoked by Secularization theory: ultramontanism and industrialization. The National Liberals found their champion in Arnold Schindler, a manufacturer in Herbolzheim who owned cigar factories throughout the region. As the employer of thousands of workers, he enjoyed wide recognition and a measure of influence over voters. Schindler's unassuming style and reputation as a devout Catholic blunted the attacks of Centre campaigners, who fell back to insisting that he would be helpless in the grip of caucus discipline.[84] Unimpressed, slates of electors in four polls where Schindler had factories, including Kappel, proclaimed that they were not National Liberal, but nevertheless for Schindler.[85]

This circumstance rendered the campaign in Kappel particularly lively. Recognizing the threat posed by the combination of residual Old Catholicism and loyalty to the firm, Hennig intervened more actively than before. For the first time, his name appeared on the ballot, as he and a future mayor led the Centre list against a slate dominated by workers. At the head of Schindler's supporters stood the manager of the sawmill, who drew on the loyalty of Kappel's fifty-member fire brigade, an organization long controlled by Old Catholics like himself.[86]

Hennig kicked off official public agitation with a late September rally, and invited Armbruster to speak at another gathering six days before the vote. With three days to go, large numbers turned out to a National Liberal rally to watch Hennig confront a big city lawyer who had been stumping for Schindler. Each side claimed victory.[87]

Hennig himself was at the centre of two campaign controversies. A special visit to Schindler's factory was denounced as trespass, and he was accused of attempting to have the factory supervisor induce workers to vote Centre. The dean insisted that he had merely urged the supervisor to remain neutral.[88] That was not Hennig's advice to clerics. In one town,[89] National Liberals attributed their defeat to the priest's intervention in the campaign at the behest of the dean.

For their parts, Schäfle and Jerger needed no encouragement. In Grafenhausen, the priest once more headed the Centre slate, on which he was joined by four of his colleagues from 1893. In Rust, the municipal council split into two slates, each supplementing its ranks with prominent citizens. As the mayor stood aloof, the clerk and one councillor led the National Liberal challenge to the treasurer and two councillors. The outcomes in the three localities were quite similar, as the Centre totals doubled its opponent's. Schindler was more successful elsewhere, but even so he fell short.[90] Industrialization was no match for ultramontanism.

Schindler's defeat in Grafenhausen was not that surprising, for factory work was less common there. In 1897 a majority of villagers stood by their priest and their Church. Two years later those loyalties were placed in conflict. Grafenhauseners' overwhelming antipathy to the Church hierarchy on that occasion demonstrates that strong bonds of communal solidarity existed beneath the political battles they fought with such enthusiasm. The episode is redolent of Secularization theory, yet also reveals the shortcomings of that model.

Throughout the 1890s, Hennig's confidential decannal evaluations of Schäfle had mentioned a hearing problem.[91] Schäfle was assigned a vicar and acquired an ear trumpet to use in hearing confessions in the sacristy. Concern about the effectiveness of his preaching and teaching persisted as the priest entered his ninth decade. Hennig found it particularly significant that young men and women—a group who normally preferred to confess to strangers—chose the old man over the vicar, and concluded that they assumed Schäfle could not make out what they were saying. Adults, both male and female, displayed the same attachment to their priest.

To Schäfle's consternation, the Freiburg curia in late 1899 forbade him to hear confessions, deliver religious education, or prepare first communicants. His parishioners were also astonished. Virtually every household, including those headed by widows, contributed a signature to a petition calling on the hierarchy to cease persecuting their pastor. When their plea was ignored, some became alienated, declaring openly that they would prefer Old Catholics or Social Democrats to the current régime in Freiburg.

Others stuck to persuasion, insisting that the sentiments of an entire community could not be ignored. In their eyes, an old man who had only a couple of years to live did not merit such harsh treatment. They argued further that Schäfle performed well in both school and confessional, and attested to his skill and understanding. When the curia responded after months of silence, it simply reaffirmed its decision, maintaining that a condition Grafenhauseners felt would move stones to sympathy was not a punishment of any kind. In a manner that fully suited his parishioners, Schäfle acquiesced publicly, but interpreted the regulation and private correspondence with the archbishop so as to maximize the scope of his activities.

Because almost all Grafenhauseners united in defence of their priest, it is not possible to analyse differences between villagers in this matter. None the less, even in isolation, examining the fertility of those petitioning on Schäfle's behalf provides useful perspectives on demographic history.[92] In numerous respects, these couples display greater family limitation than any other population studied in this chapter. Low ages at last birth (35.9) and very long final intervals (4.40 years) meant that the average wife gave birth only twice after turning thirty. In consequence, completed families were small, averaging 4.6 children.

As elsewhere, I interpret the modest total marital fertility rate (6.85 children) and underlying level of natural fertility (M = 1.09) as indirect evidence of very strong family limitation. That conclusion is borne out directly by the m index at .77. Comparison with the estimated 64 % limiting shows that family limitation was even deeper than it was wide.

One is tempted to relate the petitioners' support of Schäfle to toleration of contraception. After all, Grafenhauseners' declaration that the priest's replies in the confessional showed that he comprehended what they said comes close to the situation envisaged by Zeldin.[93] With two couples in three practising family limitation, their judgements of what constituted an appropriate response might well not be orthodox. Given independent evidence of Schäfle's attitudes towards contraception and his behaviour in the confessional, that interpretation would carry some weight. In its absence, there is no compelling reason to see the parishioners' statement as anything more than a rebuttal of the hierarchy's claims about Schäfle's hearing.

The isolation of this episode renders implausible the extension of Zeldin's hypothesis to Grafenhausen, Kappel, and Rust. At no point in any nineteenth-century election campaign, in the press, in publications, or in correspondence, did any villager, government official, or ecclesiastical figure link marital fertility and political views.[94] Criticisms of clerics were of the same character as those directed against schoolteachers or mayors, who rendered themselves popular or unpopular without hearing confessions. Overbearing priests were attacked for their attempts to influence parishioners' votes, not their sex lives.

I therefore resume my account of provincial elections, restricting myself to questions on which the data bear more directly. The 1901 campaign was half-hearted in most localities. The government did not take part with the usual energy, at least not in Ettenheim-Kenzingen, which had been written off after Schindler's defeat.[95] The National Liberals put up a Freiburg lawyer, who portrayed himself as the defender of the status quo, from property rights to religiously mixed schools, while calling for reform of the electoral and tax systems.[96] These appeals made little impact, for National Liberal organization was moribund outside Protestant territories. Armbruster took all but one of the polls dominated by Catholics, leaving the National Liberals with their smallest total ever.

The results in Kappel and Rust reflected this broader trend. Hennig was unable to rouse the Centre from a dormancy based on National Liberal inactivity.[97] With no opposition in the field, the hard core of Centre supporters turned out to deliver a one-sided verdict. In Rust, the prefect persuaded the mayor, the clerk, and other National Liberal personalities to put themselves forward, but on election day that slate failed to capture even the votes of those named on it. Instead, six of the eight Centre electors chosen in 1897 were joined by two newcomers in a comfortable victory.

In Grafenhausen, the situation was rather different. Still sulking, Schäfle declined to stand, but most of his erstwhile running-mates entered the field under the Centre banner once more. There they faced a new generation of National Liberals, including a prominent advocate of Schäfle against the curia. The contest did not arouse great interest, and as in Kappel and Rust, the turnout was not even half what it had been four years earlier. The difference was that in Grafenhausen the Centre candidates won by less than three votes.[98] Even so, this narrow victory meant that the Centre had captured all three polls for four elections running.

The Fertility of Electors

This desultory campaign marked the end of an era, for the Centre's long push for direct elections finally broke through in 1905. Before I turn to those contests, I review the patterns of notable politics from 1871 to 1901. Data from the riding's OSBs reveal social and demographic differences between leading anticlericals and ultramontanes that both support and confute Secularization theory. Underlying those differences is an enduring association between family limitation and political independence.

The occupational distributions in Table 12.2 are a useful place to begin exploring the behaviour of electors. In some respects, the differences between National Liberal and Centre are reminiscent of those between confessions in Kappel (Table 11.3) or between Radicals and Moderates around 1848 (Table 10.4). For example, the National Liberals had a very large advantage in the Affluent category, which was counterbalanced by the Centre's stronger presence in artisanal and Farming occupations. However, the affluent National Liberals were not just publicans, but manufacturers and merchants. The massive incomes they drew from industrialization diminished incentive for family limitation.

The religious dimension of political life underlay opposing trends in Commerce and the Professions. Because all the Jewish electors sided with the National Liberals, they inflate commercial activities for that party. Catholic clergy, on the other hand, entered politics only through the Centre, swelling the professions there. The priests' presence obscured the National Liberals' dominance among doctors, lawyers, and teachers. Although lay Centre electors were at first less eminent figures than their opponents, neither party consistently reached into the lowest orders for candidates, as no more than 4 % of electors rose from humble occupations.

Thus, the occupations typical of notables dominated both parties. Except for the small categories I have mentioned, politics did not split on occupational lines. Instead, this riding saw parallel movements by the élite and the general population towards the Centre. As it became clear that that party was the wave of the future, ambitious local politicians scrambled to make their careers within

TABLE 12.2
Distributions of occupations of National Liberal and Centre electors in Ettenheim-Kenzingen riding from 1871 to 1901

	National Liberal	Centre
Affluent	15 %	5 %
Craft, Fishing, Weaving	15 %	22 %
Farming	42 %	52 %
Commerce	9 %	2 %
Profession	4 %	7 %
Substantial	8 %	7 %
Local Position, Labour, Industry, Petty	4 %	3 %
None	2 %	0 %
Absolute total	180	264

Notes
(1) The sources are outlined in Benz, Thesis, appendix E.
(2) In a handful of cases where no occupation was given in the OSBs, classification was based on designations from the lists of electors.
(3) The Table includes electors who first wed after 1900, or who never married.

it. In so far as the sources of social eminence did not change during this period, what shifted were the political colours of the people controlling those sources. That reasoning would lead one to anticipate little difference between the fertility of electors from different parties. If the Centre was the unwelcome heir of the National Liberals, then the two parties should share whatever social and economic motives inclined people towards—or away from—contraception.[99]

Secularization theory, on the other hand, predicts sharp differences between parties even where economic and social circumstances are similar. Table 12.3 shows that it is right, on this point at least. Because Protestants and Jews virtually never voted for the Centre, one appropriate comparison is between the second and third columns. All the same, it is noteworthy that within the National Liberal party, religion made very little difference on almost every variable. Once political views were accounted for, whatever cultural or economic differences existed between confessions had no influence on fertility.

By contrast, political loyalties did matter. Because the Centre electors were chosen later in the century, they wed and reproduced at a time when family limitation was stronger.[100] Nevertheless, they showed a greater inclination towards natural fertility. Because of the high number of cases, even the one-year difference in age at last birth was significant.[101] In addition, National Liberals had slightly longer final intervals and marginally smaller completed families.

The differences in the lower section of Table 12.3 are attenuated, although they are all in the directions predicted by Secularization theory. I do not dwell

TABLE 12.3
Fertility of documented marriages of Electors in Ettenheim-Kenzingen riding from 1871 to 1901, by party and religion

	National Liberal All	National Liberal Catholic	Centre
For completed families			
Wife's age at last birth	37.1	37.2	38.1
Final birth interval (in years)	4.05	4.12	3.96
Number of legitimate children	5.7	5.7	6.0
Total marital fertility rate	7.96	8.33	8.67
M	1.12	1.15	1.20
m	.46	.44	.44
Percentage limiting	46 %	42 %	36 %

Notes
(1) The sources are outlined in Benz, Thesis.
(2) "Catholic" unions are those in which the husband was a Roman Catholic or an Old Catholic.
(3) Electors who switched parties appear under both of them.
(4) The electors were from Altdorf, Broggingen, Herbolzheim, Kippenheim, kippenheimweiler, Mahlberg, Münchweier, Niederhausen, Oberhausen, Orschweier, Ringsheim, and Schmieheim, as well as Grafenhausen, Kappel, and Rust. These locations are marked on Map 3.2.
(5) The Table is based on 458 marriages: 192 involving National Liberals, 135 of them Catholic, and 266 involving Centre electors.

on these slight distinctions, because they are muddied by the wide gap in dates of marriage. When that gap is controlled, the National Liberals enjoy an advantage in each marriage cohort. Throughout, family limitation was wider and deeper among them.[102]

These results cannot be pushed too far. Considerable family limitation was practised by electors of both parties. Moreover, each party claimed at least one victory in each poll with a Catholic majority, with the Centre taking larger shares as time passed. The latter trend skews the findings spatially as well as temporally. In discussing Table 12.3 I have made allowances for the later marriages of the Centre electors, but no account has been taken as yet of geographic variations in party support. If, as I have been arguing, a Catholic community's resistance to Centre hegemony was linked to its overall affinity for family limitation, the results could be accounted for without there being any contrast between National Liberal and Centre supporters within each municipality.

Most polls fell naturally into one of two categories with distinct political and demographic characteristics. In municipalities where Centre support was low, such as Grafenhausen and to a lesser extent Rust, last births came younger.[103] By contrast, in Kappel and several other locations, both the Centre's electoral vote and ages at last birth were high.[104] The lone exception to this bifurcation combined the lowest age at last birth for wives of Catholic electors with medium support for the Centre.[105]

What is most striking about these data is the closeness of ages at last birth within polls relative to the variations between them.[106] Locality outweighed politics, as it has virtually every other variable it has been compared against in this book. This parallel confirms the view that the Centre won the nominal allegiance of leading elements in village society rather than ousting them in favour of a previously powerless class or convincing them to alter their non-political behaviour.

Furthermore, the coincidence of geography and fertility establishes that a substantial part of the difference between parties in Table 12.3 resulted from the mix of localities rather than some universal ideological characteristic. Family limitation was stronger among National Liberals because they were more numerous in municipalities where it was extensive. Centre power was established earliest and most fully in localities subject to natural fertility. Individuals practising family limitation proved the most resistant to the blandishments of either party, preserving their independence as they shifted their general inclination from National Liberal to Centre over these thirty years. That independence endured beneath the one-sided results of 1901, as the campaign of 1905 revealed.

Party Politics 1905–1920

I introduced the 1905 provincial election almost two chapters ago as an illustration of what voting should look like if Secularization theory were correct. (See Table 11.1.) Critical readers are now in a position to ascertain the strengths and weaknesses of that approach. As will be seen, I maintain the link between family limitation and voting National Liberal in 1905, but independent of the supposition of Secularization.

Agitation for the 1905 election began months in advance. Gone were the days when a lightning campaign on the eve of the vote was enough to capture a poll. Gone too were the days when candidates stepped forward at the last minute to the acclamation of their hastily gathered supporters. With them went the opportunity of village leaders to barter their support for local or personal advantage. Instead, strong central party apparatuses appealed directly to mass voters who lacked the leverage to make their own wishes felt.[107] Such democratic powerlessness did not sit well with a number of local notables, and when the Centre renominated judge Armbruster, they decided that they had had enough.

The figurehead of the revolt was the mayor of Ettenheim, who declared an Independent Centre candidacy. Mayor Häfele of Grafenhausen announced that he was putting aside considerations of party to support a local man.[108] Leading Centre politicians hastened to hold rallies in the riding, denouncing the independent candidate as a National Liberal cuckoo. In the end, they did not have to face him, for he died three months before election day.[109] His place was taken by another mayor, Franz Schmidt, who owned the Sun inn in Herbolzheim. Schmidt ran openly on behalf of the liberal bloc, but retained much of the support that had built up behind the earlier candidacy.[110]

In the general campaign, each party portrayed the other as extremist. The

National Liberals claimed that the Centre planned to dissolve the public school system, while the Centre warned that the National Liberals would exclude religion from the schools altogether. When the Centre sent a circular to priests urging them to campaign on its behalf, the government seized the occasion to try to force the Church hierarchy to disavow the party publicly. This thrust was parried adroitly, but the exchange reawakened old animosities.[111]

These controversies may have influenced voters in this riding, but if so their impact was indirect. There were no complaints about illegal agitation by clerics in Grafenhausen, Kappel, or Rust.[112] The future of mixed schools was likewise not at issue, for Armbruster declared that they could be tolerated so long as they were not dechristianized. Schmidt couched his position in terms of efficiency, pointing to the increased costs that would be necessary to support separate schools for religious minorities within each municipality. Their strongest disagreement in this area came over extending the curriculum and with it teachers' hours and salaries. Armbruster maintained that the three Rs were enough for rural children.[113]

The sympathetic mayors invited Schmidt to hold rallies in their municipalities, Häfele hosting him at the Crown inn in Grafenhausen. In these speeches, Schmidt stressed his own independence and his concern for local interests. His declaration that the legislature contained more than enough officials and lawyers, but too few landed proprietors, went down particularly well in Grafenhausen, the home of his wife.[114] From all sides, Hennig reported, came the old radical cry: "we don't want a bureaucrat, but a man of the people".[115]

Schmidt's election posters[116] took a similar line. They avoided the word "liberal" entirely. Apart from a defensive insistence that Schmidt was a good Catholic, his placard was also silent on religious issues. Instead, the posters rehearsed the spiriting away of Hug, the substitution of Armbruster, and the continuing challenge to the party bosses by the mayors. In contrast to the unknown absentee jurist, Schmidt was a familiar face, a local man with practical experience in farming and business as well as administration. He would transfer the tax burden from agriculture to capital. All those who did not regard themselves as wards, paupers, or schoolchildren were called to the polls to demonstrate their independent judgement.

On election day, that appeal attracted a fair number of votes in Kappel and Rust, but the interest in this first direct election increased the Centre's support still more.[117] In Grafenhausen it was a different story, as Schmidt took the poll with a higher percentage than in his hometown. The coattails of Schmidt's fellow mayors extended National Liberal support outside Protestant and Jewish enclaves once more.[118] However, these gains were not enough to offset the Centre's margins in the parts of the constituency dyed indelibly black. Armbruster retained his seat.[119]

The results confirm several elements of my analysis. First, they reinforce the geographic patterns of the indirect elections, as the Catholic municipalities defying the Centre were the ones that had maintained the most independence from it previously.[120] If electors led their populations in adopting family limitation, then Schmidt's supporters were on the whole less subject to natural fertility than his opponents. Finally, it is worth remembering that all the Catholic polls had fallen to the Centre in the federal election two years earlier. Catholics who voted for Schmidt were not dyed-in-the-wool National Liberals, but independent spirits.

The liberal bloc offered rather less to that constituency four years later when it ran a Protestant. Armbruster had died in 1908,[121] and the Centre hastened to nominate in his place a master tanner and councillor from Ettenheim. With local sensibilities thus assuaged, the party increased its majority considerably.[122]

The new incumbent kept in close touch with local councils,[123] and beat back a Democratic challenge in 1913. When he died in January 1915, the other parties adhered to the truce in effect for the duration of World War One by allowing the Centre candidate to run unopposed.[124] With the Centre's eighth consecutive victory guaranteed, only its hard core turned out, comprising 38 % and 27 % of the electorates in Rust and Kappel, but just 6 % in Grafenhausen.[125]

Voters' lists for the five elections preceding the by-election have been preserved for Kappel and Rust. Only the 1901 contests were one-sided enough to unveil the secret ballot. Because Centre electors won 98 % of the 80 ballots cast in Kappel and 89 % of the 82 in Rust, the voters' lists distinguish committed Centre supporters from other villagers. As it happens, the documented families of these Centre voters displayed considerably stronger family limitation than those of the non-voters. In each case, voters ended childbearing two years younger.[126] Secularization theory can take no comfort from these results, but may appeal for a bigger population.

Combining elections across villages and across the years produces larger groups, but the actual tendencies of individuals become harder to pinpoint accurately.[127] Perhaps for that reason, the results show no tie between high fertility and inclination towards the Centre. The gaps in age at last birth, final birth interval, and completed family size are small and inconsistent.[128] In Kappel and Rust, both tendencies endured the increase in underlying natural fertility, which elevated total marital fertility rates even as family limitation began to take hold. In isolation, a modest difference in the percentage limiting is compatible with that process being more advanced among voters less attracted to the Centre, but values of m were identical.[129] There is little to choose between the two tendencies overall.

Their composition renders these results less surprising, although no less damaging to standard Secularization theories. A disproportionate part of National Liberal support in Kappel and Rust came from Old Catholics, who were not strong practitioners of family limitation at this time. Far more important, and decisive in its own right, is the absence of evidence from Grafenhausen. That absence leaves a lopsided distribution of cases between the two tendencies. A glance at Figure 12.4 is sufficient to establish that Grafenhauseners were far less sympathetic to the Centre from 1897 to 1913.[130] If Grafenhausen's voters'

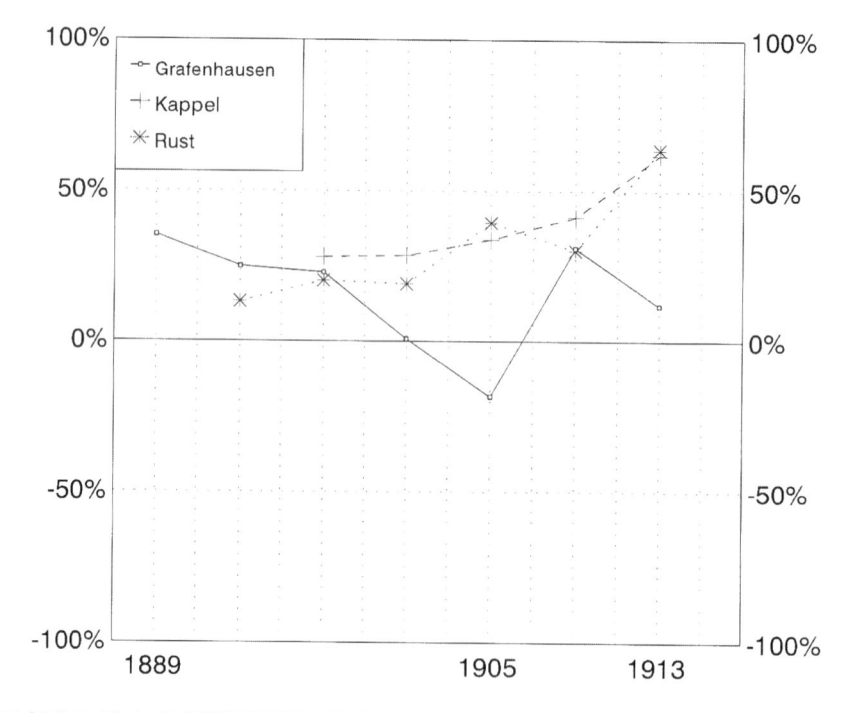

FIGURE 12.4 DIFFERENCE BETWEEN CENTRE AND NATIONAL LIBERAL VOTE AS A PERCENTAGE OF THE NUMBER OF ELIGIBLE VOTERS IN GRAFENHAUSEN, KAPPEL, AND RUST IN PROVINCIAL ELECTIONS FROM 1889 TO 1913

lists had been available, almost all the citizens named on them would have been classified as leaning away from the Centre. The inclusion of so many Grafenhauseners would have reduced the average fertility of the anticlerical tendency to a level well below its opponents'. Somewhat paradoxically, then, the absence of demonstrable differences between tendencies actually supports my argument linking politics and fertility to locality.

A brief look at election results from after World War One establishes that inter-village differences endured well into the twentieth century. Moreover, they can be observed among the newly enfranchised women as well as among the men with whom I have been concerned so far. In selecting a constituent assembly for Baden on 5 January 1919, 63 % of Kappel's voters chose Centre candidates. The Centre was also the largest party in Rust, but equally strong votes for the Social Democrats and Democrats held it to 46 % of the vote. In Grafenhausen, the Democrats pushed the Centre into second place (40 % vs. 33 %), as the Social Democrats also made a respectable showing. In keeping with prewar trends, the corresponding federal election two weeks later saw a larger Centre vote in all three localities. The most notable shift, however, was that the Social Democrats had become the strongest party in Grafenhausen, dropping the Democrats into third place.[131] Analysing these contests, in which social democracy appeared as the last hope of order and peace, would take me too far afield, but on their face the results are fully consistent with my interpretations.

Just as interesting is the manner in which villagers dealt with political differences among themselves. In local elections early in the Weimar Republic,[132] Kapplers acclaimed the lone, Centre, slate. Grafenhauseners also had only one choice, but the ticket there was drawn up through negotiation between the three parties.[133] Rusters rang yet another change on the theme of one-party dominance by entering two—and later three—distinct Centre slates, purporting to represent different economic interests. Even in their displays of solidarity, Grafenhauseners remained adventuresome bargainers, Rusters frustrated dissidents, and Kapplers cautious followers. I argue, again without detailed investigation, that these images fit rather well the picture I have built up for earlier contests.

DID POLITICS MATTER?

The shortcomings of Secularization theory have been made clear at various points throughout Chapters Eleven and Twelve, and I do not propose to recapitulate them here. Instead, I concentrate my fire on the diametrically opposed position, namely that politics and religion had no bearing on fertility. I concur with this view in so far as it rejects simplistic models of Secularization. Yet, unless I can establish that there were some links between these fields, there will be no place for the subtler views I have been urging.

Belief that politics, in anything like its conventional sense, was irrelevant to social and economic history arises from a variety of sources.[134] The underlying arguments are seldom articulated systematically, but two presumptions seem especially relevant here. The first is the idea that politics did not matter to rustics, or ordinary people generally.[135] However, the passionate campaigning and heavy participation in public struggles over power outlined in Chapters Ten through Twelve show that masses of people sometimes did get involved in politics. Questions concerning whether and how particular issues aroused such interest therefore acquire additional force.

The second popular view that I have endeavoured to undermine holds that peasants' understanding was unusually limited, and that they made their choices on the basis of local personalities without regard for programmes or policies.[136] This view would see all villages as "placid".[137] To be sure, there were periods and areas where elections were foregone conclusions, where assemblies of citizens were sparse and ill-informed, and where eminent figures enjoyed carte blanche to deal with the outside world as they saw fit. I do not deny those facts. Indeed, I insist upon them, for it is precisely by the contrast between apathy and engagement that one may judge that a genuine contest for human hearts and minds is in progress.

Although controversies were sometimes purely local, as in Grafenhausen in the 1820s, they could also have broader implications. Both in the first half of the nineteenth century when radicals disrupted the concert of Europe and later as the Centre strove to roll back the juggernaut of the modern State, two distinct worldviews confronted villagers. In each case, the three municipalities formed part of a swing riding, where both tendencies had a chance of winning. In such a situation, local disputes and general politics merged.

Organization was a key factor in these struggles. That circumstance brought to prominence those who controlled the centres of village life, most notably innkeepers. It also highlighted personal ties within communities. Because new ideas of all kinds spread along those networks, fertility and politics became intertwined. In Grafenhausen, for example, the first hints of family limitation were found among supporters of the old order in the 1824 municipal government. Demographic contrasts between factions had disappeared by 1865, as family limitation began to permeate Grafenhausen's population. That diffusion was a sign of the weakness of social barriers.

Kappel's experience in 1848 stands in sharp contrast to this pattern. There, mere endorsement by ordinary citizens of political choices made by the élite did not constitute a relationship close enough to transmit family limitation. The manner in which Kapplers subsided into quiescence after Richter's flight in September 1848 is particularly instructive. The study of Rust's Jews revealed that political ties could also be over-ridden by religion. Nevertheless, these very points strengthen my basic argument about the significance of local organizations and economic structures for the diffusion of innovations. Religion and wealth were relevant to fertility, not so much by engendering political norms as by impeding the spread of information and practices.

The indirect political system reinforced the identification of a party's cause with particular individuals, but that identification did not in itself deprive votes of political content. To suppose, for instance, that when Kappel's citizens chose Richter as an elector in 1873 and his Roman Catholic successor as an elector in 1877, they were both times simply voting for their mayor without regard for larger political or religious issues flies in the face of the facts. Moreover, as this example brings out, one needs to bear in mind how notables achieved office. Where their orientation on broader questions was one factor promoting or inhibiting their access to power, it begs the question to argue that it was their status, rather than their politics, that determined provincial or federal elections.

The argument that material local concerns,[138] and not great issues of State, dominated elections suffers from a similar flaw. In so far as larger political decisions affected taxation, conscription, and markets for produce, the distinction cannot be made out. Moreover, the ability of citizens to do more than merely pass judgement on matters put before them by others, that is, the ability to make governments respond to their local desires, can be a sign of political sophistication rather than ignorance. That ability varied from citizen to citizen, from time to time, and from place to place. As with the other points I have been making, this observation acts as a spur to examine specific historical contexts rather than lump them together.

Key features of the histories of Grafenhausen, Kappel, and Rust were their inhabitants' statistically distinct approaches to decision-making. Those approaches were fostered by distributions of wealth and reinforced by long-standing social structures. The framework of municipal government provided crucibles within which differences existing from at least the eighteenth century were maintained. Grafenhausen produced a disproportionate number of restless minds, who resisted authority and pursued the main chance even in the face of repression. They challenged monasteries and courts, reactionaries and revolutionaries, prefects and clerics, municipal leaders and government officials, often with success. This last characteristic set them apart from Rusters, who frequently saw their aspirations crushed by lord, monastery, or prefect. Most Kapplers were less willing to take the risks involved in self-assertion, and so submitted their fates to outside forces.

These approaches influenced villagers' behaviour in both political and demographic areas, producing complex relations between those fields. Solid proprietors with a history of successful innovation displayed the greatest control over their lives, through family limitation on the one hand and through political independence on the other. All these characteristics came to cluster within communities, so that differences between localities persisted even as such wider trends as the fertility transition and the rise of ultramontanism passed over them. The outcome, both federally and provincially, was that Catholic voters less bound to the Centre generally practised family limitation more assiduously. This applied equally to convinced National Liberals such as Leopold Sattler, and to those who held themselves somewhat aloof from party politics, as Ludwig Häfele did. These attitudes were linked to family limitation within particular communities—Grafenhausen for one—and between them, if one may judge from the behaviour of electors.

One link ran by way of the independence and search for control manifested in both spheres. Each party pretended that only its own supporters were using their reason to make autonomous choices,[139] but in practice voters were pressured from all sides. From the 1850s through the 1870s, for instance, the liberal government exerted more leverage over citizens, especially notables and civil servants, than the clerical opposition. Even under those circumstances, electors from Rust and Grafenhausen occasionally asserted themselves in choosing candidates. By the final decades under consideration, political independence on the local level took the form of resistance to Centre hegemony. Such resistance, possible only where citizens organized themselves outside Church and State, added a certain leaven to the personal and institutional stability of Wilhelmine society.

Even when the Centre swept all three villages, a Centre vote did not mean the same thing in each poll. In Kappel, it was a virtually automatic response, indicating only that villagers still trusted those set over them to handle political affairs. In Rust, more options were open, and even when they began to close towards the end of the nineteenth century, there was still room for disagreement within the ranks of the Centre. In Grafenhausen, support was revoked when the party hierarchy took the voters for granted. The switch to the National Liberals in 1905 after two decades in the Centre camp was merely the most dramatic manifestation of this attitude.

Grafenhausen's Centre voters who sided with Schäfle against the curia likewise demonstrated that their loyalty had limits. Much the same reasoning applied to the anticlericals who joined in the petition, as their opposition to the Church was compatible with support for the priest. That development sheds light on the failure of Old Catholicism to make great headway in Grafenhausen, where the ground seemed attractive.[140] Most liberal Catholics there saw no need to leave the local Church, because they were quite comfortable within it. By avoiding an irrevocable breach, both sides preserved freedom to manoeuvre, and demonstrated that they recognized bonds of local solidarity transcending political divisions.

That psychology reinforced realities that had origins elsewhere. Demography, politics, and economics wove local designs into which villagers fitted their lives. Because those patterns blended in complex ways, striking contrasts arose from minor differences in distributions of land, availability of by-employments, support for parties, and ages at marriage. These contours were far from rigid, and indeed sometimes accentuated the importance of individual choice. Within the historical tapestry, villagers spun the threads of their fates in ways both desired and unanticipated. Tracing some of the political strands of the web of choice and constraint has given the population histories of Grafenhausen, Kappel, and Rust a richer texture.

Notes

1. For the later phases of the struggle for civilization, see Manfred Stadelhofer, *Der Abbau der Kulturkampfgesetzgebung im Grossherzogtum Baden 1878–1918* (Mainz, 1969).
2. Lists of electors and protocols of electoral colleges for Ettenheim-Kenzingen riding throughout this period (in GLA 231/2645) provide much of the information in this section. Benz, Thesis, appendix E sets out additional sources for party affiliations.
3. To stress continuity, I occasionally drop the name Catholic People's Party a decade before the party itself did.
4. *Breisgauer Zeitung* 23 September 1871.
5. *Breisgauer Zeitung* 4 and 5 October 1871. *Oberrheinischer Courier* 7 October 1871.
6. *Breisgauer Zeitung* 10 October 1871. This accorded with a government policy to forestall splitting the liberal vote. See the 1865 circular of the Ministry of the Interior in GLA 360/1924–56/2. The self-effacing candidate was rewarded with a seat elsewhere. *Karlsruher Zeitung* 27 October 1871. *Oberrheinischer Courier* 28 October 1871.
7. GLA 236/10290 (report on county Ettenheim for 1873).
8. Andreas Jerger, *Ein Stück bad. Kulturkampfs* (Lahr, 1909). Hermann Oechsler, *"Sperrlingsleben" aus dem "badischen Kulturkampf" von 1874/76 gepfiffen zu Nutz und Trutz* (Offenburg, third edition, about 1900).
9. GLA 236/10290 (report on county Ettenheim for 1874).
10. The enactment of similar laws in Prussia, where they endured until 1887, meant

Localities and Parties 255

     that Baden also enjoyed an influx of clerics, one of whom served as vicar in Grafenhausen in 1883. GLA 360/1935-11/778 (report on 1883 inspection tour of Grafenhausen).
11. *Oberrheinischer Courier* 4 September 1873. See also *Breisgauer Zeitung* 13 December 1873.
12. *Breisgauer Zeitung* 28 September 1873.
13. *Breisgauer Zeitung* 23 September 1873. GLA 236/10290 (report on county Ettenheim for 1873). On Grafenhauseners' preference in priests, compare their response to Matthias Schäfle below.
14. Leaflet, poster, gendarmerie report, and response by prefect to an inquiry from the Ministry of the Interior in GLA 236/15068. The rally was reported in *Freiburger Zeitung* 11 September 1873.
15. *Breisgauer Zeitung* 13 September 1873.
16. Edelmann was the administrator of a religious foundation who had become embroiled in politics. Perhaps finding him insufficiently pliable, the government attempted to transfer him unilaterally. When Edelmann insisted that he was not purely a civil servant, he was locked out and detained by police. For coverage of the Edelmann Affair, see *Badischer Beobachter* 15 August to 17 October 1871, *Oberrheinischer Courier* 12 September 1871, and *Anzeiger für Stadt und Land* 11 October 1877. Edelmann had risen to the Catholic People's Party central committee and had stood twice as a candidate, losing both times. *Badischer Beobachter* 21 August and 1 October 1873. *Badische Landeszeitung* 29 October 1873.
17. A key element in their decision may have been rumours of questionable conduct by Richter with a young woman from Rust. The National Liberal county council had rejected the accusations as unproven. GLA 236/10290 (report on county Ettenheim for 1874). See also Hennig, *Chronik*, 72.
18. Not twenty-two, as erroneously reported by *Karlsruher Zeitung* 24 October 1873, and picked up by *Oberrheinischer Courier* and *Breisgauer Zeitung* 25 October 1873. See the list in GLA 231/2645.
19. *Breisgauer Zeitung* 22 and 26 October 1873. *Freiburger Zeitung* 13 November 1873.
20. *Breisgauer Zeitung* 29 October 1873.
21. GLA 236/15068 (correspondence between chief returning officer and Interior Ministry). *Badischer Beobachter* 28 October 1873.
22. His marriages are entries 235 and 237 in *OSB Herbolzheim*. He ran twice more, successfully in 1879 and unsuccessfully in 1881. See below.
23. *Badischer Beobachter* 1 November 1873. Offers and threats regarding the seats of government offices and courts were standard political fare.
24. *Karlsruher Zeitung* 21 October 1873. *Badischer Beobachter* 25 October 1873.
25. *Freiburger Zeitung* 26 September 1873 reports a joke from Grafenhausen. A pious young peasant was hastening through the streets to cast a last-minute ballot in defence of the Church. Passing by the Eagle inn, a locale notoriously dangerous for believers, he was lured inside by an appeal to check out the good red wine. By the time a second and third pint followed the first of the good red, the polls had closed. Wending his way homeward, the delinquent voter consoled himself with the thought: "the reds are better than the blacks after all".
26. There were legal pretexts, but in each case mounting criticism from the county office had preceded the dismissal. At least when defending these actions to their superiors, prefects regularly invoked political considerations.
27. GLA 236/10290 (report on county Ettenheim for 1874).
28. GLA 360/1935-11/1164 (report on 1878 inspection tour of Rust). The vicar also made himself unpopular with his fellow clerics, if his 1878 dispute with Grafenhausen's priest is any guide. (Ord A Personalia Franz Anton Schmidt.)
29. GLA 236/10292 (report on county Ettenheim for 1879).

30. GLA 236/10291 (reports on county Ettenheim for 1876 and 1877). GLA 360/1935-11/778 (report on 1883 inspection tour).
31. GLA 236/10290 (report on county Ettenheim for 1873). Gem A Grafenhausen B IV/167.
32. *Breisgauer Zeitung* 21 September 1877. *Anzeiger für Stadt und Land* 29 September 1877 rejected the accusation of political content. On the tour itself, including sacraments in Grafenhausen and Kappel, and a visit to Rust, see ibid. 13 20 and 27 September 1877.
33. *Breisgauer Zeitung* 12 October 1877. *Freiburger Zeitung* 12 October 1877. Many of them had discussed National Liberal candidates the previous May at a reunion for former county councillors. GLA 236/10291 (report on county Ettenheim for 1877).
34. *Breisgauer Zeitung* 16 October 1877.
35. Apparently unfazed by last-minute accusations that the National Liberal denied a personal God and had given his child a purely civil burial. *Anzeiger für Stadt und Land* 11 13 and 20 October 1877.
36. *Breisgauer Zeitung* 17 October 1879.
37. *Oberrheinischer Kurier* 12 and 16 October 1879. *Freiburger Zeitung* 14 and 18 October 1879. *Breisgauer Zeitung* 14 and 17 October 1879.
38. He went on to be rejected in another riding. *Oberrheinischer Kurier* 25 October 1879.
39. GLA 236/10292 (report on county Ettenheim for 1879). See also *Breisgauer Zeitung* 21 October 1879.
40. *Oberrheinischer Kurier* 16 October 1879.
41. In 1879, death and migration had reduced the ranks of the Centre's electors, while leaving those of the National Liberals almost intact. For example, Rust's vicar had been reassigned. GLA 236/15071 (24 September 1879 report from Ettenheim, after which the government decided not to replace the lost electors).
42. *Freiburger Zeitung* 8 August and 9 October 1881.
43. The victory in the Franco-Prussian War that made possible the incorporation of the south into little Germany.
44. Sepainter, *Reichstagswahlen*, 194, 325. See *Karlsruher Zeitung, Freiburger Zeitung*, and *Breisgauer Zeitung* for September–October 1881.
45. GLA 236/15221 (reports from rural commissariat 17 October 1881 and from prefect 18 November 1881). See also GLA 236/10293 (report on county Ettenheim for 1880).
46. *Freiburger Zeitung* 1 September 1881. *Breisgauer Zeitung* 2 September 1881.
47. Grafenhausen's Belfort association grew from 27 members at its 1875 founding to 69 in 1879 (St A LA Lahr 2163), and rallied to 72 in 1895 after dipping to 43 two years earlier. Kappel's organization comprised between forty-five and sixty veterans at the latter dates, while membership in Rust was well over one hundred. (The numbers come from reports on county Ettenheim for 1889–1892 and 1894–1895, in GLA 236/10490 and GLA 236/10491, respectively. The attitudes of the members can be gathered from the toasts to the pope described in the reports on county Ettenheim for 1884–1885 and 1886–1887, in GLA 236/10463 and GLA 236/10229, respectively.)
48. *Breisgauer Zeitung* 9 September 1881. Kapplers were less pleased by the celebrations, which rang in the distance as they vainly strove to stop the Rhine overflowing their fields. *Badischer Beobachter* 7 September 1881.
49. *Freiburger Zeitung* 1 and 3 September 1881. *Breisgauer Zeitung* 3 and 9 September 1881. *Badischer Beobachter* 8 September 1881. GLA 236/15221 (12 October 1881 report from rural commissariat).
50. GLA 236/15072 (correspondence of chief returning officer). *Breisgauer Zeitung* 27 September 1881. *Badischer Beobachter* 29 September and 4 October 1881.

51. *Freiburger Zeitung* 3 October 1885. *Breisgauer Zeitung* 9 October 1885. Leipf signed each Ruster's property slips for 1882 and 1883. Gem A Rust B XIII/311.
52. Rust was the only large poll not to repudiate the Catholic People's Party. It was therefore omitted from lists in *Breisgauer Zeitung* 13 October 1885 and GLA 236/15078 (report of 11 October 1885 by prefect).
53. Ibid. *Freiburger Zeitung* 14 October 1885. *Breisgauer Zeitung* 17 and 22 October 1885.
54. Hennig's hold was shaken only once. In 1899 an ex-mayor who blamed his deposition on the dean swung his support behind Old Catholic candidates municipally. Even then, such a result was possible only because the Baden government had eliminated direct municipal elections in favour of indirect ones with voting tiered by wealth. The aberration, limited to the most heavily taxed class, was neither sustained nor repeated. Hennig, *Chronik*, 173–176, 178. St A LA Lahr 2290 (report on 1900 inspection tour). See also St A LA Lahr 2295 (council elections 1883–1892) and St A LA Lahr 2297 (mayoral elections 1894–1917).
55. GLA 360/1935-11/1164 (reports on inspection tours of Rust in 1886, 1888, and 1890). GLA 236/10229 (report on county Ettenheim for 1886–1887).
56. Gem A Rust B IV/77. St A LA Lahr 3458. St A LA Lahr 3459.
57. St A LA Lahr 3454 (report on 1909 inspection tour of Rust). The workers' organization founded in 1906 had 78 active members, the youth group (founded 1900) 43 in 1914. Kremer, *Mit*, 297, 305.
58. Jerger, *Stück*, 1, 73–74, 104–105.
59. GLA 360/1935-11/778 (report on 1885 inspection tour). Just such reasoning had led the government to approve Schäfle over other applicants for the post in Grafenhausen (17 June 1884 memorandum in GLA 233/22646).
60. GLA 360/1935-11/778 (report on 1887 inspection tour). Joining Schäfle on the 1887 list were Hennig, Jerger, the mayor of Kappel, and Rust's Böcklin lord. GLA 236/14880. This behaviour could have been predicted, for Schäfle had spoken in favour of archbishop Vicari's position in 1854, resisted the use of church bells for secular purposes in 1862, disputed the State's right to ban religious schools in 1867, and led opposition to the bills on foundations and poor relief in 1869. Throughout, he encouraged other clerics to become involved in political debates, offering both tactical and strategic advice. Schäfle, *Lustren*. His book was reviewed positively in *Badischer Beobachter* 26 August 1871
61. *Breisgauer Zeitung* 9 October 1873 claims political and theological matching also took place. In *Breisgauer Zeitung* 29 January 1875, Kappel's leadership alleged that Church authorities had rejected their earlier requests for a particular priest on the grounds that he was "too lax [lau] for Kappel".
62. Though not a communist or a jacobin. Schäfle, *Lustren*, 27–29.
63. For instance, "I shall not advocate absolute academic freedom, but I shall also not condemn compulsory education [Schulzwang] outright". Ibid., 285.
64. Gem A Grafenhausen B IV/144. St A LA Lahr 2133 (mayoral elections) Chapter Three covered Häfele's economic contributions.
65. GLA 360/1935-11/778 (report on 1889 inspection tour).
66. What follows draws on the reports on county Ettenheim for 1881 (GLA 236/10427), 1884–1885 (GLA 236/10463), 1886–1887 (GLA 236/10229), 1889–1892 (GLA 236/10490), and 1894–1895 (GLA 236/10491).
67. The Rust figures are from 1911. St A LA Lahr 2131 (report on 1908 inspection tour of Grafenhausen). St A LA Lahr 2291 (report on 1908 inspection tour of Kappel). St A LA Lahr 3454 (report on 1911 inspection tour of Rust). See also other figures for 1908–1912 in those same sources.
68. GLA 360/1935-11/778 (report on 1889 inspection tour).
69. GLA 236/15075 (prefects' list of electors' leanings).
70. *Breisgauer Zeitung* 3 September 1889.

258   CHAPTER TWELVE

71. *Breisgauer Zeitung* 1 8 and 15 October 1889. Herbolzheim town archive B XIII 3/33. His marriage is entry 6337 in *OSB Herbolzheim*.
72. *Badischer Beobachter* 22 October 1889 (in GLA 236/15222). *Breisgauer Zeitung* 16 20 and 27 October 1889.
73. *Freiburger Zeitung* 13 and 20 October 1889. *Breisgauer Zeitung* 15 October 1889.
74. *Breisgauer Zeitung* 13 and 15 October 1893.
75. GLA 236/15083 (prefect's list of electors' leanings).
76. Hennig, *Chronik*, 128.
77. Reports on 1889 and 1892 inspection tours of Kappel (St A LA Lahr 2290).
78. I omit those who took part in neither contest. Their families' fertility reflected the disproportionate number of youths among them rather than any ideological bent.
79. Restricting attention to couples wed from 1850–1874 narrows the gaps in completed family size and final birth interval, but they do not close. Moreover, the floating voters' lead in age at last birth widens, despite the fact that within this cohort they wed at an earlier date.
80. Although these sub-groups were too small to differ significantly in m, the committed Centre supporters did fall significantly below the full population appearing on both voters' lists.
81. *Breisgauer Zeitung* 23 October 1897. For all that, Hug did lead Centre efforts to repeal or undermine the laws benefitting Old Catholics. Stadelhofer, *Abbau*, 248–252.
82. *Breisgauer Zeitung* 1 and 16 October 1897.
83. *Breisgauer Zeitung* 3 October 1897. (See also 17 September 1897.)
84. *Breisgauer Zeitung* 6 23 and 27 October 1897.
85. GLA 236/15098 (prefect's list of electors' leanings).
86. His contributions and those of other twenty-five-year veterans were honoured at a ceremony in Ettenheim on Friedrich's birthday. *Breisgauer Zeitung* 12 September 1897. See also Hennig, Chronik, 73.
87. Ibid., 159–160. *Breisgauer Zeitung* 28 October 1897.
88. *Breisgauer Zeitung* 21 and 28 October 1897.
89. Kippenheim. GLA 236/15098 (prefect's report of 28 October 1897).
90. GLA 236/15098. Gem A Kappel B XIII/658. Gem A Rust B XIII/297. Ringsheim municipal archive B XIII/414. Schindler's candidacy did reinvigorate provincial campaigns, for turnouts in many municipalities were the highest in years.
91. Ord A B3/519 (1892–1895 evaluations). Ord A Personalia Matthias Schäfle (1891, 1896, and subsequent evaluations). The latter source provides the material for the next few paragraphs.
92. Eleven widows signed the 15 December 1899 petition in Ord A Personalia Matthias Schäfle. Their marriages are included in the 279 documented cases I am about to discuss.
93. "Concerning his being hard of hearing: it's just not as bad as perhaps is assumed. The proof is that whenever one confessed to him, he did address each confessed sin [machte er doch nach jeder ihm gebeichtete Sünde den Zuspruch]. In addition, someone who confesses in a manner that isn't understood can pose problems for a person with good hearing as well, and someone who goes around thinking "I [man] can tell him or confess whatever I feel like", would also tell another [priest] only what he pleased and perhaps would even lie to him to boot.... Our Herr priest was already hard of hearing when he came here, that was also known then, and we were nevertheless very well satisfied with him..." Letter to curia in the name of the citizenry 20 April 1900 (Ord A Personalia Matthias Schäfle).
94. Hennig (*Chronik*, 153–155, 169, 176) made a point of noting births out of wedlock to former Old Catholics, and attributed them to negligent upbringing, but that is a rather different matter. *Badischer Beobachter* 19 June 1905 did reply circumspectly to two Social Democratic anecdotes against confession, one involving family size, from elsewhere in Germany.

Localities and Parties

95. *Breisgauer Zeitung* 8 October 1901. More generally, see GLA 236/15101.
96. *Breisgauer Zeitung* 24 September 1901.
97. Hennig, *Chronik*, 194.
98. GLA 236/15187 (prefect's list of electors and candidates).
99. There might be slight differences over time, with the Centre lagging at first where it struggled to displace an old élite. In addition, the gravitation towards the National Liberals of those made wealthy by industrialization or bureaucratic careers meant that that party recruited less and less from the landholding classes whose affinity for family limitation Chapters Eight and Nine explored.
100. On average, Centre electors wed in 1866, while National Liberals entered marriage in 1860. The average bride from either tendency first wed at twenty-four.
101. That difference actually increased when attention was restricted to young brides, even though the Centre's edge in dates of marriage widened to a full decade.
102. Among those wed before 1860: $m = .28$ and 31 % limiting for National Liberals, $m = .22$ and 15 % limiting for the Centre. Among those wed in 1860 and after: $m = .68$ and 60 % limiting for National Liberals, $m = .55$ and 45 % limiting for the Centre.
103. The other municipalities with a Centre electoral vote below 63 % and age at last birth below 37.5 were Herbolzheim, Münchweier, Kippenheim, and Schmieheim. Almost half of Kippenheim's population were Protestants or Jews, while those two religions claimed virtually all of Schmieheim's inhabitants.
104. The same was true of Oberhausen, Niederhausen, Mahlberg, and Altdorf. The last two municipalities included Protestant and Jewish minorities respectively. In each case, the Centre took over two-thirds of the electoral vote, while age at last birth averaged 38.5 or more.
105. In Ringsheim, last births came at 35.7 on average, while the Centre commanded 63% of the electoral votes. Detailed study might bring out that a strong Social Democratic vote undercut the National Liberals' chances there, but it is wisest to concede that Ringsheim's average experience between 1871 and 1901 does not match my prediction perfectly. In so far as there is anything to my arguments, Ringsheim should show less commitment to the Centre in other contests.
106. In Grafenhausen, wives of National Liberal electors and candidates gave birth for the last time at 36.9, while wives of Centre men stopped at 36.8. In Rust the figures were 37.2 and 37.8, respectively. Only in Kappel, where most National Liberals belonged to the first generation of Old Catholics, was there a clear difference (37.8 vs. 39.3).
107. I do not claim that mass politics arrived once and for all, merely that at this point there was a significant structural move in that direction.
108. Mayors in Herbolzheim, Münchweier, Ringsheim, and Munsterthal did likewise.
109. *Breisgauer Zeitung* 20 May, 6 20 and 24 June, and 20 July 1905.
110. *Breisgauer Zeitung* 26 September and 11 October 1905. Hennig, *Chronik*, 209–210.
111. GLA 48/III/6129 (government correspondence). Ord A B2-29/9 (archbishop's reply). GLA 236/15225 (newspaper controversies over campaigning by clerics).
112. GLA 236/15224 (October 1905 reports by prefect).
113. *Breisgauer Zeitung* 6 September and 6 and 17 October 1905.
114. *Breisgauer Zeitung* 17 and 18 October 1905.
115. Hennig, *Chronik*, 209–211.
116. At least the mis-dated one preserved in a drawer in Herbolzheim town archive.
117. The outnumbered minorities and superfluous majorities who had made no difference in indirect contests now contributed to the riding total regardless of the local margin.
118. Schmidt captured Ringsheim and Münsterthal, and made a respectable showing in Münchweier.
119. GLA 236/15106.

120. Moreover, they were joined this time by Ringsheim, smoothing out the one anomaly in that pattern.
121. Hennig and Fehrenbach spoke at the funeral. *Karlsruhe Zeitung* 23 September 1908 (in GLA 236/15106).
122. Since elsewhere this election saw the Centre give up ground it had won in 1905, the riding was once more bucking a trend.
123. Gem A Kappel B XIII/668 (form letter from him to council soliciting requests in December 1913).
124. GLA 236/15231.
125. GLA 236/15134.
126. Gem A Kappel B XIII/658 and *OSB Kappel*. Gem A Rust B XIII/297 and *OSB Rust*.
127. When linked to the OSBs, Gem A Kappel B XIII/658 and Gem A Rust B XIII/297 yield 543 documented marriages beginning before 1900. 96 involve husbands leaning away from the Centre and 447 involve husbands leaning towards it.
128. When the results are broken down by marriage cohort, eliminating a seven-year gap in date of marriage to the disadvantage of the Centre's opponents, there are still no differences between the two tendencies.
129. Percentage limiting: 35 % vs. 24 % and m: .36 vs. .36.
130. In Grafenhausen, the Centre's average margin was only 9 % of the eligible voters, but its lead swelled to 35 % in Rust and 40 % in Kappel.
131. Gem A Grafenhausen B XIII/758. Gem A Kappel B XIII/668. Gem A Rust B XIII/294.
132. St A LA Lahr 1246. St A LA Lahr 1298. Gem A Kappel B IV/141. Gem A Grafenhausen B IV/175. Gem A Grafenhausen B IV/176. Gem A Rust B IV/81.
133. Council seats were divided in accordance with the rough parity existing in the wider votes.
134. French historians have debated related issues. For two opposing positions, see Eugen Weber, "Comment la Politique Vint aux Paysans: A Second Look at Peasant Politicization", *American Historical Review*, 87 (1982), 357–389, and Peter McPhee, *The Politics of Rural Life* (Oxford, 1992), 260–276. For an older view, see André Siegfried, *Tableau politique de la France de l'ouest sous la Troisième République* (Paris, 1913).
135. For an example, see Rinderle and Norling, *Impact*, 57.
136. This is the interpretation of Bernhard Vogel, Dieter Nohlen, and Rainer-Olaf Schultze, *Wahlen in Deutschland* (Berlin, 1971), 79–81, and Kramer, *Fraktionsverbindungen*, 61–62, among others. (Compare Sperber, *Popular*, 100 and 113 on 1850–1866.) Hörner, *Vormärz*, 225–231, 341–346, and elsewhere, offers a more nuanced position closer to the evidence.
137. Richard Hamilton, *Who Voted For Hitler?* (Princeton, 1982), 367.
138. Even those such as Moeller ("Peasants"), James Hunt ("Peasants, Grain Tariffs, and Meat Quotas: Imperial German Protectionism Reexamined", *Central European History*, 7 (1974), 311–331), and Steven Webb, ("Agricultural Protectionism in Wilhelmian Germany: Forging an Empire with Pork and Rye", *Journal of Economic History*, 42 (1982), 309–326), who are anxious to deny that peasants were simple dupes, give them credit only for a narrow economic rationality. In this connection, see also David Blackbourn, *Class, Religion and Local Politics in Wilhelmine Germany* (Wiesbaden, 1980).
139. A few examples: *Breisgauer Zeitung* 16 February 1868, *Badischer Beobachter* 23 February 1868, *Badischer Beobachter* 30 September 1873, *Karlsruher Zeitung* 27 September 1873, and *Oberrheinischer Kurier* 13 September 1881.
140. In January–February 1875, the county prefect and Kappel's Old Catholics claimed that there were Old Catholics in Grafenhausen who would attend their services. GLA 360/1935–11/829.

13

Innovation and Diffusion

It is said[1] that at one point during the Thirty Years War, Swedish troops came riding down a road through two villages, both of which they set afire. The inhabitants of the first village hid in their root cellars, emerging to extinguish the blaze after the soldiers had passed. The residents of the second village simply fled, leaving their homes and belongings to be consumed.

Three centuries later, Allied troops were poised to invade Baden in the waning months of World War Two. Exchanges of artillery fire demolished buildings on both sides of the Rhine. The priest in the first village urged gunners in the battery there to direct their fire away from the enemy. They were eventually won over by the point that the war was lost in any case. When the Allied gunners recognized that the shells from the first village were falling harmlessly, they concentrated their own barrage on other sites, including the second village. The first village therefore emerged from the war in far better shape. For instance, its church dates to 1789, while the one in the second village had to be rebuilt after 1945.

Readers who have followed my arguments will not be surprised to learn that the first village in these stories is Grafenhausen, while the second is Kappel. Indeed, they may be able to fill in what is supposed to have happened midway between these two events, when the soldiers of revolutionary France overran the area.[2] These tales fit well the images conjured up in earlier chapters. From field clearances to electrification, Grafenhauseners blazed trails for the rest. Moreover, they did so together, in their successful court cases, in their thriving cooperatives, in their defence of their priest, and so on. From that perspective, family limitation was just one more innovation taken up throughout Grafenhausen.

In dealing with outside authorities, villagers were not so quick to trumpet these qualities. In 1852, Grafenhausen's municipal council blandly assured the central government that "the character of the inhabitants in no way stands out from that of the other Rhine residents... Peculiar mores and customs [Sitten und Gebräuche] are unknown here".[3] The latter point was reiterated in 1855.[4] The responses from Rust[5] were equally unassuming, as were those from Kappel,[6] perhaps with greater reason. In the aftermath of the revolutions of 1848–1849, no community wished to call attention to itself.

Those who came up against Grafenhauseners were less reluctant to portray them as exceptional. Grating under the accusation that a ruthless monastery had taken advantage of simple peasants, exploiting their ignorance for centuries, the monks of Ettenheimmünster insisted that these villagers were fully capable of understanding legal language—and of exploiting its ambiguities.[7] Half a century later, prefect Donsbach echoed the monks' sentiments: "the inhabitants of Grafenhausen . . . can all read and calculate quite well, perhaps better than is fitting".[8] Envious communities noted Grafenhausen's wealth; approving agronomists commented on its dynamism. Whether they wrote of "restless minds", "a progressive peasantry", or "a nest of hamsters", observers agreed that these villagers were somehow extraordinary.

What can the historian make of this individuality? Tracing connections between facets of village history multiplies anecdotes and speculations, but systematic understanding remains elusive. That Michel Ott and Philipp Werner, the mayor and treasurer of rebellious Rust, wed two sisters and produced three children between them illustrates intermarriage within the notability and perhaps the peculiar fecundity of one family. That the Old Catholic Karl Richter, like other restless minds in Kappel, numbered Grafenhauseners among his ancestors is interesting, but hard to evaluate. That women inherited equally with men all along the Rhine plain says something about their economic rôles, but nothing direct about how they viewed childbearing. That trader and malcontent Damas Rauch acted as agent for the Lotzbeck firm and later headed Grafenhausen's People's Club in 1849 links tobacco and radicalism, but the seven births in his first marriage prevent any strong tie to family limitation. That eight years elapsed between the second and third births to the republican wife of Nepomuk Winkler may indicate only that two such assertive personalities formed a rocky partnership.[9] That the OSBs themselves emerged from the same nexus of prosperity and independence likewise raises only inchoate suspicions.[10] It is all very well to insist as I have that history comprises just such individual events, but if they do not fall into patterns, the discipline is condemned to recapitulate the virtually endless variety of human experience.

That prospect distresses me rather less than it might a social scientist. Moreover, in so far as one can advance beyond the level of individuals, it is by appreciating the full import of starting there. At the end of the nineteenth century, family limitation was found in all three villages, among landed proprietors and day labourers, among mayors and humble citizens, among women who owned breweries and women who rolled cigars, among rich and poor, among Catholics and Jews, among anticlericals and ultramontanes. Furthermore, the popularity of contraception across such lines in the twentieth century suggests that what these people had in common was simply family limitation, not some more amorphous social, economic, or political characteristic. If the spread of family limitation must be conceived as part of modernization, it is worth stressing that the demographic components of that transformation possessed their own dynamic.

That does not mean that contraception struck at random. Indeed, I have been at considerable pains to trace variations in its frequency. Those variations fit basic models of the diffusion of innovations[11] rather better than they do more complex theories about the affinities of different classes for fertility control.[12] In their strong forms, popular accounts of automatic adaptation have been shown to be inadequate. The changes they postulate, declining infant mortality, urbanization, younger marriage, rising prosperity, Secularization, and the like, either never took place or came about in the wake of family limitation. If one finds local psychologies implausible, then one natural response is to fall back all the way to simple innovation.[13] At various points I have called such interpretations banal and coincidental, but that need not make them false.

Indeed, descriptive theories have been considerably more successful than those that set out to explain fertility by reducing it to more fundamental factors. Thus, the European marriage pattern applied comfortably to these villages, but there is no sign of the Oedipal mechanisms that are supposed to make it work. Likewise, there is abundant support for the classical theory of family limitation, but none for the demographic transition. In a similar vein, I have narrated how fertility became linked to politics and religion, while showing the inadequacy of models of Secularization. In each case, the search for a simple causal explanation has proven sterile, while the attempt at comprehensive description has borne fruit.[14]

To be sure, one case-study could not refute—or establish—global theories outright. It is always open to their proponents to flee from testing by amending their claims. A general Oedipal model can invoke any death as the trigger for a marriage, rather than the father's death, a demographic transition can key on deaths in childhood rather than infancy, and so on, patching the new data into the old stories. For that matter, the notion of local cultures has much the same, less testable character. There need be nothing illegitimate about amendments. They are a common feature of ongoing research programmes, and sometimes accompany creative integration of new domains and even sharper predictions. The refined morcellement hypothesis is a case in point.[15]

Yet such strategic amendments in themselves win their theories no new credibility. On the one hand, they abandon the straightforward dynamics that had initially brought them plausibility. On the other hand, their compatibility with the data is openly contrived; they are evading falsification, not earning confirmation. Moreover, in all these cases, an historian wonders whether the logical end of this amending, generalizing, and complicating is not renewed appreciation that individuals acted for their own reasons. The more reasons a theory allows, the more intricate the circumstances under which those reasons operate, the more articulated the links between cause and effect, the more scope there is for individual decision-making. Why not proceed to the individual level directly?

Let me illustrate how such an approach might highlight innovation in analysing the fertility transition. I start from the classical theory of family limitation, an independently successful hypothesis, as I just noted. There is no firm evidence that anyone in these villages was stopping births within marriage before the nineteenth century. The classic measures of family limitation are all unremarkable at that point, as is my modest addition to that battery.[16] Land was relatively abundant and a backlog of agricultural improvements had accumulated which permitted the population to rise above the level where the wars of the seventeenth century had held it. Over the next century, division of holdings among heirs gradually ate away these gains, while lengthening adult lifespans meant that the smaller inheritances were received later in life. Feeling the pressure, villagers and governments responded by intensifying Malthusian controls,[17] increasing ages at marriage first in Grafenhausen, then in Rust, and finally in Kappel.

Although eighteenth-century births were separated more widely than they might have been, that spacing reflected breastfeeding customs independent of the number of children a woman had already borne. That those practices were unrelated to specific desires concerning family size is borne out by the falling off in breastfeeding and consequent rise in underlying natural fertility at a time when population pressure was greater than ever. In the early nineteenth century, with spacing unquestioned and starting already near its limit, stopping constituted a breakthrough. The rapidity with which family limitation was taken up thereafter further testifies to its novelty, as does the range of couples to whom it appealed.

The variations in that appeal were reminiscent of simple diffusion.[18] Take the massive differences between villages in levels of family limitation. Throughout the second half of the book, I have confronted locality with other variables to test whether its relation to fertility was artefactual. Time after time, locality has come out on top.[19] The interactions of village life were far more important in promoting family limitation than any feature shared across municipal boundaries.

Moreover, many of the social, economic, and political regularities that have been uncovered do not betray intrinsic affinities for family limitation. Occupation, wealth, and party affiliation ran in families, and so when one tests for relations between them and fertility, one is selecting subsets of villagers whose members dealt with one another more often than with non-members.[20] Those encounters themselves fostered the transmission of novel ideas and behaviour quite independent of the particular characteristic that brought people into contact.[21]

This reasoning accounts for the possible association between family limitation and political faction in Grafenhausen in the 1820s rather better than postulating that contraception predisposes one to defence of embezzlement, or vice versa. On a larger scale, there is as much truth in the suggestion that the predominance of Grafenhauseners among landed proprietors produced early and strong family limitation within the farming category as there is in the idea that Grafenhausen's occupational distribution explains the fertility of its inhabitants. Likewise, the rising fecundity of artisans and of workers owed something to the fact that those livelihoods were most common in Rust. Again, the advantage of National Liberals over Centre supporters in family limitation has been seen to grow out of local patterns rather than to underlie them. The same logic worked in reverse, as a limited range of ties for a time insulated Rust's Jews and the bulk of Kappel's population from the practices spreading around them.

On the simplest level then, regarding family limitation as an innovation diffusing through structures of varying density clarifies how dramatic contrasts between localities were possible.[22] Even if each village had possessed the same internal structure, its being an independent municipality was enough to open the possibility of differentiation. Because the German municipality was a social community, with its peculiar laws and customs, its own church and assembly hall, its distinct markets and guilds, citizens encountered one another far more often than they did outsiders. They measured their fortunes, and their opportunities, by their neighbours. Once there was one innovator, for whatever reason, the innovation was more apt to pass to a fellow citizen than to someone in a distant municipality, no matter how similar qualitatively.[23]

The picture becomes still more interesting when one takes account of varying internal structures as well. On this deeper level, still within the framework of innovation theory, certain relations facilitate—or impede—picking up new information from outside and still other relations facilitate—or impede—transmitting that information within segments of a community. The more connections there are, regardless of their character, the more potential there is for a rich associational life, stimulating economic cooperation and competition, social solidarity and rivalry, political alliances and controversies. On that score, inhabitants of Grafenhausen, Kappel, and Rust were well-positioned to begin with: on geographic thoroughfares rather than isolated backwaters, in nucleated villages rather than dispersed homesteads, sharing property between siblings and between the sexes rather than freezing out the disinherited. Entwined in dense local kin nests biologically and economically, key citizens[24] were at the same time open to developments elsewhere. This is much the sort of environment in which new practices catch on.

The preceding paragraphs have argued that innovation was possible and that it might diffuse unevenly. Perhaps that was all there was to it. Yet innovation theory is not limited to coincidence in explaining the divergence between the three villages. There were also differences between their social structures, differences that make sense of the patterns formed as family limitation spread. Where networks became cleavages, as in Kappel between the elite and the mass, diffusion ground to a halt. Where all were bound together in subordination, as in Rust, innovation was slower and subject to countervail. Where past experiments had met success, as in Grafenhausen, venturers looked for new worlds to conquer.

These suggestions may not satisfy those thirsty for governing laws. They may then take the still more speculative step of restoring to the analysis elements from adaptation theory that have proven relevant even where there was no adaptation. After all, social and economic characteristics might conceivably promote acquiring ideas and practices regarding contraception, as distinct from information in general.[25]

It is not always easy to specify what direct contribution social factors made to family limitation. Notables and innkeepers everywhere were drawn towards it earlier than ordinary citizens, perhaps because of their wealth, perhaps merely because of the extensive ties they maintained with the wider world. Their domination of the public life of the county and their leading rôles within the community gave a political coloration to demographic behaviour, but the borders between tendencies were far from rigid. For instance, the notability ultimately swung its allegiance to the Centre and relinquished its lead in family limitation without sacrificing social prestige or political power.

Economics seems to have exerted rather more impact on fertility, but only as mediated through the distribution of wealth within a community and individual psychology. The relative equality and prosperity in Grafenhausen manifested themselves in many ways, from low rates of emigration and massive shifts in age at marriage, to the rapidity with which innovations of all kinds spread. Manifold and variegated ties rendered Grafenhauseners particularly outward-looking and forward-looking. It was no accident that a population that distinguished itself by family limitation also stood out in adopting and marketing cash crops and in experimenting with political parties. Solidarity was forged from similar economic interests and tempered in shared struggles against the outside world.

That experience had a three-fold influence on fertility. First, it meant that morcellement was actively perceived as a danger by wide sectors of the population. Second, that circumstance rendered them alive to ways to forestall the danger, and so new ideas circulated readily. Finally, the solid proprietors who were threatened were confident of their power and open to qualitative change.[26] For them contraception proved just one more discipline through which they could control the world.

These attitudes were by no means limited to Grafenhausen, nor were they universal there. Rather, it was simply that one natural constituency of family limitation was larger there, and well-connected. New ideas were more apt to occur to one of Grafenhausen's citizens and to spread fast once they did. Elsewhere, couples took longer to catch wind of innovations and were less enthusiastic about experimenting. That too might be a function of economics, for poverty undercut villagers' ability to assert themselves. For people like the Sartoris, it was already the height of boldness to petition prefects and councils for residence rights or to cohabit without benefit of a marriage ceremony. Some found it hard enough to create a family and keep it together without having to plan its size. By contrast, solid peasants did not allow themselves to be treated like the rootless poor. Mastery of one's destiny rested on material resources as well as psychological ones.

However, these attitudes depended less on current economic circumstances than on past ones.[27] What mattered was the psychology created by economic independence, by agricultural improvement, by victory in the judicial arena. Instead of practising family limitation, couples could have postponed marriage, emigrated, tightened their belts, lowered their expectations, dropped their hopes for their children. Those alternatives were rejected by solid citizens who had invested too much to abandon their holdings, who were accustomed to social perquisites, and who refused to accept a lower standing. Family limitation met their needs, and acquired a larger body of adherents as its efficacy became evident.

These reflections emphasize once more the importance of individual decisions. Demographic change did not occur independent of human will or beyond human ken. Villagers did not behave as a unit, responding by well-practised or unconscious rote to external stimuli. Nor were they cyphers, randomly generating irrational behaviour. Peasants were not universally sunk in benighted ignorance, pursuing tradition blindly, or eschewing innovation for security. Some of course were all those things and more, but others were eager and curious, dynamic and creative, determined that they themselves and not outside forces should control their fates.

The forces they acknowledged were concrete: biology, climate, soil, rivers, dues, armies, the desires and actions of their families, neighbours, and leaders. As they confronted these forces, now succumbing, now compromising, now emerging victorious, now surviving to face new challenges, the inhabitants of Grafenhausen, Kappel, and Rust marked the passage of time even as it marked them. After all, that is what it means to start something.

Notes

1. I am vouching for the fact that these stories are told, rather than for their truth.
2. According to *Lahrer Zeitung* 8 May 1935 in St A LA Lahr 2131, Grafenhausen was to be burnt in retaliation for the slaying of a French requisitioner. The village was spared through the efforts of one French-speaking citizen who negotiated a fine instead, and a second peasant who sacrificed his personal fortune to pay it.
3. GLA 360/1935–11/778. Ecclesiastical authorities were equally oblivious. "No particular dangers to morality [sittliche] were detected" during an 1889 visitation. Ord A B4/3742.
4. Report on 1855 inspection tour of Grafenhausen in GLA 360/1935–11/778.
5. GLA 360/1935–11/1164 (1852 return) and GLA 360/1935–11/1163 (report on 1855 inspection tour of Rust).
6. GLA 360/1935–11/822 (1852 return).
7. *OSB Grafenhausen* page 197 (1774 complaint).
8. Ibid., page 89. Incidentally, I found no notable relation between early family limitation and the literacy of either spouse (indicated by signing the marriage registers in Pf A Grafenhausen from 1780 to 1810).
9. The priest Steiger (testimonial of 28 April 1847 in GLA 264/5) and the Grafenhausen municipal council (testimonial of 16 September 1849 in GLA 264/7—its 28 April 1847 evaluation in GLA 264/5 had reported nothing of the kind) asserted that Winkler's marriage was bad. All the same, the police did find the couple in bed together at 7:30 the morning of 20 April 1847. GLA 264/5.

10. Albert Köbele credited his interest in genealogy to his grandmother Frieda Sattler, only daughter of the National Liberal mayor Leopold Sattler.
11. In which family limitation is seen as an underground movement with potentially universal appeal. Readers insisting on a more systematic and explicit model may prefer Everett Rogers, *Diffusion of Innovations* (New York, 1983). The innovation may be a practice, or information, or a value. It spreads as a new crop, a new tool, or a new technique would.
12. For a variety of interpretations of what innovation and adjustment mean when applied to fertility declines, see Gösta Carlsson, "The Decline in Fertility: Innovation or Adjustment Process", *Population Studies*, 20 (1966), 149–174, Etienne van de Walle, "Motivations and Technology in the Decline of French Fertility", in Wheaton and Hareven, *Family*, 135–178, Knodel and van de Walle, "Lessons", Bean, Mineau, and Anderton, *Frontier*, 4, 11–33, and Adrian Raftery, Steven Lewis, and Akbar Aghajanian, "Demand or Ideation? Evidence from the Iranian Marital Fertility Decline", *Demography*, 32 (1995), 159–182. My own understanding of the issues accords perfectly with none of these.
13. A second would be to specify, in a way subject to genuine testing, another aspect of life to which fertility was supposedly adjusting.
14. For parallel debates in the philosophy of science, see Bas van Fraassen, *The Scientific Image* (Oxford, 1980) and Paul Churchland and Clifford Hooker (ed.), *Images of Science* (Chicago, 1985).
15. The recognition that the European marriage pattern generated ranges of ages at marriage, differentiated by wealth, economic trends, and gender, is another good example, as is Henry's increasing emphasis on the crucial importance of stopping. In both cases, the more developed theory highlights individual choice and specifies empirical claims more precisely than ever.
16. In no case did I trace a lineage with young second-last births back past the 1780s.
17. That such adaptive fertility control did take place highlights the absence of family limitation, and strengthens the case for regarding it as an innovation in the other times and groups where it did appear.
18. Diffusion need not mean trickling down from the top. Rather, it connotes spreading outward from one or more starting-points.
19. The ranking of localities was by no means fixed. From the trends just before 1900, one can imagine fertility in Kappel falling below that in Rust in the twentieth century. Similarly, the very same distinctive homogeneity that at first blocked the penetration of family limitation among Jews later assisted its very rapid spread, which plunged their fertility below the Christians' averages by the twentieth century.
20. Compare Coale, "Reconsidered", 67.
21. A dramatic example of how the content of an association may be less relevant than the association itself is Martine Segalen's suggestion ("Exploring a Case of Late French Fertility Decline: Two Contrasted Breton Examples", in Gillis, Tilly, and Levine, *Experience*, 240–244) that information and values fostering contraception spread in parts of Brittany under the aegis of Catholic organizations.
22. Neither absolutism in politics nor capitalism in economics enjoyed such full success as to smooth villagers and villages into equal subjects and uniform consumer markets.
23. When diffusion swamps adaptation in this fashion, standard multiple regression cannot capture the dynamics at work.
24. I have in mind peasants with produce to market, the affluent, and horseowners, rather than professionals or townspeople.
25. Such characteristics may be quite heterogeneous. Those displaying them would become similar only after their various paths led them to contraception.

26. Quantitative changes like the acquisition of Reichenweier or the reclaiming of tithes had been played out, and there was no realistic prospect of expanding towards the Rhine or expropriating the lords.
27. Just as they corresponded more to future allegiances than to contemporary politics.

Bibliography

Archival Sources

Archives départementales du Bas-Rhin (ADBR): Files from series 3E, 4E, and G.
Böcklin family archive (BvB A, currently in Staatsarchiv Freiburg): Documents as coded in Schwarz, "Freiherrlich".
Altdorf midwife's diary 1846–1859.
Ettenheim town archive: Files from section B.
Grafenhausen section of Kappel-Grafenhausen municipal archive (Gem A Grafenhausen): Documents, files, and books as coded in Walter Ziemann and Walter Fischer, *Archivverzeichnis Grafenhausen Gemeinde Kappel-Grafenhausen* (1977).
Herbolzheim town archive: Files and books.
Kappel section of Kappel-Grafenhausen municipal archive (Gem A Kappel): Documents, files, and books, as coded in Walter Ziemann and Walter Fischer, *Archivverzeichnis Kappel Gemeinde Kappel-Grafenhausen* (1977).
Münchweier section of Ettenheim municipal archive: File B XIII 3/1.
Ringsheim municipal archive: Files and books.
Rust municipal archive (Gem A Rust): Documents, files, and books as coded in *Inventare Badischer Gemeindearchive Rust a/Rh Kreis Lahr* (1951).
Generallandesarchiv Karlsruhe (GLA): Files from sections 27a, 33, 48, 60, 61, 66, 126, 138, 229, 231, 233, 236, 237, 239, 240, 264, 313, 314, 315, 353, 360, 390, and H. Items from sections 264, 315, 353, 360, and 390 dealing with periods after 1806 are now stored in Staatsarchiv Freiburg.
Freiburg archdiocesan archive (Ord A): Files from sections B2, B3, B4, B8, Dekanatsarchiv Lahr, Finanzkammer, Konstanz, and Personalia.
Grafenhausen parish archive (Pf A Grafenhausen): Announcement books and parish registers beginning 15 March 1686.
Kappel parish archive (Pf A Kappel): Parish registers beginning 29 September 1699, and Hennig, Michael, *Chronik der Pfarrei Kappel am Rhein* (1890 with additional notes through 1913).
Rust parish archive (Pf A Rust): Parish registers beginning 16 August 1652 with indices by Anton Uhrenbacher.
Staatsarchiv Freiburg (St A): Files from Landratsamt Lahr and Bezirksamt Ettenheim.

Newspapers

Badischer Beobachter 1868 and 1873 in Freiburg university library; 1871, 1874–1875, and 1881 in Karlsruhe provincial library.
Badische Landeszeitung 1873 and 1874–1875 in Karlsruhe provincial library.
Breisgauer Zeitung 1865, 1868, 1871, 1873, 1874–1875, 1877, 1879, 1881, 1885, 1889, 1893, 1897, 1901, 1905 in Freiburg university library.
Freiburger Zeitung 1865, 1871, 1873, 1877, 1879, 1881, 1885, 1889 in Freiburg university library.
Herbolzheimer Zeitung 1937 in Herbolzheim municipal archive.
Karlsruher Zeitung 1871, 1873, 1877, 1879, 1881 in Freiburg university library.
(Lahrer) Anzeiger für Stadt und Land 1877 in Karlsruhe provincial library.
Oberrheinischer Courier 1871, 1873, 1877 in Freiburg university library.
Oberrheinischer Kurier 1879, 1881, 1885 in Freiburg university library.

Works

Abel, Wilhelm, *Agrarkrisen und Agrarkonjunktur* (Hamburg: Parey, 1966).
Anderson, Barbara, "Regional and Cultural Factors in the Decline of Marital Fertility in Europe", in Coale and Watkins, *Europe*, 293–313.
Anderson, Margaret, *Windthorst A Political Biography* (Oxford: Clarendon Press, 1981).
Anderton, Douglas, and Lee Bean, "Birth Spacing and Fertility Limitation: A Behavioral Analysis of Nineteenth Century Frontier Populations", *Demography*, 22 (1985), 169–183.
Andorka, Rudolf, "Birth control in the eighteenth and nineteenth centuries in some Hungarian villages", *Local Population Studies*, 22 (1979), 38–43.
―――, "Un exemple de faible fécondité légitime dans une région de la Hongrie L'Ormansag à la fin du XVIIIe et au début du XIXe siècle: contrôle des naissances ou faux-semblants?", *Annales de Démographie Historique*, 1972, 25–53.
―――, "La prévention des naissances en Hongrie dans la région 'Ormansag' depuis la fin du XVIIIe siècle", *Population*, 16 (1971), 63–78.
Andorka, Rudolf and Sandor Balazs-Kovacs, "The Social Demography of Hungarian Villages in the Eighteenth and Nineteenth Centuries (With Special Attention to Sarpilis, 1792–1804)", *Journal of Family History*, 11 (1986), 169–192.
Backmann, Gaston, "Die beschleunigte Entwicklung der Jugend", *Acta Anatomica*, 4 (1948), 421–480.
Baden Handels-Ministerium, *Beiträge zur Statistik der inneren Verwaltung des Grossherzogthums Baden*, 20 (1865).
―――, *Beiträge zur Statistik der inneren Verwaltung des Grossherzogthums Baden*, 35 (1874).
Baden Handelsministerium, *Beiträge zur Statistik der inneren Verwaltung des Grossherzogthums Baden*, 37 (1878).
Baden Ministerium des Innern, *Beiträge zur Statistik der inneren Verwaltung des Grossherzogthums Baden*, 1 (1855).
―――, *Beiträge zur Statistik der inneren Verwaltung des Grossherzogthums Baden*, 5 (1857).
Baden Statistisches Bureau, *Beiträge zur Statistik des Grossherzogthums Baden*, N.F. 6 (1893).
Baden Statistisches Landesamt, *Beiträge zur Statistik des Grossherzogtums Baden*, N.F. 20 (1921).
―――, *Badische Gemeindestatistik* (1927).
―――, *Ergebnis der Volkszählung vom 16. Juni 1933* (1936).
―――, *Gemeindestatistik des Landes Baden* (1949).
Baden *Inventare Badischer Gemeindearchive Rust a/Rh Kreis Lahr* (1951).
(Bader, Carl), "Die badischen Wahlen zum Zollparlament", *Historisch-politische Blätter für das katholische Deutschland*, 61 (1868), 760–793.
Baier, Hermann, "Die Ortenau als Auswanderungsgebiet", *Badische Heimat*, 22 (1935), 144–150.
―――, "Wirtschaftsgeschichte der Ortenau", *Die Ortenau*, 16 (1929), 217–286.
Bardet, Jean-Pierre, "Les incertitudes de l'explication", in Jacques Dupâquier and others (ed.), *Histoire de la population française*, vol. 3 (Paris: Presses Universitaires de France, 1988), 364–378.
Bauer, Sonja-Maria, *Die verfassungsgebende Versammlung in der badischen Revolution von 1849* (Düsseldorf: Droste, 1991).
Bean, Lee, Geraldine Mineau, and Douglas Anderton, *Fertility Change on the American Frontier* (Berkeley: University of California Press, 1990).
Becht, Hans-Peter, *Badische Parlamentarier 1867–1874* (Düsseldorf: Droste, 1995).
Becker, Josef, *Liberaler Staat und Kirche in der Ära von Reichsgründung und Kulturkampf* (Mainz: Grünewald, 1973).
Bender, Karl Ludwig, Joachim Krämer, and Eugen Eble, *Ortssippenbuch Nonnenweier* (Grafenhausen: Köbele, 1971).

Benz, Ernest, "Fertility in Three Baden Villages 1650–1900", Ph.D. dissertation at the University of Toronto 1988.
Berkner, Lutz, "Peasant Household Organization and Demographic Change in Lower Saxony (1689–1766)", in Lee, *Patterns*, 53–69.
———, "The Stem Family and the Developmental Cycle of the Peasant Household: an Eighteenth-Century Austrian Example", *American Historical Review*, 77 (1972), 398–418.
Bideau, Alain, and Jean-Pierre Bardet, "Fluctuations chronologiques ou début de la révolution contraceptive?", in Jacques Dupâquier and others (ed.), *Histoire de la population française*, vol. 2 (Paris: Presses Universitaires de France, 1991), 373–398.
Bischoff-Luithlen, Angelika, *Von Amtsstuben, Backhäusern und Jahrmärkten* (Stuttgart: Kohlhammer, 1979).
Blackbourn, David, *Class, Religion and Local Politics in Wilhelmine Germany* (Wiesbaden: Steiner, 1980).
Blankenhorn, Erich, "Badens Wehr in den Jahren 1848/49", *Mein Heimatland*, 27 (1940), 188–206.
Blum, Jerome, "The European Village as Community: Origins and Functions", *Agricultural History*, 45 (1971), 157–178.
———, "The Internal Structure and Polity of the European Village Community from the Fifteenth to the Nineteenth Century", *Journal of Modern History*, 43 (1971), 541–576.
Bonfield, Lloyd, "Normative Rules and Property Transmission: Reflections on the Link between Marriage and Inheritance in Early Modern England", in Bonfield, Smith, and Wrightson, *Gained*, 155–176.
Bonfield, Lloyd, Richard Smith, and Keith Wrightson (ed.), *The World We Have Gained* (Oxford: Blackwell, 1986).
Boserup, Ester, *The Conditions of Agricultural Growth* (Chicago: Aldine, 1965).
Bouchard, Gérard, *Le village immobile Sennely-en-Sologne au XVIIIe siècle* (Paris: Plon, 1972).
Bourke, Paul, and Donald DeBats, "Individuals and Aggregates: A Note on Historical Data and Assumptions", *Social Science History*, 4 (1980), 229–249.
Bourgière, André, "De Malthus à Max Weber: le mariage tardif et l'esprit de l'entreprise", *Annales Economies Sociétés Civilisations*, 27 (1972), 1128–1138.
Broström, Göran, "Practical Aspects of the Estimation of the Parameters in Coale's Model for Marital Fertility", *Demography*, 22 (1985), 625–631.
Broström, Göran, and Kenneth Lockridge, "Coale and Trussell's "m" visits Sweden, or, why do we get such lousy fits?", in Lockridge, *Sweden*, 98–110.
Buchenberger, Adolf, "Die Lage der bäuerlichen Bevölkerung im Grossherzogthum Baden", in *Bäuerliche Zustände in Deutschland* (Leipzig: Duncker and Humblot, 1883), 237–303.
Burgdorf, Dagmar, *Blauer Dunst und Rote Fahnen* (Bremen: Brockkamp, 1984).
Butterfield, Herbert, *The Whig Interpretation of History* (London: Penguin, 1973).
Carlsson, Gösta, "The Decline in Fertility: Innovation or Adjustment Process", *Population Studies*, 20 (1966), 149–174.
Chaunu, Pierre, "Réflexions sur la démographie normande", in *Sur la population française au XVIIIe et au XIXe siècles* (Paris: Société de démographie historique, 1973), 97–117.
Chiniquy, Charles, *The Priest, The Woman, and the Confessional* (Chick edition).
Churchland, Paul, and Clifford Hooker (ed.), *Images of Science* (Chicago: University of Chicago Press, 1985).
Coale, Ansley, "Age Patterns of Marriage", *Population Studies*, 25 (1971), 193–214.
———, "The Decline of Fertility in Europe from the French Revolution to World War II", in Samuel Behrman, Leslie Corsa, and Ronald Freeman (ed.), *Fertility and Family Planning* (Ann Arbor: University of Michigan Press, 1969), 3–24.
———, "The Decline of Fertility in Europe since the Eighteenth Century As a Chapter in Demographic History", in Coale and Watkins, *Europe*, 1–30.

―――, "The Demographic Transition Reconsidered", in *International Population Conference Liège 1973* (Liège: International Union for the Scientific Study of Population, 1973), 53–72.

―――, "Factors associated with the development of low fertility: an historical summary", *Proceedings of the World Population Conference* (Belgrade, 1965), II, 205–209.

Coale, Ansley, and Roy Treadway, "A Summary of the Changing Distribution of Overall Fertility, Marital Fertility, and the Proportion Married in the Provinces of Europe", in Coale and Watkins, *Europe*, 31–181 plus maps.

Coale, Ansley, and James Trussell, "Erratum", *Population Index*, 41 (1975), 572.

―――, "Model fertility schedules: variations in the age-structure of childbearing in human populations", *Population Index*, 40 (1974), 185–258.

―――, "Technical Note: Finding the Two Parameters that Specify a Model Schedule of Natural Fertility", *Population Index*, 44 (1978), 203–213.

Coale, Ansley, and Susan Watkins (ed.), *The Decline of Fertility in Europe* (Princeton: Princeton University Press, 1986).

Cooper, Patricia, *Once a Cigar Maker* (Urbana: University of Illinois Press, 1987).

Davis, Kingsley, "The Theory of Change and Response in Modern Demographic History", *Population Index*, 29 (1963), 345–366.

Debacher, Karl-Heinz, "Hanfbereitung in Rust—Eine Pflanze in der Geschichte der Gemeinde", *Die Ortenau*, 71 (1991), 397–401.

Dees, Thomas, "Ettenheim in den Revolutionsjahren 1848 und 1849", *Die Ortenau*, 62 (1982), 140–174.

Demleitner, Josef, and Adolf Roth, *Der Weg zur Volksgenealogie* (Munich: Oldenbourg, 1937).

Derouet, Bernard, "Une démographie différentielle: clés pour un système auto-régulateur des populations rurales d'Ancien Régime", *Annales Economies Sociétés Civilisations*, 35 (1980), 3–41.

―――, "Famille, ménage paysan et mobilité de la terre et des personnes en Thimerais au XVIIIe siècle", *Etudes rurales*, 86 (April 1982), 47–56.

Deuchert, Norbert, *Vom Hambacher Fest zur badischen Revolution* (Stuttgart: Theiss, 1983).

Diefenbacher, Karl, *Ortssippenbuch Weingarten* (Grafenhausen: Köbele, 1980).

Döring, Gerhard, "The Incidence of Anovular Cycles in Women", *Journal of Reproduction and Fertility*, supplement no. 6 (1969), 77–81.

Dorneich, Julius, "Die Entstehung der badischen 'Katholischen Volkspartei' zwischen 1865 und 1869 im Tagebuch von Baurat Dr. Karl Bader", *Freiburger Diözesan-Archiv*, 84 (1964), 272–399.

―――, "Die Führungsschicht der Katholischen Volkspartei in Baden 1869 nach ihrer Sozialstruktur", *Zeitschrift für die Geschichte des Oberrheins*, N.F. 85 (1976), 363–368.

―――, "Der Kirchenkampf in Baden (1860–1876) und die Katholische Gegenbewegung", *Freiburger Diözesan-Archiv*, 94 (1974), 517–588.

Dupâquier, Jacques, "De l'animal à l'homme: le mécanisme autorégulateur des populations traditionelles", *Revue de l'Institut de Sociologie* (Free University of Brussels), 45 (1972), 177–211.

Dupâquier, Jacques, and Marcel Lachiver, "Du contresens à l'illusion technique", *Annales Economies Sociétés Civilisations*, 36 (1981), 489–492.

Eaton, Joseph, and Albert Mayer, "The Social Biology of Very High Fertility Among the Hutterites. The Demography of a Unique Population", *Human Biology*, 25 (1953), 206–264.

Eble, Eugen, *Ortssippenbuch Istein und Huttingen* (Grafenhausen: Köbele, 1970).

Eble, Eugen, and Bernd Sandhaas, *Ortssippenbuch Wittenweier* (Grafenhausen: Köbele, 1970).

Ell, Emil, "War Kippenheims Kronenwirt ein Revoluzzer?", *Altvater*, 36 (May 1978), 37–39, 41–43.

Engler, Wilhelm, *Freiburg, Baden und das Reich* (Stuttgart: Theiss, 1991).
Fehse, Helmut, *Ortssippenbuch Eimeldingen* (Eimeldingen: Gemeinde Eimeldingen, 1979).
Ferdinand, Johannes, "Ettenheim", *Badische Heimat*, 22 (1935), 308–321.
———, "Die revolutionäre Bewegung 1848–1849 in Ettenheim", *Die Ortenau*, 30 (1950), 46–59.
Fessler, August, "Mark- und Waldgenossenschaften der Ortenau", *Badische Heimat*, 22 (1935), 95–102.
Fleury, Michel, and Louis Henry, *Nouveau manuel de dépouillement et d'exploitation de l'état civil ancien* (Paris: Editions de l'institut national d'études démographiques, 1965).
Galenson, David, *White Servitude in Colonial America* (Cambridge: Cambridge University Press, 1981).
Gall, Lothar, *Der Liberalismus als regierende Partei* (Wiesbaden: Steiner, 1968).
Gänshirt, Adolf, Klaus Siefert, and Erich Reinbold, *Ortssippenbuch Friesenheim* (Lahr: Köbele Nachfolger, 1986).
Gaunt, David, "Family Planning and the Preindustrial Society: Some Swedish Evidence", in Kurt Agren (ed.), *Aristocrats, Farmers, Proletarians* (Uppsala: Almqvist, 1973), 28–59.
Gautier, Etienne, and Louis Henry, *La population de Crulai paroisse normande* (Paris: Presses Universitaires de France, 1958).
Gillis, John, Louise Tilly, and David Levine (ed.), *The European Experience of Declining Fertility* (Cambridge, Massachusetts: Blackwell, 1992).
Glass, David, and David Eversley (ed.), *Population in History* (London: Arnold, 1968).
Golde, Günter, *Catholics and Protestants Agricultural Modernization in Two German Villages* (New York: Academic Press, 1975).
Goldstein, Alice, "Aspects of Change in a Nineteenth-Century German Village", *Journal of Family History*, 9 (1984), 145–157.
———, *Determinants of Change and Response among Jews and Catholics in a nineteenth century German village* (New York: Conference on Jewish Social Studies, 1992).
———, "Some Demographic Characteristics of Village Jews in Germany: Nonnenweier, 1800–1931", in Paul Ritterband (ed.), *Modern Jewish Fertility* (Leiden: Brill, 1981), 112–143.
———, "Urbanization in Baden, Germany Focus on the Jews, 1825–1925", *Social Science History*, 8 (1984), 43–66.
Goody, Jack, "Inheritance, property and women: some comparative considerations", in Jack Goody, Joan Thirsk, and Edward Thompson (ed.), *Family and Inheritance* (Cambridge: Cambridge University Press, 1976), 1–36.
Gothein, Eberhard, "Die oberrheinischen Lande vor und nach dem dreissigjährigen Kriege", *Zeitschrift für die Geschichte des Oberrheins*, N.F. 1 (1886), 1–45.
Goubert, Pierre, *Louis XIV and Twenty Million Frenchmen* (New York: Vintage, 1972).
Greer, Germaine, *Sex and Destiny* (New York: Harper and Row, 1984).
Greule, Joseph, "Archivalien des Amtsbezirks Ettenheim", *Zeitschrift für die Geschichte des Oberrheins*, N.F. 3 (1888), m68–m79.
Griesmeier, Josef, "Die Entwicklung der Wirtschaft und der Bevölkerung von Baden und Württemberg im 19. und 20. Jahrhundert", *Jahrbücher für Statistik und Landeskunde von Baden-Württemberg*, 1 (1954), 121–242.
Grotefend, Hermann, *Taschenbuch der Zeitrechnung des deutschen Mittelalters und der Neuzeit* (Hannover: Hahn, 1960).
Guinane, Timothy, Barbara Okun, and James Trussell, "What Do We Know About the Timing of Fertility Transitions in Europe?", *Demography*, 31 (1994), 1–20.
Habakkuk, H. J., "The Economic History of Modern Britain", in Glass and Eversley, *Population*, 147–158.
Haemmerle, Albert, *Alphabetisches Verzeichnis der Berufs- und Standesbezeichnungen* (Hildesheim: Olms, 1966).
Haepler, Rolf, "Die erste Volkswahl in Baden vor 130 Jahren", *Baden*, 1 (1949), 33–35.

Hahn, Karl, "Visitationen und Visitationsberichte aus dem Bistum Strassburg in der zweiten Hälfte des 16. Jahrhunderts", *Zeitschrift für die Geschichte des Oberrheins*, N.F. 26 (1911), 204–249, 501–543, 572–598.

Hajnal, John, "European Marriage Patterns in Perspective", in Glass and Eversley, *Population*, 101–143.

———, "Two Kinds of Pre-industrial Household Formation System", *Population and Development Review*, 8 (1982), 449–494.

Hales, Edward, *Pio Nono* (New York: P.J. Kenedy, 1954).

Hamilton, Richard, *Who Voted For Hitler?* (Princeton: Princeton University Press, 1982).

Hansjakob, Heinrich, *Bauernblut* (Stuttgart: Benz, 1922).

Hassinger, Hellmich, *Der oberbadische Tabakbau und seine wirtschaftliche Bedeutung* (Karlsruhe: Braun, 1911).

Hebbel, Friedrich, Wolfgang Collum, and Willy Hartmann, *Sippenbuch der Stadt Philippsburg* (Grafenhausen: Köbele, 1975).

Hecht, Moritz, *Die Badische Landwirtschaft am Anfang des XX. Jahrhunderts* (Karlsruhe: Braun, 1903).

Helleiner, Karl, "The Vital Revolution Reconsidered", in Glass and Eversley, *Population*, 79–86.

Helmreich, Ernst (ed.), *A free church in a free state? The Catholic Church, Italy, Germany, France 1864-1914* (Boston: Heath, 1964).

Hennig, Michael, *Geschichte des Landkapitels Lahr* (Lahr: Schömperlin, 1893).

Henripin, Jacques, *La population canadienne au début du XVIIIe siècle* (Paris: Presses Universitaires de France, 1954).

———, *Trends and Factors of Fertility in Canada* (Ottawa: Statistics Canada, 1972).

Henry, Louis, *Anciennes Familles Genevoises* (Paris: Presses Universitaires de France, 1956).

———, "Concepts actuels et résultats empiriques sur la fécondité naturelle", in *International Population Conference Mexico 1977* (Liège: International Union for the Scientific Study of Population, 1977), 5–15.

———, *On the Measurement of Human Fertility* (New York: Elsevier, 1972).

———, *Population Analysis and Models* (London: Arnold, 1976).

———, "Some Data on Natural Fertility", *Eugenics Quarterly*, 8 (1961), 81–91.

Hesselbarth, Hellmut, *Revolutionäre Sozialdemokraten, Opportunisten und die Bauern am Vorabend des Imperialismus* (Berlin: Dietz, 1968).

Hofmann, D., and T. Soergel, "Untersuchungen über das Menarchen- und Menopausenalter", *Geburtshilfe und Frauenheilkunde*, 32 (1972), 969–977.

Hofmann, Manfred, Albert Köbele, and Robert Wetekam, *Von der Kirchenbuchverkartung zum Ortssippenbuch* (Limburg a. d. Lahn: Starke, 1957).

Hohlfeld, Johannes, "Die Dorfsippenbücher", *Familiengeschichtliche Blätter*, 42 (1944), 65–90.

Holderness, B. A., "Widows in pre-industrial society: an essay upon their economic functions", in Smith, *Life-Cycle*, 423–442.

Hörner, Manfred, *Die Wahlen zur badischen zweiten Kammer im Vormärz (1819-1847)* (Göttingen: Vandenhoek und Ruprecht, 1987).

Houdaille, Jacques, "Fécondité des mariages dans le quart nord-est de la France de 1670 à 1829", *Annales de Démographie Historique*, 1976, 341–392.

———, "La Population de Remmesweiler en Sarre aux XVIIIe et XIXe siècles", *Population*, 20 (1970), 1183–1192.

———, "Quelques résultats sur la démographie de trois villages d'Allemagne de 1750 à 1879", *Population*, 20 (1970), 649–654.

Hundsnurscher, Franz, and Gerhard Taddey, *Die jüdischen Gemeinden in Baden* (Stuttgart: Kohlhammer, 1968).

Hunt, James, "Peasants, Grain Tariffs, and Meat Quotas: Imperial German Protectionism Reexamined", *Central European History*, 7 (1974), 311–331.

Ifele, Otto, "Die Bevölkerung der Ortenau im 17. Jahrhundert", *Die Ortenau*, 19 (1932), 7–14.
Jerger, Andreas, *Ein Stück bad. Kulturkampfs* (Lahr: Bosch, 1909).
Kähni, Otto, "Geschichte der Offenburger Judengemeinde", *Die Ortenau*, 49 (1969), 80–114.
Kalbach, Warren, and Wayne McVey, *The Demographic Bases of Canadian Society* (Toronto: McGraw-Hill, 1979).
Kalkoff, Hermann, *Nationalliberale Parlamentarier 1867–1917 des Reichstags und der Einzellandtagen* (Berlin: Selbstverdienststelle der nationalliberalen Partei Deutschlands, 1917).
Katterman, Hildegard, *Geschichte und Schicksale der Lahrer Juden* (Lahr: Stadtverwaltung Lahr, 1976).
Kintz, Jean-Pierre, "Anthroponymie en pays de lange germanique. Le cas d'Alsace, XVIIe–XVIIIe siècles", *Annales de Démographie Historique*, 1972, 311–317.
Kistler, Franz, *Die wirtschaftlichen und sozialen Verhältnisse in Baden, 1849–1870* (Freiburg: Eberhard Albert Universitäts-Buchhandlung, 1954).
Knodel, John, "Breast feeding and population growth", *Science*, 198 (1977), 1111–1115.
———, "Child Mortality and Reproductive Behaviour in German Village Populations in the Past: A Micro-Level Analysis of the Replacement Effect", *Population Studies*, 36 (1982), 177–200.
———, *The Decline of Fertility in Germany, 1871–1939* (Princeton: Princeton University Press, 1974).
———, *Demographic behavior in the past A study of fourteen German village populations in the eighteenth and nineteenth centuries* (Cambridge: Cambridge University Press, 1988).
———, "Demographic Transitions in German Villages", in Coale and Watkins, *Europe*, 337–389.
———, "Espacement des naissances et planification familiale: une critique de la méthode Dupâquier-Lachiver", *Annales Economies Sociétés Civilisations*, 36 (1981), 473–488.
———, "Family Limitation and the Fertility Transition: Evidence from Age-Patterns of Fertility in Europe and Asia", *Population Studies*, 31 (1977), 219–249.
———, "From Natural Fertility to Family Limitation: The Onset of Fertility Transition in a Sample of German Villages", *Demography*, 16 (1979), 493–521.
———, "Historische Demographie und Genealogie", *Genealogie*, 11 (1972), 65–70.
———, "Law, Marriage, and Illegitimacy in Nineteenth Century Germany", *Population Studies*, 20 (1967), 279–294.
———, "Natural Fertility: Age Patterns, Levels, and Trends", in Rodolfo Bulatao and Ronald Lee (ed.), *Determinants of Fertility in Developing Countries* (New York: Academic Press, 1983), 61–102.
———, "Natural Fertility in Pre-industrial Germany", *Population Studies*, 32 (1978), 481–510.
———, "Ortssippenbücher als Daten für die historische Demographie", *Geschichte und Gesellschaft*, 1 (1975), 288–324.
———, "Réponse de John Knodel à Jacques Dupâquier", *Annales Economies Sociétés Civilisations*, 36 (1981), 493–494.
———, "Starting, Stopping, and Spacing During the Early Stages of Fertility Transition: The Experience of German Village Populations in the Eighteenth and Nineteenth Centuries", *Demography*, 24 (1987), 143–162.
———, "Two and a Half Centuries of Demographic History in a Bavarian Village", *Population Studies*, 24 (1970), 353–376.
Knodel, John, and Steven Hochstadt, "Urban and rural illegitimacy in Imperial Germany", in Laslett, Oosterveen, and Smith, *Bastardy*, 284–312.
Knodel, John, and Hallie Kintner, "The Impact of Breast Feeding on the Biometric Analysis of Infant Mortality", *Demography*, 14 (1977), 391–409.
Knodel, John, and Mary Jo Maynes, "Urban and Rural Marriage Patterns in Imperial Germany", *Journal of Family History*, 1 (1976), 129–168.

Knodel, John, and Edward Shorter, "The Reliability of Family Reconstitution Data in German Village Genealogies (Ortssippenbücher)", *Annales de Démographie Historique*, 1976, 115–154.
Knodel, John, and Etienne van de Walle, "Breast Feeding, Fertility and Infant Mortality: An Analysis of some Early German Data", *Population Studies*, 21 (1967), 109–131.
———, "Lessons from the Past: Policy Implications of Historical Fertility Studies", in Coale and Watkins, *Europe*, 390–419.
Knodel, John, and Chris Wilson, "The Secular Increase in Fecundity in German Village Populations: An Analysis of Reproductive Histories of Couples Married 1750–1899", *Population Studies*, 35 (1981), 53–84.
Köbele, Albert, "Die deutschen Ortssippenbücher", manuscript.
———, *Dorfsippenbuch Egringen* (Grafenhausen: Köbele, 1957).
———, *Dorfsippenbuch Freiamt* (Grafenhausen: Köbele, 1954).
———, *Dorfsippenbuch Kappel am Rhein* (Grafenhausen: Köbele, 1969).
———, *Dorfsippenbuch Meissenheim* (Grafenhausen: Köbele, 1969).
———, *Dorfsippenbuch Ringsheim* (Grafenhausen: Köbele, 1956).
———, "Einwohnerzahlen der 42 Gemeinden des Landkreises von 1813–1957", *Geroldseckerland*, 1 (1958–1959), 51.
———, "Freiherr Franz von Böcklin, Bannbrecher für die Landwirtschaft schon vor der französischen Revolution", *Geroldseckerland*, 8 (1965–1966), 174–177.
———, *Ortssippenbuch Grafenhausen* (Grafenhausen: Köbele, 1971).
———, *Ortssippenbuch Haltingen* (Grafenhausen: Köbele, 1965).
———, *Ortssippenbuch Müllen* (Grafenhausen: Köbele, 1981).
———, *Ortssippenbuch Münchweier* (Grafenhausen: Köbele, 1977).
———, *Ortssippenbuch Ottoschwanden* (Grafenhausen: Köbele, 1966).
———, *Ortssippenbuch Ringsheim Fortführung 1956–1968* (Grafenhausen: Köbele, 1969).
———, *Ortssippenbuch Rust* (Grafenhausen: Köbele, 1969).
———, *Sippenbuch der Stadt Herbolzheim im Breisgau* (Grafenhausen: Köbele, 1967).
———, *Sippenbuch der Stadt Hüfingen* (Grafenhausen: Köbele, 1962).
Köbele, Albert, and Erich Hentschke, *Ortssippenbuch Kippenheimweiler* (Grafenhausen: Köbele, 1980).
Köbele, Albert, and Margarete Kirner, *Ortssippenbuch Rheinhausen* (Grafenhausen: Köbele, 1975).
Köbele, Albert, and Hans Scheer, *Ortssippenbuch Altdorf* (Grafenhausen: Köbele, 1976).
———, *Ortssippenbuch Dundenheim* (Grafenhausen: Köbele, 1977).
———, *Ortssippenbuch Ichenheim* (Grafenhausen: Köbele, 1978).
Köbele, Albert, Hans Scheer, and Emil Ell, *Ortssippenbuch Schmieheim* (Grafenhausen: Köbele, 1979).
Köbele, Albert, and Fritz Schleicher, *Ortssippenbuch Oberweier* (Grafenhausen: Köbele, 1964).
Köbele, Albert, and Fritz Schülin, *Ortssippenbuch Efringen-Kirchen* (Grafenhausen: Köbele, 1968).
Köbele, Albert, Fritz Schülin, and others, *Ortssippenbuch der Gemeinden Binzen und Rümmingen* (Grafenhausen: Köbele, 1967).
Köbele, Albert, and Klaus Siefert, *Ortssippenbuch Mahlberg-Orschweier* (Grafenhausen: Köbele, 1977).
Köbele, Albert, Klaus Siefert, and Hans Scheer, *Ortssippenbuch Kippenheim* (Grafenhausen: Köbele, 1979).
Kopp, Adolf, *Zehentwesen und Zehentablösung in Baden* (Freiburg: Volkswirtschaftliche Abhandlungen der badischen Hochschulen, 1899).
Kramer, Helmut, *Fraktionsverbindungen in den deutschen Volksvertretungen 1819–1849* (Berlin: Duncker and Humblot, 1968).
Krebs, Manfred, supplemented by L. Lauppe, "Politische und kirchliche Geschichte der Ortenau", *Die Ortenau*, 40 (1960), 133–246.

Kremer, Hans-Jürgen (ed.), *Mit Gott für Wahrheit, Freiheit, und Recht* (Stuttgart: Kohlhammer, 1983).
Kuntzemüller, Albert, "Achtzig Jahre Eisenbahnen in der Ortenau", *Die Ortenau*, 13 (1926), 21–40.
Labisch-Benz, Elfie, *Die jüdische Gemeinde Nonnenweier* (Freiburg: Mersch, 1981).
Lachat, P., *Lateinische Bezeichnungen in alten Kirchenbüchern* (Neustadt: Degener, 1960).
Lagneau, G., "Recherches comparatives sur la menstruation en France", *Bulletins de la Société d'Anthropologie de Paris*, 6 (1865), 724–743.
Laslett, Peter, "The bastardy-prone sub-society", in Laslett, Oosterveen, and Smith, *Bastardy*, 217–240.
Laslett, Peter, and Klara Oosterveen, "Long-term Trends in Bastardy in England", *Population Studies*, 27 (1973), 255–286.
Laslett, Peter, Klara Oosterveen, and Richard Smith (ed.), *Bastardy and its Comparative History* (London: Arnold, 1980).
Lavely, William, "Age Patterns of Chinese Marital Fertility, 1950–1981", *Demography*, 23 (1986), 419–434.
Le Bras, Hervé, "Parents, Grands-parents, Bisaieux", *Population*, 28 (1972), 1–38.
Lee, Loyd, *The Politics of Harmony Civil Service, Liberalism, and Social Reform in Baden 1800–1850* (Newark: University of Delaware Press, 1980).
Lee, Robert, "Tax Structure and Economic Growth in Germany (1750–1850)", *Journal of European Economic History*, 4 (1975), 153–178.
Lee, Ronald, "Introduction", in Lee, *Patterns*, 1–17.
——— (ed.), *Population Patterns in the Past* (New York: Academic Press, 1977).
———, "Short-term variation: vital rates, prices, and weather", in Wrigley and Schofield, *England*, 356–401.
Le Play, Frédéric, *On Family, Work, and Social Change* (Chicago: University of Chicago Press, 1982).
Leridon, Henri, *Human Fertility* (Chicago: University of Chicago Press, 1977).
Lerner, Robert, Standish Meacham, and Edward Burns, *Western Civilizations* (New York: Norton, 1988), vol. 2.
Le Roy Ladurie, Emmanuel, "Demography and the "Sinful Secrets": The Case of Languedoc in the Late Eighteenth and Early Nineteenth Centuries", in *The Territory of the Historian* (Hassocks: Harvester, 1979), 239–254.
———, "From Waterloo to Colyton", Ibid., 223–234.
———, "L'histoire immobile", in *Le territoire de l'historien*, vol. 2 (Paris: Gallimard, 1978), 7–34.
Lesthaeghe, Ron, *The Decline of Belgian Fertility 1800–1970* (Princeton: Princeton University Press, 1977).
———, "On the Social Control of Human Reproduction", *Population and Development Review*, 6 (1980), 527–548.
Lesthaeghe, Ron, and Chris Wilson, "Modes of Production, Secularization, and the Pace of the Fertility Decline in Western Europe, 1870–1930", in Coale and Watkins, *Europe*, 261–292.
Levine, David, *Family Formation in an Age of Nascent Capitalism* (New York: Academic Press, 1977).
———, ""For Their Own Reasons": Individual Marriage Decisions and Family Life", *Journal of Family History*, 7 (1982), 255–264.
———, "The Reliability of Parochial Registration and the Representativeness of Family Reconstitution", *Population Studies*, 30 (1976), 107–122.
Levine, David, and Keith Wrightson, "The Social Context of Illegitimacy in Early Modern England", in Laslett, Oosterveen, and Smith, *Bastardy*, 158–175.
Lewis-Faning, Ernest, *Family Limitation and its influence on human fertility during the past fifty years* (London: His Majesty's Stationery Office, 1949).

Lively, Jack (ed.), *The Works of Joseph de Maistre* (New York: Macmillan, 1965).
Livi-Bacci, Massimo, *A Century of Portuguese Fertility* (Princeton: Princeton University Press, 1971).
———, *A History of Italian Fertility During the Last Two Centuries* (Princeton: Princeton University Press, 1977).
———, "Social Group Forerunners of Fertility Control in Europe", in Coale and Watkins, *Europe*, 182–200.
Lockridge, Kenneth, *The Fertility Transition in Sweden* (Umea: Demographic Data Base Umea University, 1984).
Lowenstein, Steven, "The Rural Community and the Urbanization of German Jewry", *Central European History*, 13 (1980), 218–236.
Ludwig, Theodor, *Der badische Bauer im achtzehnten Jahrhundert* (Strasbourg: Trübner, 1896).
MacFarlane, Alan, *Reconstructing Historical Communities* (Cambridge: Cambridge University Press, 1977).
Maehl, William, "German Social Democratic Agrarian Policy, 1890–1895, Reconsidered", *Central European History*, 13 (1980), 121–157.
Manschke, R., "Beruf und Kinderzahl", *Schmollers Jahrbuch*, 40 (1916), 1867–1937.
Marschalck, Peter, *Bevölkerungsgeschichte Deutschlands im 19. und 20. Jahrhundert* (Frankfurt: Suhrkamp, 1984).
Matthiessen, Poul, and James McCann, "The Role of Mortality in the European Fertility Transition: Aggregate-Level Relations", in Samuel Preston (ed.), *The Effects of Infant and Child Mortality on Fertility* (New York: Academic Press, 1978), 47–68.
McDonald, Peter, "Nuptiality and Completed Fertility: A Study of Starting, Stopping, and Spacing Behavior", *World Fertility Survey Comparative Studies*, 35 (1984).
McKay, John, Bennett Hill, and John Buckler, *A History of Western Society* (Boston: Houghton Mifflin, 1991).
McPhee, Peter, *The Politics of Rural Life* (Oxford: Clarendon Press, 1992).
Meisner, Franz, "Der Tabakbau in der Ortenau", *Badische Heimat*, 22 (1935), 547–557.
Mineau, Geraldine, and James Trussell, "A Specification of Marital Fertility by Parents' Age, Age at Marriage and Marital Duration", *Demography*, 19 (1982), 335–349.
Moeller, Robert, "Peasants and Tariffs in the *Kaiserreich*: How Backward Were the *Bauern*?", *Agricultural History*, 55 (1981), 370–384.
Mohr, Alexander, "Karl Zittel (1802–1871), Pfarrer und liberal Politiker in der II. Ständekammer und im Paulskirchen-Parlament", in Gerhard Schwinge (ed.), *Protestantismus und Politik* (Karlsruhe: Badische Landesbibliothek, 1996), 132–140.
Morrow, Richard, "Family Limitation in Pre-Industrial England: A Reappraisal", *Economic History Review*, second series, 31 (1978), 419–428.
Müller-Dietz, Heinz, *Das Leben des Rechtslehrers und Politikers Karl Theodor Welcker* (Freiburg: Eberhard Albert Universitäts-Buchhandlung, 1968).
Netting, Robert, *Balancing on an Alp* (Cambridge: Cambridge University Press, 1981).
Neu, Heinrich, Albert, and Benedikt Schwarz, "Archivalien aus Orten des Amtsbezirks Ettenheim", *Zeitschrift für die Geschichte des Oberrheins*, N.F. 22 (1907), m101–m104.
Noonan, John Jr., *Contraception* (Cambridge: Belknap, 1965).
Norton, Susan, "The Vital Question: Are Reconstituted Families Representative of the General Population?", in Bennett Dyke and Warren Morrill (ed.), *Genealogical Demography* (New York: Academic Press, 1980), 11–22.
Ochs, Ernst, *Badisches Wörterbuch* (Lahr: Schauenburg, 1925-present).
Oechsler, Hermann, *"Sperrlingsleben" aus dem "badischen Kulturkampf" von 1874/76 gepfiffen zu Nutz und Trutz* (Offenburg: Zuschneid, third edition, about 1900).
Ohlin, G., "Mortality, Marriage, and Growth in Pre-Industrial Populations", *Population Studies*, 14 (1961), 190–197.
Perrenoud, Alfred, "Malthusianisme et protestantisme: «un modèle démographique wébérien»", *Annales Economies Sociétés Civilisations*, 29 (1974), 975–988.

Person, Hans, "Parlamentarisches aus 150 Jahren Abgeordnete aus dem Kreis Lahr", *Geroldseckerland*, 7 (1964–1965), 20–29.
Pfister, Christian, *Bevölkerungsgeschichte und historische Demographie 1500–1800* (Munich: Oldenbourg, 1994).
Poos, L. R. and R. M. Smith, "'Legal Windows Onto Historical Populations'? Recent Research on Demography and the Manor Court in Medieval England", *Law and History Review*, 2 (1984), 143.
Raferty, Adrian, Steven Lewis, and Akbar Aghajanian, "Demand or Ideation? Evidence from the Iranian Marital Fertility Decline", *Demography*, 32 (1995), 159–182.
Razi, Zvi, *Life, Marriage and Death in a Medieval Parish* (Cambridge: Cambridge University Press, 1980).
Reinbold, Erich, *Ortssippenbuch Broggingen* (Grafenhausen: Köbele, 1981).
Reinfried, Karl, "Visitationsberichte aus der zweiten Hälfte des 17. Jahrhunderts über die Pfarreien des Landkapitels Lahr (Schluss)", *Freiburger Diözesan-Archiv*, 31 (N.F. 4, 1903), 255–297.
Rest, Josef, "Zustände in der südlichen Ortenau im Jahr 1802", *Die Ortenau*, 11 (1924), 19–30.
Riff, Michael, "The Anti-Jewish Aspect of the Revolutionary Unrest of 1848 in Baden and its Impact on Emancipation", *Leo Baeck Institute Yearbook*, 21 (1976), 27–40.
Rinderle, Walter and Bernard Norling, *The Nazi Impact on a German Village* (Lexington: University Press of Kentucky, 1993).
Rogers, Everett, *Diffusion of Innovations* (New York: Free Press, 1983).
Roth, Adolf, and Paul Thorbecke, *Die badischen Landstände* (Karlsruhe: Braun, 1907).
Sabean, David, *Property, production, and family in Neckarhausen, 1700–1870* (Cambridge: Cambridge University Press, 1990).
———, "Young bees in an empty hive: relations between brothers-in-law in a south German village around 1800", in Hans Medick and David Sabean (ed.), *Interest and Emotion* (Cambridge: Cambridge University Press, 1984), 171–186.
Samuelsson, Kurt, *Religion and Economic Action* (Stockholm: Svenska bokförlaget, 1961).
Schäfle, Matthias, *Vier Lustren oder zwanzig Jahre im conferenziellen Leben eines Geistlichen* (Rastatt: Bernhard, 1870).
Schauff, Johannes, *Das Wahlverhalten der deutschen Katholiken im Kaiserreich und in der Weimarer Republik* (Mainz: Grünewald, 1975).
Scheer, Hans, and Albert Köbele, *Ortssippenbuch Sexau* (Grafenhausen: Köbele, 1974).
Schneider, Jane and Peter Schneider, "Going Forward in Reverse Gear: Culture, Economy, and Political Economy in the Demographic Transitions of a Rural Sicilian Town", in Gillis, Tilly, and Levine, *Experience*, 146–174.
Schofield, Roger, "Representativeness and Family Reconstitution", *Annales de Démographie Historique*, 1972, 121–125.
Schubnell, Hermann, *Der Kinderreichtum bei Bauern und Arbeitern* (Freiburg: Eberhard Albert Universitätsbuchhandlung, 1941).
Schwarz, Benedikt, "Archivalien der Gemeinde Rust, Bezirksamt Ettenheim", *Zeitschrift für die Geschichte des Oberrheins*, N.F. 26 (1911), m140–m142.
———, "Freiherrlich Böcklin von Böcklinsauisches Archiv in Rust, Bezirksamt Ettenheim", *Zeitschrift für die Geschichte des Oberrheins*, N.F. 25 (1910), m14–m121.
Seccombe, Wally, "Starting to Stop: Working-Class Fertility Decline in Britain", *Past and Present*, 126 (February 1990), 151–188.
Segalen, Martine, "Exploring a Case of Late French Fertility Decline: Two Contrasted Breton Examples", in Gillis, Tilly, and Levine, *Experience*, 227–247.
———, "The Family Cycle and Household Structure: Five Generations in a French Village", in Wheaton and Hareven, *Family*, 253–271.
———, "Mentalité populaire et remariage en Europe occidental", in Jacques Dupâquier and others (ed.), *Marriage and Remarriage in Populations of the Past* (London: Academic Press, 1981), 67–77.

Sepainter, Fred, *Die Reichstagswahlen im Grossherzogtum Baden* (Frankfurt: Lang, 1983).
Sheehan, James, *German Liberalism in the nineteenth century* (Chicago: University of Chicago Press, 1978).
Shorter, Edward, "L'âge des premières règles en France, 1750–1950", *Annales Economies Sociétés Civilisations*, 36 (1981), 495–511.
———, "Bastardy in South Germany: A Comment", *Journal of Interdisciplinary History*, 8 (1978), 459–469.
———, "Capitalism, Culture, and Sexuality: Some Competing Models", *Social Science Quarterly*, 53 (1972), 338–356.
———, "Female Emancipation, Birth Control, and Fertility in European History", *American Historical Review*, 78 (1978), 605–640.
———, "Has a desire to limit fertility always existed? The question of drug abortion in traditional Europe", manuscript prepared for the International Union for the Scientific Study of Population's Conference on Determinants of Fertility Trends, held in Bad Homburg in 1980.
———, *A History of Women's Bodies* (New York: Basic Books, 1982).
———, "Illegitimacy, Sexual Revolution, and Social Change in Modern Europe", *Journal of Interdisciplinary History*, 2 (1971), 237–272.
———, *The Making of the Modern Family* (New York: Basic Books, 1975).
———, "Middle-Class Anxiety in the German Revolution of 1848", *Journal of Social History*, 2 (1969), 189–215.
———, "On Writing the History of Rape", *Signs*, 3 (1977), 471–482.
———, "«La vie intime» Beitrage zu seiner Geschichte am Beispiel des kulturellen Wandels in den bayerischen Unterschichten im 19. Jahrhundert", *Kölner Zeitschrift für Sociologie und Sozial-psychologie*, 16 (1973), 530–549.
Shorter, Edward, John Knodel, and Etienne van de Walle, "The Decline of Non-Marital Fertility in Europe, 1880–1940", *Population Studies*, 25 (1971), 375–393.
Siefert, Klaus, *Ortssippenbuch Mietersheim* (Grafenhausen: Köbele, 1975).
Sieger, Jörg, *Kardinal in Schatten der Revolution* (Kehl: Morstadt, 1986).
Siegfried, André, *Tableau politique de la France de l'Ouest sous la Troisième République* (Paris: Colin, 1913).
Smith, Daniel, "A Homeostatic Demographic Regime: Patterns in West European Family Reconstitution Studies", in Lee, *Patterns*, 19–51
———, "Parental Power and Marriage Patterns: An Analysis of Historical Trends in Hingham, Massachusetts", *Journal of Marriage and the Family*, 35 (1973), 419–428.
Smith, Richard (ed.), *Land, Kinship and Life-Cycle* (Cambridge: Cambridge University Press, 1984).
———, "Some Reflections on the Evidence for the Origins of the 'European Marriage Pattern' in England", in Chris Harris (ed.), *The Sociology of the Family: New Directions for Britain* (Keele: University of Keele, 1979), 74–112.
Späth, Fritz, *Wyhl am Kaiserstuhl Einst und Jetzt* (Endingen: Wild, 1963).
Specht, Fritz and Paul Schwave, *Die Reichstags-Wahlen von 1867 bis 1907* (Berlin: Heymann, 1908).
Sperber, Jonathan, *Popular Catholicism in Nineteenth-Century Germany* (Princeton: Princeton University Press, 1984).
Spuler, Bertold, *Regenten und Regierungen der Welt* (Würzburg: Ploetz, 1962), pt. 2, vol. 3, 65–71.
Stadelhofer, Manfred, *Der Abbau der Kulturkampfgesetzgebung im Grossherzogtum Baden 1878-1918* (Mainz: Grünewald, 1969).
Staudenmaier, P., "Mittheilungen aus den Capitelsarchiven Offenburg und Lahr", *Freiburger Diözesan-Archiv*, 14 (1881), 268–279.
Stengers, J., "Les pratiques anticonceptionnelles dans le mariage au XIXe et au XXe siècles: problèmes humains et attitudes religieuses", *Revue belge de philologie et d'histoire*, 49 (1971), 403–481, 1119–1174.

Störk, Wilhelm, "Archivalien der Pfarreien", *Zeitschrift für die Geschichte des Oberrheins*, N.F. 3 (1888), m80–m84..
Straus, Albert, *Der Tabakbau im Grossherzogtum Baden und seine natürlichen Vorbedingungen* (Halle a. S.: Paalzow, 1909).
Tentler, Thomas, "The Summa for Confessors as an Instrument of Social Control", in Charles Trinkaus and Heiko Oberman (ed.), *The Pursuit of Holiness in Late Medieval and Renaissance Religion*, (Leiden: Brill, 1974), 103–126.
Thestrup, Poul, "Methodological Problems of Family Reconstitution Study in a Danish Rural Parish before 1800", *Scandinavian Economic History Review*, 20 (1972), 1–26.
Tilly, Charles, "Demographic Origins of the European Proletariat", in David Levine (ed.), *Proletarianization and Family History* (Orlando: Academic Press, 1984), 1–85.
Tilly, Charles in "Review Symposium Ansley J. Coale and Susan Cotts Watkins (eds.) The Decline of Fertility in Europe", *Population and Development Review*, 12 (1986), 323–340.
Tilly, Louise, Joan Scott, and Miriam Cohen, "Women's Work and European Fertility Patterns", *Journal of Interdisciplinary History*, 6 (1976), 447–476.
Uttenweiler, Bernhard (ed.), *Schicksal und Geschichte der jüdischen Gemeinden Ettenheim Altdorf Kippenheim Schmieheim Rust Orschweier* (Ettenheim: Historischer Verein für Mittelbaden, 1988).
———, *'s Ettenheimer Bähnle* (Ettenheim: Historischer Verein Ettenheim, 1992).
Van de Walle, Etienne, "Motivations and Technology in the Decline of French Fertility", in Wheaton and Hareven, *Family*, 135–178.
Van de Walle, Francine, "Infant Mortality and the European Demographic Transition", in Coale and Watkins, *Europe*, 201–233.
Van Fraassen, Bas, *The Scientific Image* (Oxford: Clarendon Press, 1980).
Viazzo, Pier Paolo, "Illegitimacy and the European Marriage Pattern: Comparative Evidence from the Alpine Area", in Bonfield, Smith, and Wrightson, *The World We Have Gained*, 100–121.
Vilar, Pierre, "Réflexions sur la «crise de l'ancien type», «inégalité des récoltes» et «sous-developpement»", in *Conjoncture économique, structures sociales* (Paris: Mouton, 1974), 37–58.
Vogel, Bernhard, Dieter Nohlen, and Rainer-Olaf Schulze, *Wahlen in Deutschland* (Berlin: De Gruyter, 1971).
Von Arnswaldt, Werner, *Familiengeschichtliche Quellen in den Archiven und ihre Benutzung* (Leipzig: Degener, 1933).
Walker, Mack, "Home Towns and State Administrators: South German Politics, 1815–30", *Political Science Quarterly*, 82 (1967), 35–60.
Wall, Richard, "Real property, marriage and children: the evidence from four pre-industrial communities", in Smith, *Life-Cycle*, 443–479.
Watkins, Susan, "Conclusions", in Coale and Watkins, *Europe*, 420–449.
Webb, Steven, "Agricultural Protection in Wilhelmian Germany: Forging an Empire with Pork and Rye", *Journal of Economic History*, 42 (1982), 309–326.
Weber, Eugen, "Comment la Politique Vint aux Paysans: A Second Look at Peasant Politicization", *American Historical Review*, 87 (1982), 357–389.
Wecken, Friedrich, and Johannes Krause, *Taschenbuch für Familiengeschichtsforschung* (Schellenberg bei Berchtesgaden: Degener, 1951).
Weir, David, "Fertility Transition in Rural France, 1740–1829", *Journal of Economic History*, 44 (1984), 612–614.
———, "Fertility Transitions in Rural France 1740–1829", Ph.D. dissertation at Stanford University 1983.
Weiss, Volkmar, "Die Verwendung von Familiennamenhäufigkeiten zur Schätzung des genetischen Verwandtschafts", *Mitteilungen der Deutschen Gesellschaft für Bevölkerungswissenschaft*, 55 (December 1978), 1–16.

Welti, Manfred, "Abendmahl, Zollpolitik und Sozialistengesetz in der Pfalz. Eine statistisch-quantifizierende Untersuchung zur Verbreitung von liberal-aufklärerischem Gedankengut im 19. Jahrhundert", *Geschichte und Gesellschaft*, 3 (1977), 384–405.

Wheaton, Robert, and Tamara Hareven (ed.), *Family and Sexuality in French History* (Philadelphia: University of Pennsylvania Press, 1980).

Wilson, Chris, Jim Oeppen, and Mike Pardoe, "What is Natural Fertility? The Modelling of a Concept", *Population Index*, 54 (1988), 4–20.

Windell, George, *The Catholics and German Unity 1866–1871* (Minneapolis: University of Minnesota Press, 1954).

Wrigley, Anthony, "Family Reconstitution", in Anthony Wrigley (ed.), *An Introduction to English Historical Demography* (New York: Basic Books, 1966), 96–159.

——, "Fertility Strategy for the Individual and the Group", in Charles Tilly (ed.), *Historical Studies of Changing Fertility* (Princeton: Princeton University Press, 1978), 135–154.

——, "Marital Fertility in Seventeenth-Century Colyton: A Note", *Economic History Review*, second series, 31 (1978), 429–436.

——, *Population and History* (New York: McGraw-Hill, 1969).

Wrigley, Anthony, and Roger Schofield, *The Population History of England 1541–1871* (London: Arnold, 1981).

Wülfrath, Karl, "Das Dorfsippenbuch", *Heimat und Reich*, October 1938, 361–365.

Zangerl, Carl, "Courting the Catholic Vote: The Center Party in Baden, 1903–1913", *Central European History*, 10 (1977), 220–240.

Zeldin, Theodore, "The Conflict of Moralities. Confession, Sin and Pleasure", in Theodore Zeldin (ed.), *Conflicts in French Society* (London: Allen and Unwin, 1970), 13–50.

Ziemann, Walter, and Walter Fischer, *Archivverzeichnis Grafenhausen Gemeinde Kappel-Grafenhausen* (1977).

——, *Archivverzeichnis Kappel Gemeinde Kappel-Grafenhausen* (1977).

Zier, Hans Georg, "Die Wirtschaft der Ortenau im 19. und 20. Jahrhundert", *Die Ortenau*, 40 (1960), 252–320.

Zittel, Karl, "Der badische Landtag", *Jahrbücher der Gegenwart*, 1848, 62–64.

——, "Die politischen Partheiungen in Baden", *Jahrbücher der Gegenwart*, 1847, 347–378.

Index

Abortion, induced 90, 105n.10, 222n.2; spontaneous 91
Absolutism 268n.22
Abstinence (method of birth control) 77, 94, 133, 195n.33
Accumulation 55, 58, 60–61, 77, 133, 136, 142, 148
Adaptation or adjustment 170, 263, 265, 268n.12–13n.17n.23
Adolescents 43–44, 53, 169
Adolescent sterility 104n.2
Adultery 70, 83n.6
Affluent (occupational category) defined 48n.65; 34, 37, 110, 115–118, 123, 127, 131, 137, 140, 189, 192–193, 207, 209, 225n.54, 244–245, 268n.24
Age at first marriage 8, 98–99, 135–136, 153–154, 158, 163–164, 173n.3, 188–189, 254, 263–264, 266; by faction or tendency 189, 195n.37, 197n.91, 229n.136, 240, 259n.100; by occupation 113–115; by religion 206; by sex 114–115; by status 123; by village 80–82; by wealth 153, 159, 166; distorts other measures 97, 170, 192, 195n.34, 205, 212, 224n.38, 226n.85–86, 240
Age at last birth 89, 94–97, 103, 108n.60; by faction or tendency 184–185, 191–192, 204–205, 220–221, 229n.136, 245–247, 258n.79, 259n.103–106; by occupation 111–112, 116–117; by religion 206, 211–212, 225n.49; by status 124, 129n.32, 188–189; by village 98–99, 101, 243; by wealth 152–155, 158–160, 165–167
Age at second-last confinement 8, 93, 96, 103, 264, 268n.16; by occupation 112, 116; by status 124; by tendency 229n.133, 249; by wealth 154–156, 160–161, 164–165
Age gap between spouses 114–115, 119, 123, 128n.8–9, 206
Agrarian question 145
Agricultural Union 47n.44, 238

Algeria 18
Alsace map 5; 30, 42, 74–75, 79, 85n.45, 194n.6, 236, 239
Altdorf (village) map 32; 22n.6, 26n.60, 74, 141, 206, 218, 224n.41, 259n.104
Anti-Catholicism 223n.18
Anticlericals 9, 41, 199–202, 208, 213–217, 223n.23, 224n.31, 226n.83, 227n.89, 233, 235, 237, 254, 262; see also liberals
Anti-Semitism 206, 223n.18, 224n.46
Apathy 197n.89, 224n.35, 251
Apprentices 37–38, 49n.84n.88, 53, 61–62
Archbishop of Freiburg 203–204, 208, 224n.35, 235, 242; see also Vicari
Archbishop of Strasbourg 6, 16, 30, 179–180, 194n.21, 202
Armbruster, Emil (Centre member of parliament) 241, 243, 247–249
Auctions 137–138, 183

Baden (State) map 5; 4, 6, 16, 30, 40, 74–76, 78–79, 85n.33, 122, 144, 150n.32, 175, 181, 182, 186–187, 190–192, 194n.6, 199, 202, 204, 207–208, 214–216, 218, 261; constitution 187–188
Bakers 37, 64n.26, 145
Bands 195n.36, 233
Bargees 36, 48n.79
Basket-weavers 39, 75
Beans, lentils, peas 29
Beet root 31, 34
Belgium 222n.2
Benthamite calculation 132, 148n.4
Berstett (noble family) 140
Birth control 105n.10, 222n.6; passim
Birth intervals defined 107n.41; 92–95, 120
Bischeim bei Hönheim/Alsace (town) 13
Bismarck, Otto von (Prussian chancellor) 215, 216, 217
Black Forest (region) 135–136
Blacksmithing 177, 209

284

Bleaching 35, 48n.69
Böcklin von Böcklinsau (lords in Rust) 6, 13, 16, 19, 25n.50, 30, 140, 164, 178–180, 194n.16n.19, 195n.30, 216–217, 257n.60
Bookbinders 35, 187; see also Winkler
Border guards 39, 83n.11, 225n.54, 227n.103
Brazil 18
Breastfeeding 90–91, 104n.7, 107n.45, 120–121, 125, 128n.18, 169, 264
Brentano, Lorenz (revolutionary) 189, 190
Brewers 36–37, 43, 231, 262
Brickmakers 43, 50n.188
Brittany 268n.21
Brokers 19, 39, 145
Buchenberger, Adolf (finance minister) 150n.32
Burg, Vitus (priest in Kappel) 203, 207–208, 213, 223n.24
Butchers 37, 40, 49n.83, 226n.83
By-elections 190, 197n.90, 235
By-occupations 21, 28, 38, 44, 45n.4, 134, 164, 254

Canada 92, 97–99, 107n.33
Capitalism 129n.23, 145, 268n.22
Carpenters 51n.121
Cartwrights 36
Catholic associations 108, 226n.66, 232, 234, 238, 268n.21
Catholic People's Party 216, 228n.11, 231–237, 254n.3, 255n.16; see also Centre
Celibacy 8, 52–53, 65n.8, 90
Censuses 23n.26, 52–53, 135, 151n.47, 200; agricultural 151n.46; animal 154–155
Centre party 9, 129n.34, 200–202, 210–211, 214, 217–218, 222n.8, 223n.10n.13–14n.17, 226n.84, 227n.107, 228n.111n.113n.120, 237–251, 264, 266; see also Catholic People's Party
Chicory 30–31, 33
Child care 121, 129n.22
Child labour 44, 218
Child mortality 17, 120, 263
Choirs 236
Christian Democrats (party) 197n.79, 226n.84
Church assets 45n.13, 138, 144, 193n.5, 203, 207–208, 210–211, 225n.56
Church-State relations 2, 193, 201–204, 207, 216–219, 230–232, 238, 254n.1
Cigarmakers see factory workers
Citizens, local 16, 19, 37, 42, 146, 175, 177–180, 191, 206, 237, 252, 265
Citizens' assembly 122, 181, 251
Citizens' committee 13, 122, 186, 203, 224n.31
Civil liberties 187–188, 195n.45, 215, 218
Clerks 41
Clover or lucerne 29, 31
Coale, Ansley and James Trussell (demographers) 92, 156; see also M index, m index
Colonialism 216
Commerce 39–40, 45n.8, 119, 139, 207, 209, 244–245
Common fields 29–30, 42, 44n.23
Completed families defined 107n.43; 97, 149n.16, 156
Completed family size defined 104n.6; 95; by faction or tendency 184–185, 188–189, 191–192, 195n.34, 204–205, 220–221, 229n.136, 240, 245–246, 249, 259n.79, 260n.128; by occupation 112, 117, 120–121; by religion 206, 211–212, 243; by status 124, 129n.52; by village 98–99, 101; by wealth 152–155, 158–160, 165–167, 169
Concordat 204, 215, 224n.31
Confession 199–200, 213, 222n.4, 227n.88n.93, 242–243, 258n.93
Conscription 13, 18, 24n.42, 215, 217, 252
Contraception distinguished 105n.10; 9n.6, 52, 69, 79, 89, 95, 114, 132–133, 175, 199, 207, 213, 240, 243, 264, 266
Contraceptive failure 103, 108n.56
Control 1–3, 133, 143, 146, 177, 182, 253, 266–267
Cooperatives 31, 33, 40, 132, 238, 261
Corruption 178, 182
County councillors 234, 255n.17, 256n.33
Crafts 34–35, 76, 115–118, 123
Credit 137, 140; credit unions 31, 33, 140

INDEX

Crises 12–14, 17–18, 53, 115, 150n.32, 193n.5
Crops 146, 266; see also grains and specific crops
Customs union 195n.45, 214
Czechoslovakia 92

Dancing 80, 86n.56, 236
Day labourers 27–28, 34–35, 42–44, 45n.2, 46n.24, 50n.111, 74, 76, 78, 141, 145, 209, 218, 262; fertility 111–115, 126; fertility and mortality 119–121, 124–125, 128n.17
Dealers 33, 39–40, 47n.53, 119, 127, 217
Deans 186, 189, 203, 208, 211, 241; see also Hennig, Steiger
Death 57–58, 63, 67n.27, 150–151n.39, 263
Deferred gratification 132
Democrats or Progressives (party) 216–217, 220, 228n.133, 237, 249, 250
Demographic transition 17, 263
Differentiation 3–4, 21–22, 27, 121, 131–132, 134, 145–147, 201, 223n.11, 252–253
Diffusion distinguished 268n.11n.18; 3, 162, 194n.6, 252, 263–266, 268n.23; spread 3–4, 142, 155, 157, 160–163, 168–172, 173n.4, 175, 213, 225n.52, 229n.138, 268n.11; plateaus 90, 98, 154, 163, 169, 172; reverses 124, 160, 163–164, 172, 211
Divorce 222n.2
Doctors 40–41, 121, 137, 225n.54, 244
Documented marriages defined 10–11n.19; 7, 206, *passim*
Donsbach, Christian (county prefect) 182–184, 186, 262
Drinking 37, 80, 86n.56, 137, 236
Dues 30, 37, 46n.27, 49n.83, 123, 178

Edelmann, Carl (Centre member of parliament) 232–233, 235, 255n.16
Education systems 204, 222n.2, 232, 243, 248, 257n.60n.63
Elections 188, 201, 209, 226n.84, 252; to Baden constituent assembly 1849 190, 197n.93, 227n.100; to Baden constituent assembly 1919 250; to Baden parliament 189, 191, 195n.46, 200–201, 216, 222, 223n.10, 228n.100, 230–251, 258n.90; to customs parliament 208, 214–215; to district council 204–205, 208; to Erfurt parliament 191; to federal parliament 200–201, 206, 210, 214–221, 226n.83, 236, 250; to Frankfurt parliament 189; municipal 154, 183–186, 194n.27, 197n.86, 208, 210, 234–235, 251, 257n.54; schoolboard 204, 206, 224n.35
Electoral colleges 189–191, 197n.90, 231, 233, 235–237, 239, 254n.2
Electors 189–193, 195n.45, 231–247, 252, 254n.2
Electrification 34, 42, 261
Elite in Kappel 81–82, 86n.59, 100, 125, 129n.34, 130n.37, 149n.18, 152, 158, 162–163, 176, 182, 189, 207, 209, 212–213, 225n.54, 237, 252, 265; elsewhere 139, 231, 244, 247
Elz river map 5, 15; 29, 31, 36, 42, 146
Emancipation 19, 40, 119, 204, 206, 219
Emigration 7, 11n.19, 12, 16, 18–20, 24n.37–40, 24–25n.42–47, 34, 71, 73–76, 79–80, 137, 146, 162–163, 167, 170–171, 193n.5, 206, 266–267
Emmendingen (town) map 5; 31, 200
Engelmann, Alois (baker from Rust) 61–62
Engler, Wilhelm (Social Democratic candidate) 222n.9
Enlightened 180, 202–203, 216, 223n.23
Entrepreneurship 40, 50n.98, 138
Entry fees 16, 23n.22–25, 85n.38
Equilibrium or homeostasis 20, 46n.20, 53, 63–64
Ettenbach stream 36
Ettenheim (town) map 5, 15, 32; 6, 14, 31, 51n.127, 75, 180, 182–183, 196n.68, 214, 224n.43, 228n.109, 235–237, 247, 249, 258n.86
Ettenheim county map 32; 24n.40, 186, 231, 233; county office 41, 182, 187
Ettenheim-Emmendingen-Lahr riding 200, 247–249
Ettenheim forest map 5; 42
Ettenheim-Kenzingen riding map 32; 197n.90, 231–247
Ettenheimmünster (monastery) 25n.50, 180–181, 262

Ettenheim riding map 32; 189, 195n.43–46
Europa-Park Rust 194n.19
European marriage pattern 8, 52–53, 64, 80, 128n.9, 263, 268n.15
Exam requirement for ecclesiastical functions 204, 232

Factions 177, 184–186, 264
Factories 43–44, 51n.17In.126–129n.133, 72, 79, 117, 162, 169, 171, 218, 236, 241–242
Factory workers 72, 76, 83n.8, 84n.16, 119–121, 124–125, 128n.16n.21, 135–136, 145, 149n.17, 241, 257n.57
Family limitation defined 88, 90; *passim*; classical theory of 87, 89–90, 92, 94–96, 103, 105n.9, 108n.58, 263–264; *see also* m index
Family reconstitution 6–7, 10n.14
Farmhands 26n.63, 53; *see also* servants
Fecundity defined 104n.1; 87, 91, 94, 97–98, 101, 120, 157, 164, 262, 264; *see also* M index
Feedback between m and M 98, 107n.35, 121, 157, 240, 243
Fehrenbach, Konstantin (Centre member of parliament) 228n.113, 260n.121
Fertility control defined 90; *passim*
Fertility rates 87–88; age-specific defined 88; 89–91, 98; total marital fertility rate defined 88; 91, 97; by faction or tendency 185, 188–189, 191–192, 221, 249; by occupation 111, 117, 119–120; by religion 206, 211–212, 225n.49, 243; by status 124, 129n.33; by village 99–101; by wealth 156–157, 161, 167
Fertility transition defined 90; 2–4, 90, 93, 95, 103, 105n.10, 161, 225n.51, 253, 263
Fertilizer 30–31, 132
Feudal reaction 180
Field clearance 31, 261
Field-wardens 42, 210
Final birth intervals 93–97, 103; by faction or tendency 184–185, 188–189, 191–192, 204–205, 220–221, 240, 245–246, 249, 259n.79, 260n.128; by occupation 112, 117; by status 124, 129n.32; by village 98–99, 101; by wealth 152–155,
159–160, 165–167; by religion 206, 211–212, 243
Fire brigades 233, 241, 258n.86
Fishing 29, 34–36, 45n.78, 68n.42, 115–117, 123, 147, 151n.50, 209
Flax 29, 35, 45n.19
Flexibility 29, 140, 176, 202, 217; *see also* independence
Floods 27, 148, 236, 256n.48
Fodder 29, 34, 36
Foresters 41–42, 178–179
For their own reasons 3, 20n.8, 263
France 1, 4, 14, 19, 187, 194n.6, 196n.47, 215
Franchise 187, 195n.33n.42, 206, 214, 250
Franco-Prussian War 215–216, 256n.13
Frankfurt Parliament 189–190, 196n.68, 197n.90
Freiburg (city) map 5; 31, 203, 207–208, 210, 223n.25, 225n.55, 232, 235–237, 239, 242–243
French Revolution 30, 72, 74, 79, 261, 267n.2
Frequency of intercourse 91, 106n.23n.28, 108n.47
Fridolin (saint) 35
Friedrich I (grand duke) 204, 233, 236, 258n.86
Fruit 33

Geese 30, 42
Gendarmes 39, 218, 255n.14
German empire 18, 193, 218, 253, 256n.43
German question or national question 187–189, 214–216, 218
Goats 121
Goldstein, Alice (demographer) 26n.60
Government officials 137, 139 140, 145, 150n.28, 183, 187, 191, 235, 248, 253; *see also* prefects
Government party 187, 191, 195n.46, 201, 206, 208, 215, 224n.43, 230
Grafenhausen (village) map 5, 15, 32; *passim*
Grains 29–31, 34, 36, 45n.15, 145, 180
Grand dukes 24n.43, 215; *see also* Friedrich
Great Depression (1873–1896) 236
Guardians 233

Guilds 34–37, 40, 48n.76, 61–63, 122, 204, 265
Gurs/France (internment camp) 26n.57

Habsburg monarchy 84n.15, 214–215, 223n.23, 227n.104
Häfele, Ludwig (mayor of Grafenhausen) 31, 33, 238–239, 247–248, 253, 257n.64
Hecker, Friedrich (revolutionary) 196n.65
Heidelberg 208
Hemp 29, 31, 33, 35, 45n.17
Hennig, Michael (priest in Kappel) 23n.11–12, 86n.51, 211, 220, 222n.8, 226n.83, 229n.125n.127, 257n.54n.60, 241–243, 248, 258n.94, 260n.121
Henry, Louis (demographer) 268n.15
Herbolzheim (town)   map 5, 15, 32; 10n.9, 43, 73–75, 193n.1, 233, 235, 239, 241, 247–249, 259n.103n.108
Herders 42, 50n.109, 75, 178
Herzog, Anton (mayor of Grafenhausen) 182–183, 186, 194n.30
Holy Roman Empire 122, 179–181
Home village or locality 3, 8, 101, 110, 121–122, 126–127, 131, 147–148, 181, 206, 221–222, 229n.128, 231, 247, 250, 253, 261–266
Hops 33
Horses 31, 33–34, 36, 39, 179, 268n.24
Hug, Friedrich (Centre member of parliament) 239, 241, 248, 258n.81
Hungary 24n.38, 74, 92
Hunting 42, 188
Hutterites 88, 104n.3

Ig index of marital fertility 104n.3–5n.7
Illegitimacy defined 83n.1; 8, 10n.10, 19, 24n.30, 52, 69–80, 107n.44, 110, 119, 175, 258n.94, 266
Illegitimacy ratio defined 83n.4; 70, 77, 79, 163
Im index of nuptiality 65n.6, 104n.5
Immigration 14, 16, 23n.21, 146
Independence distinguished 193n.2; 4, 9, 104, 176, 182, 202, 214, 220–221, 231–232, 244, 247–248, 253, 262, 267
Independents or uncommitted politically 185, 217, 233, 235, 237, 240–241, 247, 248
Indirect elections 187, 191, 216, 230–231, 252, 259n.117

Individualism 129n.23
Industrialization 3, 134, 241–242, 244, 259n.99
Industry 34, 41–44, 118–121; *see also* factories
Infant mortality 2, 17, 24n.32, 91, 119–121, 127, 263
Inheritance 4, 17, 19, 35, 37, 40, 53–54, 67n.30, 132, 141–143, 147–148, 150n.35; impartible 55, 66n.14, 69, 136, 265; *see also* partible inheritance
Innkeepers 8, 37, 68n.42, 115, 123, 137, 138, 177, 187, 190, 192, 197n.83, 211, 214, 231, 244, 252, 266; *see also* Schmidt, Winkler
Innovations 1, 3–4, 27, 29, 31, 34, 44, 132, 170, 175, 177, 192, 207, 221, 227n.90, 252–253, 261, 263–267, 268n.11–13n.17
Inns 182, 187, 190–191, 195n.36, 218, 229n.124, 232–233, 236–237, 247–248
Inspection tours 28
Intensive agriculture 21, 134–135, 145–146
Interior ministry 187
Intermarriage 40
Irrigation projects 31, 145, 208
Italy 222n.2, 227n.104
Itinerant (occupational category) 16, 39, 73–75, 85n.34n.43, 119, 126
Itzstein, Adam von (opposition member of parliament) 187

Jerger, Andreas (priest in Rust) 232, 238–239, 241–242, 256n.60
Jews 19–20, 25–26n.48–58, 40, 45n.8, 49n.83, 50n.100n.103, 62, 68n.51, 85n.45, 119, 201, 204–207, 219, 223n.14, 224–225n.41–51, 228n.112, 229n.126, 230, 236, 244–245, 248, 252, 259n.103–104, 262, 265, 268n.19
Josephism 203, 223n.23
Journeymen 38, 61–63, 68n.44
Judges 208, 235, 239, 241, 247; *see also* Armbruster

Kappel (village) map 5, 15, 32; *passim*; river crossing 6, 12
Karlsruhe (capital city) 235
Kenzingen (town) map 5, 32; 235
Kiefer, Friedrich (National Liberal

Index

politician) 214–216, 227n.96n.98, 228n.109, 235
Kippenheim (town) map 5, 32; 22n.6, 31, 141, 187, 224n.41n.43, 258n.89, 259n.103
Kippenheimweiler (village) 197n.75
Knifegrinders 39
Knodel, John (demographer) xv–xvi, 96, 101, 109n.65
Köbele, Albert (genealogist from Grafenhausen) xv, 48n.78, 147, 194n.7, 268n.10
Koch, Felix (priest in Kappel) 208–211, 213
Konstanz (town) 203, 223n.25, 236, 239

Lahr (town) map 5; 6, 30–31, 43, 200, 214, 217; rural chapter 203
Laissez-faire or free trade 37–38, 49n.89, 79, 187, 202, 204
Landed proprietors or peasants 8, 27–29, 34, 44, 45n.1–2, 110–115, 123, 127, 131, 139, 147, 217, 232, 248, 262; peasants 135, 149n.17, 158, 163, 262, 264, 267, 267n.2, 268n.24
Land hunger 21, 137, 207
Landlessness 28, 134–135
Land surveys 141–142, 144, 155, 173n.8, 174n.20
Lawyers 41, 232, 235–236, 239, 241, 243–244, 248
Leaflets or pamphlets 208, 214, 220, 227n.102
Leasing 30, 33, 46n.25, 140, 151n.42n.46
Legal proceedings 179–181, 183–186, 189, 217, 225n.55, 253, 261–262, 267; appeals 179–180, 182–186, 191, 196n.50n.52
Leipf, Stefan (surveyor) 237, 239, 257n.51
Leo XIII (pope) 239, 256n.37
LePlay, Frédéric (sociologist) 131
Levine, David (historian) xvi, 10n.8, 26n.50, 86n.58
Liberal Catholics 221, 230, 241, 254
Liberals 79, 129n.34, 201–202, 204, 207–208, 214–216, 220, 230, 232–234, 237, 248; liberalism 202, 213, 217, 236
Lifespan 17

Liguori, Alphonsus (theologian) 199, 222n.5
Literacy 262, 267n.8
Livestock or cattle 29–31, 33–34, 40, 42, 46n.23, 121, 133, 146, 179, 226n.83
Livi-Bacci, Massimo (demographer) 86n.54, 223n.19, 225n.51
Local positions 41–42, 50n.106n.109n.111n.113, 76, 119, 122, 209–210
Lords 6, 10n.12, 16, 30, 45n.13, 139–140, 172, 174n.23, 177–181, 193n.5, 217, 219, 253, 269n.26; see also Böcklin, archbishop of Strasbourg, Ettenheimmünster
Lotharingia 4
Lotzbeck (firm) 31, 217, 262
Louis XIV (king of France) 12, 72

Mahlberg (town) map 5, 15, 32; 6, 22n.6, 51n.127, 196n.68, 259n.104
Malthusian fertility control 17, 52–54, 61, 64, 65n.2, 68n.41, 69, 76–82, 88, 99, 111, 114–115, 133, 135, 162, 167, 169, 264, 267
Managers or agents 37–38, 40, 177, 241
Manufacturers 37, 43, 214, 217, 239, 241, 244; see also Schindler
Markets 31, 39, 52, 145, 252, 264, 268n.24; in land 136–140, 145, 149n.22–23; in marriage 141, 162–163, 171
Marriage 2, 44, 53, 56–60, 133, 137, 148n.7, 204, 210, 212, 226n.82; cohorts 10n.18, 173n.4, 260n.128; contracts 54, 62; strategies 55, 68n.55, 123, 141, 211
Marsh 29, 144, 146
Masons 35, 51n.121, 209; Freemasons 226.65
Masters (in guild) 34, 48n.66, 49n.88, 53, 61, 68n.41n.44–45
Mature marriages defined 142–143, 155; 10n.10, 109n.80, 144, 148, 150n.38, 151n.42, 156, 164, 173n.4
Mayors 24n.38, 33, 122–123, 141, 179, 196n.48, 189–190, 197n.86, 210, 214, 224n.31, 231–239, 241–243, 247–248, 252, 257n.54n.60, 262; see also Häfele, Herzog, Ott, Richter, Sattler
Members of parliament 187, 189–190,

217, 226n.67, 228n.113; candidacies 231–233, 235–236, 239, 241, 247, 254n.6, 256n.33; *see also* Armbruster, Edelmann, Fehrenbach, Hennig, Hug, Kiefer, Leipf, Richter, Rosshirt, Sander, Welcker, Zittel
Menarche   52, 91
Menopause   2, 64n.5, 91, 174n.24
Merchants   36–37, 39, 132, 140, 214, 233, 235, 244
Messengers   41, 210
Metternichean system   187, 251
Midwives   41, 121, 128n.18, 226n.76
Migration   16, 36–38, 47–49n.80, 119, 127, 133, 137, 225n.48, 256n.41
Militarism   215–218, 229n.125
Milk   33, 121
Millers   36, 145
m index of family limitation   defined 91; 90, 92, 96–97, 155; by faction or tendency   185, 188–189, 192, 205, 220–221, 229n.136, 240, 249, 259n.102, 260n.129; by occupation   113, 118; by religion   211–212, 225n.49, 243; by status   125, 129–130n.36–37; by village   98–102; by village and occupation   126; by wealth   171, 173n.12
M index of underlying natural fertility defined   90–91; 93, 97, 101, 119, 264; by faction or tendency   185, 188–189, 191–192, 221; by occupation   111, 117–121, 128n.12; by religion   211–212, 225n.49, 243; by status   124, 129n.33; by wealth   157, 161, 167
Moderates defined   197n.90; 191–193, 197n.91–92, 224n.28
Modernization   4, 90, 199, 223n.14, 230, 262
Money   137–138
Morcellement   defined 148n.1; 22, 77, 113, 133–135, 141, 144–148, 148–149n.10, 149n.13, 155, 158, 163, 169–171, 264, 266
Mortgages   137–140, 150n.27
Münchweier (village) map 32; 74–75, 259n.103n.108n.118
Municipal accounts   178, 182–183
Municipal clerk   122–123, 138, 184, 186, 190, 214, 231, 234, 237, 239, 242, 243
Municipal councils   77, 178, 191, 203, 207–208, 260n.133, 261, 266, 267n.9

Municipal councillors   121–122, 183–187, 191, 208, 210, 226n.80, 231–235, 237–239, 242, 249
Municipality   4, 16, 35, 41, 76, 110, 146, 154, 167, 176–186, 193n.3, 217, 253, 265
Münsterthal (village)   map 32; 31, 43, 259n.108n.118
Mutschler, Ignaz (treasurer of Grafenhausen)   182–186, 195n.35n.38

Napoleonic Code   85n.33
Napoleonic Wars   18, 24n.36, 30
Natalist   175
Nationalists   187, 202–203, 208, 214–215, 217, 236
National Liberals party   216, 227–228n.109n.111; 200–202, 208, 210, 214, 218, 223n.13, 224n.43, 228n.113, 230–250, 265
Natural fertility   defined 89–90; *passim*; *see also* M index
Nazism   6, 20, 197n.79, 202
Neckarhausen/Württemberg (village) 66n.16, 149n.23
Neo-Malthusian fertility control   52, 69, 80–82, 95, 115
Nest of hamsters   50n.98, 262
Netting, Robert (anthropologist) 226n.78
Networks   175, 177, 185–186, 221, 231, 252, 264–266
Newspapers   80, 177, 208–209, 230, 243; pro-government   204, 208, 214, 233, 235–236; opposition   226n.67
Night roaming   80, 86n.56
Nonnenweier (village) map 32; 19, 206, 224n.40, 235n.46
Non-citizens   16, 39, 75
Notables   8, 35–36, 48n.77, 77, 104, 110, 119, 121–127, 131, 138, 158, 175, 178–179, 185, 188–189, 203–205, 209, 214, 220, 231, 234, 237, 244, 247, 252–253, 262, 266
Notaries   233
Nucleated villages   265
Nurses   121

Oath of allegiance   24n.43, 195n.31
Occupational distributions overall   28; by cohort   35–36, 47n.60–61; by religion   207–209; by status   123; by tendency   192–193, 244–245; by village   45n.6, 111, 127n.4, 164; for

lovers, fathers, and husbands of unwed mothers 71–73, 76–78; for fathers of workers 51n.128; for young stoppers 104, 110–111, 127n.2–3
Occupations 3, 7–8, 27–28, 60–61, 110–121, 126–127, 195n.33, 264
Oedipal model 53–54, 61–64, 64n.10, 68n.50, 128n.9, 263
Offenburg (town) map 5; 6, 31, 75, 207, 216
Oilseed, poppyseed, rapeseed 29, 31
Old Catholics 201–202, 205–213, 219, 221, 226n.81–82n.85–86, 227n.88, 229n.133, 231–232, 235, 237, 241–242, 246, 249, 254, 257n.54, 258n.81n.94, 260n.140, 262
Order (occupational category) 39, 119, 126; see also border guards, gendarmes, soldiers
Orders 203, 226n.65, 232; Jesuits 208, 226n.65
Organists 41, 203, 210
Organization 177, 193, 204, 214, 218, 220, 229n.130, 230–232, 252–253, 268n.21
Orschweier (village) map 5, 32; 53, 73–75, 141, 189, 224n.43
Ortenau (region) 6, 12, 22n.3, 28
OSBs (local genealogies) 6–7, 10n.13.15–16, 109n.71, 126, 194n.7, 262
Ott, Michel (mayor of Rust) 24n.38, 178–181, 194n.8n.18–19, 262

Palatinate 228n.117
Parity defined 89; 88–89, 105–106n.16, 264
Parliament 187–191, 216, 230; see also elections
Parliamentary opposition 187, 189, 204–205, 214–215, 227n.103–104, 232, 253
Paris (city) 40, 191
Parish 207; committees 203
Parish registers 6, 10n.13, 270
Partible inheritance rules 54; 8, 54–64, 77, 82, 131, 141, 146–147, 150n.31n.33, 262, 264–265; see also inheritance
Patrols 42, 50n.106, 210
Patronage 38, 42, 137–138, 176–177, 182, 209, 231, 233
Peasants Union 47n.44, 238–239, 241
Pedlars 19, 39–40

Pensions 138, 145, 188
Percentage limiting defined 108n.57; 8, 10n.10, 95–97, 108n.59, 129n.35, 167, 174n.27; by faction or tendency 185, 188–189, 192, 205, 221, 229n.136, 240, 249, 259n.103, 260n.129; by village 99–102; see also shape of family limitation
Petitions 183–184, 187–189, 191, 196n.57–59, 206, 216, 224n.31n.41n.43, 225n.56
Petty trades 39, 73–77, 119, 126
Pigs 30, 42, 49n.97, 178–179
Pius IX (pope) 204, 211, 224n.34
Plumbers 74–75
Polarization political 190, 205, 209–210, 216, 226n.72n.78, 230; religious 200–201, 226n.78; social 147
Police 42, 183, 214, 237, 267n.9
Political Catholicism see Centre, ultramontanes
Political culture 215
Poll-book or register of public vote 184
Poor defined 133, 142–143, 147, 150n.38, 155, 173n.8n.14; 135, 152–174, 185
Poor relief 16, 18, 23n.18, 138, 204, 257n.60
Popes 204, 207–208, 239, 256n.47; see also Leo XIII, Pius IX
Population decline 146, 170, 175
Population pressure 7, 12, 16–18, 20–22, 81, 103, 113, 133, 146, 176–177, 264
Population totals 13
Posters 248, 255n.14
Potato 29, 31, 34, 36, 45n.18, 180
Poultry 30, 33, 47n.53
Poverty 19, 21, 44, 50n.100, 79, 115, 120–121, 128n.10, 142, 145, 151n.50, 163, 266
Prague (city) 40
Prefects 28, 33, 40, 78, 80, 121, 137, 173n.7, 182–187, 190, 194n.30, 203, 210, 231–235, 238–230, 243, 253, 255n.14n.126, 260n.140, 262, 266; see also Donsbach
Pregnant brides 77, 93, 106n.27, 107n.35n.39
Priests 41, 80, 121, 137, 177, 188, 199–200, 202–204, 207–208, 215, 220, 224n.28, 225n.57, 228n.119, 231–232, 238, 241–244, 248, 253, 255n.28, 257n.61, 261; vicars 207–208, 211,

227n.103, 232, 234–235, 242, 255n.10n.28, 256n.41; Old Catholic pastors 208, 210, 226n.79; see also Burg, Hennig, Jerger, Koch, Schäfle, Schleyer, Steiger, Uebelin
Processions 203, 208, 211, 236, 239
Professionals 38, 40–41, 119, 123, 127, 128n.15, 139–140, 150n.28, 244–245, 268n.24
Professors 208, 225n.55, 239
Progressive peasantry 33, 262
Proletariat 79, 218
Promethean 177
Property qualification for marriage 71, 76–82, 85n.37, 86n.56, 90, 165–166, 204, 212
Prosperity 37, 118, 123, 146, 176, 218, 262, 263, 266
Prostitution 90
Protestants 19, 25n.50, 41, 201, 205, 211, 214–217, 219, 223n.14, 227n.103, 228n.112, 243, 245, 248–249, 259n.103–104
Protest vote 216, 218
Prussia 190, 215–216, 254n.10

Quadrilateral 227n.104
Qualitative changes 2, 12, 16, 134, 146, 171, 176, 266
Quality of land 144, 146
Quantitative changes 12, 16, 133–134, 146, 269n.26

Radicals defined 197n.90; 176, 187–193, 194n.6, 197n.86n.91, 198n.92, 202, 216–218, 227n.107, 235, 237, 239, 248, 251, 262
Railroad map 5; 43, 189–190, 196n.68, 223n.19, 238
Rallies 220, 231–233, 236, 241, 247–248; see also Social Democrats
Rape 72, 84n.13–15
Rauch, Damas (trader from Grafenhausen) 183–186, 188–191, 196n.68, 262
Reclamation 31, 146, 162–163, 167, 181, 269n.26
Red and black 228n.19, 234, 248, 255n.25
Refined morcellement hypothesis defined 134–135; 141, 146, 152, 154, 158, 161, 163, 167–172, 263
Refugees 14, 22n.6–7, 23n.16, 179

Regression analysis 150n.37, 268n.23
Reichenweier (deserted village) map 15; 14, 23n.13–15, 146, 180–181, 269n.26
Religiosity 3, 199, 211, 213, 226n.80, 256n.35
Remarriage 123, 153, 174n.28, 197n.41
Replacement effect 2, 9n.2, 94, 103
Republicanism 187, 189–191, 194n.6, 262
Restless minds or malcontents defined 184–185, 194n.30; 9, 182–187, 215, 253, 262
Retailers 39
Retallack, James (historian) xvi, 49n.97
Retirement 53–54, 60–61, 133, 143
Returning officers 186, 191, 204, 234
Revisionism 218
Revolution 182, 185, 194n.7, 228n.29; revolution of 1848 9, 18, 122, 176, 186–193, 198n.93, 206, 215, 225n.56, 252, 261–262; 48ers 177, 191, 208, 215, 253; see also Brentano, Hecker, Rauch, Richter, Struve, Winkler
Rheinhausen (villages of Niederhausen and Oberhausen) 49n.88, 57, 74–75, 259n.104
Rhinau/Alsace (town) map 5, 15; 14, 23n.16, 29, 42–43, 46n.23, 85n.46
Rhine river map 5; 4, 12, 14, 23n.6, 36, 39–40, 42, 50n.115, 53, 146, 167, 171, 203, 256n.48, 261, 269n.26; correction 31, 36, 42, 147; Rhine plain map 5; 21, 42, 64, 72, 135–136, 262
Rich defined 143, 147, 150n.38, 155, 173n.8; 60, 81, 104, 129n.34, 135–136, 139, 141–143, 149n.18–19, 152–174, 180, 185, 195n.35
Richter, Karl (mayor of Kappel) 188–190, 196n.64, 208–211, 215–216, 219, 226n.80, 227n.109, 231–233, 235, 252, 255n.17, 262; brother Franz Joseph 190, 196n.64
Riff, Michael (historian) 225n.44
Ringsheim (village) map 5, 15, 32; 14, 19n.88, 43, 51n.127, 73–75, 84n.23, 190, 218, 259n.105n.108n.118, 260n.120
Rittmatten (field) map 15; 14, 23n.13, 31, 36, 47n.41, 238
Roman Catholic Church 151n.43, 175, 177, 193n.1, 199, 202, 204, 208, 215–216, 222n.6, 227n.103, 238,

242–244, 248; see also Church-State relations
Roman Catholics 6, 9, 19, 40, 175, 200–201, 203–213, 216, 223n.14, 228n.112, 229n.128n.130, 235, 237, 239, 246, 262
Rosshirt, Franz (clerical member of parliament) 215, 227n.96
Rousseauite patriotism 188
Rust (village) map 5, 15; passim; market 31, 39; 1747 rebellion 178–180, 195n.30

Saddlers 36
Sander, Ferdinand (independent member of parliament) 217–219, 228n.115n.118–120, 236
Sartori lineage 73–75, 77–78, 84–85n.21–32, 266
Sattler, Georg (mayor of Grafenhausen) 183–186
Sattler, Leopold (mayor of Grafenhausen) 234–235, 237–238, 253, 268n.10; daughter Frieda 268n.10
Schäfle, Matthias (priest in Grafenhausen) 238–239, 241–243, 254, 255n.13, 257n.59–60
Schindler, Arnold (manufacturer from Herbolzheim) 241–243, 258n.90
Schleswig-Holstein 208
Schleyer, Peter Anton (priest in Kappel) 203, 207, 225n.55
Schmidt, Franz (mayor of Herbolzheim) 247–249
Schmieheim (village) map 32; 200–201, 224n.41n.43, 225n.46, 228n.112, 259n.103
Scholarship funds 138
Schubnell, Hermann (demographer) 135–136
Schuttertal (village) map 32; 200–201
Secret ballot 214, 220, 224n.37n.39, 227n.101, 249
Secularization 2, 199–202, 206–207, 213, 216–218, 220–221, 223n.21, 224n.39, 227n.89, 228n.122, 229n.133, 230–231, 241–242, 244–245, 247, 249, 251, 263
Sedan (battle) 236, 256n.43
Seduction 70, 78
Seed 132–133
Servants or menials 23n.26, 38, 44, 49n.90, 51n.131, 53, 64n.6n.8,

66n.14, 72, 76, 83n.8, 119, 127, 147
Sextons 41, 215, 238
Shape of family limitation defined 99, 109n.66; by occupation 113, 118; by status 125; by tendency 246; by village 100, 102; by wealth 157–158, 161–162, 167–168
Shorter, Edward (historian) xv–xvi, 129n.23
Slanderers and rioters 183–186
Slovenia 187
Social Democrats or socialists 187, 202, 213–219, 222n.9, 228n.113, 228–229n.123–125, 238, 242, 250–251, 258n.94, 259n.105
Social legislation 217
Soldiers or troops 39, 44, 53, 71–72, 76–77, 179–181, 183, 186, 188, 190, 194n.12, 197n.81, 261; militia 190, 197n.81
Solid peasants 8, 33, 135, 146, 152, 155–156, 158, 163, 168, 171–172, 174n.22, 176–177, 202, 253, 259n.99, 266–267
Solidarity 55, 172, 176–177, 181, 221, 242, 251, 254, 265–266
Songs 181, 198n.93, 203
Spacing between births 2, 8, 9, 91, 93–95, 97, 105n.12–14, 264
Starting childbearing 93–95, 264
Statistical significance 105n.8, 106–107n.30, 107n.35–36, 109n.64, 127n.5, 129n.36, 161, 173n.2n.18, 196n.59, 220, 226n.87, 258n.80
Status 8, 121–127, 188–189, 207, 252; see also notables
Steiger, Franz Sales (priest in Grafenhausen) 189–191, 197n.78, 203, 213, 224n.28–29, 267n.9
Step-relatives 57–58, 67n.24, 171n.28
Stöhr, Catharina (landholder from Rust) 56–57
Stopping childbearing 89–90, 93–95, 105n.12, 264, 268n.15
Strasbourg/Alsace (city) map 5; 6, 13, 31, 35, 52, 178, 202; see also archbishop
Strips 30
Struve, Gustav (revolutionary) 196n.67
Students 53
Subjects 175, 179
Substantial artisans defined 48n.65;

34, 36–37, 115–118, 127, 131, 137, 140, 207, 209, 225n.54
Sugar-beet 30, 33, 36
Surety 137–138
Surgeons 41
Surveyors 41, 237; see also Leipf
Sweden 261
Swing riding 231, 235–237, 239, 252
Switzerland 85n.47, 187, 222n.2

Tailors 35, 209
Tanners 249
Target family size 90, 94, 106n.19–20, 264
Taxation 37, 123, 144–146, 154, 159, 163, 173n.15, 174n.20, 180, 188, 195n.45, 207, 215, 217, 225n.56, 228, 232, 236, 238, 240, 248, 252
Tax-collectors 37, 123
Tax rolls or cadastres 56, 142, 195n.31
Teachers 40–41, 133, 137, 145, 188, 190, 196n.68, 197n.78n.81, 208, 210, 224n.29, 235, 243–244
Terrorism 190
Textiles 35, 39
Thirty Years War 12, 22n.3, 25n.48, 261
Three-field system 29, 42, 45n.14, 170
Tinkers 39, 73–74
Tithes 29–30, 45n.15, 46n.28, 123, 137, 144, 180–181, 188, 269n.26
Tobacco 31, 33–34, 40, 43, 46n.35, 52, 132, 146, 176, 215, 217, 236, 262
Toleration 217
Towns or urbanism 2–3, 19, 24n.41, 86n.54, 202, 216, 223n.19, 233, 263, 268n.24
Traders 19, 39–40, 119, 183, 262; see also Rauch
Treasurers 122–123, 194n.27, 231, 242; see also Mutschler, Werner
Troupers 39
Twins 91, 107n.41

Uebelin, Baptist (priest in Kappel) 207, 213, 227n.88
Ultramontanes or clericals 9, 86n.51, 199–205, 207–208, 214–216, 220, 223n.19, 227n.89, 240–242, 253, 262
Underemployment 21, 137

United States of America 18–19, 24n.43, 39, 74, 187, 190, 208
Usury 86n.56

Vatican Council (1870) 207, 210
Venezuela 18
Veterans 24n.36, 236, 257n.47
Veterinarians 41
Vicari, Hermann von (archbishop of Freiburg) 203, 257n.60
Victorianism 86n.51
Vienna (city) 181
Vineland 141
Visitations 23n.17, 193n.1, 267n.3
Voters' lists 51n.135, 154

Wacker, Theodor (Centre politician) 222n.8
Wage labour 28, 34, 121, 129n.23, 149n.26; see also factory workers, servants
Wages 34, 44, 41n.132
Wallburg (village) map 5, 32; 31
War debts 24n.36, 30, 46n.29
War of Polish succession 23n.16
Wealth 7, 27, 127, 131, 143, 152–174, 192, 195n.33, 207, 213, 252, 262, 264, 266; distribution of wealth 4, 8, 46n.13, 69, 144, 147, 253–254, 266; by village 144–146, 164, 172, 174n.21; less even 139, 147, 158–159, 161–163, 182; more even 82, 138, 140–141, 153, 164, 168, 221, 266
Weaving 34–36, 44, 115–117, 128n.16, 209
Weber thesis 223n.14–15
Weimar Republic 228n.113, 251
Welcker, Karl Theodor (opposition member of parliament) 195n.43n.45–46
Well-documented marriages defined 11n.20; 103, 108n.57, 109n.78
Werner, Philipp (treasurer of Rust) 178–179, 194n.15n.18, 262
Wessenberg, Ignaz (administrator of archdiocese) 203, 208
Widowhood 54–60, 66n.21–22, 85n.42, 129n.31, 141, 174n.28, 242, 258n.92; see also remarriage
Winkler, Nepomuk (bookbinder from Grafenhausen) 187–191, 194n.6,

196n.47–53n.68, 197n.82, 262, 267n.9
Withdrawal (coitus interruptus) 2, 94, 133, 193n.1, 195n.33, 199, 222n.6
Wittenweier (village) map 15, 32; 227n.103
Women's political activity 177, 179, 183–184, 186–187, 215, 226n.80, 233, 248, 250, 262
Women's property rights 8, 28, 54, 57–64, 66n.17, 67n.23n.26n.30, 68n.40n.50, 83n.6, 116, 128n.10, 139, 141, 177, 186, 191, 262, 265; *see also* Stöhr
Women working for wages 34–35, 42–44, 51n.129n.132, 52, 55, 83n.8, 84n.16, 107n.45, 121, 125, 128n.71, 169, 218, 262
World War One 47n.49, 50n.115, 213–214, 249–250
World War Two 261
Wrigley, E.A. (demographer) 68n.47

Yarn 31, 35
Young families selected 103; 8, 103–104, 110–111, 123–124, 136, 149n.18–19

Zeldin, Theodore (historian) 199–200, 212–213, 243
Zittel, Karl (member of parliament) 195n.46